RESEARCH IN
THE HISTORY OF
ECONOMIC THOUGHT
AND METHODOLOGY

*Volume 12* • 1994

# RESEARCH IN THE HISTORY OF ECONOMIC THOUGHT AND METHODOLOGY

*Editors:*     WARREN J. SAMUELS
*Department of Economics*
*Michigan State University*

JEFF BIDDLE
*Department of Economics*
*Michigan State University*

VOLUME 12 • 1994

 JAI PRESS INC.

*Greenwich, Connecticut*                    *London, England*

# CONTENTS

# LIST OF CONTRIBUTORS

*Timothy Alborn*

Department of History
Harvard University

*Roger Backhouse*

Department of Economics
University of Birmingham

*Kenneth E. Boulding*

Institute of Behavioral Science
University of Colorado

*James M. Buchanan*

Center for Public Choice
George Mason University

*Richard X. Chase*

Department of Economics
University of Vermont

*A.W. Coats*

Department of Economics
Duke University

*Allin Cottrell*

Department of Economics
Wake Forest University

*John B. Davis*

Department of Economics
Marquette University

*Thomas R. DeGregori*

Department of Economics
University of Houston

*Brian Fay*

Department of Philosophy
Wesleyan University

*Sasan Fayazmanesh*

Department of Economics
California State University

*Rendigs Fels*                          Department of Economics
                                        Vanderbilt University

*Alon Kadish*                           Department of History
                                        Hebrew University

*S. Todd Lowry*                         Department of Economics
                                        Washington and Lee University

*Ray Petridis*                          Department of Economics
                                        Murdoch university

*Salim Rashid*                          Department of Economics
                                        University of Illinois

*William D. Sockwell*                   Department of Economics
                                        Berry College

*Charles E. Staley*                     Department of Economics
                                        State University of New York

*Edward J. Sullivan*                    Department of Economics
                                        Fordham University

*E. Roy Weintraub*                      Department of Economics
                                        Duke University

*Timothy M. Weithers*                   Department of Economics
                                        Fordham University

*Charles J. Whalen*                     Department of Economics
                                        Hobart and William Smith Colleges

# EDITORIAL BOARD

# ACKNOWLEDGMENTS

The editors wish to express their gratitude for assistance in the review process and other consultation to the members of the editorial board and to the following persons:

| | |
|---|---|
| *Richard Baillie* | *Arjo Klamer* |
| *Peter Boettke* | *Julie Matthaei* |
| *Larry Boland* | *Philip Mirowski* |
| *Tim Brennan* | *Mary Morgan* |
| *Charles Clark* | *Ted Porter* |
| *John Davis* | *Edward Puro* |
| *Donald Dewey* | *David Ruccio* |
| *Ross Emmett* | *Andrea Salanti* |
| *Jerry Evensky* | *Janet Seiz* |
| *Wade Hands* | *Margaret Schabas* |
| *Geoff Hodgson* | *Stephen Stigler* |
| *E.K. Hunt* | *Dan Suits* |
| *Rajani Kanth* | *Donald Walker* |

# WILLIAM ELLIS:
## CONTRIBUTIONS AS A CLASSICAL ECONOMIST, ECONOMIC EDUCATOR, ECONOMIC POPULARIZER, AND SOCIAL ECONOMIST

W. D. Sockwell

## I. INTRODUCTION

William Ellis (1800-1881) contributed to classical economic thought both as an original economic thinker and as a popularizer of economic ideas. Ellis's efforts were wide-ranging, broad-based and relatively successful for a time, but they are almost unknown today. Yet, Ellis deserves to be recognized for several reasons. As a member of J.S. Mill's study group Ellis was a central figure in the discussions about classical political economy and made some minor theoretical contributions during the 1820s. After the 1820s, Ellis concentrated on his business career, but his influence on political economy continued. As his financial condition improved, Ellis contributed large sums of money and considerable time to spreading classical economic ideas. Ellis published a series

Research in the History of Economic Thought and Methodology, Volume 12, pages 1-29.
Copyright © 1994 by JAI Press Inc.
All rights of reproduction in any form reserved.
ISBN: 1-55938-747-5

of economic lectures, as well as numerous books, pamphlets, and articles on economics. Ellis was also one of the first economists to implement a plan to remove economic illiteracy. His unique contribution was the founding of the Birkbeck Schools in 1848. Through the Birkbeck Schools, which emphasized the laws of classical political economy, Ellis attempted to teach young children of all economic or social classes the lessons of political economy so they could understand and act on its laws. In addition, he tried to refocus the direction of political economy; indeed, he was one of the few economists of his day to use the phrase "social economy" to describe the science.[1] This paper seeks to bring recognition to Ellis's accomplishments by recounting his early theoretical contributions, describing his role as an economic popularizer, noting his use of the term "social economy," and discussing his efforts to promote economic literacy among children.

## II.   EARLY ECONOMIC WORKS

Ellis was introduced by his father's friend, Thomas Tooke, to James Mill, Jeremy Bentham, and John Stuart Mill around 1820 and later wrote that it was the two Mills that "set me thinking for myself" (Blyth, 1892, pp. 4, 11, 140).[2] From 1822 to 1827, Ellis was a part of John Stuart's inner group of associates that met regularly, first at Jeremy Bentham's, then at George Grote's house, to discuss political economy and other issues. Late in his life Ellis observed, "I am more indebted to the two Mills ... than to anybody with whom I ever came in contact. I have been their disciple, but certainly not their blind follower" (Blyth, 1892, p. 305). J.S. Mill echoed the sentiment that Ellis was neither a "blind follower" nor a passive observer in the study groups. In his autobiography, Mill wrote, "those among us [the Grote study group] with whom new speculation chiefly originated, were Ellis, Graham, and I" (Mill, 1924, p. 84-85).

Other evidence that Ellis was a central figure and leading thinker in J.S. Mill's study groups is found in Ellis's early contributions to the *Westminster Review*, which was founded by Jeremy Bentham in 1824 "to challenge the aristocratic bias of the existing reviews and to promote the philosophy and the policy proposals of the Utilitarians and Philosophical Radicals" (Fetter, 1962, p. 570). Of the first thirteen economic articles in the *Westminster Review* of which the author is known, four each were written by Ellis and J.S. Mill, and these two co-authored another (Fetter, 1962, pp. 583-584). In these early *Westminster Review* articles, Ellis and the other contributors promoted the Benthamite philosophy along with mainly Ricardian economics as propagated by the textbooks of James Mill and J.R. McCulloch.[3]

Two of Ellis's early articles were, in fact, glowing reviews of the textbooks written by Mill and McCulloch.[4] Ellis opined that Smith's *Wealth of Nations* "did not attain perfection," and that although Ricardo's *Principles* "was the dawn of a new era in the science," it did "not afford a clear and well-arranged view of the science." He added that, with the publication of Mill's *Elements* "all complaints ... may now cease.... Every body henceforward, who denies the truth of any of the principles, is bound to refute the proposition as stated in this work." Ellis heartily recommended Mill's book: "This is a work, which all who have not read ought to read, and which all who have, should read again and again" (Ellis, 1824b, pp. 289-291).[5]

McCulloch's *Principles* was similarly praised by the joint authors Ellis and J.S. Mill.[6] They noted that McCulloch did not claim any originality in his book, but suggested the book "was written evidently with a view to attract those who as yet are strangers to the science.[7] In this [McCulloch] has more than succeeded." They added, "of all who have hitherto been engaged in this meritorious employment [writing about political economy], there is no one who has distinguished himself more than the author of the Discourse which we have before us" (Ellis and Mill, 1825, pp. 90-91).

As a part of his review of Mill's book, Ellis discussed what he believed to be the cornerstone of political economy, namely, the principle that "every man is desirous of his own happiness." He suggested happiness was, in fact, "the end of all sciences;" political economy was merely the study of wealth as the source of that happiness (Ellis, 1824b, pp. 292, 297, 309). Echoing Adam Smith, Ellis believed the best way for self-interested individuals to attain happiness was through minimal government interference, both in the production of goods and in the foreign and domestic interchange of these goods.

Ellis stated (1824b, p. 298) "that the improvements of the new school of political economy [began] to manifest themselves" in the area of functional distribution of wealth. The "improvements of the new school" to which Ellis referred were the Ricardian concepts of rent and profit, the population principle of Malthus, and the iron law of wages. As to the latter, Ellis (1824b, p. 299) asserted:

> there is no proposition in Euclid more clearly established than that theorem in political economy which shews, that the command of the labouring classes over the necessaries and conveniences of life, depend upon the ratio which their number bears to the means of employment.

An increase in population without an accompanying increase in the means of employment (capital) would be detrimental to society.

Another point that Ellis felt was "particularly necessary to bear in mind" was "that every thing which is produced is consumed." He added, "this is so plain as almost to appear as a truism." This emphasis on the importance of the law of the markets—that supply creates its own demand—refuted, he believed, Malthus's belief in the possibility of gluts. Ellis indicated that one of the few revisions to Mill's second edition was an extended illustration of the principle, that "consumption is co-extensive with production," which had made, "if possible, the refutation of the fallacy of the universal glut still more complete than it was in the former edition" (Ellis, 1824b, pp. 292, 306-307).

Each of the above themes—Bentham's greatest happiness principle, Smith's self-interested individuals and call for laissez-faire, the new ideas about functional distribution of wealth, and the law of the markets—became familiar themes propagated by the promoters of the new political economy. But, before the popularizers' version of the classical doctrine was complete, they needed to face a difficulty presented in the third edition of Ricardo's *Principles*.

In 1821, when Ricardo issued his third edition, he added a chapter on machinery that shocked his supporters by its retraction of his earlier view that the introduction of machinery benefited all classes. Prior to this time, the classical economists, including Ricardo, generally favored the exportation of machinery on free trade grounds and assumed that since supply created its own demand, the possibility of unemployment due to new machinery could be ignored. Ricardo's new conclusion, however, was:

> that the opinion entertained by the labouring class, that the employment of machinery is frequently detrimental to their interests, is not founded on prejudice and error, but is conformable to the correct principles of political economy (Ricardo, 1951-1973, vol. 1, p. 392).

Because of the increasing agitation of workers, periodic out breaks of machinery-breaking, and recent attention given to the machinery question in Parliament, Ricardo's acolytes were compelled to explain this conundrum.[8]

Ellis's "Employment of Machinery" (1826) confronted the problem presented by Ricardo. He acknowledged (1826, p. 102) that Ricardo's *Principles* indicated the use of machinery might be detrimental to the working classes in some cases, but added "we think his arguments are inconclusive." Using the basic Ricardian framework Ellis argued:

> The strongest case ... which can, with any appearance of plausibility, be stated against any given improvement in machinery is, that, by a sudden absorption of that portion of capital devoted to the payment of wages, *wages* MAY *be temporarily reduced*. It is evident that they MUST *be ultimately raised*, unless the rise be counteracted by an increase in population (1826, p. 116).

After acknowledging this "strongest case," Ellis disputed "the probability even of a temporary depression." He asserted (1826, p. 106) that the anticipation of greater profits due to the improvements in machinery prevented even a temporary decline in wages.

Despite Nesbitt's complaint (1934, p. 58) of "Ellis's laborious defense of machinery,"[9] this article made several significant contributions. Not only did the article confront the problem presented by Ricardo, but as Berg notes (1980, pp. 89, 106), Ellis also recognized the power of anticipated profits. The recognition of the power of anticipated profits was important, for by arguing that fresh savings could be induced by the expectation of greater profits, Ellis rejected the fixed wages fund analysis of the classical school and separated savings from investment. Viner notes (1937, pp. 194-195) Ellis was the

> only member of the Ricardian School [he had] found who gave any attention to the fact that saving might have other motives than securing interest on current investment and who showed some recognition that the "transmission of savings into capital" was not an automatic and certain process.

Ellis's analysis suggested that the original investment did not need to come from the "wages fund," and furthermore, the process was self-perpetuating:

> when that additional capital is introduced, motives in abundance are presented for still further accumulation, since profits will have risen in as much as the same number of labourers, aided by more powerful instruments, will be able to produce a larger quantity of commodities (1826, p. 116).

He continued,

> The grand source of all the false reasoning upon machinery is to be found in the supposition that every new application of capital to other purposes than that of paying wages is a deduction from the fund devoted to that purpose (1826, p. 119).

In another *Westminster Review* article, "Exportation of Machinery" (1825), Ellis addressed the issue that, in 1824, Parliament had left unresolved—whether English-made machinery should be exported. The article is notable for its doctrinaire support of free trade and for using, for its time, a sophisticated example of comparative advantage to illustrate the benefits from trade.[10] To Ellis, the export of machinery was essentially a free trade issue, and he assumed that free trade was an accepted doctrine by anyone who did not seek to advance a special interest. Suggesting that this issue should have already been settled by Parliament, he opined that the "examination of any additional witnesses would be a mere waste of time" (1825, p. 386).

Ellis affirmed his strong free trade sentiment in his 1826 article on machinery. He asserted that not only was it acceptable for capitalists to sell machinery abroad to take advantage of higher profits, but that any other investment abroad that improved the profits of capitalists would be beneficial to the home country. He concluded (1826, p. 130):

capitalists ought not to suffer themselves to be diverted from any profitable employment
of their capitals by a fear of injuring the working classes. Wherever their capitals can be
most profitably employed for themselves, whether in machinery or horse-labour, or in
foreign countries, there it is most for the interest of the labouring classes that they should
be invested.

Ellis's conclusion concerning the export of capital also differs sharply from
that of Ricardo. Ricardo asserted that, while investing capital in machinery
would be detrimental to workers because it would lower demand for labor,
the export of capital would be far worse. He wrote (1951-1973, vol. 1, p. 397),
"by investing part of a capital in improved machinery, there will be a diminution
in the progressive demand for labour; by exporting it to another country, the
demand will be wholly annihilated."

It is evident from Ellis's two articles on the machinery question that the
doctrine presented by Ellis and the Millian group had already deviated
significantly from that of Ricardo. Nevertheless, Ellis's analysis was generally
within the Ricardian framework. Ellis was merely more optimistic about the
means of avoiding the declining rate of profit. Whereas Ricardo felt that
improvements in machinery could delay a stationary state in which profits had
declined to the lowest possible level such that no additional investment could
be induced, Ellis thought that not only would machinery improvements
postpone the stationary state, but that the improvements would directly benefit
all classes. In Ellis's mind there was true harmony of interests among all classes,
while Ricardo's chapter on machinery at best left this in doubt. J.S. Mill later
wrote that he regarded Ellis's 1826 article on the tendency of profits to reach
a minimum to be "the most scientific treatment of the subject which I have
met with" (Mill, 1965, p. 748).[11]

Another article during this period that was important, at least as a forerunner
of much of Ellis's later interest in education, was his July, 1824 piece,
"Charitable Institutions." While conceding the usefulness of some charities,
such as those providing for the care of the deaf and mute and indigent blind
or hospitals that cared for wounds, fractures, highly contagious diseases or
other bodily hurts, he cautioned individuals not to allow the evil arising from
the consequences of their benevolent actions to outweigh the positive benefits
achieved. It was important to remember "every increase of the funds for the
maintenance of the poor, has a tendency to raise up such an additional supply
of persons to be fed, that each individual shall be no better provided than
before" (1824a, pp. 99, 103, 114-120). In an attempt to demonstrate that
economists were not hard-hearted when they refused to help the indigent poor,
Ellis asked (1824a, p. 105): is it "better to relieve the indigent, or so to order
things that there shall be no indigent to relieve." His remedy was to educate
the poor so they could understand their situation and develop the prudence
and forethought necessary to avoid destitution.[12]

## III. EARLY POPULARIZING

After his initial flurry of articles in the *Westminster Review*, Ellis devoted most of his time and energy to his insurance company.[13] Nevertheless, he continued to be interested in promoting the ideas of the classical economists. During the late 1820s and 1830s, Ellis particularly was interested in propagating economic ideas among the adult population.[14] He gave numerous lectures during the period and held informal discussions with the working men of the London Mechanics' Institute.[15] Ellis compiled his lectures and informal discussions in 1829 into a pamphlet, *Conversations upon Knowledge, Happiness, and Education between a Mechanic and a Patron of the London Mechanics' Institution*. In the discussions, Ellis stressed the Malthusian population doctrine and the importance of prudence and forethought, topics that would be major components of his later teaching.

While the *Conversations* provided a framework for Ellis's later educational efforts, a more important statement of his economic principles during this period was embodied in the set of economic lectures he presented to the City of London Literary Institution in 1835. They are one of the better examples of the state of the science that was being propagated in the 1830s.

As was usual with Ellis, he scrupulously guarded his identity as author of these lectures and, consequently, they were often attributed to Henry Brougham. Brougham was, in fact, accused of being a plagiarist when he had the lectures read at the Mechanics' Institutes, but he merely circulated the lectures among various Institutes after receiving Ellis's permission to do so.[16] Brougham thought so highly of the lectures that twenty-five years later he inquired of Ellis, "would you have any objection to their forming, with such additions or alterations as you may please to make, a part of the unpublished portion of my *Political Philosophy?*" By this time, however, Ellis "thought them not of sufficient value to be worth publishing" (Blyth, 1892, p. 54).

The message of the lectures was that of the orthodox classical school as popularized by both Mill and McCulloch. Ellis emphasized that the lessons reflected his own opinions, "but while I claim your attention as if to the exposition of my individual opinions, it must be understood that I pretend to have made no discovery. In these lectures there will be found little or nothing original" (Ellis, 1836, p. 1). While it is true that Ellis presented little original material in these lectures, they are, nevertheless, an important rendering of the state of the science that was being popularized at the time.

The lectures began by defining political economy as "the science of the laws which regulate the production, distribution, and consumption, of those material products which have exchangeable value, and which are either necessary, useful, or agreeable to man" (1836, p. 1). Ellis divided the "laws or principles" of political economy into those relating to the physical world and those relating to human nature. The law regulating human nature was that of Smith or Bentham; that is, everyone desired his or her own happiness and tried to pursue pleasure and avoid pain. On the other hand, the laws relating to the physical world were derived from Ricardian and Malthusian political economy. In their simplest form, the physical laws can be stated as four propositions: first, labor is necessary for human existence; second, some land is more fertile than other lands; third, as labor is added to land, diminishing returns operate; and, fourth, if workers are adequately provided for, the population will double every twenty to twenty-five years. To these propositions, Ellis added that happiness was not possible without wealth, so the goal of political economy was to create as much wealth as possible. Then, "if wealth is judiciously distributed, the progress of wealth is the progress of civilization" (1836, pp. 3-4).

From these basic postulates, Ellis elaborated on an economic system that was essentially Ricardian in nature. As had Ricardo, Ellis emphasized the importance of repealing the Corn Laws and the role of taxation in the economy. Like Ricardo, Ellis concluded that the Corn Laws and high taxes were the major governmental policies that were inhibiting wages, and thus, the well-being of workers. If one could assume good government with no Corn Laws and low taxation, Ellis maintained, the only worry would arise from the tendency of population to increase faster than the rate of capital (1836, pp. 34-35).

The possibility that population might increase faster than capital was the greatest concern of Ellis and many popularizers of political economy. The role of the government in attacking the population problem, as well as in the economy in general, was easily definable; government should "do nothing more than secure the faithful performance of contracts, and provide a cheap and convenient medium of exchange." The most critical mistake the government had made with regard to the population problem, Ellis wrote, was to encourage population growth through the Poor Laws (1836, pp. 97-98).

Ellis identified (1836, pp. 37-38) as possible solutions to the population problem an increased awareness and prudence on the part of the populace, an increase in the quantity of available food (either through increased domestic production or through importation), and emigration. Only the former was deemed to be a long-term solution. For Ellis, as for other classical economists, this justified an exception to the general principle of laissez-faire. He felt it was critical for all classes to be educated so they could understand that "the rate of wages is dependent upon the rate which the number of labourers bears to capital, and upon nothing else" (1836, p. 100). Ellis continued:

> the science of Political Economy, if it taught no other truth than this, would be well deserving of attention; and if this truth were once universally acknowledged, most of the other improvements, so much to be desired for the good of society, would follow as a matter of course.

To enable all classes to learn and understand this principle, Ellis favored free schools to teach reading and writing to all classes (Ellis, 1836, p. 87, 1824a, p. 12).

Like Ricardo and James Mill, Ellis believed in the Law of the Markets. In no uncertain terms Ellis stated (1836, p. 82):

> there can never be too much produced. The mere supposition of such a thing as overproduction is too ridiculous to admit of its being expressed in language. Men produce because they want more than they have. Since this is always the case, the general case is there cannot be overproduction.

Ellis conceded that there could be temporary overproduction of a particular commodity, but it would be counterbalanced by underproduction of another commodity.

While Ellis's lectures were Ricardian in most respects, they contained some differences that he, as well as other popularizers of the period, often noted.[17] For example, the Ricardian concept of value posed problems for Ellis, who suggested (1836, p. 49), "much of the confusion and difficulty which have heretofore prevailed in the science of Political Economy may be traced to the word value."[18] Ellis departed from Ricardo's attempt to establish a labor theory of value and returned to a Smithian cost of production analysis. He indicated that price was synonymous with value, although expressed in money terms. Price or value was determined in the shortrun by fluctuations in demand and supply, but, ultimately, value depended "entirely" on cost of production.[19]

In his lecture on "Interchange," Ellis presented some of the strongest arguments of his day for free trade. Though Ellis had originally presented his ideas in 1825 and 1826 articles in which he attacked the Ricardian position that machinery might be detrimental to labor, his ideas, nevertheless, were consistent with Ricardo's goal of repealing the Corn Laws. Ricardo, however, did not foreclose the possibility of restricting the export of machinery because it could harm labor, while Ellis strongly asserted that "restrictions never fail to check commerce in general—they may extend particular branches [at the expense of other branches], but that is all" (1836, p. 79).

Although Ellis maintained that labor "is the source of all wealth," in his chapters on distribution, he carefully explained why the entire produce of labor should not be divided among laborers. Not only did capitalists and landlords deserve a share in the produce of the country, but the profits and rents they received were necessary inducements to call forth additional capital (Ellis, 1836, pp. 9, 26, 28, 43).

Ricardo had suggested that population pressure and diminishing returns in agriculture led to the inevitable tendency of profits to fall and capital to cease to accumulate. Ellis, however, believed that "this tendency is constantly checked by the various improvements in science which are brought to light, day by day." The possibility of technological improvements was one more reason to encourage a general diffusion of education. "The greater the number of instructed people, the greater the number of those from whom the improvements in science are to be expected." Ellis further asserted that education was necessary to improve the skill of the workmen and that to acquire the necessary knowledge workers needed "the power of purchasing assistance, and leisure" to learn (Ellis, 1836, pp. 44-45). Increased skill and the leisure to learn would not be possible with low wages, so Ellis maintained that it behooved both the capitalist and the laborer to keep wages as high as possible.

In general, Ellis was more optimistic than Ricardo. While Ricardo indicated, and Ellis agreed, that technological improvements, along with low taxation and repeal of the Corn Laws, could ward off declining profits and the stationary state, Ellis thought a stationary state could be avoided solely by improved technology. Ellis even suggested, as J.S. Mill (1965, p. 746-751) stated more elaborately some years later, that as long as population did not continue to increase, the stationary state was not necessarily bad. Ellis indicated (1836, p. 42), "it must not be supposed, however, that such a state of things [a stationary state] would be at all inconsistent with the utmost perfection of happiness of which the human race is susceptible." Ellis cautioned that the stationary state must not be achieved prematurely or just for the sake of achieving it. The goal of society was to attain perfect happiness, and he merely suggested that perfect happiness and the stationary state could coexist. In addition, Ellis attempted to preserve the ideas of harmony of interest among the classes, whereas Ricardo did not deny that there might be a temporary conflict of interests. For Ellis, the accumulation of capital was of primary importance. If more capital were accumulated, all classes would benefit, regardless of whether or not the accumulation resulted from machinery improvements, export of machinery, or any other method.

Ellis concluded by insisting that legislative reforms were insufficient to raise the living standards of the working class. The goal of increasing the productivity of the population could only be achieved through individual initiative. Political institutions could help only indirectly by

> giving to each individual a motive so to regulate his conduct as to further the general interests—they may be instrumental also in diffusing knowledge; and knowledge is the source of all happiness which we enjoy (Ellis, 1836, p. 102).

Government could motivate individuals by educating them, by protecting their property, and by staying out of the marketplace. Individual initiative and good conduct were the only other major ingredients needed to promote the well-being of society.

As stated above, after 1826 Ellis turned his attention to his family and business interests, and his theoretical contributions in the late 1820s and 1830s were minor. He did, however, remain active as a popularizer of classical economics. Ellis's *Lectures* stressed the importance of education, primarily as a vehicle for disseminating knowledge about political economy. Education of the masses had long been a dream of many classical economists, but, as of the 1830s, little progress had been realized.[20] Secular reading material had been introduced to a larger segment of the adult population through organizations such as the Mechanics' Institutes and the Society for the Diffusion of Useful Knowledge, but many individuals felt this process would not be complete until secular knowledge was introduced to young children.[21] When his family and business demands eased in the 1840s, Ellis made this his cause. That effort is the subject of the next section.

## IV.  LATER ECONOMICS, ECONOMIC EDUCATION AND POPULARIZING

Ellis's initial experience in educating young children was in 1846 when he gave a series of lectures on Social Economy at a British and Foreign Society School in Cold Harbour Lane, Camberwell. He wanted to demonstrate that political economy could be taught easily and effectively to ordinary school age children. His experiment apparently succeeded beyond his expectations and inspired him to devote as much time, energy, and resources as possible to ensuring that social economy was taught in all schools.

When Ellis completed his lectures, he immediately incorporated them in a book for teachers, *Outlines of Social Economy* (1846). The *Outlines* were, in essence, a shortened and simplified version of his 1836 *Lectures* presented to adults at Mechanics' Institutes. Like the earlier *Lectures* and his articles for the *Westminster Review*, Ellis's *Outlines* were written anonymously. He hoped his book would be circulated among teachers who would use it in their schools, much as his earlier *Lectures* had been circulated among the Mechanics' Institutes. Publishers were instructed to make it available at low cost to any school that accepted voluntary contributions. The *Outlines* attracted a good deal of attention, eventually going through three editions as well as French, Dutch, and Japanese translations (Blyth, 1892, p. 121 Morris-Suzuki, 1989, p. 50).

Beginning with *Outlines*, Ellis attempted to characterize economics as a moral science that concerned all segments of the population, including young children, rather than an abstruse science that could only be understood by the middle and upper classes. He hinted at this change in *Outlines* by using the term "social economy" instead of "political economy." Although Ellis did not explain in *Outlines* what the term meant, his later writings make it clear that he felt that "social economy" better reflected the connection between economics and individual conduct than did "political economy." Social economy was related to, indeed a part of, social science, a term used by Ellis to imply consideration "not only of the means of supplying physical wants ... but of the teaching and training, and self discipline, without which the desirable qualifications are not to be had in perfection" (Ellis, 1863, p. 10). Ellis (1849b, pp. 10-14, 89) later defined social science as "knowledge of the effects produced upon human well-being by human acts as causes," and social economy or economical science as "all that is known or knowable of the consequences of different lines of human action or conduct in the production, accumulation, and distribution of wealth, as bearing upon the general well-being or happiness of society." In other words, social economy was that part of social science concerned with promoting well-being through production, distribution and accumulation of wealth. Ellis's emphasis on social economics placed him at the forefront of what Nitsch (1990, pp. 13-14) refers to as the "positive law" or "moral philosophical" vein of social economists that influenced England in the 1840s.

Ellis concluded *Outlines* by suggesting that only the power of reason allowed men and women to conquer their basic desires. Ellis felt the ability to reason could best be taught at an early age; thus, it was unfortunate that many children did not receive enough early training to develop their reasoning. While he recognized training in social economy was only one part of a proper education, Ellis maintained:

> without a knowledge of social economy, it is utterly impossible for any body to form a correct judgement either upon the tendency of his own individual conduct, or of the acts of society ... Without it, the causes of the privation and suffering by which he is surrounded and to which he is exposed, must ever remain a mystery to him.

While completing his successful experiment teaching young children and writing *Outlines*, Ellis developed a lasting interest in using social economy as the foundation of a secular education for children. But, to prove the practicality of his theory, he needed schools to adopt his techniques. In 1846 he inquired, through Francis Place, about starting a school under the superintendence of William Lovett. The school eventually opened on February 28, 1848, with Ellis providing the desks, books, apparatus, and the salary for the schoolmaster. By October of that year, the school had over 200 students. Ellis personally taught a course on social science, while Lovett taught physiology in addition to providing superintendence (Blyth, 1892, pp. 83-87).[22]

## A. Birkbeck Schools

While many classical economists had commented on the lack of education among the working class and had lamented that the economy would work more efficiently if only the lower classes were aware of the principles of political economy, only Ellis founded schools based on this principle.[23] Soon after opening the school under the superintendence of Lovett, Ellis opened the first school in which he truly demonstrated the practicality of his ideas on teaching social economy. Ellis secured the building, guaranteed its expenses for five years, and persuaded his friend, John Runz, to be master of the school (Blyth, 1892, pp. 89-91).[24] In addition, Ellis agreed to teach three lessons a week on social economy to the children and two such lessons a week to adults at night. The school, which opened on July 17, 1848, was named the Birkbeck School in honor of George Birkbeck, the founder of the Mechanics' Institutes.[25] The first Birkbeck School was an immediate success. By 1850 it was teaching 340 boys; soon thereafter it opened a school for girls. The school was also used for many years as a training ground for many of the teachers who later became masters at other schools (Blyth, 1892, pp. 91-92, 95-96).

Ellis eventually founded seven Birkbeck Schools with enrollments of between 300 and 900 students (Blyth, 1892, pp. 104-111). He hoped to establish schools in different districts throughout London to serve as models for other schools. Ellis was confident that once his method had been demonstrated, other schools would readily adopt it. He was encouraged in this endeavor by a number of individuals, including Francis Place, who wrote, "you are going on in the right way all together and will by means of the secular schools produce a new era" (Place, 1849).

The unique feature of Ellis's Birkbeck Schools was their emphasis on teaching laws of conduct as well as traditional courses in reading, writing, and arithmetic. Ellis based his laws of conduct on the laws of classical political economy. In his prospectus for the first Birkbeck School, he wrote that, in addition to traditional courses, the children

> are to be made acquainted with the laws of their own organisation in order that they may understand how much their health, general energy, physical happiness, and length of life are dependent on their own conduct, also with the laws of social economy, that they may properly understand their own position in society, and their duties towards it (Blyth, 1892, p. 92).

Though most educators thought political economy was "abstruse and difficult to understand," Ellis was determined to demonstrate that the subject could be "brought down to the comprehension of children of the ordinary school age" (Blyth, 1892, p. 80). He firmly believed that if children understood the laws of classical economics or social economy, as they grew older they would more willingly accept the existing system and work diligently to improve their condition.

Ellis further elaborated on the intent of his teaching in a circular describing the Birkbeck School at Peckham, in which he stated that particular attention would be focused on teaching social economy including:

(1) Instruction in the means by which wealth or the comforts and necessaries of life are produced; this inquiry leading to the conviction in the minds of the pupils, that industry, skill, economy and security to property must prevail in society, in order that this production be abundant: (2) Instruction in the advantages of the division of labour and capital, and in the arrangements which facilitate interchange; the study of these subjects furnishing the pupils with arguments which demonstrate beyond all doubt how honesty, sobriety, punctuality, and moral discipline must obtain amongst a people for these arrangements to be fully serviceable: and (3) Instruction in the influence upon the general well-being, of the prevalence of parental forethought or of parental improvidence (E.E. Ellis, 1888, pp. 67-68).

Ellis maintained that his schools were not modeled on any existing schools but took the best parts from several different methods. The circular issued upon the opening of the Peckham Birkbeck School said, "the monitorial system of Bell and Lancaster, the collective-lesson system of Stowe, and the arrangements incident to the object-lesson system of Pestalozzi, have a place in the Birkbeck School" (E.E. Ellis, 1888, p. 66).

Other distinguishing features of the Birkbeck Schools included the elimination of corporal punishment, a questioning or Socratic style of teaching, and the omission of all subjects that Ellis did not feel were necessary. He dismissed the classics, for example, as "groping among the rubbish, and filth, and superstition of by-gone times" (Ellis, 1850b, p. 409).

Assessing the overall impact of Ellis's schools is difficult. His seven Birkbeck schools were certainly successful, attaining enrollments of between 300 and 900 and some remaining open long after the passage of the Education Act of 1870, notwithstanding the fact that they relied on fees to pay part of the expenses and received no support from the state or from churches. C.T. Bartley (1871, p. 26) indicated that of the 1,384,203 students in school in 1869 approximately 1,100,000 were in church schools and most of the remaining students were educated by the War Department, the Home Office, or the Poor Law Board. The only exception to this general pattern was provided by the six remaining Birkbeck Schools. Despite the modest fees, which nevertheless could be burdensome for a relatively poor working-class family, students from such families did attend the Birkbeck Schools. Bartley reported (1871, p. 421):

several interesting examples have been adduced of the appreciation shown by comparatively poor parents of the value of an advanced education to their children. It frequently happens that great sacrifices are made to enable at least one of a family to have the benefit of a year or two at the Birkbeck School, which is regarded in the neighborhood as one giving a sort of finishing education. If one of the boys in a family shows great promise, he is sent there after leaving the Elementary School.

Though the Birkbeck Schools were successful, Ellis never gained broad-based support for his ideas. The major obstacles that Ellis was not able to overcome were the dominance and opposition of the church schools and the reluctance of the lower classes to submit to education perceived to be provided by the middle or upper classes.[26]

Although church schools had always been dominant providers of education, they became even more prominent in the 1840s and 1850s. Churches had significantly more resources to fund schools than any other private group; in addition, when the government began to subsidize private education in the 1830s, the bulk of governmental support went to church schools. Though the church schools began to introduce some secular subjects into their curricula, they required secular subjects to be tempered by heavy doses of religious training. There seemed to be little hope that the church schools would provide adequate training in secular subjects. For this reason, many of the classical economists, including J.S. Mill, had acceded to the reality that only a state-supported system could provide universal secular education, and supported such a system, even if it did not offer political economy as a subject.[27]

The other obstacle facing Ellis and his schools was the resistance by the lower classes of any effort by the upper or middle classes to educate the lower classes. The distrust by the lower classes was rooted in their perception of increasing poverty due to industrialization and previous attempts by political economists to explain their situation. Writers with sympathies for the laboring class soon began to recognize that "political economy in the hands of [classical economists] was an ideological buttress of the inequitable status quo; it was a theoretical rationalisation of the impoverishment of labor" (Thompson, 1984, p. 21).

Initially, labor movement sympathizers were at a disadvantage in the contest for the support of the working class because they had no complete economic theory to combat the classical school in its own terms. In the mid-1820s, however, William Thompson, Thomas Hodgskin, and John Gray provided a theoretical foundation for an anticapitalist critique of the classical school. In addition, in the early 1830s numerous working-class newspapers appeared specifically to criticize the methods and concepts of the classical economists and to promote those of Hodgskin, Thompson, or Gray.

In this environment, many classical economists began to view schools as having the greatest potential for molding attitudes and future policy because they were one of the few vehicles through which a middle- or upper-class ideology could be presented directly to the people with little competition or resistance from the lower class. J.F.C. Harrison (1961, p. 40) put it this way:

> The working classes had no distinctive educational ideology of their own.... there was no alternative but to accept the instruction offered in the middle-class Sunday and day schools.... The Schools were not the people's institutions, but rather instruments for shaping society according to dominant middle-class views.

The common view of Senior, Longfield, Whately, and other classical economists was that schools should carefully "train" students to accept the "correct" principles of political economy. According to Senior, education has two functions, teaching and training:

> As between teaching and training, there can be no doubt that training is by far the more important.... Training, therefore, or the formation of habits, rather than teaching, or the imparting of knowledge, is the great business of society (Senior, quoted in Blaug, 1975, pp. 578-579).

Longfield reminded his beginning students of

> their obligation to educate the working class in the "true" principles of political economy so that they would learn what types of legislation would further their interests and what types would hinder them.... specifically, the worker must learn that he cannot raise his wages by "violent demolition of the capital destined to his support," or by advocating laws that promise to increase his share of national product by limiting profit (Moss, 1976, p. 19).

Similarly, Whately argued

> that workers were equivalent to the "savages" in the colonies, and that their education should be equivalent to that which attempted to "civilize" those peoples—acceptance of England's colonial domination (Henry, 1990, p. 142).

With these expressed attitudes, there is little wonder that the efforts of Ellis and others were commonly perceived as propagandizing or worse. For example, one of Ellis's disciples whose teaching was based on Ellis's principles was "accused by the parents of his children...of being 'a special pleader for the capitalists,' and had been informed that the political economy lessons would be refuted at home" (Stewart and McCann 1967, p. 330). There is also little doubt that Dickens' fictional Gradgrind school portrayed in *Hard Times* (1854) was a satirical treatment of the genre of schools to which the Birkbeck Schools belonged, and such writings reinforced the lower-class skepticism of schools promoted by the upper classes.[28]

## B.   Other Popularizing Methods

Because of the obstacles cited above, Ellis's most optimistic hopes for the Birkbeck Schools were not fulfilled. Ellis's influence, however, was much broader than the accomplishments of the Birkbeck Schools. A significant number of other schools copied Ellis's methods or were otherwise directly influenced by Ellis. Other schools were indirectly influenced by Ellis or used his lessons in social economy.[29] Moreover, his financial assistance supported many schools and allowed them to teach classes based on his principles. Miller (1882, p. 233) estimates he gave a quarter of a million pounds in support of other schools, but even this estimate may be low because Ellis tried to keep his contributions confidential. In addition, Ellis propagated his ideas through teacher training colleges, lectures at various schools across the country, classes for adults, and numerous books and pamphlets.

Ellis tried to establish social economy as a subject taught at the British and Foreign Society School and Church of England Training Colleges, but when they declined his offers to establish and teach these classes, Ellis started his own training classes for teachers. The classes began in 1847 and were maintained, with the help of John Runz, for two or three years. The classes met on Saturdays and had as many as fifty teachers attending at one time. In these classes, teachers and aspiring teachers not only learned how to teach in general but also learned Ellis's method of teaching social economy. When these teachers were employed at various schools across Britain, they assuredly carried some of Ellis's ideas with them.[30]

In addition to the Birkbeck Schools and teacher training schools, Ellis taught classes for adults who wanted to learn how the science of conduct might be taught. The adult classes not only served the middle and lower classes but also attracted members of Parliament and the nobility. Among other well-known attendees were Richard Cobden, Lady Byron, and Florence Nightingale. Noted educationists, such as George Combe, came directly to the Birkbeck Schools to observe Ellis's methods (Blyth, 1892, p. 65).

Another aspect of Ellis's propagation of classical economics consisted of the many books, pamphlets, and articles he produced. Ellis appealed to as many different audiences as possible with his publications. Some were written in the questioning style Ellis thought appropriate for the classroom. These books, which often stated a proposition followed by several questions that might be appropriate to help understand the proposition, were aimed at those who were interested in teaching social economy or those who wanted to learn how it may be effectively taught. Other publications contained standard discussions of the principles of social economy, which always included liberal doses of classical political economy as well as Ellis's theories concerning the role of good moral conduct. His *Religion in Common Life* (1857) argued that the moral principles he taught were similar to the principles taught by the Church. In other works, which were published anonymously, he assumed the role of an objective outsider, who, of course, concluded that society needed more education in social economy.[31]

In addition to the books Ellis wrote, many of his associates wrote books adopting or incorporating his ideas. Lovett's books have already been noted. Other writers who were strongly influenced by Ellis included several who had worked in the Birkbeck Schools, such as Benjamin Templar, W.A. Shields, and James Runz, as well as Dean Dawes, who was Dean of Hereford from

1850 to 1867 and had established several large, successful schools on his own, physician and author, Dr. M.R. Leverson and Ellis's good friend, educational reformer and political economist, W. B. Hodgson (Blyth, 1892, pp. 356-358; Jolly, 1879, pp. 196-200). In addition to writers who incorporated his theory, associates recommended Ellis's original works. For example, the educationist George Combe constantly recommended Ellis's works as good introductions to social and political science, and William Jolly referred to Ellis as the founder of "the Science of Human Well-being." He continued (1879, pp. 194-195):

> to Mr. William Ellis is due the merit, not only of introducing the subject into our common schools, but of so broadening it as to make it truly "the Science of Human Well-being," and of simplifying what was previously a dry and abstruse subject, and rendering it easily understood by children.

Recommendations of Ellis's books and the many books based on Ellis's method are an indication of the acceptance of his teaching.

Ellis's teaching was, in fact, so well known and regarded that in 1855 Prince Albert, who had read some of his books, asked Ellis to teach the principles of social economy to the Royal children. For almost a year, Ellis gave two sets of lessons, one to the older children and one to the younger, on Saturday afternoons.

In addition, as previously noted, Ellis's teaching extended beyond Britain; his textbooks were translated into French, Dutch, and Japanese. Morris-Suzuki reports (1989, pp. 49-50) that the 1867 translation of Ellis's *Outlines* was:

> the first Japanese translation of a general economics text ... Its translator was Kanda Takahira (1830-98), a well-established political and economic thinker who ... had been an articulate advocate of the opening of Japan to foreign trade. Kanda was a scholar of Dutch Learning and a language teacher at the *Bansho Shirabesho*, and he translated Ellis's book, not from the original English, but from a Dutch version which had in turn been translated by Simon Vissering.

Morris-Suzuki also notes that Ellis's text was still popular in the 1870s when two lecturers at the *Bansho Shirabesho* were sent by the government to study law and economics under Vissering (1818-1888), who was professor of economics at Leiden University. Ellis's influence also extended to Italy, where in 1864 Madame Salis Schwabe established a school based on his teaching. She noted that her headmaster had received all his training from the Birkbeck school in Peckham and that the headmaster taught "all the classes above the Kindergarten in the principles of social economy and right conduct as taught by Mr. Ellis." She regarded Ellis as "the pioneer of most of what is attempted in [Italy] as regards middle class education" (Blyth, 1892, pp. 250, 347-348).

Notwithstanding Ellis's successes, he never gained broad support for establishing schools centered around the principles of social economy nor established social economy as an integral part of the curriculum. His last hope of gaining support for his proposals was through the Royal Commission that was appointed in June of 1858 to examine the state of popular education in England. The Commission, which is often referred to as the Newcastle Commission, laid the foundation for the system of national education that was passed in Parliament in 1870. Ellis had several friends on the Commission and was granted a preliminary interview with the Commissioners. Ellis's pleading, however, had minimal effect, and the prospects for making social economy a part of the curriculum for all schools began to wane at this time.[32]

Even so, Ellis and his supporters continued to promote his ideas whenever possible. The Birkbeck Schools, as well as many other private schools, continued teaching social economy even after the Education Act of 1870 regimented the curriculum for public schools.[33] One of Ellis's friends, Rosamond Davenport-Hill, introduced social science into the Board Schools in London in the 1880s. Stewart and McCann (1967, p. 340) note, "she found that in some cases headmasters had already been teaching social science for some years on the Ellis plan." They further suggest, "Ellis's social science was the forerunner of the civics courses introduced into the elementary system ... in the 1890s, and the parent of all social studies courses that exist in schools and colleges today." Thus, Ellis's teaching continued to have a lasting impact long after his death in 1881.

## C.  Content of Ellis's Later Works

The later works of William Ellis do not substantially add to or alter the economic doctrines he presented earlier in *Westminster Review* articles and the 1836 *Lectures*. His works contained all the usual accouterments of classical economics—laissez-faire, Malthus's population principle, diminishing returns in agriculture, the equalization of profits, the iron law of wages, the law of the markets, harmony of interests among all classes, and free interaction of self-interested individuals as the best means to attain the greatest happiness for society. Ellis also returned to Smith's cost of production theory of value rather than Ricardo's labor theory, which made it easier to discuss the harmony of interests between different classes. He suggested (1868, pp. 111-112):

> the tendency of the efforts of each [capitalist and laborer] is to bring together the labourer who can tender the service required, and the employers who can best pay for it, and best turn it to profitable account: the struggle, if the term must be used, being rather of labourer against labourer, and employer against employer, than of employer against labourer.

As noted previously, however, Ellis attempted to broaden the study of economics and shift the focus to its moral dimensions. One of the clearest examples of the evolution of his work is a comparison of the first edition of

*Outlines of Social Economy* (1846) to the third edition (1860). The first edition is little more than a shortened and simplified version of the 1836 *Lectures,* whereas the third edition contains numerous passages emphasizing training individuals in moral conduct. Ellis conveyed the general message that good conduct—mainly industry, economy, and forethought—were instrumental in promoting the well-being of society. He stressed that it was the individual's responsibility to determine how prosperous he or she was and that individuals who worked hard and saved were the ones who would be most successful. An individual could improve his or her wages by becoming more useful. The best land went to the individual who could best use it, and this individual was willing to pay the highest rent. Likewise, the highest profits went to those willing to take the greatest risk or those whose skill of superintending capital were the greatest (Ellis, 1860, pp. 25, 71, 77).

In addition, in the third edition Ellis strongly cautioned laborers against using credit. He recognized credit was very important for the well-being of society, but recommended that laborers should only come into contact with credit as lenders. He maintained (1860, p. 76), "a borrowing workman—a workman who not only neglects to save from his present earnings—but actually uses credit in order to live upon his future earnings, is foredoomed to misery."

In the 1860 edition of *Outlines,* Ellis encouraged competition *and* cooperation, emphasizing that both were necessary for human progress. He suggested (1860, p. 83) that cooperation was one of the best means of producing present and future wealth and added, "as cooperation must be ranked among the most efficient of producers, so must competition be ranked among the most efficient distributors." Ellis was referring to cooperation among employees and between workers and their employers. If cooperation among these groups existed, workers would be more productive and the well-being of society would be enhanced. This reasoning could also be found among other classical economists, but Ellis shifted the emphasis from competition to a balance between cooperation and competition.

Finally, in the third edition, Ellis emphasized forethought, particularly parental forethought, more than any other individual characteristic. Though he still maintained that for wages to increase, population must increase at a slower rate than capital accumulated, Ellis stressed (1860, p. 26) that "parental forethought ... may be said to be the one thing needful to establish an 'average rate of wages' compatible with a state of well-being." Parental forethought was the means to limit population and, most importantly, to ensure that children received the proper education.

Other substantive alterations appearing in Ellis's later works relate more to the changes that had taken place in England than to any fundamental change in philosophy. By the 1850s, the Corn Laws had been repealed, laissez-faire legislation was in vogue, and the country was relatively prosperous. While Ellis viewed laissez-faire legislation as a major factor in Britain's prosperity and a vindication of the classical policies, he no longer devoted attention to the issue; for the most part, he considered the battle won.

Perhaps Ellis's greatest change in his later works was his softened attitude toward the destitute. Britain's prosperity and recent empirical evidence made the Malthusian specter of a crushing population problem less imminent; at the same time, however, England had a large number of destitute citizens. Evidence of Ellis's evolving attitude toward population and the poor is plentiful. The question had become not what to do about the destitute caused by overpopulation but what were the factors that were causing poverty. Ellis reasoned that it was the character of the population, rather than sheer numbers, that caused destitution. As he noted in *Education as a Means of Preventing Destitution* (1851, pp. 115-122), undereducation, not overpopulation, caused destitution. Likewise, more and better quality education was the solution for destitution, not more emigration.

As for treatment of the destitute, in his April, 1850 *Westminster Review* article, Ellis went so far as to defend the Poor Laws against an attack in the *Edinburgh Review*. The *Edinburgh* reviewer maintained the Poor Laws were a cause of destitution and said the government should only intervene "for salvation of life." Ellis responded saying he could not blame those who had a tendency "to consider Political Economists as opposed to humanity" if they thought this type of thinking to be the norm for political economists. Ellis further asserted that destitution existed long before the Poor Laws, so destitution was a cause of the Poor Laws, not the reverse as the *Edinburgh* reviewer had stated. While Ellis did not advocate being overly lenient with the poor, he thought it absurd to intentionally inflict harsh treatment on those receiving poor relief. When it came to giving out aid, he said:

> The building, the diet, the clothing, the arrangements should be so applied as to afford the *maximum* of comfort out of the *minimum* of means. The steady and intelligent application of this principle would rid us of a great deal of rubbishy talk about "*labour-tests*," and all of those offensive attempts, by malconstruction of buildings and by harshness of treatment, to make life in a poor-house unbearable (Ellis, 1850a, pp. 155, 157-158, 162).

Elsewhere, Ellis (1850c, p. 80) contended, "destitution unrelieved is intolerable to a humane people. Where it has not been prevented, it must be relieved."

Despite his softened views toward the poor, Ellis remained an ardent supporter of the general population doctrine of Malthus and the wages fund doctrine. He continued to argue against indiscriminate alms-giving, reminding workers they would have to share the burden for supporting the poor. He clearly hoped that the laborers would take a proprietary interest in seeing destitution eradicated.

Ellis's later works were also different than his earlier works because they focused on teaching children about practical issues, rather than solely presenting economic theory. For this reason, he addressed topics such as Britain's system of money, the workings of the banking and credit system, the importance of insurance, and the system of taxation.[34] He also moralized to a much greater degree, never hesitating to teach children which traits were necessary to succeed in life.[35] These traits, of course, were consistent with Ellis's economics and could be taken as mere proselytizing to appease the lower classes. There is every indication, however, that Ellis firmly and in good faith believed that if only all economic classes could understand the economic and social forces around them, they would act in accordance with economic laws and cooperate with one another, thus benefiting the entire society. Ellis's devotion to teaching people about the relationship between individual conduct, societal well-being, and economics made his social economy unique and distinguished him from other economists.

The impact of Ellis's schools did not fully meet his expectations, but his influence was still substantial. In addition to founding the Birkbeck Schools, Ellis was involved in many other activities to promote his ideas. His many activities certainly made him one of the leading propagators of the economic ideas that permeated the middle and upper classes by the 1850s and led Stewart and McCann (1967, p. 339) to assert:

> Ellis was probably the most influential educator of the mid-nineteenth century. Not only was he always ready to endow schools that followed his principles, but the success of his methods and the persuasiveness of his manner assured him of a number of disciples who endeavoured to put into practice all or some of his teachings.

# V. CONCLUSION

While Ellis did not continue to contribute novel economic theories throughout his career, it is nevertheless curious that Ellis's contributions have been largely ignored or forgotten, while other popularizers of economics, such as Jane Marcet and Harriet Martineau, are remembered.[36] As Madame Schwabe, who brought Ellis's method to Italy, reflected a scant seven years after Ellis's death:

> To us who have sat at his feet, to learn, not abstruse formulas, but some of the life-bringing principles which ought to direct the conduct of man..., the fact may well seem inexplicable that so few years after the close of William Ellis's career, his name...is almost forgotten and, among the younger generation, utterly unknown. We all remember to what extent Ellis courted obscurity during life and oblivion after death. But it is surprising, nevertheless, that the nation should allow one of its patriarchal teachers of political economy as applied to the education of the people to be thus lost to memory (Blyth, 1892, p. 346).

Ellis's obscurity can be attributed partially to Ellis's desire to remain anonymous, but because so many well-placed individuals were aware of his efforts, this hardly accounts for his anonymity. A more likely explanation lies in the culture of England during Ellis's life. The Church, always a powerful force, jealously guarded its position in all matters, including education, and resisted any tampering with its curriculum. Similarly, the lower classes suspected the motives of the middle and upper classes in all matters, and the proselytizing nature of Ellis's approach may have served only to confirm their suspicions. At the same time, progressive leaders were promoting the idea of a publicly provided secular school system, and they likely were unwilling to jeopardize their goal by getting mired down in the issues presented by Ellis.

Given England's culture, perhaps it is surprising that Ellis accomplished as much as he did. He certainly deserves recognition as a forerunner in the movement to eliminate economic illiteracy. Contemporary educators have been pursuing the goal of economic literacy since at least the 1930s and, even though they do not face obstacles as significant as those faced by Ellis, have not succeeded fully. For example, as late as 1970, George Stigler (1970) raised serious questions about teaching economics even in high schools, suggesting that "economics is not yet ready to be made a part of the basic curriculum of all educated men." He continued, "economics belongs in everyone's education once we have learned to teach it," which, he argued we have not.[37]

Ellis also deserves recognition for broadening the subject of economics and his use of the term "social economy" instead of political economy in his later writings. The origin and use of the term "social economy" is just beginning to be explored by Nitsch and others, but Ellis's extensive later writings, and his change in focus in these writings, suggest that he was a leader in the movement to develop a social economics. Among the important elements of his later works were his focus on the well-being of society, rather than production of material wealth, his emphasis on ethical matters, and the attention he gave to cooperation as well as competition.

Thus, although his theoretical contributions were minor, Ellis deserves to be recognized for these contributions as well as his significant role as popularizer of classical economic doctrines, his efforts to provide economic education to all classes, and his attempts to broaden economics as a subject. He was undoubtedly influential in his day, but perhaps only now can his contributions be appreciated.

# NOTES

1.  A history of the early use of the term "social economics" is found in Nitsch (1990).
2.  See also Packe (1954, p. 52) who suggests that it was William Eyton Tooke, the son of Thomas Tooke, who first brought Ellis to J.S. Mill's study group in 1822.
3.  Although it is conventional to class Smith, Malthus, Mill, Ricardo, McCulloch, and Ellis as part of the classical economic tradition, it should be noted that some authors, such as Henry (1990, pp. 85, 121, 125, 161-165), would class the works of James Mill and J.R. McCulloch as anti-Ricardian or anticlassical. In this view, there were two separate traditions, and Ellis would

be labeled anti-Ricardian for his cost of production rather than labor theory of value. Also note that it is likely that the ideas presented by Ellis in the early *Westminster Review* articles were a direct result of the study group discussions. Nesbitt (1934, p. 26) suggests "it is not at all unlikely that most of the articles done for that journal by members of the [Utilitarian] Society were ... submitted to the entire group." He maintains "this concerted thinking" is probably responsible for the "evident confidence and authority that characterizes the papers."

4.   Ellis reviewed Mill's *Elements of Political Economy* (London, 1821) and McCulloch's *Principles of Political Economy* (London, 1825) in his *Westminster Review* articles of (1824b, 1825).

5.   Despite Ellis's contention (1824b, p. 289) that the book presented a "masterly and logical argument," he cautioned that the book should be read as one "would read Euclid" and not as "a novel." McCulloch (1964 [1845], pp. 17-18) later stated that Mill's book was "too abstract to be either popular or of much utility" and rated Jane Marcet's *Conversations on Political Economy* (1816) to be "on the whole, perhaps, the best introduction to the science that has yet appeared."

6.   It should be noted that Mill and Ellis were dissatisfied with the final version of their article on McCulloch. In a letter to McCulloch, James Mill wrote, Ellis and J.S. Mill "say that several important things were left out, and the article, by that and other editorial operations, disfigured" (Blyth, 1892, p. 36).

7.   McCulloch, as well as James Mill, has been criticized over the years for adding nothing original to the classical views. Schumpeter (1954, pp. 476-478), for example, refers to McCulloch and James Mill as "unconditional adherents and militant supporters of Ricardo's teaching" who added nothing substantial. For a discussion of the literature on this issue and reassessments of James Mill, see O'Brien (1988, pp. 188-193, 1970).

8.   The most notable outbreaks of worker agitation were during the Luddite riots of 1811-1812, the antimachinery riots of 1825-1826, and the later Swing riots of the early 1830s. The machinery question was discussed as a policy issue in 1824; as a result, the prohibition against the emigration of skilled artisans was repealed. Left unresolved was the question of whether English-made machinery should be exported.

9.   Elsewhere, Nesbitt (1934, p. 26) contradicts his own assessment when he notes: "Ellis wrote four excellent articles" (including the article "Employment of Machinery") in the *Westminster Review*.

10.   Ellis's example of comparative advantage is found on page 392. It should be noted that Ellis only asserted that the loss from not trading; by inference, the gain from trading would be divided between the two countries. It would be left for J.S. Mill to point out that the gains or losses depended on the supply and demand of the two countries. Ellis's argument regarding the benefits of trade is important, however, because he was the first to use three countries in an arithmetical example to demonstrate the doctrine of comparative costs. Viner (1937, p. 462) notes that though Ellis was the first to do this, his example was not completely satisfactory. For a discussion of the early use and development of comparative advantage see Thweatt (1976, 1986).

11.   Mill continued, the "essay excited little notice, partly from being published anonymously in a periodical, and partly because it was much in advance of the state of political economy at the time."

12.   Ellis later softened his position toward the poor. For a discussion of this issue see the section of this paper titled "Content of Ellis's Later Works."

13.   Ellis had married in 1825 and was living frugally. In 1827, he accepted the position of manager of the Indemnity Mutual Marine Assurance Company, which was tottering on the brink of bankruptcy. Although he was successful in rescuing the company and ensuring his financial security, undertaking such a position left him little time for political economy. E.E. Ellis (1888, p. 52) later observed, "not only did their new manager rescue the company from impending ruin, but he raised it into one of the most remarkable successes on record in the City."

14.   The effort to propagate classical economic ideas among the adult population is discussed in Sockwell (forthcoming).

15.   Although similar organizations existed in the past, the beginning of the Mechanics' Institute is generally dated at 1823 with the founding of the London Mechanics' Institutes. They were formed to provide lectures and access to books primarily for the artisan and working classes who otherwise may not have access to these materials. For a discussion of the origins of the Mechanics' Institutes, see Kelly (1957, pp. 58-76).

16.   Several letters from James Mill to Lord Brougham make it clear that Ellis was the author of the lectures and suggest that the charges of plagiarism were "ridiculous" (see Bain, 1966, pp. 389-392). Bloomfield still attributed this set of lectures (which had been delivered at the Glasgow Mechanics' Institution in 1835) to Brougham in his 1984 article in which he noted (pp. 187-193), Brougham repeats Ellis's examples and conclusions, "but without acknowledgement." In reality, it was Ellis himself who had simply lifted sections from his previous work. Brougham had borrowed the lectures from Ellis and paid to have them read throughout Britain on the condition that their author remain anonymous. Some examples of Ellis copying whole passages from his earlier works with little or no modification are *Lectures* (pp. 69-71) from Ellis (April 1825, pp. 388-393); *Lectures* (pp. 4-5) from Ellis (1824b, pp. 293-297); and *Lectures* (pp. 86-87) from Ellis (1824a, pp. 104-105, 112-113).

17.   Some writers note that by the 1830s, the popularizers had deviated so significantly from the Ricardian line that they should not be considered Ricardian economists. Schumpeter (1954, p. 478), for example, stated that by the 1830s, Ricardian economics was "no longer a living force." It is significant to note that when Ellis wrote of the knowledge he would like to disseminate, he omitted Ricardo from his list of economists. He stated (1849a, p. 391), "the future rate of progressive improvement among mankind depends greatly upon the success which awaits the efforts of those who are now engaged in making what there is of truth in the philosophy of Adam Smith, Malthus and the two Mills ... we look forward with confidence to see the great truths of social science transferred ... into common-places and unquestioned regulations of human conduct."

18.   McCulloch had written as early as 1824 that Ricardo's value theory was a "mere chimera" that was "entitled to no more respect, and, we believe, will be crowned with no better success, than the search after the philosopher's stone" (J.R. McCulloch, *The Scotsman*, [February 21, 1824], p. 114, quoted in O'Brien, 1970, p. 146.)

19.   Ellis (1836, p. 52) did make certain exceptions to his cost of production theory of value. He said there were some goods, such as rare books, in which there was no way to counteract an increase in demand. In these cases, value was determined solely by the proportion of demand to supply. In addition, he argued that the cost of production theory only applied when there was free competition, not when monopoly existed.

20.   Early classical economists and their views on education are discussed in Sockwell (1992, pp. 163-172).

21.   See, for example, Henry Brougham's 1835 speech on education (Brougham, 1838, p. 233-238).

22.   In many ways, Ellis and Lovett were a strange pair to start such an endeavor. Lovett was a journeyman carpenter who became involved in the worker's movement of the late 1830s and 1840s, and was primarily responsible for drawing up the document that became known as the People's Charter. What they had in common was that both believed in the power of education and that education or knowledge was the key to providing happiness for the working classes. Lovett was so impressed with Ellis's work that in 1852 he wrote his own book, *Social and Political Morality*, based on Ellis's teaching. Additionally, in the summer of 1868 Lovett wrote a series of articles appearing in the *Beehive* that were based on Ellis's lessons in political economy (Lovett, 1920, pp. 370, 390-391, 407-408). Francis Place worked himself up to the position of master tailor and later became friends with many classical economists and other intellectuals. Place drafted

the People's Charter in 1838 and served as a mediator between the working class and intellectuals in efforts for Parliamentary reform and to legalize trade unions. For more information on the life of Place, see Wallas (1919).

23. The opinions of the classical economists are referred to in Sockwell (1992, pp. 163-172).

24. Runz previously worked with Ellis to help give lessons on social economy to teachers. In addition, Runz studied teaching at a British and Foreign Society training school, taught at one of these schools, and attended University College in London.

25. Birkbeck College, also named after George Birkbeck, began as a Mechanics' Institute in 1823 and was gradually converted into an educational institution. For a history of Birkbeck College, see Burns (1924). A biography of George Birkbeck is provided by Kelly (1957).

26. For more information on these obstacles, see Sockwell (1992, pp. 170-171).

27. Blaug (1975, p. 592) suggests that the classical economists became increasingly disenchanted with the prospects for private schools that had to compete with better funded state schools. Also see the comments of J.S. Mill (1965, pp. 953-956) and West (1964, p. 170).

28. For an account of the connection between the Birkbeck Schools and Dickens' Gradgrind school, see Gilmour (1967).

29. Indications of Ellis's direct and indirect influence on other schools are found in Blyth (1892, pp. 111-119) and Sockwell (1989, pp. 314-317).

30. Examples of Ellis's influence on other teachers are provided by E.E. Ellis (1888, p. 93) and Stewart (1967, pp. 310-316).

31. Examples of books for teachers that were written in the questioning style are *Questions and Answers* (1848b), *Progressive Lessons* (1850a), and *Philo-Socrates* (1861-1864). *Outlines of Social Economy* (1846) and *Lessons on the Phenomena of Industrial Life* (1854) provide standard discussions of political economy along with Ellis's ideas concerning moral conduct. Ellis adopts the persona of an outside observer in *Reminiscences and Reflections of an Old Operative* (1852) and *Studies of Man, by a Japanese* (1874).

32. For more information on Ellis's efforts to influence the Newcastle Commission, see Blyth (1892, pp. 197-209).

33. The Education Code only allowed social economy to be taught through reading books (Miller, 1882, 250-251).

34. Some of these practical issues did, of course, overlap into Ellis's economic theory, most notably in the area of monetary theory and taxation. Again, there was very little new. One exception to this was in the area of taxation, where Ellis generally favored the property tax and constantly called for reform of the inheritance taxes. He felt a large portion of government revenue could be raised if the government received all intestate property (see *A Few Questions* [1848a, pp. 69-71]; see also *Introduction to the Study of the Social Sciences* [1849b, p. 49], *Lessons on Industrial Life* [1854, pp. 166-167], and *Philo-Socrates* [1861-1864, vol. 3, p. 137]).

35. In *Religion in Common Life* (1857, pp. 155, 269, 275, 299) Ellis went so far as to refer to his topics as the morals of wages, the morals of money, the morals of buying and selling, the morals of credit, and so on.

36. For a comparison of Ellis with Marcet, Martineau, and other educational popularizers, see Sockwell (1992, pp. 157-176).

37. Crucial problems facing the modern movement to provide economic education are similar to the problems Ellis faced: lack of properly trained teachers, lack of training materials, and perceptions of bias. These problems have yet to be solved. For example, although a number of states now require economics in high school, studies suggest that little economics is being learned and that teachers are poorly trained in economics. State mandates for economic education are discussed in Brennan (1986), Becker, Green, and Rosen (1990, pp. 234-235), and Marlin (1991, pp. 5-14). Poor performance on economic literacy tests and inadequate teacher training is discussed by Walstad and Soper (1988, p. 251) and Baumol and Highsmith (1988, pp. 259-260).

# REFERENCES

Bain, A. 1966. *James Mill: A Biography.* New York: Augustus M. Kelley.

Bartley, George C.T. 1871. *The Schools for the People.* London: Bell and Daldy.

Baumol, William J., and Robert J. Highsmith. 1988. "Variables Affecting Success in Economic Education: Preliminary Findings from a New Data Base." *American Economic Review* (May): 257-262.

Becker, William, William Greene, and Sherwin Rosen. 1990. "Research on High School Economic Education." *Journal of Economic Education* (Summer): 231-245.

Berg, Maxine. 1980. *The Machinery Question and the Making of Political Economy: 1815-1846.* Cambridge: Cambridge University Press.

Blaug, Mark. 1975. "The Economics of Education in English Classical Political Economy: A Re-Examination." Pp. 568-599 in *Essays on Adam Smith,* edited by A.S. Skinner and T. Wilson. Oxford: Clarendon Press.

Bloomfield, Arthur. 1984. "Effect of Growth on the Terms of Trade: Some Earlier Views." *Economica* (May): 187-193.

Blyth, E.K. 1892. *Life of William Ellis.* 2nd edn. London: Kegan Paul.

Brennan, Dennis C. 1986. *A Survey of State Mandates for Economics Instruction, 1985-1986.* New York: Joint Council on Economic Education.

Brougham, Henry. 1838. *Speeches of Henry Lord Brougham upon questions relating to public rights, duties, and interest,* 4 vols. Edinburgh, UK: A.C. Black.

Burns, C. Delisle. 1924. *A Short History of Birkbeck College.* London: University of London.

Ellis, Ethel E. 1888. *Memoir of William Ellis.* London: Longmans.

[Ellis, William]. 1824a. "On Charitable Institutions." *Westminster Review* 2(3, July 1824): 97-121.

_____. 1824b. "James Mill's *Elements of Political Economy.*" *Westminster Review* 2(4, October): 289-310.

_____. 1825. "On Exportation of Machinery." *Westminster Review* 3(6, April): 386-394.

_____. 1826. "On the Employment of Machinery." *Westminster Review* 5(9, January): 101-130.

_____. 1829. *Conversations upon Knowledge, Happiness, and Education between a Mechanic and a Patron of the London Mechanics Institution.* Baldwin and Craddock.

_____. 1836. *Lectures on Political Economy.* Glasgow: Privately printed.

_____. 1846. *Outlines of Social Economy.* 1st edn. London: Smith, Elder, and Co. (1st edn. 1846, 3rd edn. 1860).

_____. 1848a. *A Few Questions on Secular Education.* London: Smith, Elder, and Co.

_____. 1848b. *Questions and Answers Suggested by a Consideration of some of the Arrangements and Relations of Social Life.* London: Smith, Elder, and Co.

_____. 1849a. "The Distressed Needlewomen and Cheap Prison Labour." *Westminster Review* 50(99, January): 371-394.

_____. 1849b. *Introduction to the Study of the Social Sciences.* London: Smith, Elder, and Co.

_____. 1850a. "Relief Measures." *Westminster Review* 53(104, April): 145-164.

_____. 1850b. "Classical Education." *Westminster Review* 53(105, July): 393-409.

_____. 1850c. *Progressive Lessons in Social Science.* London: Smith, Elder, and Co.

_____. 1851. *Education as a Means of Preventing Destitution.* London: Smith, Elder, and Co.

_____. 1852. *Reminiscences and Reflections of an Old Operative.* London: Smith, Elder, and Co.

_____. 1854. *Lessons on the Phenomena of Industrial Life and the Conditions of Industrial Success,* edited by Richard Dawes. London: Groombridge and Sons.

_____. 1857. *A Layman's Contribution to the Knowledge and Practice of Religion in Common Life.* London: Smith, Elder, and Co.

————. 1860. *Outlines of Social Economy*. 3rd edn. London: Smith, Elder, and Co.

————. 1861-1864. *Philo-Socrates*. 4 vols. London: Smith, Elder, and Co.

————. 1863. *Instruction in Elementary Social Science, what it is and why and how it ought to be given in schools*. London: Smith, Elder, and Co.

————. 1868. *What Stops the Way?* London: Smith, Elder, and Co.

————. 1874. *Studies of Man, by a Japanese*. London: Trubner and Co.

[Ellis, William, and J.S. Mill]. 1825. "McCulloch's *Political Economy*." *Westminster Review* 4(7, July): 88-92.

Fetter, Frank W. 1962. "Economic Articles in the *Westminster Review* and Their Authors, 1824-1851." *Journal of Political Economy* 70(6, December): 570-596.

Gilmour, Robin. 1967. "The Gradgrind School: Political Economy in the Classroom." *Victorian Studies* (December): 207-224.

Harrison, J.F.C. 1961. *Learning and Living, 1790-1960*. London: Routledge and Paul.

Henry, John F. 1990. *The Making of Neoclassical Economics*. Boston: Unwin Hyman.

Jolly, William. 1879. *Education: Its Principles and Practice as Developed by George Combe*. London: Macmillan.

Kelly, Thomas. 1957. *George Birkbeck, Pioneer of Adult Education*. Liverpool, UK: University Press.

Lovett, William. 1920. *Life and Struggles of William Lovett, with introduction by R.H. Tawney*. New York: Alfred Knopf.

Marcet, Jane. 1816. *Conversations on Political Economy*. London: Longman, Hurst, Rees, Orme, and Brown.

Marlin, James W. 1991. "State-Mandated Economic Education, Teacher Attitudes, and Student Learning." *Journal of Economic Education* (Winter): 5-14.

McCulloch, J.R. 1964. *The Literature of Political Economy*. New York: Augustus M. Kelley (first printed 1845).

Mill, J.S. 1924. *Autobiography of John Stuart Mill*. New York: Columbia University Press.

————. 1965. *Principles of Political Economy*. New York: A.M. Kelley (originally published 1848).

Miller, Florence Fenwick. 1882. "William Ellis and his Work as an Educationist." *Fraser's Magazine* (February): 233-252.

Morris-Suzuki, Tessa. 1989. *A History of Japanese Economic Thought*. London: Routledge.

Moss, Laurence S. 1976. *Mountifort Longfield: Ireland's First Professor of Political Economy*. Ottawa, IL: Green Hill Publishers.

Nesbitt, George L. 1934. *Benthamite Reviewing: The First Twelve Years of the Westminster Review, 1824-1836*. New York: Columbia University Press.

Nitsch, Thomas O. 1990. "Social Economics: The First 200 Years." Pp. 5-90 in *Social Economics: Retrospect and Prospect*, edited by Mark A. Lutz. Boston: Kluwer.

O'Brien, D.P. 1970. *J.R. McCulloch. A Study in Classical Economics*. London: Allen and Unwin.

————. 1988. "Classical Reassessments." Pp. 179-220 in *Classical Political Economy: A Survey of Recent Literature*, edited by William O. Thweatt. Boston: Kluwer.

Packe, Michael St. John. 1954. *The Life of John Stuart Mill*. London: Secker and Warburg.

Place, Francis. Add. MSS, 35151. April 29, 1849.

Ricardo, David. 1951-1973. *The Works and Correspondence of David Ricardo*. 11 vols, edited by P. Sraffa. Cambridge: Cambridge University Press.

Schumpeter, Joseph A. 1954. *History of Economic Analysis*. New York: Oxford University Press.

Sockwell, W.D. 1989. *Contributions of Henry Brougham and William Ellis to Classical Political Economy*. Unpublished Ph.D. dissertation, Vanderbilt University.

Sockwell, W.D. 1992. "Popularizing Classical Economic Ideas in Nineteenth Century Britain: The Education Movement." *Perspectives on the History of Economic Thought*. Vol. 7 edited by S. Todd Lowry. Aldershot, England: Edward Elgar.

Stewart, W.A.C., and W.P. McCann, eds. 1967. *The Educational Innovators: 1750-1880.* New York: Pantheon.

Stigler, George J. 1970. "The Case, if Any, for Economic Literacy." *Journal of Economic Education* (Spring): 77-84.

Thompson, Noel W. 1984. *The People's Science: The Popular Political Economy of Exploitation and Crisis, 1816-34.* Cambridge: Cambridge University Press.

Thweatt, William O. 1976. "James Mill and the Early Development of the Law of Comparative Advantage." *History of Political Economy* 8(2, Summer): 207-234.

_____. 1986. "James and John Mill on Comparative Advantage." Pp. 33-43 in *Trade in Transit*, edited by H. Visser and E. Schoorl. Dordrecht, The Netherlands: Martinus Nijhoff.

Viner, Jacob. 1937. *Studies in the Theory of International Trade.* New York: Harper & Brothers.

Wallas, Graham. 1919. *The Life of Francis Place.* 3rd ed. New York: Alfred A. Knopf.

Walstad, William B., and John C. Soper. 1988. "A Report Card on the Economic Literacy of U.S. High School Students." *American Economic Review* (May): 25-56.

West, E.G. 1964. "Private versus Public Education: A Classical Economic Dispute." *Journal of Political Economy* 72(5, October): 465-475.

# THE HISTORY AND DEVELOPMENT
# OF THE OPTION PRICING FORMULA

Edward J. Sullivan and Timothy M. Weithers

## I. INTRODUCTION

Shortly after its publication, the Black-Scholes option pricing model was recognized as one of the great success stories in financial economics. Like many seemingly "overnight" successes, however, this story reflects the culmination of years of effort. The purpose of this paper is to give a more complete understanding of the history and development of the option pricing formula. While some minimal literature dealing with options existed before the turn of this century, three remarkable advances have been made since that time in the specification of the option pricing formula; these are associated with the names of Bachelier, Boness, Black, and Scholes. This historical survey acknowledges the original contributions of these individuals to the current state of option pricing theory.

In addition to a historical survey, this paper provides a comparative study of the three pricing formulas by assessing their respective predictive content using modern financial data. Presumably, the most recent pricing formula

Research in the History of Economic Thought and Methodology, Volume 12, pages 31-43.

would perform best, while the earliest would be expected to yield the least accurate results. The simultaneous testing of the three formulas, then, provides an empirical yardstick of the progress made since 1900.

## II.  A PRECURSOR

In tracing the development of option pricing theory before the work of Bachelier (1964), the trail begins with Charles Castelli's *The Theory of Options in Stocks and Shares*, which was published in London in 1877. A stock and share broker, Castelli wrote this short treatise with the proximate goal of affording the general public an understanding of the beneficial trades which options provide. In his rare little (77 page) book, Castelli explains the speculative and hedging aspects of options trading with an emphasis on practical application. Using numerical examples that abstract from transactions costs, he analyzes the gains and losses associated with long and short positions in calls and puts; he also analyzes a variety of more involved positions using combinations of these contracts.

Although a useful primer for the options investor, Castelli's work is absent a theoretical model of option pricing. Nonetheless, his work displays some theoretical insight. For example, there is the recognition that the option price or premium will fluctuate "according to the variations of the Stock to be contracted; if the fluctuations are violent and numerous, and its future course liable to a great rise or great fall, then the (call) premium asked is very heavy; if, however, the Stock has evenly kept its quotation, Options can be negociated for a very trifling premium" (Castelli 1877, pp. 7-8). Further, after a significant rise (fall), there is generally held to be an expectation of a fall (rise).

The modern theory of option pricing identifies five variables that determine the price of a call stock option. Three of the variables—the price of the underlying stock, the time to option expiration, and the stock return's standard deviation—are positively related to the value of the contract. Conversely, the exercise price and the risk-free rate of return are negatively related to its value. In his book, Castelli identified two of these variables—the stock price and the dispersion of returns—as important determinants of option prices.

## III.  BACHELIER

In a truly prescient fashion, many of the insights and techniques used to solve the option pricing problem were anticipated or developed at the beginning of the twentieth century by the French mathematician Louis Bachelier. Born seven years before the appearance of Castelli's work, Bachelier proved, early on, to be somewhat of a mathematical prodigy. He pursued formal statistical and mathematical studies at the Academy of Paris and wrote his doctoral thesis under the distinguished probabilist Henri Poincaré. His choice for a dissertation topic was far from the norm; Bachelier chose to derive and apply mathematical models to value the securities traded on La Bourse—the Paris Stock Market. Titled *Théorie de la Spéculation,* Bachelier's thesis was successfully defended on March 19, 1900. Mandelbrot (1987) claims Poincaré failed to comprehend the import of Bachelier's contribution. As a result, Bachelier had some difficulty securing an academic post and his Sorbonne dissertation had very little impact at the time. This was to remain the case until some fifty years later.

One of Bachelier's innovations in explaining options was his graphical presentation. Castelli had given numerous tabular examples, but Bachelier first graphed the (now) standard textbook option payoff diagram.[1] Figure 4 from his thesis was the first graphical representation of a long position in a European call option. This has been reproduced as our Figure 1.[2]

The vertical axis measures the profit derived from a long position in a European call option which is contingent upon the terminal price of the underlying stock, as depicted along the horizontal axis. *B* denotes the exercise or strike price. A terminal stock price below *B* will abrogate the option's usefulness, and the loss will be equal to the price of the option contract. Any terminal stock price above *B* will result in the option being employed or exercised. A terminal stock price above *S* will yield a positive profit.

Much more important than visual presentations, though, was Bachelier's insight that option prices depend on the prices of the underlying stocks. While Castelli understood this fact, it was Bachelier who attempted to explicitly model

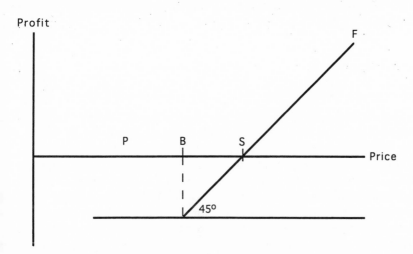

*Figure 1.*   Backelier's Payoff Diagram for a Call Option

this phenomenon. Since the manner in which options contracts are priced depends critically on the distribution of stock price changes, there must be a formal link associating the stock price and the option price. Bachelier made the primary assault on this problem.

In formulating a mathematical description of stock price changes, Bachelier anticipated the later efficient market hypothesis by assuming that stock price movements are identically and independently distributed. The particular stochastic process employed by Bachelier is now known as arithmetic Brownian motion (or a Wiener process). Incremental changes in stock prices are, thus, assumed to be normally distributed independent random variables with zero means and variances that are proportional to time. The law of motion is identical to the Fourier equation of heat diffusion.

The intuition behind the selection of Brownian motion (named for the botanist Robert Brown who, in 1828, observed and reported the seemingly random, frenetic paths followed by pollen in a suspension medium) to model stock price changes is that a rise is as likely as a fall and a huge change is less likely than a small one over some fixed time horizon. Further, future movements along a sample Brownian motion path are independent of any past movements; tomorrow's stock price depends only on where the price is today. Five years later, Albert Einstein independently discovered the same theory of Brownian motion and applied it to the movement of molecular particles. In 1923, the formal mathematical foundation of this process was presented by Norbert Wiener (hence, "Wiener process").[3]

Bachelier's model of option pricing incorporates as essential elements the stock price and its increments, the variance of the underlying stock, and the strike or exercise price. His pricing equation may be written as follows (Bachelier, 1964, p. 54):

$$C = \int_{X}^{\infty} (S - X)\, p(S)\, dS. \tag{1}$$

In essence, his equation states that the call premium, $C$, is equal to the expected difference between the stock price, $S$, and the exercise price, $X$, where $p(S)$ denotes the probability of the stock assuming a value of $S$.

Upon deriving a theoretical model, Bachelier established a tradition among option theorists—he tested the model. Looking at options traded on French government bonds for the time period 1894-1898, he compared the calculated and observed quotes on contracts with different premiums and times to maturity. In general, Bachelier seemed quite satisfied with his results noting, "The observed and calculated figures agree on the whole, but they show certain discrepancies which must be explained."[4] An examination of his results suggest that his model generated smaller forecast errors for more distant contracts.

Nonetheless, Bachelier's work represents one of the earliest tests in financial economics.

While Bachelier's work seems to have had little immediate impact, he was not altogether unknown. Samuelson wrote an unpublished paper on "Brownian Motion in the Stock Market" in 1955 and accepted, as thesis supervisor, Richard J. Kruizenga's (1956) M.I.T. dissertation *Put and Call Options: A Theoretical and Market Analysis* the next year. Kruizenga cites Bachelier in his dissertation. Further, Samuelson recollects mention of Bachelier by the mathematician Stan Ulam and recalls a "patronizing reference" in a work by Feller and Kolmogorov (see Samuelson, 1982). Around 1957, the noted statistician L. Jimmie Savage wrote to Samuelson and several other economists asking whether they might be able to supply information about Bachelier (a request echoed by Mandelbrot in *The New Palgrave* some 30 years later). In 1960, Osborne, who had independently derived some of Bachelier's results, noted the difficulty encountered in obtaining Bachelier's thesis (which he found only in the Rare Book Room of the Library of Congress); Samuelson had access to the Widener Library copy. Thus, the evidence indicates that while Bachelier was perhaps not obscure in 1960, he was certainly not familiar.[5]

# IV.  BONESS

The next pivotal figure in the development of option pricing theory is A. James Boness. His efforts bridge the works of Bachelier, and Black and Scholes, for several reasons. First, Boness notes that his model "bears a strong and conscious resemblance" to Bachelier's model (Boness, 1964, 163). Second, Boness popularized Bachelier's work by translating the 1900 dissertation into English; that translation appeared in Paul Cootner's edition of *The Random Character of Stock Market Prices* in 1964. Finally, the Black-Scholes model more closely resembles that of Boness than any of the other derivative asset pricing models published in the 1960s.[6]

As a graduate student, A. James Boness took up Bachelier's pursuit of a valuation formula that would describe option prices. In his 1962 Ph.D. thesis at the University of Chicago, under the direction of Lawrence Fisher, Boness (who was obviously aware of Bachelier's results) extended the option pricing equation to include explicitly the expected rate of growth of the stock price underlying the option in question and the time to option expiration.

Boness rests his theory of stock-option valuation on four assumptions: (1) equally risky assets having, via competition, equal expected yield rates, (2) the percentage stock price changes being lognormal, (3) variances that are proportional to the time horizon, and (4) risk neutrality among investors.

The improvements from a theoretical point of view are not minor. The most serious difficulty with Bachelier's model stems, ironically, from his innovative modeling of stock price movements. Bachelier's assumption that stock prices followed an arithmetic rather than a geometric Brownian motion process had several important drawbacks. For example, Bachelier's assumption implies both a positive probability of a negative stock price (an impossibilty given limited liability) and the possibility that an option price could exceed the price of the underlying stock.[7] By assuming that the probability distribution of the expected percentage change in a stock price is lognormally distributed, Boness adopted a geometric Brownian motion process which yields a continuous-time random walk.[8] We can summarize Boness's formula as follows:[9]

$$C = S\,N(d_1) - X\,e^{-rt}\,N(d_2) \qquad (2)$$

where, as before,  C  = the option price or premium,
                   X  = the strike or exercise price,
                   S  = the current stock price,
                   N(.) = the cumulative normal probability,
                   t  = the time to option expiration,
                   r  = the expected appreciation in the stock price, or the market discount rate
                   $\sigma$  = the stock return's standard deviation,
                   $d_1$ = { $[\ln(S/X) + (r + \sigma^2/2)\,t]/\sigma\sqrt{t}$ } , and
                   $d_2$ = { $[\ln(S/X) + (r - \sigma^2/2)\,t]/\sigma\sqrt{t}$ } .

Incorporation of the random walk model into option pricing theory reflected the econometric studies of Cowles and Jones (1937), Working (1939), Davis (1941), Kendall (1953), Granger and Morgenstern (1963), and Moore (1969). These studies lent statistical support to the random walk hypothesis. Although the less restrictive submartingale process superceded this model by the early 1970s, most option models, including the Black-Scholes model, assume a random walk.[10]

Like Bachelier, Boness also tested his model on market data. Looking at 89 contracts over a two-and-a-half year period from February 1958 to August 1960, he tested his model against "the alternative hypothesis that the variables are simply independent members of a linear function which determines option values" (Boness, 1964, p. 173). By comparing the relative effectiveness of each model in explaining the variance of option prices, he concludes that the theoretical model is superior because of a higher $R$-square statistic.

While Boness's approach clearly advanced option pricing theory, his model provided no method for determining the correct discount rate. Boness's *ad hoc* solution was to "locate the rate of appreciation most nearly consistent with the market data" (Boness, 1964, p. 170).[11] Boness's lack of a theoretical solution to this free parameter problem is not surprising. Capital market theory, in particular, the capital asset pricing model (CAPM) of Sharpe (1964), Lintner (1965), and Mossin (1966), was only emerging. Black and Scholes later used CAPM to provide a theoretically rigorous closed-form solution to the problem.

## V. BLACK-SCHOLES

While the late 1950s and early 1960s generated a growing literature on warrant and option pricing, it was not until 1973 that a clear successor to the Boness model emerged. At that time, Fischer Black and Myron Scholes (1973) published (after considerable referee difficulties) a model which addressed the discount rate problem and reshaped the analysis of contingent claims. The development of their equation is clearly and fascinatingly chronicled by Black (1989).

Maintaining the assumption of lognormality, Black and Scholes gave two theoretical justifications for the use of the risk-free rate of return as the correct discount rate in the option pricing formula. One approach, suggested by Robert Merton, which employed an arbitrage argument, demonstrated that a long position in an equity could be continuously hedged by writing call options. Such a portfolio must yield a risk-free rate of return. By implication, the cash flow from a call option should be discounted at the risk-free rate. In their second approach, they used the capital asset pricing model to derive the same valuation equation. The significance of the second approach is that it linked capital market theory with option pricing theory.

A cursory examination of the Boness and Black-Scholes models suggest that they are quite similar. Indeed, Equation (2) becomes the Black-Scholes formula when the risk-free rate is used for discounting (i.e., when $r$ is taken to be the risk-free rate as opposed to the expected stock appreciation rate). The models, however, are different in several important respects. First, having provided a theoretical justification for the use of a risk-free discount rate, Black and Scholes removed the arbitrary parameter, $r$, which characterized Boness's model. Second, the Black-Scholes option pricing equation is completely independent of investors' preferences; Boness relied on the assumption of risk neutrality. According to the Black-Scholes model, then, the call premium depends on only five factors: the current stock price, the exercise or strike price, the risk-free rate, time (or time to maturity), and the volatility of the stock's underlying return.

Black and Scholes used their formula to estimate the theoretical values for contracts on 545 securities between 1966 and 1969. Their results indicated that option buyers paid prices consistently higher than those predicted by the formula, while option writers received prices that were approximatley equal to the theoretical price. They attribute this discrepancy to "large transaction costs, all of which are effectively paid by option buyers" (Black and Scholes, 1973, p. 653). Finally, they conclude that when transaction costs are included, the option market is efficient.

Since its publication, the Black-Scholes model has been tested extensively and some mispricing has been detected. In one well-known study, for example, MacBeth and Merville (1979) tested the model to determine if it over- or underpriced options. They concluded that, on average, the model's prices were lower than market prices for in-the-money options and higher than market prices for out-of-the-money options.[12] Also, the mispricing decreased as the time to expiration decreased. Hence, the model's mispricing appears most severe for long-term options that are deeply in- or out-of-the-money.[13]

Spurred on, at least in part, by these kinds of empirical findings, theorists have attempted to improve the model by either respecifying the underlying stochastic process of security prices or by relaxing the assumption of a constant variance for the security's return. These efforts produced the Cox-Ross (1975) pure jump model, the Merton (1976) mixed diffusion model, the Cox-Ross (1976) constant elasticity of variance diffusion model, the Geske (1979) compound option diffusion model, and the Rubinstein (1983) displaced diffusion model. In comparing the relative performance of these models, Rubinstein (1985) concluded that none of these newer models was consistently free of pricing bias. In other words, no one model was clearly superior to another. Thus, the Black-Scholes model has held its own against the more recent models.

## VI.   AN EMPIRICAL TEST OF THE OPTION PRICING MODELS

All of the option pricing theorists—Bachelier, Boness, and Black-Scholes—felt obliged to confront their respective option pricing models with data. In order to compare the three main formulas, an empirical test was carried out calculating the hypothesized option prices. A comparison between the predicted prices and the actual option prices was undertaken to assess their forecasting abilities.

To test the accuracy of each model, Digital Equipment call option prices with 15 days to expiration were collected for each month in 1989. This nondividend-paying stock was selected because all these models assume no dividends are paid over the life of the option. The closing prices, the exercise prices, and the risk-free rates of return were obtained from the *Wall Street Journal*.[14] The standard deviations of the stock's return—used in the Black-Scholes and Boness models—were calculated from the ten previous closing day prices.[15] The discount rate used in the Boness model was calculated using the

*Table 1.* Digital Equipment Call Estimations

| | January (S = 99.625, X = 90) | February (S = 119.25, X = 90) | March (S = 112.25, X = 100) | April (S = 97.375, X = 90) | May (S = 95.875, X = 90) | June (S = 125, X = 90) |
|---|---|---|---|---|---|---|
| Actual Value | 9.75 | 29.50 | 11.875 | 8.25 | 6.75 | 3.875 |
| Bachelier Value | 7.93 | 25.13 | 13.03 | 7.56 | 6.43 | 3.11 |
| Black-Scholes Value | 9.94 | 29.57 | 12.62 | 7.72 | 6.52 | 3.81 |
| Boness Values | 10.59 | 30.21 | 13.34 | 8.36 | 1.89 | 4.33 |

| | July (S = 95.75, X = 90) | August (S = 95.25, X = 90) | September (S = 100.375, X = 100) | October (S = 91.625, X = 85) | November (S = 89.5, X = 85) | December (S = 85, X = 85) |
|---|---|---|---|---|---|---|
| Actual Value | 6.50 | 6.125 | 2.875 | 7.25 | 5.00 | 1.8125 |
| Bachelier Value | 3.90 | 3.58 | 1.775 | 7.025 | 5.30 | 2.71 |
| Black-Scholes Value | 6.87 | 5.89 | 2.90 | 7.08 | 5.67 | 1.83 |
| Boness Value | 7.45 | 6.40 | 3.93 | 7.60 | 6.28 | 2.18 |

*Note:* S denotes the closing price of the stock 15 days before the option matures, and X is the exercise price. These data were obtained from various issues of the *Wall Street Journal.*

capital asset pricing model.[16] The value for the beta coefficient, 1.1, was obtained from *Value Line*, and the actual 1989 return on the New York Stock Exchange was used to proxy the market portfolio's expected return. The results of these estimations are presented in Table 1.

An examination of Table 1 reveals that the Black-Scholes formula provides call prices closest to the actual values in 10 out of 12 months. It is outperformed by the Boness model in April and the Bachelier model in November. A comparison of the Bachelier and Boness models shows the latter model to be more accurate. Specifically, the Boness model gives closer estimates 8 out of 12 times. In terms of ranking, the Black-Scholes model yields the lowest average standard error of the forecast with a value of 0.36. The standard error approximately doubles for the Boness model with a value of 0.73, while the Bachelier model forecast error is 2.7—nearly eight times larger than the Black-Scholes value. Finally, even though the Bachelier model ranked last, in half of the estimations, its forecast error was less than one dollar.

In general, these results confirm the expected improvements in the option pricing formula. Bachelier's 90-year-old model performs reasonably well using contemporary data, but Boness's model performs better. Why? Boness benefited from the intervening years of stock market research. Rather than assuming that stock price changes are normally distributed, he opted for a lognormal distribution. Similarly, Black and Scholes benefited from advances in capital asset pricing theory; they employed a risk-free discount rate, thereby eliminating the arbitrary rate which compromised Boness's model. While the empirical results do support the notion of progress in option modeling, Black (1989, p. 8) ventured an alternative explanation for the success of the Black-Scholes equation:

> [T]raders now use the formula and its variants extensively. They use it so much that market prices are usually close to formula values even in situations where there should be a large difference.

Ideally, a three-faceted test should be employed whereby each option pricing formula is tested not only against current financial data but also against the data used by the other option theorists. Such a test is not feasible, however. Bachelier's data is not extant. Further, the data used in the Boness and Black-Scholes studies, which came from the over-the-counter options market (OTCOM), had several deficiencies including the lack of standardized exercise prices, maturity dates, and a secondary market. The primary advantage of using current data based on an actively traded, standardized contract is that the potential for biased price quotes is minimized.

# VII.  CONCLUSION

The Black-Scholes option pricing formula serves today as the cornerstone for contingent claims valuation theory. Like other advances in economics, the theoretical insights gained in option pricing theory provided applications well beyond the problem originally considered. In their remarkable paper, Black and Scholes foresaw this, noting that the formula could be applied to to the valuation of common stock, corporate bonds, and warrants. Since then, option pricing theory has been applied to a variety of topics, including the analysis of insurance contracts, variable rate mortgages, and capital budgeting. Option pricing theory has evolved considerably since its origins in Bachelier's Sorbonne thesis.

## ACKNOWLEDGMENT

An earlier draft of this paper was presented at the American Economic Association Meetings in Washington, D.C. in December 1990. The authors wish to thank Jeff Biddle, Zvi Bodie, Robert Dorfman, Robert A. Strong and two anonymous referees for their insightful comments.

## NOTES

1.  Castelli is the sole reference in Bachelier's dissertation.
2.  This diagram is seen on p. 24 of A. James Boness's translation of Bachelier's "Theory of Speculation" found in Cootner (1964).
3.  Albert Einstein's papers on this topic are found in his *Investigations on the Theory of The Brownian Movement* (1926). For a rigorous derivation of this process, see Wiener (1923).
4.  Found in its original notation in Cootner (1964, p. 43).
5.  For further information on Bachelier and his remarkable contributions, see Paul Cootner's introduction to Part I of *The Random Character of Stock Price Movements* (1964, pp. 1-6) titled "Origins and Justification of the Random Walk Theory," Osborne (1960), Mandelbrot (1987), and Sullivan and Weithers (1991).
6.  Although Sprenkle (1964) and Samuelson (1965) published models on warrant pricing, both possessed serious drawbacks. Sprenkle's model, for example, lacked a discount rate but required an adjustment factor for risk aversion (absent in the subsequent Black-Scholes model). Samuelson's model introduced separate growth rates for the stock and warrant prices but failed to reconcile their values under capital market equilibrium. For a more detailed analysis of these shortcomings and some other difficulties involving Bachelier's model, see Smith (1976).
7.  Sprenkle (1964) and Samuelson (1965) introduced geometric Brownian motion into the pricing of warrants. For an analysis of the bounds on option prices, see Merton (1973).
8.  The random walk model states that tomorrow's return is equal to today's return plus an error term with an expected value of zero.
9.  The original notation can be seen in Equation (4) of Boness (1964, p. 170).
10.  Recently, Fama and French (1988) have argued that stock prices follow a mean-reverting random walk.
11.  Using the stocks in his sample, Boness regressed the actual percentage change of the stock on the theoretical value using a variety of assumed rates of stock price appreciation. His criterion

for selecting the appreciation rate most consistent with the option prices is the size of the standard error of estimate. For more details, see Boness (1964, pp. 170-173).

12.   A call option is in-the-money when the price of underlying stock exceeds the exercise price. Conversely, it is out-of-the-money when the stock price is below the exercise price.

13.   For a summary of the empirical research on option pricing models, see Copeland and Weston (1988, chap. 8).

14.   The risk-free rate was based on the 13-week Treasury bill rate quoted in the "Money Rates" column.

15.   The exact method for calculating these inputs is described in Kolb (1991, pp. 128-131).

16.   CAPM states that the expected return on a security, E(R), is equal to the risk-free rate, Rf, plus a risk premium, $[E(Rm)\text{-}Rf] \times \beta$, where $E(Rm)$ is the expected return on the market portfolio and $\beta$ is the "beta" coefficient which measures the sensitivity of the security's return to movements in the market portfolio. Thus, the CAPM equation is $E(R) = Rf + [E(Rm) - Rf] \times \beta$. Because of its theoretical superiority, the CAPM discount rate would, in general, improve the performance of Boness's model.

# REFERENCES

Bachelier, Louis. 1964. "*Théorie de la spéculation.*" Trans. by A.J. Boness. Pp. 17-78 in *The Random Character of Stock Market Prices*, edited by P. Cootner. Cambridge: MIT Press (originally published by Gauthier-Villars, Paris, 1900).

Black, Fischer. 1989. "How We Came Up With The Option Formula." *The Journal of Portfolio Management* (Winter): 4-8.

Black, Fischer, and Myron Scholes. 1973. "The Pricing of Options and Corporate Liabilities." *Journal of Political Economy* 81: 637-654.

Boness, A. James. 1962. "A Theory and Measurement of Stock Option Value." Unpublished Ph.D. dissertation, Economics, University of Chicago.

————. 1964. "Elements of a Theory of Stock-Option Value." *Journal of Political Economy* 72: 163-175.

Castelli, Charles. 1877. *The Theory of Options in Stocks and Shares.* London: Mathieson.

Cootner, Paul, ed. 1964. *The Random Character of Stock Market Prices.* Cambridge: MIT Press.

Copeland, Thomas E., and J. Fred Weston. 1988. *Financial Theory and Corporate Policy.* 3rd edn. New York: Addison-Wesley.

Cowles, Alfred, and H.E. Jones. 1937. "Some Posteriori Probabilities in Stock Market Action." *Econometrica* 5: 280-294.

Cox, John C., and Steven Ross. 1975. "The Pricing of Options for Jump Processes." Working Paper No. 2-75, Rodney L. White Center Center for Financial Research. Philadephia: University of Pennsylvania.

————. 1976. "The Valuation of Options for Alternative Stochastic Processes." *Journal of Financial Economics* 3: 145-166.

Davis, Harold T. 1941. *The Analysis of Economic Time Series.* Bloomington, IN: Principia.

Einstein, Albert. 1926. *Investigations on the Theory of the Brownian Movement.* London: Methuen.

Fama, Eugene F., and Kenneth R. French. 1988. "Permanent and Temporary Components of Stock Prices." *Journal of Political Economy* 96: 246-274.

Geske, Robert. 1979. "The Valuation of Compound Options." *Journal of Financial Economics* 7: 63-81.

Granger, Clive W.J., and Oskar Morgenstern. 1963. "Spectral Analysis of the New York Stock Market Prices." *Kyklos* 16: 1-27.

Kendall, Maurice G. 1953. "The Analysis of Economic Time Series, Part 1: Prices." *Journal of the Royal Statistical Society* 96: 11-25.

Kolb, Robert W. 1991. *Options An Introduction.* Miami: Kolb.

Kruizenga, Richard J. 1956. "Put and Call Options: A Theoretical and Market Analysis." Unpublished Ph.D. dissertation, Economics, MIT.

Lintner, John. 1965. "The Valuation of Risk Assets and the Selection of Risky Investments in the Stock Portfolios and Capital Budgets." *Review of Economics and Statistics* 47: 13-37.

MacBeth, James D., and Larry J. Merville. 1979. "An Empirical Examination of the Black-Scholes Call Option Pricing Model." *Journal of Finance* 34: 1173-1186.

Mandelbrot, Benoit. 1987. "Louis Bachelier." Pp. 168-169 in *The New Palgrave: A Dictionary of Economics.* New York: Stockton.

Merton, Robert C. 1973. "Theory of Rational Option Pricing." *Bell Journal of Economics and Management Science* 4: 141-183.

————. 1976. "Option Pricing When Underlying Stock Returns Are Discontinuous." *Journal of Financial Economics* 3: 1173-1186.

Moore, A. 1969. "Some Characteristics of Changes in Common Stock Prices." Pp. 139-161 in *The Random Character of Stock Market Prices,* edited by P. Cootner. Cambridge: MIT Press.

Mossin, Jan. 1966. "Equilibrium in a Capital Asset Market." *Econometrica* 34: 768-783.

Osborne, M.F.M. 1959. "Brownian Motion in the Stock Market." *Operations Research* 7: 145-173.

————. 1960. "Reply to 'Comments on Brownian Motion in the Stock Market.'" *Operations Research* 8: 806-810.

Rubinstein, Mark. 1983. "Displaced Diffusion Option Pricing." *Journal of Finance* 38: 213-217.

————. 1985. "Nonparametric Tests of Alternative Option Pricing Models Using All Reported Trades and Quotes on the 30 Most Active CBOE Option Classes from August 23, 1976 through August 31, 1978." *Journal of Finance* 35: 455-480.

Samuelson, Paul A. 1965. "Rational Theory of Warrant Pricing." *Industrial Management Review* 6(Spring): 13-29.

————. 1982. "Paul Cootner's Reconciliation of Economic Law with Chance." Pp. 101-118 in *Financial Economics: Essays in Honor of Paul Cootner,* edited by W.F. Sharpe and C.M. Cootner. Englewood Cliffs, NJ: Prentice-Hall.

Sharpe, William. 1964. "Capital Asset Prices: A Theory of Market Equilibrium under Conditions of Risk." *Journal of Finance* 19: 425-442.

Smith, C.W., Jr. 1976. "Option Pricing: A Review." *Journal of Financial Economics* 3: 3-51.

Sprenkle, Case M. 1964. "Warrant Prices as Indicators of Expectations and Preferences." Pp. 412-474 in *The Random Character of Stock Market Prices,*edited by P. Cootner. Cambridge: MIT Press.

Sullivan, Edward J., and Timothy M. Weithers. 1991. "Louis Bachelier: The Father of Modern Option Pricing Theory." *Journal of Economic Education* 22: 165-171.

Wiener, Norbert. 1923. "Differential Space." *Journal of Mathematics and Physics* 2: 165-171.

Working, Holbrook. 1939. "Prices of Cash Wheat and Futures at Chicago Since 1883." *Wheat Studies of the Stanford Food Institute* II: 75-129.

# RESEARCH STRATEGIES IN
# ECONOMICS JOURNALS

Rendigs Fels

*...in discussions on method and scope, a man is nearly sure to be right when affirming the usefulness of his own procedure, and wrong when denying that of others.*

— Alfred Marshall (1936, p. 771n)

## I. INTRODUCTION

In accordance with modern thinking on such questions as how to do research, how to appraise theories, and how to persuade others, the choice of research strategies is a subject for investigation.[1] We must examine the work of economists, expecting to find that what they do is mostly sound but sometimes less than ideal.[2]

In that spirit, I have reviewed the strategies in one issue of each of nine mainstream economics journals. The sample includes the three top-rated journals in S.J. Liebowitz and J.P. Palmer (1984) and six others selected for variety.[3] Though the articles are high in quality, there are no Nobel Prize

**Research in the History of Economic Thought and Methodology, Volume 12, pages 45-63.**
**Copyright © 1994 by JAI Press Inc.**
**All rights of reproduction in any form reserved.**
**ISBN: 1-55938-747-5**

*Tabel 1.* Research Strategies in Nine Economics Journals

| | AER | BPEA | Econometrica | EJ | IJIO | JEH | JPE | Review of Economics and Statistics | Review of Economics Studies | Total |
|---|---|---|---|---|---|---|---|---|---|---|
| Cause-to-Effect | 5 | 0 | 5 | 4 | 4 | 0 | 4 | 0 | 6 | 28 |
| Search for Regularities | 12 | 1 | 1 | 0 | 4 | 2 | 1 | 13 | 0 | 34 |
| Explanatory Modeling* | 6 | 0 | 0 | 0 | 1 | 0 | 2 | 1 | 0 | 10 |
| Theory Testing | 4 | 2 | 0 | 3 | 0 | 1 | 1 | 5 | 0 | 16 |
| Eclectic | 0 | 1 | 0 | 0 | 0 | 0 | 0 | 0 | 0 | 1 |
| Applications | 1 | 2 | 0 | 3 | 0 | 7 | 2 | 5 | 0 | 20 |
| Other | 1 | 3 | 5 | 3 | 0 | 1 | 0 | 2 | 3 | 18 |
| Total | 29 | 9 | 11 | 13 | 9 | 11 | 10 | 26 | 9 | 127 |

*Note:* *Without testing. Explanatory modeling with testing is included in next line.

winners among the authors and no past presidents of the American Economic Association.[4] Nor are there any major breakthroughs in the 127 articles. The sample represents normal, everyday science at work.[5] Good research, not great research.

Table 1 summarizes the research strategies. I shall say little about the 20 papers classified as "applications," a category used sparingly. Some of them apply economic theory to measuring magnitudes like elasticities or rates of return as distinct from developing and testing theories; Akira Goto and Kazuyaki Suzuki (1989) estimate the rate of return to R&D in Japanese manufacturing industries as around 40 percent. The applications category includes historical and institutional papers, like the one by Gary D. Libecap (1989) that explains how the U.S. oil cartel worked between 1933 and 1972. The number of papers in the applications category may seem small but results in part from the journals chosen for study.[6] Dropping the three journals with no applications and adding three in applied fields would have changed the picture, as would, I suspect, a study of the working papers of the National Bureau of Economic Research. Including journals devoted to radical, institutional, or Austrian economics might have led to a different story.

Eighteen papers are listed in Table 1 as "other." Twelve of them are on econometric methods, two are on the history of economic thought, one on the elasticity of substitution, and several are surveys or discussions that do not report original research.

## II. FROM CAUSE TO EFFECT

The traditional approach of economics is deductive. The theory of comparative advantage provides an exemplar. It consists of a set of assumptions from which logical conclusions are deduced. The assumptions play two roles: they both simplify reality and capture some important aspect of it. In the case of the initial comparative advantage model, still taught in elementary courses, the simplification was drastic: two countries, two commodities, constant costs, barter, and so forth. The analysis took the form of a numerical example; it was (and is) implied or asserted that the specific numbers chosen made no difference; any set of numbers such that one country had a comparative advantage would lead to the conclusion that trade increased world production. Since models are simpler than reality, the method as usually practiced requires reviewing the assumptions to make sure the simplifications merely get rid of irrelevant details and do not seriously damage the conclusions. Often, this step leads to replacing one or more of the assumptions and complicating the model to get a closer approximation to reality. In the case of comparative advantage, the process of relaxing assumptions and complicating the model went on for many decades, leading to new and valuable insights. In the meantime, the very simple model was applied to real-world problems, such as justifying repeal of the corn laws. The traditional approach, thus, involves four steps (five if definition of special terms is counted): assumptions, deductions, complications, and applications.

The traditional approach is pursued in two different ways. The theorist may select a set of assumptions and follow them wherever they lead. Or, the theorist may start with stylized facts and invent a model that explains them. The second, to be discussed later, is modeled on the natural sciences.

As Table 1 shows, 28 of the papers in my sample follow the cause-to-effect strategy. Of them, 12 have no immediate empirical relevance.[7] They are, it may be inferred, expected to be stepping stones. The models do not directly help understand the economic world, but they may be a start in the right direction. Later theorizing, building on them, may lead to improved understanding of how the economic system works. The twelve such papers are given an empirical relevance rating of 1, signifying almost none (see Table 2).

A typical example of a paper with an empirical relevance rating of 1 is Ariel Rubinstein and Asher Wolinsky (1990).[8] They initially assume a market with more buyers than sellers, where every agent wants to buy or sell one unit. The buyers are willing to pay a maximum price of 1 (so the competitive equilibrium price is 1). "Prices are determined in direct contacts between pairs of agents" (p. 63.) The pairing is random. One member of the pair proposes a price, which the other accepts or rejects. Such bargaining takes place between the various pairs simultaneously. Those who do not make deals in the first period go on with the game in the next. Three cases are initially distinguished. In one, the agents know everything that has happened in past periods but not what is going on in the present. Some buyers are privileged for reasons not specified. The competitive equilibrium price is not necessarily the result, and so on.

Situations of pairwise bargaining are common in real life: you negotiate with one buyer or seller and either conclude a deal or not. Consequently, modeling

*Table 2.*   Empirical Relevance Ratings for Papers Classified as
"Cause-to-Effect"

| Journal | 1 | 2 | 3 | Total |
|---|---|---|---|---|
| American Economic Review | 1 | 4 | 0 | 5 |
| Econometrica | 3 | 2 | 0 | 5 |
| Economic Journal | 0 | 4 | 0 | 4 |
| International Journal of Industrial Organization | 2 | 1 | 1 | 4 |
| Journal of Political Economy | 1 | 3 | 0 | 4 |
| Review of Economic Studies | 5 | 1 | 0 | 6 |
| Total | 12 | 15 | 1 | 28 |

such cases has some point. But the empirical relevance of Rubinstein and Wolinsky's model seems remote. Whether such papers will ever lead to a better understanding of how the economic world works may be doubted. But as Marshall said (quoted in the epigraph to this paper), it is safe to praise your own strategy, unsafe to damn somebody else's.

Sixteen of the papers in Table 2 get an empirical relevance rating of 2, meaning that they have obvious relevance for empirical work. An example is Philip E. Graves, Dwight R. Lee, and Robert L. Sexton (1989), who assume that a lower speed limit and more policing are alternative ways to reduce average speed and therefore (a proposition questioned by Charles A. Lave [1989]) highway fatalities; since additional policing costs money and lowering the limit does not, the limit should be set as low as politically feasible. In another example, David I. Levine (1989) concludes, without using data, that government policies requiring a show of just cause for firing promote efficiency by introducing an externality: firing workers increases hiring rates to replace the dismissed workers.

One paper, by Xavier Vives (1989), in a close decision gets the highest empirical relevance rating, 3.[9] Vives sets out "to understand the channels through which an improvement in the accuracy of the information available to a firm fosters its competitive position" and "to know...what is the effect on the profitability of a firm of better information for the *rivals* in the industry" (p. 18). In his model, a firm that acquires better information is always better off. The rivals will be hurt in the case of quantity competition, benefited in the case of price competition. The empirical context that begins and ends the paper is the advantage Japan has attained from the government policy of encouraging and subsidizing collection, exchange, and propagation of industrial information.

The papers rated 2 and 3 illustrate what cause-to-effect can lead to and why, despite doubts, those rated 1 should be tolerated. Typically, model builders do not start from scratch. They start from a model already published and introduce new assumptions that make the model a closer approximation to reality. This procedure is not limited to papers classified as cause-to-effect. It generally characterizes explanatory models and papers that include econometric or other testing. As Herbert A. Simon (1979, p. 510) put it, "We are committed to a strategy of successive approximations."

## III. FROM EFFECTS TO CAUSES AND BACK AGAIN

Cause-to-effect starts with a set of premises and follows wherever they lead. The opposite procedure, preached and practiced by Milton Friedman and discussed at length by Abraham Hirsch and Neil de Marchi (1990), starts with facts, creates a model that explains them, tests the model by its predictions of other facts, and modifies the model if necessary.[10] A good example of this process of inquiry is the well-known article by Friedman and L. J. Savage (1948) on risk. They start with the observation that people, often the same people, take out insurance and gamble, both at unfavorable odds. Their model explaining these stylized facts includes as its centerpiece a wiggly curve of the total utility of money with marginal utility first diminishing, then increasing, and ultimately diminishing again. They suggest other tests of the model. The most casual reading of scientists' writings for laymen confirms that this is similar to what goes on in the natural sciences except for an important omission. In the natural sciences, the implications of the theory stimulate a search for new data and observations. The importance of this step, and the failure of economists to take it, has been stressed by Wassily Leontief (1971), who wrote, "True advances can be achieved only through an iterative process in which improved theoretical formulation raises new empirical questions and the answers to these questions in turn lead to new theoretical insights" (p. 5). Leontief (1982) complained that economists do little data gathering; instead, they use the same data over and over. My investigation supports his criticism. In 127 articles, only eight or nine (eight clear cases, one questionable) presented or used new data. Two of them reported the results of experiments (not the kind of data Leontief had in mind). None had data gathering as the main purpose of the research. None is a clear case of Leontief's iterative process. One paper (Lave, 1989) suggested the kind of data needed to settle the dispute over highway speed discussed in the next subsection and referred to an unpublished exploratory study of the right kind. But to get the data needed would require a major, expensive study of a kind economists are not likely to undertake even though its social value would be great.

In my sample, I found no paper that was as good an exemplar of Friedman's research strategy as the Friedman-Savage article. Instead, I found a number of papers that fit one or two parts of the pattern: search for regularities, explanatory modeling, and theory testing. They may belong to ongoing research programs that follow the Friedman-Savage natural-science pattern.

## A. Search for Regularities

Finding empirical regularities or stylized facts is an important task of research. Stylized facts can (but need not) provide the starting point for a Friedman-Savage process of inquiry. Thirty-four of the papers in my sample (see Table 1) pursue this task.

Four of the papers in the category of searching for regularities come to the same conclusion, namely, the greater the variance of highway speed, the greater the number of accidental deaths.[11] None of them tries to explain the finding; none provides a model. Lave, however, in the original article (1985) that stimulated the three comments and his reply included in my sample, pointed out that greater variance of speed means more passing and more collisions, and he cited Ezra Hauer (1971) as having provided a theoretical foundation for earlier findings in the traffic engineering literature showing the danger of deviating in either direction from average speed.

Other regularities discovered or confirmed include: the duration of strikes is countercyclical in Canadian as well as American data (Alan Harrison and Mark Stewart, 1989; Susan B. Vroman, 1989); strike incidence is procyclical and positively related to unexpected inflation (Vroman, 1989); demand disturbances have a temporary effect on output and employment, supply disturbances a permanent effect (Olivier Blanchard and Danny Quah, 1989); participants in a series of committee meetings in an experiment advanced from myopic to strategic voting, taking account of the voting behavior of others to get their second choice approved when their first choice could not win (Catherine Eckel and Charles A. Holt, 1989); firms adjust their demand for labor to exogenous shocks in jumps, rather than smoothly (Daniel S. Hamermesh, 1989); strikes are not accidents but give union members information about the rents of the firm (Sheena McConnell, 1989).

Few of these regularities involve economic theory either as a tool of analysis or as contribution to theoretical advance. The finding that the variance of highway speed is associated with fatalities could have been made by any competent statistician.

## B.  Rational Expectations

A special problem arises with key assumptions of economic theory. Such assumptions may be tested directly or indirectly. In the Friedman-Savage (1948) article on risk, the wiggly curve of the marginal utility of money is tested only indirectly. That is, the model is tested by its implications. If the model passes the tests, it is provisionally accepted, as is the set of assumptions underlying it. The authors, in keeping with the much-criticized position of Friedman (1953), do not propose any direct test of the wiggly curve. But direct tests of key assumptions of economic theory such as rationality (George A. Akerlof, 1991) and profit maximization do get made. Such attempts might be regarded as a search for regularities of economic behavior or as tests of theories in which they appear.

Four papers in my sample test the rational expectations hypothesis (REH), which is often used as an assumption in models. Robert W. Rich (1989), using University of Michigan survey data, finds expectations of inflation "consistent with both weak and strong forms of rationality." (In another paper [Rich, 1990, not part of my sample] he used a different set of survey data, this one of economists' forecasts of inflation, and found the evidence inconsistent with rational expectations. He was too tactful to point out the implication: laymen's expectations of inflation are rational but economists' are not.) Karen K. Lewis

(1989) shows that mispredictions of the foreign exchange market in the early 1980s were consistent with rational expectations. Yoon Dokko and Robert H. Edelstein in "How Well Do Economists Forecast Stock Market Prices? A Study of the Livingston Surveys" (1989) also find the predictions rational. Benjamin M. Friedman and David I. Laibson (1989, p. 169), on the other hand, find evidence inconsistent with rational expectations.

All four papers come closer to a search for regularities (which is how they are listed in Table 1) than a test of models that assume rational expectations. The mixed results—three papers favorable to REH, one unfavorable—are just what should always be expected when key assumptions are tested directly. Such assumptions perform both of the classic functions of assumptions: they simplify and they embody something important about the way the world works. Direct tests of them inevitably show that they are more or less correct, on target but not in the bull's-eye.

Direct tests of assumptions are useful for pointing the way to better models. Economics advances by relaxing the initial simplifications to get better approximations to reality. Direct tests of assumptions tell us in what specific ways they do and do not differ from reality. We know that people are not always rational. We know that departures from rationality are not all random: there are patterns—regularities—of irrational behavior. They may need to be taken into account.

Whereas direct tests of assumptions are useful, they are no substitute for tests of models by their implications. Testing assumptions is one thing; testing theories, another. Since we know that a model is a simplification, the only way we can find out if it is oversimplified is to test it by its implications. In my sample of 127 papers, there are no tests of models built on rational expectations. Tests of models include John M. Abowd (1989), who finds evidence that "investors behave as if they believe managers make profit-maximizing employment decisions" and who "cannot reject the strong efficiency model for most of the analyses" (p. 793); and Martin Eichenbaum (1989), who tests alternative explanations for holding inventories, to smooth production rates (rejected) or to smooth production costs.

## C.  Replication

I follow Nancy Cartwright (1991) in distinguishing routine checking, replication, and reproduction. Routine checking means making sure there were no errors in a study. The work of W.G. Dewald, J.G. Thursby, and R.G. Anderson (1986) comes under the heading of routine checking (though they called it replication).[12] Another example is the discovery of Dean Leimer and Selig Lesnoy (1982) of a programming error in Martin Feldstein (1974). There are no examples of it in my sample. But as H.M. Collins (1991) argues, it is doubtful if finding and correcting all the errors in published econometric studies would make a significant difference for the advance of economics. The errors exposed by Dewald, Thursby, and Anderson (1986) do not seem earthshaking.

Replication goes beyond checking. It means doing the same thing as the original study in different circumstances or with different data. In my sample, Glenn W. Harrison (1989) conducted experiments on first-price auctions that essentially replicated those of previous writers with a different set of subjects; he got the same results, thus strengthening the evidence. As mentioned previously, A. Harrison and Stewart (1989) use Canadian data to confirm an earlier finding in American data that the duration of strikes is countercyclical. The four studies showing positive correlation between variance of highway speed and fatalities do not count as replication. They used different equations as well as different data sets to come to the same conclusion.

Replication shades off into reproduction, which means getting the same (or different) results from an entirely different approach, using different auxiliary assumptions. The paradigm comes from physics: the existence of atoms and molecules was established by calculating Avogadro's number in thirteen different ways, all with the same result. The four different ways of studying highway speed in my sample do not count as reproduction because the auxiliary assumptions are not independent. The studies of rational expectations come closer to reproduction.

As Cartwright (1991) explains, "the argument from coincidence" makes the evidence from reproduction much more convincing than that from replication. Unless there were atoms and molecules, the experimental results from thirteen different measures of Avogadro's number would be an astonishing coincidence. The element of coincidence is much less when different functional forms are used as in different measures of the wage elasticity of hours worked (Cartwright's [1991] example) or the four studies of highway speed.

My sample tends to confirm what any economists' ordinary reading of journals would lead them to expect: except for economic historians, economists rely too heavily on one kind of evidence, econometric, and devote too little effort to mobilizing other kinds of information. In my sample, William H. Nordhaus (1989), discussed below, is the chief exception.

## D. Explanatory Models

In Table 1, ten papers are listed as explanatory modeling without testing. These papers stop short of what Friedman regarded as an essential step.

The illuminating model of Alex Cukierman and Allan H. Meltzer (1989) explains why rational people support federal deficits in spite of the Ricardian equivalence principle, according to which the choice between deficits and taxes does not matter. Some people would like to reduce bequests to heirs but can— not because they have no assets. Such people can rationally support deficits as a way to increase their own consumption at the expense of future generations. Also, those with large wealth benefit from higher interest rates resulting from crowding out of capital by government deficits. The authors discuss other implications of their model, for example, "deficit financing is more likely when government expenditures increase, and surpluses are more likely when expenditures decline" (pp. 730-31). They do not point out that this implication could be used to test their model, let alone carry out the test themselves. Economists are apt to assume that if a model is plausible, its implications provide reliable predictions and explanations. It is not clear whether this is the case with Cukierman and Meltzer.

Other papers in the category of explanatory models without tests include Jon W. Faust (1989), whose model helps explain why people accept fiat money even though it has no intrinsic value; Kenneth A. Froot and Paul D. Klemperer (1989), who explain why, in response to dollar appreciation in the early 1980s, foreign firms increased profit margins in the United States, creating differentials between prices here and elsewhere; Boyan Jovanovich and Saul Lach (1989), who account for S-shaped diffusion of innovation; Dale O. Stahl, II (1989), who improves on a model explaining why stores charge different prices for identical items; and Jere R. Behrman and Anil Deolalikar (1989), who show that consumers seem to increasingly value food variety as their incomes increase.

As the examples given above show, explanatory modeling by itself can produce interesting, plausible results. But it would be useful for such papers to suggest tests that they or others could do in the future. Friedman's 1951 complaint about "all too much emphasis on the derivation of hypotheses, all too little on testing their validity" may be less true now than then but finds support in my sample.[13]

## E.   Theory Testing

Seventeen of the papers surveyed (six each from the *American Economic Review* and the *Review of Economics and Statistics*, none at all from *Econometrica*, the *Journal of Economic History*, or the *Review of Economic Studies*) test models by their implications. Thomas F. Cooley and Gary D. Hansen's "The Inflation Tax in a Real Business Cycle Model" (1989), like many papers, introduces a new assumption into an old model: it modifies an earlier business cycle model of the second author to introduce money.[14] The model is then simulated, "using parameter values based on growth observations and the results of studies using microeconomic data." Simple correlations are calculated between output and six other aggregate variables for both actual U.S. data and the simulations; the simulation with an erratic money supply comes closer to U.S. data than the one with a constant money supply. In the model and in data for 23 countries, employment rates are lower with higher inflation. It thus compares the predictions of the model with reality. The results "suggest that the phenomenon displayed in our model economy may not be counterfactual." The paper falls short of the ideal process of inquiry because it does not start with the full and comprehensive investigation of the facts that Friedman advocates. Neither did Friedman and Savage. But in their case, the stylized facts they started with (people gamble, people take out insurance, both at unfavorable odds) seem sufficiently well-founded in everyday observation. Cooley and Hansen, on the other hand, (and the same is true of the real-business-cycle research program generally) are dealing with a subject that has been extensively investigated empirically. They seem to ignore a wealth of available detail that a business cycle theory ought to account for. Their tests of their theory show only that it is consistent with the broad features of business cycles. Moreover, it does not pit its theory against any other theory of the business cycle. All in all, the paper seems to be an interim report on an ongoing research program. All research is to some extent a steppingstone: no finding puts an end to the investigation. But the steppingstone element is greater in some papers like this one than in others like Friedman and Savage. Because real business cycle theory starts with such a limited set of facts, I doubt if it will succeed better than the several approaches to business cycles that have come to a dead end. But that remains to be seen.

## F.  New Data

As already noted, the process of inquiry common in natural science calls for gathering new data and making new observations as a follow-up to theorizing. The implications of a model suggest empirical tests. The tests require information not previously available. Einstein's theory of relativity stimulated astronomers to observe and measure the bending of light during an eclipse of the sun. The Alvarez hypothesis that a giant asteroid hit the earth 65 million years ago, causing a drastic change in the weather that wiped out the dinosaurs, was based in part on finding at one site an iridium layer in rocks 65 million years old. The hypothesis suggested that a similar iridium layer would be found around the world. It was. Examples from the natural sciences could easily be multiplied, but they seem less frequent in economics. There is no clear example in my sample and only two papers that come close.

Fred S. Inaba and Nancy E. Wallace (1989) modify a previous model and apply it to wheat shipping in the Pacific Northwest, using data from a survey apparently conducted by the authors. The econometric results confirmed three hypotheses: "market boundary should be a significant predictor of mode choice"; "the conditional quantity shipped distributions are positively truncated and...transit time is probably not a good proxy for the interest and storage costs of holding inventory" (p. 624). Since the hypotheses confirmed by the paper do not amount to much, it can hardly be regarded as an example of the research strategy discussed above.

The other paper that comes close is C.W.F. Baden-Fuller (1989). The interviews he conducted can be regarded as providing a test of his model only by stretching a good deal.

# IV.  ECLECTIC RESEARCH

All but one of the 127 papers in my sample fit reasonably well into one or the other categories of research strategy.[15] The one paper that does not fit into a single category is Nordhaus.[16] Despite its shortcomings, Nordhaus's "Alternative Approaches to the Political Business Cycle" (1989) is a model of economics research at its best.[17] He uses a variety of approaches: historical-institutional, conceptual exploration, and theory testing. First, he summarizes five kinds of models of the political business cycle. Next, he discusses, using mathematical modeling, the issue of whether political parties are opportunistic or ideological. The third section presents a formal (mathematical) analysis applicable to models of political business cycles generally. The fourth section examines historical evidence to try to narrow down the issues, using Gallup polls on presidential performance. This results in discrediting one of the five classes of models, the one based on ultrarationality. A subsection on the opportunism-ideology question concludes that much of the previous discussion has been wide of the mark. "The major difference introduced by ideology is that parties specialize in different policies. Just as you go to dentists to get your teeth drilled, you go to conservatives to root out inflation." This explains why "Republican presidents often begin their tenure with a recession while Democrats start by expanding the economy" (p. 42). A final section, titled "Do Political Cycles Exist?,"[18] says, "A review of the evidence finds a rich array of possible linkages between macroeconomics and politics and a wide variety of cycles in different times and places." Nordhaus is not surprised:

> Politics, after all, is constantly evolving. An obviously manipulative economic policy, for example, will elicit political reforms that ultimately control it. In reaction to the manipulative 1972 Nixon reelection campaign, Congress took steps [which Nordhaus details] to impede future attempts to manipulate the economy for political purposes. (p. 48). [L]ike any evolving creature, the political business cycle is likely to emerge in the future in unexpected shapes and with unanticipated dynamics. (p. 49).

This is the only paper in my sample that recognizes the difficulty for economic research of dealing with behavior and institutions that evolve in response to experience, making it almost impossible to find new regularities that are dependable other than those few fundamental regularities already incorporated in basic economic theory.

# V. CONCLUSIONS

1.   The presumption that what economists do is mostly sound is justified. But, their practice could be improved.

2.   There is limited evidence to support the charge of too much modeling that is remote from reality. The twelve papers with an empirical relevance rating of 1 contribute more to the reputations of the authors than to the advance of economics. They are the least interesting (except to those economists doing that kind of thing) but require the high technical expertise that economists love and admire. They constitute less than 10 percent of my sample and very likely an even smaller proportion of all published research. Since there is always the possibility that such papers will ultimately lead to something valuable, my evidence on this matter does not suggest a serious misallocation of resources.

3.   Economists rely too heavily on one kind of evidence, namely, econometric. Many of the econometric studies evoke the old metaphor of mountains laboring to bring forth mice. Like the papers with an empirical relevance rating of 1, they demonstrate admirable technical skill of the authors, but the conclusions are often nugatory.

4.   My study confirms what should never have been in doubt: testing theories by their assumptions can be useful. Sometimes a particular model can be refuted by showing that a key assumption is wrong. Directly testing the basic assumptions used generally in economics—profit maximization, downward sloping demand curves, rationality in general, rational expectations in particular—are useful for showing the limits of the undoubted generalizations they embody.

5.   Testing models by their predictions is useful but infrequent. More would be desirable.

6.   Few authors in my sample present new data. Those few did so because the data were needed for a particular problem. There are no articles devoted primarily to increasing the stock of data. The charge that economists neglect this kind of research is supported by my study.

7.   Economists are mainly engaged in telling more or less plausible stories. Very little gets proved beyond a reasonable doubt and, at least in my sample, much of that little can be called economics only by stretching the term. If economics is defined as whatever gets published in economics journals, then the finding that variability of highway speed increases fatalities is economics. But the four studies that reached this conclusion made no use of economic theory; they could have been done by anybody competent in statistics.

8.   As might have been expected, the most interesting and illuminating journals are the *American Economic Review* and the *Journal of Political Economy*.

9.   Robert M. Solow (1990) and W. Lee Hansen[19] have lamented that knowledge in economics does not cumulate as much as we would like. My

sample suggests that this may be in part because economists too often think in terms of their own research projects rather than an ongoing research program to which they and many others are contributing. The result is numerous contributions that are connected only by the kind of literature review at the beginning of a typical paper. The concluding section summarizing the paper makes no reference to the literature reviewed at the beginning. Authors do not define how they have advanced the broad research program. Eventually, to be sure, somebody will write a review article to try to put the pieces together, but it is apt to result in "some say this, some say that" without any clear picture of what all the contributions add up to. Or, the review article will show that most or all of the studies have reached the same conclusion, implying that the various studies reinforce each other, when in fact they may be vulnerable to Cartwright's critique. Replication is rare. It would help if authors in their conclusions defined what they have done to advance the broad research program. It would help even more if economists made a greater effort to choose research projects by their potential for such advance. Sometimes economists choose topics because they have a data set nobody else has used or they know of econometric methods superior to those used by their predecessors. An economist I know has published two articles on an important hypothesis. The two papers, which used different data sets, came to opposite conclusions. When I asked him where this left the hypothesis, I got no answer. He had never been interested in the subject of the hypothesis and had moved on to other subjects. He had done two projects on it because he knew of data sets that offered him an opportunity to use his econometric skills. As Paul Diesing (1991) pointed out, social science research workers are engaged in monopolistic competition, each trying to produce a differentiated product, a kind of endeavor not conducive to cumulating knowledge.

## ACKNOWLEDGMENTS

The author thanks those who in one way or another helped him with this paper or the project that it grew out of. They are, in alphabetical order, Jeff Biddle, Henry W. Chappell, Jr., William Guthrie, Daniel M. Hausman, C. Elton Hinshaw, Theodore Morgan, Warren J. Samuels, John J. Siegfried, William O. Thweatt, and three anonymous referees.

## NOTES

1.   I shall avoid using the word *methodolgoy* for my subject. Sometimes words get worn out from overuse, misuse, and loose use. Such is the case with *methodology*. Sometimes it means ways of theory appraisal (Hausman, 1989; M. Friedman, 1953, both of whom commendably make clear that is what they mean). Sometimes it means process of inquiry or research strategy (Hirsch and de Marchi, 1990, who leave the reader in doubt what they mean until p. 70). Sometimes it

means what Fritz Machlup (1963) and Donald N. McCloskey (1985) call method, as in Faik Koray and William D. Lastrapes (1989) and in Gerard Debreu (1991, p. 6). The subject of this paper is research strategy or process of inquiry in the phrase used by Hirsch and de Marchi, terms I use as synonyms.

Though I avoid *methodology*, there is no objection to others using it. There *is* objection to the popular phrase, "the official methodology." The phrase is a metaphor; no official body such as the American Economic Association has promulgated the methodology economists should follow. It is a bad metaphor; it implies that there a consensus among economists. Actually, methodology is a controversial subject. That is what makes it interesting. References to the official methodology of economics should be banned.

2.   If, as used to be asserted, there is a gap between what economists do and what they say, the remedy may not be for them to practice what they preach, but for them to preach what they practice (cf. Hausman, 1980.)

3.   The top three in the rankings by impact-adjusted citations to articles published in 1975-1979 were *American Economic Review, Journal of Political Economy*, and *Econometrica*. Of the other six, one specialized in industrial organization, one in economic history, one in macroeconomics, one in econometrics, and one in model-building. The *Economic Journal* was included to reduce the emphasis on American journals. A tenth journal, *Industrial and Labor Relations Review*, was dropped from the study because it had little to do with economic theory.

4.   This differentiates my study from McCloskey (1985) and Arjo Klamer (1983), who have reported on the work and conversation of leading lights in the profession.

5.   I use the word *science* in its general sense, bypassing the much-discussed "demarcation" question of how to draw the line between science and nonscience. The question is wrongly stated. It commits the common fallacy of confusing a question of degree with a question of kind. It is easy to draw up a long list of the characteristics of sciences and then (though this is not so easy) to classify fields into groups that are more or less scientific. In such a classification, physics and chemistry are in the top group, economics in a middle group, and history in a lesser scientific group (though not lesser in any invidious sense), with literature among the least scientific.

6.   It also results from the decision to use the category "applications" sparingly. An econometric test of a theory could be ragarded as an application but is not in Table 1.

7.   A separate paper (Rendigs Fels, 1992) deals with the complaint of Leontief (1982) against mathematical models without data. He found that two-thirds of the articles in the *American Economic Review* during a ten-year period fell into this category. Theodore Morgan (1988) more or less supported his complaint. In my sample of 127 papers, I found only 37 cases of models without data, including all 28 listed in Tables 1 and 2 of the present paper as cause-to-effect. Moreover, the important objection is not to models without data but to models remote from reality, in other words, to the twelve I have given an ampirical relevance rating of 1. The other twenty-five models without data are clearly relevant to empirical questions. Those rated 3, such as Cukierman and Meltzer (1989) (summarized in the text below), are illuminating.

8.   Another example, Philippe Weil (1989), is summarized in Fels (1992).

9.   Papers that more clearly deserve a rating of 3 typically start out to explain a stylized fact rather than starting with a set of assumptions and seeing where they lead.

10.   Friedman described the procedure as follows:

The approach that is standard in the physical sciences is to use theory to derive generalizations about the real world. The theorist starts with some set of observed and related facts, as full and comprehensive as possible. He seeks a generalization that will explain these facts; he can always succeed; indeed, he can always find an indefinitely large number of generalizations. The number of observed facts is finite, and the number of possible theories is infinite; infinitely many theories can therefore be found that are consistent with the facts. The theorist therefore calls in some arbitrary principle such as

"Occam's razor" and settles on a particular generalization of theory. He tests this theory to make sure that it is logically consistent, that its elements are susceptible of empirical determination, and that it will explain adequately the facts he started with. He then seeks to deduce from his theory facts other than those he used to derive it and to check these deductions against reality. Typically some deduced "facts" check and others do not; so he revises his theory to take account of the additional facts. The ultimate check of deduced against observed facts in essential in this process Friedman (pp. 282-283).

Friedman believed that this was Marshall's procedure and, in fact Marshall (1936, p. 781) gives a broadly similar description of the process of inquiry in economics. The association of Marshall with the Friedman-natural science approach is doubted by two commentators on an earlier draft of this paper.

11. The four papers, Peter Asch and David T. Levy (1989), Richard Fowles and Peter D. Loeb (1989), Donald W. Snyder (1989), and Charles A. Lave (1989), differ on the question of whether greater speed per se increases deaths. The first three papers conclude that it does. Lave gives convincing reasons for doubt. Pending further research, the issue must be regarded as open.

12. Cartwright's terminology is an improvement. "Routine checking" conveys the idea better than "replication" even though Dewald et al. have shown that checking other economists' work is anything but routine. Cartwright's terms for the other two categories are less happy choices.

13. Testing theories by their predictions has at best limited value in any field. The limitations are especially great in economics. But it is useful to try.

14. It is disconcerting, it not brain-boggling, to learn that as late as 1989 economists could make a contribution to business cycle theory by adding money to their analysis. Sic transit gloria de Joseph Schumpeter (1934, 1939), Gottfried Haberler (1937), M. Friedman, and Anna J. Schwartz (1963).

15. The papers in the "other' category are not genuine exeptions since they fit neatly into the subcategories given near the beginning of this paper.

16. I estimate that Nordhaus's paper is about 10 percent longer than Abowd, the longest in the September 1989 issue of the *American Economic Review*. Abowd is an outlier, being 35 percent longer than the second longest. The length permitted by the *Brookings Papers* facilitates the variety of research methods in Nordhaus.

17. Its principla shortcoming is neglect of the literature cited by Alberto Alesina (1989) in his comment. It is not an exemplar of ideal research strategy because it is mainly a review of the literature with the addition of some original research, but it is the nearest thing to an exemplar in my sample.

18. As this section title suggests, Nordhaus's paper could reasonably be classified as a search for regularities: he is trying to find out if there is a political business cycle and if so, in what sense. But that classification does not do justice to the paper as a whole. A referee has suggested that Nordhaus could be classified as effect-to-cause. True enough, but that is just the point—Nordhaus did not confine himself to one approach.

19. Oral comment by W. Lee Hansen at the annual meeting of the Midwestern Economic Association, 1991.

# REFERENCES

Abowd, John M. 1989. "The Effect of Wage Bargains on the Stock Market Value of the Firm." *American Economic Review* 79(September): 774-800.

Akerlof, George A. 1991. "Procrastination and Obedience." *American Economic Review* 81 (May; Papers and Proceedings): 1-19.

Alesina, Alberto. 1989. "Comments and Discussion." *Brookings Papers on Economic Activity* 2: 50-56.

Asch, Peter, and David T. Levy. 1989. "Speeding, Coordination, and the 55-MPH Limit: Comment." *American Economic Review* 79(September): 913-915.

Baden-Fuller, C.W.F. 1989. "Exit from Declining Industries and the Case of Steel Castings," *Economic Journal* 99(December): 949-961.

Behrman, Jere R., and Anil Deolalikar. 1989. "Is Variety the Spice of Life? Implications for Calorie Intake." *Review of Economics and Statistics* 71 (November): 666-672.

Blanchard, Olivier Jean, and Danny Quah. 1989. "The Dynamic Effects of Aggregate Demand and Supply Disturbances." *American Economic Review* 79(September): 655-673.

Cartwright, Nancy. 1991. "Replicability, Reproducibility, and Robustness: Comments on Henry Collins." *History of Political Economy* 23(Spring): 143-155.

Collins, H.M. 1991. "The Meaning of Replication and the Science of Economics." *History of Political Economy* 23(Spring): 123-142.

Cooley, Thomas F., and Gary D. Hansen. 1989. "The Inflation Tax in a Real Business Cycle Model." *American Economic Review* 79(September): 733-748.

Cukierman, Alex, and Allan H. Meltzer. 1989. "A Political Theory of Government Debt and Deficits in a Neo-Ricardian Framework." *American Economic Review* 79(September): 713-732.

Debreu, Gerard. 1991. "The Mathematization of Economic Theory." *American Economic Review* 81(March): 1-7.

Dewald, W.G., J.G. Thursby, and R.G. Anderson. 1986. "Replication in Empirical Economics: The Journal of Money, Credit and Banking Project." *American Economic Review* 76(September): 587-603.

Diesing, Paul. 1991. *How Does Social Science Work? Reflections on Practice.* Pittsburgh: University of Pittsburgh Press.

Dokko, Yoon, and Robert H. Edelstein. 1989. "How Well Do Economists Forecast Stock Market Prices?" *American Economic Review* 79(September): 865-871.

Eckel, Catherine, and Charles A. Holt. 1989. "Strategic Voting in Agenda-Controlled Committee Experiments." *American Economic Review* 79(September): 763-773.

Eichenbaum, Martin. 1989. "Some Empirical Evidence on the Production Level and Production Cost Smoothing Models of Inventory Investment." *American Economic Review* 79(September): 853-864.

Faust, Jon W. 1989. "Supernovas in Monetary Theory: Does the Ultimate Sunspot Rule Out Money?" *American Economic Review* 79(September): 872-881.

Feldstein, Martin. 1974. "Social Security, Induced Retirement, and Aggregate Capital Accumulation." *Journal of Political Economy* 82(September/October): 905-926.

Fels, Rendigs. 1992. "An Update on Leontief's Complaint." *Journal of Economic Perspectives* 6(Winter): 201-204.

Fowles, Richard, and Peter D. Loeb. 1989. "Speeding, Coordination, and the 55-MPH Limit: Comment." *American Economic Review* 79(September): 916-921.

Friedman, Benjamin M., and David I. Laibson. 1989. "Economic Implications of Extraordinary Movements in Stock Prices." *Brookings Papers on Economic Activity* 2: 137-172.

Friedman, Milton. 1946. "Lange on Price Flexibility and Unemployment: A Methodological Criticism." *American Economic Review* 36(September): 613-631.

————. 1951. "Comment." Pp. 107-114 in *Conference on Business Cycles.* New York: National Bureau of Economic Research.

————. 1953. *Essays in Positive Economics.* Chicago: University of Chicago Press.

Friedman, Milton, and L.J. Savage. 1948. "The Utility Analysis of Choices Involving Risk." *Journal of Political Economy* 56(August): 279-304.

Friedman, Milton, and Anna J. Schwartz. 1963. *A Monetary History of the United States, 1867-1960.* Princeton: Princeton University Press.

Froot, Kenneth A., and Paul D. Klemperer. 1989. "Exchange-Rate Pass-Through When Market Share Matters." *American Economic Review* 79(September): 637-654.

Goto, Akira, and Kazuyaki Suzuki. 1989. "R & D Capital, Rate of Return on R & D Investment and Spillover of R & D in Japanese Manufacturing Industries." *Review of Economics and Statistics* 71(November): 555-564.

Graves, Philip E., Dwight R. Lee, and Robert L. Sexton. 1989. "Statutes versus Enforcement: The Case of the Optimal Speed Limit." *American Economic Review* 79(September): 932-936.

Haberler, Gottfried. 1937. *Prosperity and Depression.* Geneva: League of Nations.

Hamermesh, Daniel S. 1989. "Labor Demand and the Structure of Adjustment Costs." *American Economic Review* 79(September): 674-689.

Harrison, Alan, and Mark Stewart. 1989. "Cyclical Fluctuations in Strike Durations." *American Economic Review* 79(September): 827-841.

Harrison, Glenn W. 1989. "Theory and Misbehavior of First-Price Auctions." *American Economic Review* 79(September): 749-762.

Hauer, Ezra. 1971. "Accidents, Overtaking and Speed Control." *Accident Analysis and Prevention.* 3(January): 1-12.

Hausman, Daniel M. 1980. "How to Do Philosophy of Economics." Pp. 353-362 in *PSA 1980,* edited by P. D. Asquith and R. Giere. East Lansing, MI: Philosophy of Science Association.

_____. 1989. "Economic Methodology in a Nutshell." *Journal of Economic Perspectives* 3(Spring): 115-128.

Hirsch, Abraham, and Neil de Marchi. 1990. *Milton Friedman: Economics in Theory and Practice.* Ann Arbor: The University of Michigan Press.

Inaba, Fred S., and Nancy E. Wallace. 1989. "Spatial Price Competition and the Demand for Freight Transportation." *Review of Economics and Statistics* 71(November): 614-625.

Jovanovich, Boyan, and Saul Lach. 1989. "Entry, Exit, and Diffusion with Learning by Doing." *American Economic Review* 79(September): 690-699.

Klamer, Arjo, 1983. *Conversations with Economists: New Classical Economists and Opponents Speak Out on the Current Controversy.* Totowa, NJ: Rowman and Allanheld.

Koray, Faik, and William D. Lastrapes. 1989. "Real Exchange Rate Volatility and U. S. Bilateral Trade: A VAR Approach." *Review of Economics and Statistics* 71(November): 708-712.

Lave, Charles A. 1985. "Speeding, Coordination, and the 55 MPH Limit." *American Economic Review* 75(December): 1159-1164.

_____. 1989. "Speeding, Coordination, and the 55-MPH Limit: Reply." *American Economic Review* 79(September): 926-931.

Leimer, Dean, and Selig Lesnoy. 1982. "Social Security and Private Saving: New Time-Series Evidence." *Journal of Political Economy* 90(February): 606-629.

Leontief, Wassily. 1971. "Theoretical Assumptions and Nonobserved Facts." *American Economic Review* 61(March): 1-7.

_____. 1982. "Academic Economics." *Science* 217(July 9): 104-107.

Levine, David I. 1989. "Just-Cause Employment Policies When Unmemployment Is a Worker Discipline Device." *American Economic Review* 79(September): 902-905.

Lewis, Karen K. 1989. "Changing Beliefs and Systematic Rational Forecast Errors with Evidence from Foreign Exchange." *American Economic Review* 79(September): 621-636.

Libecap, Gary D. 1989. "The Political Economy of Crude Oil Cartelization in the United States, 1933-1972." *Journal of Economic History* 49(December): 833-855.

Liebowitz, S.J., and J.P. Palmer. 1984. "Assessing the Relative Impacts of Economics Journals." *Journal of Economic Literature* 22(March): 77-88.

Machlup, Fritz. 1963. "Problems of Methodology: Introductory Remarks." *American Economic Review* 53(May; Papers and Proceedings): 204.

Marshall, Alfred, 1936. *Principles of Economics.* 8th edn. London: Macmillan.

McCloskey, Donald N. 1985. *The Rhetoric of Economics, Series in the Rhetoric of Human Sciences.* Madison: University of Wisconsin Press.

McConnell, Sheena. 1989. "Strikes, Wages, and Private Information." *American Economic Review* 79(September): 801-815.

Morgan, Theodore. 1988. "Theory versus Empiricism in Academic Economics: Update and Comparison." *Journal of Economic Perspectives* 2(Fall): 159-164.

Nordhaus, William D. 1989. "Alternative Approaches to the Political Business Cycle." *Brookings Papers on Economic Activity* 2: 1-49.

Rich, Robert W. 1989. "Testing the Rationality of Inflation Forecasts from Survey Data: Another Look at the SRC Expected Price Change Data." *Review of Economics and Statistics* 71(November): 682-686.

_____. 1990. "Another Look at the Rationality of the Livingston Price Expectations Data." *Applied Economics* 22(April): 477-485.

Rubinstein, Ariel, and Asher Wolinsky. 1990. "Decentralized Trading, Strategic Behavior and the Walrasian Outcome." *Review of Economic Studies* 57(January): 63-78.

Schumpeter, Joseph A. 1934. *The Theory of Economic Development: An Inquiry into Profits, Capital, Credit, Interest, and the Business Cycle.* Translated from the German by Redvers Opie. Cambridge: Harvard University Press.

_____. 1939. *Business Cycles, A Theoretical, Historical, and Statistical Analysis of the Capitalist Process.* New York: McGraw-Hill.

Simon, Herbert A. 1979. "Rational Decision Making in Business Organizations." *American Economic Review* 69(September): 493-513.

Snyder, Donald W. 1989. "Speeding, Coordination, and the 55-MPH Limit: Comment." *American Economic Review* 79(September): 922-925.

Solow, Robert M. 1990. "Discussion." *American Economic Review* 80(May; Papers and Proceedings): 448-450.

Stahl, Dale O., II. 1989. "Oligopolistic Pricing with Sequential Consumer Search." *American Economic Review* 79(September): 700-712.

Vives, Xavier. 1989. "Information and Competitive Advantage." *International Journal of Industrial Organization* 8(April): 17-35.

Vroman, Susan B. 1989. "A Longitudinal Analysis of Strike Activity in U.S. Manufacturing: 1957-84." *American Economic Review* 79(September): 816-826.

Weil, Philippe. 1989. "Increasing Returns and Animal Spirits." *American Economic Review* 79(September): 889-894.

# MARX'S SEMANTICS AND THE LOGIC OF THE DERIVATION OF VALUE

Sasan Fayazmenesh

## I. INTRODUCTION

One of the oldest and yet still unresolved controversies in the history of economic theory centers around the first few pages of *Capital*, where Marx derives his concept of value. This controversy began with Bohm-Bawerk's famous work, *Karl Marx and the Close of His System* (1949). In this work, Bohm-Bawerk praised the middle parts of the Marxian system as "masterly." These parts, he argued, "by their extraordinary logical consistency, permanently establish the reputation of the author as an intellectual force of the first rank" (Bohm-Bawerk, 1949, pp. 88-89). However, he contended that the beginning of Marx's system, where he derives the concept of value, and the end of his system, where he transforms market values into prices of production, are logically flawed. In these two "most decisive places," Bohm-Bawerk argued, Marx resorted to sophistry in order to achieve his desired results (p. 90). The beginning was "a subtle and artificial afterthought contrived to make a preconceived opinion seem a natural outcome of a prolonged

Research in the History of Economic Thought and Methodology, Volume 12, pages 65-91.
Copyright © 1994 by JAI Press Inc.
ISBN: 1-55938-747-5

investigation" (p. 69). Marx, said Bohm-Bawerk, "knew the result that he wished to obtain, and must obtain, and so he twisted and manipulated the long-suffering ideas and logical premises with admirable skill and subtlety until they actually yielded the desired result in a seemingly respectable syllogistic form" (p. 79). The end, contended Bohm-Bawerk, was written by Marx when "he could not venture to write clearly and definitely without open contradiction and retraction" (p. 100). This explained, according to Bohm-Bawerk, Marx's logical blunders that appear at the beginning and the end.

A few years later Hilferding wrote a countercritique in which he argued that Bohm-Bawerk's critique of Marx's *Capital* represented the clash of two "mutually exclusive outlooks upon the whole of social life" (Hilferding, 1949, p. 187). This clash, according to Hilferding, had created for Bohm-Bawerk a perception of contradictions in Marx's theory where none existed. Hilferding applied this general line of defense against Bohm-Bawerk's argument that there was an open contradiction between the two volumes of *Capital*. He showed that this contradiction existed not in Marx's theory but in Bohm-Bawerk's interpretation of the theory. This argument was coupled with pointing out a major factual error in Bohm-Bawerk's contention. The third volume of *Capital*, he reminded Bohm-Bawerk, was written before the publication of the first volume and thus could not have been a cunning postscript (p. 155). The debate over the apparent contradiction between the two volumes came to an end. However, Hilferding was not as successful in defending the logical consistency of the beginning of *Capital*. He failed to address the important charge made by Bohm-Bawerk that the beginning of *Capital* was an artificial afterthought. He also failed to convince many future critics that Bohm-Bawerk's perception of logical blunder in the derivation of value was due to his interpretation of Marx's method and economic concepts. This left the controversy on the beginning of *Capital* unresolved. Since then, every few years, the debate over Marx's derivation of value erupts. In this periodic debate, the critics argue, à la Bohm-Bawerk, that this derivation is logically flawed and the countercritics argue otherwise, mainly by quoting Marx and repeating what has been said before.[1] So far, there seems to be no resolution in sight.

Toward resolving this century-old controversy, I would like to make the following points: Bohm-Bawerk's assertion that the beginning of *Capital* was merely "an artificial afterthought" was factually incorrect; and the derivation of value, contrary to his claim, was actually the result of a prolonged amount of work by Marx. Thus, any logical error in the derivation, perceived or actual, could not have been the result of sophistry on Marx's part. This is demonstrated in the third section of this paper. Moreover, both Bohm-Bawerk's criticism of Marx's derivation and the later countercriticisms of Bohm-Bawerk's work by Marxist writers are for the most part irrelevant because neither side has correctly understood the thrust of Marx's argument. This issue is discussed in the fifth and the last section of the present paper. However, I will argue in the fourth section that Marx himself is at least partially responsible for the misunderstandings that may arise, and have arisen, on the part of the reader because some of the terms that he employs, such as "use-value," are not clearly defined. Furthermore, ill-defined or fuzzy concepts used by Marx, such as "exchange-value" and the "exchange relation," result in a fallacious argument at the most decisive point in the derivation. This fallacy, so far as I know, has never been pointed out in any previous criticism of Marx's derivation. But before dealing with these issues in detail, let me first outline the main points of the controversy.

## II.   MARX'S DERIVATION AND BOHM-BAWERK'S CRITIQUE

The focus of the controversy has usually been on a few consecutive paragraphs that appear in the first few pages of either the third German edition or the English edition of the first volume of *Capital*. Given the importance of these paragraphs to the previous debates and to my own attempt to analyze them in the fourth section of this article, I reproduce them in their entirety, numbering them for convenience.

(1)   A given commodity, a quarter of wheat for example, is exchanged for x boot-polish, y silk or z gold, etc. In short, it is exchanged for other commodities in the most diverse proportion. Therefore the wheat has many exchange-values instead of one. But x boot-polish, y silk, z gold, etc., each represent the exchange-value of one quarter of wheat. Therefore x boot-polish, y silk, z gold, etc., must, as exchange-values, be mutually replaceable or of identical magnitude. It follows from this that, firstly, the valid exchange-values of a particular commodity express something equal, and secondly, exchange-value cannot be any thing other than the mode of expression, the 'form of appearance', of a content distinguishable from it.

(2)   Let us now take two commodities, for example corn and iron. Whatever their exchange relation may be, it can always be presented by an equation in which a given quantity of corn is equated to some quantity of iron, for instance 1 quarter of corn = x cwt of iron. What does this equation signify? It signifies that a common element of identical magnitude exists in two different things, in 1 quarter of corn and similarly in x cwt of iron. Both are therefore equal to a third thing, which in itself is neither the one nor the other. Each of them, so far as it is exchange-value, must therefore be reducible to this third thing.

(3)   A simple geometrical example will illustrate this. In order to determine and compare the areas of all rectilinear figures we split them up into triangles. Then the triangle itself is reduced to an expression totally different from its visible shape: half the product of the base and the altitude. In the same way the exchange-values of commodities must be reduced to a common element, of which they represent a greater or a lesser quantity.

(4)   This common element cannot be a geometrical, physical, chemical or other natural property of commodities. Such properties come into consideration only to the extent that they make the commodities useful, i.e. turn them into use-values. But clearly, the exchange relation of commodities is characterized precisely by its abstraction from their use-values.

Within the exchange relation, one use-value is worth just as much as another, provided only that it is present in the appropriate quantity. Or, as old Barbon says: 'One sort of wares are as good as another, if the value be equal. There is no difference or distinction in things of equal value... One hundred pounds worth of lead or iron, is of as great a value as one hundred pounds worth of silver and gold.'

(5) As use-values, commodities differ above all in quality, while as exchange-values they can only differ in quantity, and therefore do not contain an atom of use-value.

(6) If then we disregard the use-value of commodities, only one property remains, that of being products of labor. But even the product of labor has already been transformed in our hands. If we make abstraction from its use-value, we abstract also from the material constituents and forms which make it a use-value. It is no longer a table, a house, a piece of yarn or any other useful thing. All its sensuous characteristics are extinguished. Nor is it any longer the product of the labor of the joiner, the mason or the spinner, or of any other particular kind of productive labor. With the disappearance of the useful character of the products of labor, the useful character of the kinds of labor embodied in them will also disappear; this in turn entails the disappearance of the different concrete forms of labor. They can no longer be distinguished, but are all together reduced to the same kind of labor, human labor in the abstract.

(7) Let us now look at the residue of the products of labor. There is nothing left of them in each case but the same phantom-like objectivity; they are merely congealed quantities of homogeneous human labor, i.e. of human labor-power expended without regard to the form of its expenditure. All these things now tell us is that human labor-power has been expended to produce them , human labor has been accumulated in them. As crystals of this social substance, which is common to them all, they are values— commodity values (Marx, 1977, pp. 127-28).

Bohm-Bawerk's critique was centered mainly around paragraphs 2, 4, and 6. In reference to the second paragraph, Bohm-Bawerk argued that:

the first assumption, according to which an "equality" must be manifested in the exchange of two things, appears to me to be very old fashioned, which would not, however, matter much were it not also very unrealistic. In plain words, it seems to me to be a wrong idea. Where equality and exact equilibrium obtain, no change is likely to occur to disturb the balance (Bohm-Bawerk, 1949, p. 68).

This argument against Marx's conceptualization of exchange relation as an equation has been repeated in different ways in almost all the subsequent criticisms of Marx.

Bohm-Bawerk's next arguments were directed against paragraphs 4 and 6, simultaneously. Marx, contended Bohm-Bawerk, having conceived of exchange as equality, then searches for a "common factor" in the following way:

He passes in review the various properties possessed by the objects made equal in exchange, and according to the method of exclusion separates all those which cannot stand the test, until at last only one property remains, that of being the product of labor (p. 69).

This method of derivation reminded Bohm-Bawerk of "one who urgently desiring to bring a white ball out of an urn takes care to secure this result by putting in white balls only." In other words, "he limits from the outset the field of his search for the substance of exchange-value to 'commodities... and limits it to the products of labor against gifts of nature" (p. 70).

However, according to Bohm-Bawerk, even if we accept this narrow definition of commodities, the logic of Marx is still false. In disregarding "the value in use of commodities," Marx confuses "abstraction from the genus, and abstraction from the specific forms in which the genus manifest itself."

> The special forms under which the value in use of the commodities may appear, whether they serve for food, shelter, clothing, etc., is of course disregarded, but the value in use of the commodity as such is never disregarded (p. 74).

But this is not all, argued Bohm-Bawerk. "The second step" in Marx's argument "is still worse" (p. 75). "If the use-value of commodities be disregarded," Bohm-Bawerk quoted Marx, "there remains in them only one other property, that of being products of labor" (p. 75). But is this so, asked Bohm-Bawerk.

> Is not the property of being scarce in proportion to demand also common to all exchangeable goods? Or that they are the subjects of demand and supply? Or that they are appropriated? Or that they are natural products? (p. 75)

This argument, too, appears in almost all the subsequent criticisms of Marx's derivation.

All of these "obvious faults of logic and method" were attributed by Bohm-Bawerk to the artificial nature of the beginning of *Capital* (p. 66). Marx was convinced that "labor is the source of value," said Bohm-Bawerk, thus leading him to concoct an argument, a "dialectical hocus-pocus," and to present it as though it were the result of a long period of thinking and investigation (p. 77).

## III.  THE HISTORY OF MARX'S DERIVATION OF VALUE

Bohm-Bawerk was not the first critic of Marx's derivation of value. Even during Marx's own lifetime, some writers had expressed their dissatisfaction with his derivation, and Marx was well aware of these criticisms (see, for example, Marx, 1975). This of course raises an important question: Why did Marx not start *Capital* with "value," rather than beginning with "the commodity" and then trying to derive "value"? A meaningful answer to this question would require a thorough analysis of the development of Marx's concepts not only of "commodity" and "value," but of science and scientific method as well, particularly as this concerns the proper point of departure for political economy. Such an analysis, although helpful in dispelling the charge that the beginning of *Capital* was merely an artificial afterthought, lies beyond the scope of this paper. Suffice it to say that the issue of the point of departure is both posed and settled by Marx in his notebooks of 1857-1858, better known now as the *Grundrisse* (1973). Here, at the end of these writings, we encounter Marx's first attempt to formally derive the concept of value. In a section which still bears the title of "Value," he states:

> The first category in which bourgeois wealth presents itself is that of the *commodity*. The commodity itself appears as the unity of two aspects. It is *use-value*, i.e. object of the satisfaction of any system whatever of human needs. This is the material side, which the most disparate epochs of production have in common, and whose examination therefore lies beyond political economy. Use-value falls within the realm of political economy as soon as it becomes modified by the modern relations of production... Now how does use-value become transformed into commodity? Vehicle of *exchange-value* [*Marx, 1973, p. 881*].[2]

So far, this attempt at the derivation of value is very similar to that which we saw earlier in *Capital*. At this point, however, the two texts begin to differ considerably, particularly when, within the discussion of the process of exchange, a digression appears on the historical development of exchange. Shortly thereafter, Marx's manuscript comes to an abrupt end, without either an explanation of the meaning of "exchange-value" or any actual derivation of the concept of "value."

The second attempt at the derivation of value appears in *A Contribution to the Critique of Political Economy* (1970, hereafter *A Contribution*) published in 1859. This derivation is very similar to the first attempt. There are, however, certain modifications. The title of the first chapter now reads "The Commodity," and the opening sentences are modified:

> The wealth of bourgeois society, at first sight, presents itself as an immense accumulation of commodities, its unit being a single commodity. Every commodity, however has a twofold aspect—*use-value* and *exchange-value*.
>
> To begin with, a commodity, in the language of the English economists, is "anything necessary, useful or pleasant in life", an object of human wants, a means of existence in the widest sense of the term. Use-value as an aspect of the commodity coincides with the physical palpable existence of the commodity (Marx, 1970, p. 27).

These opening sentences are followed by further discussion of the concept of "use-value" and, similarly to the first attempt, the place of this concept in political economy. The analysis then leads to the relation between the concepts of "use-value" and "exchange-value," and the definition of "exchange-value":

> Use-value is the immediate physical entity in which a definite economic relation—*exchange-value*—is expressed.

> Exchange-value seems at first to be a *quantitative relation*, the proportion in which use-values are exchanged for one another. In this relation they constitute equal exchangeable magnitudes (p. 28).

Two sets of "use-values" are then used by Marx to elucidate the point. The first set is "snuff and elegies" and the second, "tins of boot polish" and a "palace." These peculiar sets are chosen to show that:

> quite irrespective, therefore, of their natural form of existence, and without regard to the specific character of the needs they satisfy as use-values, commodities in definite quantities are congruent, they take one another's place in the exchange process, are regarded as equivalents, and despite their motley appearance have a common denominator (p. 28)

What is this common denominator? The answer is given, rather imperceptibly, in the next two paragraphs:

> Use-values serve directly as means of existence. But, on the other hand, these means of existence are themselves the products of social activity, the result of expended human energy, *materialized labor*. As objectification of social labor, all commodities are crystallization of the same substance. The specific character of this substance, i.e., of labor which is embodied in exchange-value, has now to be examined.
>
> Let us suppose that one ounce of gold, one ton of iron, one quarter of wheat and twenty yards of silk are exchange-values of equal magnitude. As exchange-values in which the qualitative difference between their use-value is eliminated, they represent equal amounts of the same kind of labor. The labor which is uniformly materialized in them must be uniform, homogeneous, simple labor.... Labor which creates exchange-value is thus *abstract general* labor (pp. 28-29).

Even though the term "value" is not used in the above passages, the derivation of value is nonetheless complete at this point, since materialized "abstract general labor" is another expression for Marx's concept of "value."

This constitutes Marx's second attempt to derive value. The derivation is short and to the point, occupying no more than two- and-a-half pages. From here, Marx goes on to analyze various aspects of the concept of labor, such as the distinction between "concrete" and "abstract labor," and the measurement of labor.

The third derivation of value is found in the first edition of *Capital* (1983), published in 1867, that is, almost eight years after the publication of *A Contribution*. The first few paragraphs of this derivation are very similar to the previous work. But even here, there are some minor changes that should be noted. The title of the chapter is, of course, fixed now as "The Commodity." In the opening paragraph, Marx paraphrases the first sentence of *A Contribution* and proceeds directly to an analysis of the commodity, without mentioning the twofold aspect of the commodity, "use-value and exchange-value." The commodity now is defined as an "external object, a thing which satisfies through its qualities human needs of one kind or another" (Marx, 1976, p. 7). Next, the concept of "use-value" is presented:

> It is the utility of a thing for human life that turns it into a *use-value*. By way of abbreviation let us term the useful thing itself (or *commodity-body*, as iron, wheat, diamond, etc.) *use-value*, good, article (p. 7).

After some continued discussion of the concept of "use-value" and without any further mention of the place of this concept in the sphere of investigation of political economy, Marx proceeds to the concept of "exchange-value,' repeating verbatim what he had stated earlier about this concept in *A Contribution*. At this point, however, the two texts begin to differ perceptibly. Immediately after defining "exchange-value," Marx casts doubt on the concept of "valeur intrinsique" by arguing that the relation of exchange "constantly changes in accordance with time and place," and thus the existence of an intrinsic value appears to be a "contradictio in adjecto" (p. 8). In order to "examine the matter more closely," he then adds three new paragraphs that do not appear in *A Contribution*. These new paragraphs differ from paragraphs 1-3 quoted earlier from the third edition of *Capital* only in certain minor details, too small to mention. The following three paragraphs, however, are substantially different from those of the third edition:

> The fact that the substance of the exchange-value is something utterly different from and independent of the physical-sensual existence of the commodity or its reality as a *use-value* is revealed immediately by its exchange relationship. For this is characterized precisely by the *abstraction* from the *use-value*. As far as the exchange-value is concerned, one commodity is, after all, quite as good as every other, provided it is present in the correct proportion.
>
> Hence, commodities are first of all simply to be considered as *values*, independent of their exchange-relationship or from the *form*, in which they *appear* as *exchange-values*.
>
> Commodities as objects of use or goods are corporeally different things. Their reality as *values* forms, on the other hand, their *unity*. This unity does not arise out of nature but out of society. The common social substance which merely manifests itself differently in different use-values, is—*labor* (pp. 8-9).

After these paragraphs, Marx declares commodities to be nothing, as values, but "crystallized labor." The derivation of value in the first edition of *Capital* is completed at this point. From here, Marx goes on to discuss the unit of measurement of labor and the dual nature of labor. In relation to this latter issue, Marx repeats what he had stated at the beginning of *A Contribution*, but not actually in *Capital*, that is: "Originally, the *commodity* appeared to us as a two-sided entity, use-value *and* exchange-value" (p. 11).

Before discussing the next derivation, let me briefly explain why, I believe, Marx extended the derivation in *Capital* beyond that in *A Contribution*. Between publishing *A Contribution* and the first edition of *Capital*, Marx wrote his notes on the history of economic theory, better known now as *Theories of Surplus Value* (1971, hereafter *Theories*). Certain passages in these notes indicate that the changes in the derivation may have been simply a reaction to Samuel Bailey's *A Critical Dissertation on the Nature, Measure and Causes of Value* (see also Rubin, 1972, pp. 107-110). In this work, Bailey argued that although in the act of exchange "one A is in our estimation equal to two B," this is not an expression of "positive but relative esteem" (Bailey, 1967, pp. 2-3). In other words, value denotes "nothing intrinsic, but merely the relation in which two objects stand to each other as exchangeable commodities" (pp. 4-5). In support of this argument, Bailey drew an analogy between exchange-value and distance. According to this analogy, "a thing cannot be valuable in itself without reference to another thing, any more than a thing can be distant in itself without reference to another thing" (p. 5). Marx devoted a considerable number of pages in his *Theories* to refuting Bailey's argument. He argued that Bailey does not understand the difference between the concepts "object," "product," and "commodity," as is evident from Bailey's interchangeable use of these concepts. According to Marx, "if only two products existed, the products would never become commodities, and consequently the exchange-value of commodities would never evolve either" (Marx, 1971, p. 144). Therefore, the exchange of two "objects" or "products" does not turn them into commodities, and hence there can be no talk of commensurability. In order to derive the concept of value, Marx argued, it is necessary to assume that A and B are commodities, and this requires the regularity of exchange.

With regard to Bailey's analogy, Marx contended that the distance between two objects has nothing to do with the relation of the type $1A = 2B$. Instead of this "insipid" geometric analogy, Marx gave a geometric analogy of his own in which he attempted to compare the reduction of "exchange-values" of commodities to a common property to the reduction of the areas of parallelograms to a "common element" (pp. 143-144).

All of these arguments seem to find their way into the first few pages of *Capital*. The doubt cast on the concept of intrinsic value, the assumption of the regularity of exchange in the first paragraph, the equation of exchange in the second paragraph, and the geometric analogy in the third paragraph appear all to be responses to Bailey's arguments.

The next derivation of value is found in both the French edition, published in installments between 1872-1875, and the second edition of *Capital*, published in 1872. In the postface to the second edition, Marx himself alludes to the changes made in the derivation vis-à-vis the first edition: "In Chapter 1, Section 1, the derivation of value by analysis of the equations in which every exchange-value is expressed has been carried out with greater scientific strictness" (Marx 1977, 94). He does not, however, elaborate on this issue. So what does he have in mind by "greater scientific strictness"?

A comparison of the second and the third editions of *Capital* reveals that the derivation is almost identical in the two works. The major difference is paragraph 1, which in the third edition is slightly longer than the corresponding paragraph in the two earlier editions. Thus, for all practical purposes the differences in the derivation of value between the first and the second editions are almost identical to the differences between the first and the third editions. Therefore, from what has been said earlier, we can conclude that the "greater scientific strictness" must refer to the changes that occur in the derivation after the paragraph containing the geometric analogy, since up to this point the two derivations are almost identical. After this, as we saw earlier, the derivation in the first edition is completed in three short paragraphs, while in the second and third editions this is done in four, relatively more elaborate, paragraphs.

We have now examined Marx's derivation of value in its different stages and various shapes and can conclude that, contrary to Bohm-Bawerk's assertion, the derivation was not an artificial afterthought. What Bohm-Bawerk read in the third edition of *Capital* was at least 25 years in the making and the result of many years of thinking and rethinking. Bohm-Bawerk, who was completely unaware of this, simply assumed that the whole thing was a hoax and this assumption, like his other concerning the end of *Capital*, is factually incorrect.

However, the fact that the derivation of value in the third edition of *Capital* was the result of a prolonged effort does not necessarily make it right. Actually, it is in the process of looking back at this effort that some of the problems with the derivation become apparent. A comparative analysis of the texts mentioned above reveals that this derivation, particularly in the third edition of *Capital*, may not only be misleading but logically flawed. This is shown in the next section.

## IV.  SEMANTICS AND LOGIC

One of the greatest obstacles to understanding the logic of Marx's derivation of value is his semantics. The entire derivation seems to turn around such seemingly simple concepts as "commodity," "use-value," "exchange-value," "exchange relation," and "value." Yet these concepts, despite all that has been written on Marx's economic theory, remain to this day largely ambiguous. In this section, I concentrate on three of these, showing how their ambiguities can adversely affect not only the reader's understanding of Marx's logic of the derivation but Marx's own logic as well. This discussion is then followed by an analysis of the paragraphs quoted earlier from the third edition of *Capital*.

### A.  Use-value

The evolution of the concept of "use-value" from Adam Smith to Marx is an interesting issue. However, since I have dealt with this subject elsewhere,

I do not wish to go deeply into this issue here (Fayazmanesh, 1992). By way of summary, however, I would like to say that Smith and, following him, David Ricardo considered "value in use" to be one meaning of the word "value," the other meaning being "value in exchange" (Smith, 1965, p. 28; Ricardo, 1976, p. 5.). Moreover, both Smith and Ricardo used the expression "value in use" in the sense of usefulness or utility. Marx, up until the early part of the *Grundrisse*, considers "use-value" to be a "form of value," a concept similar to that of Smith and Ricardo (Marx, 1973, p. 177). However, beginning in the middle of the *Grundrisse*, Marx changes the meaning of the term. From here onward, use-value is no longer considered to be a form of value but rather to be one aspect of the commodity, along with the other, exchange-value. Moreover, the term "use-value" is used, again from here onward, primarily in the sense of "a useful thing," rather than usefulness. This is perhaps best exemplified in "Notes on Adolf Wagner" (1879-1880), where Marx states clearly that a commodity in its natural form is "*a useful thing, alias a use-value*" (Marx, 1975, p. 198).[3] But there are numerous other passages which show the term "use-value" being employed in the sense of a useful object, some of which have been already cited in this article. For example, as noted earlier, Marx writes in *A Contribution*: "Use-value as an aspect of the commodity coincides with the physical palpable existence of the commodity" (Marx, 1970, p. 27). Or, in the first edition of *Capital*, he states: "By way of abbreviation let us term the useful thing itself (or commodity-body, as iron, wheat, diamond, etc.) use-value" (Marx, 1976, p. 7).

Before going on any further, let me emphasize the distinction between the classical use of the term "use-value" and that of Marx. "Use-value" in the classical sense of "usefulness" expresses a relationship between an object and human needs. "Use-value" in Marx's sense of "a useful thing," however, refers to the object itself, but of course only insofar as the object, by virtue of its properties, satisfies some kind of human needs.[4]

Marx, however, fails to state clearly and explicitly his shift in the meaning of the term "use-value." Moreover, the detection of such a shift is hampered by the following problems. First, in using the term in the sense of "a useful thing," sometimes the indefinite article "a" in front of "a use-value" is missing in Marx's writings, blurring the distinction between his concept of "use-value" and that of the classical economists. This is clearly evident in some of the passages quoted earlier. Second, Marx uses certain expressions in which use-value appears to mean usefulness rather than a useful object, even though it is the other way around. Take, for example, the expression "the use-values of commodities," which is found more than once in the derivation of value (e.g., Marx, 1977, pp. 126, 128). There is a natural tendency to interpret this expression as meaning the usefulness of commodities, particularly if one is reading Marx after reading the classical economists. Yet, this is not what Marx intends. The "use-values of commodities" is rather his shorthand expression for the "use-value aspect of commodities," that is, looking at commodities from the perspective of being useful objects rather than "exchange-values." Third, on a few occasions, Marx does seem to use the term use-value in the classical sense of usefulness.[5]

The above problems can adversely affect the reader's understanding of Marx's logic of the derivation of value. For example, look back at paragraph 4 in the derivation of value in *Capital*. The following statement, which is, as I show later, the most important link in Marx's overall logic, appears here: "the exchange relation of commodities is characterized precisely by its abstraction from *their use-values*." How is this sentence to be understood? Does the expression "their use-values" refer to the use-value aspect of commodities or to the usefulness of commodities? In other words, is the relation of exchange characterized by abstraction from the *useful object* or the *usefulness of the object*? Obviously, this makes a great deal of difference. In the first case, we abstract not only from the relation between the object and human needs but from the object itself altogether. In the second case, however, only the relation between the human needs and the object is abstracted from. So, which one is it? There is, again, a natural tendency to interpret the expression "their use-values" to mean the usefulness of commodities and, as we shall see in the last section of this paper, this is how it usually has been understood. In other words, the usual interpretation of this sentence has been that Marx abstracts from the usefulness of commodities. But this interpretation is not correct. In the discussion of "exchange-value," I will show in greater detail that it is actually the useful object itself that Marx is trying to abstract from. For the time being, however, let me remind the reader that in the 1867 edition of *Capital* (Marx, 1983), the same sentence reads this way: "This [the exchange relation] is characterized precisely by the abstraction *from the use-value*."[6] This sentence seems to support my interpretation, and if this is the case, the ambiguous expression "their use-values" in the later editions must refer not to the usefulness of commodities but to the use-value aspect of commodities.

It appears, therefore, that the sentence in the third edition of *Capital* should read as follows: The exchange relation of commodities is characterized precisely by its abstraction from the use-value aspect of the commodities, or, to put it simply, abstraction from useful objects themselves. Having resolved the ambiguity, however, the question now becomes this: What does Marx mean by "the exchange relation" and why does he say that this relation is characterized by abstraction from useful objects? The answer to this important question— which to the best of my knowledge has never been asked in the previous debates on the logic of Marx's derivation—should become clear after we have analyzed Marx's concepts of "exchange relation" and "exchange-value."

Before proceeding to this analysis, however, I would like to call attention to an additional source of confusion in *A Contribution* and *Capital*. Following his derivation of value, Marx attempts to draw a parallel between this derivation and the process of arriving at the concept of "abstract labor." He thus writes, in *A Contribution*: "As exchange-values in which the qualitative *difference between their use-values is eliminated*, they [exchange-values of equal magnitude] represent equal amounts of the same kind of labor" (Marx, 1970, p. 29). Similarly, he writes in *Capital* that "just as *one is abstracting*, in the case of the values of coat and linen, *from the difference between their use-values*, just so, in the case of the labor which these values represent" (Marx, 1976, p. 14).[7] The expression "their use-values" that appears in these statements has been discussed above and should no longer pose any problem: it simply refers to the use-value aspect of commodities. What is problematic in these statements is the word "difference." Earlier, Marx was talking about abstraction from useful objects. Now, however, he is talking about abstraction from the "difference" between useful objects. But these abstractions conceptually are not the same. In the first case, useful objects vanish altogether.[8] In the second case, however, we are left, presumably, with the similarities of useful objects. So which abstraction does Marx have in mind? If we look at *Theories*, the answer seems to be only the first, and not the second, abstraction. Here, in response to Bailey, Marx argues that in the process of exchange one use-value is exchanged with "an infinite mass of other things which have nothing in common with it—and even if there are *natural or other similarities between those things, they are not considered in the exchange*" (Marx, 1971, p. 128). This means, once again, that from Marx's perspective the exchange relation is characterized by total abstraction from useful objects and not simply abstraction from the difference between useful objects. Thus, it appears that the statements concerning the abstraction from the "difference between their use-values" are due either to Marx's carelessness or to his own conceptual confusion.

To summarize, Marx changes the meaning of the classical expression "use-value" from usefulness to a useful object; and when in the derivation of value he argues that the exchange relation of commodities is characterized by abstraction from "their use-values," what he has in mind is that the relation of exchange is characterized by abstraction from useful objects themselves. The reader, however, may misunderstand the above statement to mean that the exchange relation is characterized by abstraction from the usefulness of commodities. This misunderstanding is partly due to Marx's own failure to state clearly and explicitly his shift in the meaning of the term "use-value."

## B. The Exchange Relation

The most striking and visible expression of the exchange relation in Marx is, of course, the so-called equation of exchange which we saw in paragraph 2 of *Capital*: "1 quarter of corn = x cwt of iron," translated by Marx to mean: "a given quantity of corn *is equated* to some quantity of iron." This conceptualization of the relation of exchange in terms of an equation, with the symbol "=" used in the sense of equality, has been criticized, one way or another, in almost all critiques of Marx's derivation. However, what seems to have escaped the critics is that this is not the only mode of representation of the exchange relation that appears in Marx. The relation of exchange is also conceptualized by Marx in terms of the expression "is worth," and he has used the same symbol "=" to express this relation. This is evident in *Capital*, where the same type of equation "x commodity A=y commodity B" is translated by Marx to mean "x commodity A *is worth* y commodity B" (Marx, 1977, p. 139). In addition to this concept, Marx uses, among others, the concepts of "as good as," "replaceable," "congruence," "parity," and "identity" to express the relation of exchange (see, respectively, Marx 1976, p. 9, 1977, p. 127, 1970, p. 28, 1971, pp. 139, 144). These many concepts of the exchange relation and multiple use of the same symbol can be quite problematic if "=" is employed in any strict mathematical sense. The symbol "=" is used in mathematics to express a relation defined on the set of numbers, and if used in any other way, the two sides of the symbol must have the same dimension. This relation is an equivalence relation in the sense that it is reflexive, symmetric, and transitive. But consider the relation "is worth," which, as an expression that is actually used in practice, seems to be Marx's most reasonable expression of the exchange relation. Realistically, the two sides of this relation do not have the same dimension. Hence, this relation is not an equivalence relation since it is not reflexive. It therefore follows that the two relations "is equal" and "is worth," strictly speaking, are not identical and cannot be represented by the same symbol. The question then becomes: How strictly was Marx using the relation of equality? To answer this question, we need to examine Marx's equation of exchange in greater detail.

It has been rightly argued in recent years that Marx's equation of exchange is a nonsensical equation: it makes no sense to say a given quantity of a use-value is equal to some quantity of another use-value (see, for example, Krause 1982, pp. 28-29; Carling, 1984-1985, p. 409, 1986, p. 60). I would argue, however, that Marx himself seems to have been aware of this and his logic of the derivation appears to be based on this issue. In *Theories*, he contends, again in reference to Bailey, that "if y yards of linen equal x lbs. of straw, this [implies] a *parity between two unequal things*—linen and straw—making them equal magnitudes" and that it "is not as straw and linen that they are equated, but as equivalents" (Marx 1971, 139).[9] These statements show that Marx was aware of the fact that use-values cannot be physically equal to each other. But the statements also seem to show a great deal of confusion. He first writes an equation in which use-values are physically equated, then he argues that since these use-values are not physically equal, they must be equal as something else. But if use-values are not physically equal to each other, why write them as such?

The answer to the above question may lie partially in the writings of some of the classical political economists. These economists, when speaking of exchange, often stated that something is exchanged for, or can be exchanged for, something else.[10] From the perspective of modern algebra, the relation of exchange embedded in such statements is simply the expression "is exchanged for" or "can be exchanged for," a relation which from now on I will symbolize by the letter E.[11] But this was not, of course, the way that classical economists viewed the exchange relation. The concepts of intrinsic value and exchange of equivalence led many of these economists to view the relation of exchange as a relation of equality. Even Bailey, who did not believe in the concept of intrinsic value, as we saw earlier, expressed the relation of exchange as such. Marx, I believe, inherited the classical concept of exchange relation as a relation of equality and adopted it without any hesitation. However, I argue in the next section that Marx's own concept of exchange-value, which is ill-defined, reinforces the idea that relation of exchange is one of equality.

## C. Exchange-value

Smith and, again following him, Ricardo defined the "value in exchange" of a good as the "power of purchasing other goods" (Smith, 1965, p. 28; Ricardo, 1976, p. 5). This definition is, of course, quite ambiguous, since it is not clear what is meant by "power of purchasing." But the subsequent examples that they provided make it apparent that what they had in mind by "value in exchange" of a good was quantities of other goods that can be exchanged for it.

Marx also used the term "exchange value" at times in the same way that it was used by Smith and Ricardo. For example, consider the following statement in *A Contribution*: "The exchange-value of a palace can be expressed in a definite number of tins of boot polish" (Marx, 1970, p. 28). Here, by exchange-value of a palace, Marx clearly means certain quantities of tins of boot polish. This concept of exchange-value is in fact generalized in *Theories*, where in response to Bailey, Marx writes (in English) that "If we speak of the *value in exchange of a thing*, we mean in the first instance of course the *relative quantities of all other commodities that can be exchanged for the first commodity*" (Marx, 1971, p. 128). Note that the relation of exchange, "can be exchanged for," or as I referred to it earlier, E, appears in this statement, as well.

But this is not the only sense in which the term "exchange-value" appears in Marx's writings. In the *Grundrisse*, as was mentioned earlier, Marx changed the meaning of the classical expression "value in use," and in so doing he also changed the meaning of the expression "value in exchange." Here, he began to view "use-value" as the "content" of a commodity and "exchange-value" as the "form" of this content (Marx, 1973, p. 267). In this sense, the "form," or "exchange-value," was a "relation" between use-values (267). This concept of exchange-value as a relation is also present in Marx's later writings. For example, consider this statement, which we saw earlier in *A Contribution* and *Capital*: "Exchange-value seems at first to be a *quantitative relation*, the proportion in which use-values are exchanged for one another." Here, it is apparent that by "exchange-value" Marx means a relation between use-values.

There is also an additional third sense in which Marx uses the term "exchange-value": a use-value that is being exchanged. This is most clearly expressed in the "Notes on Adolph Wagner," when Marx writes that insofar as a use-value is "a bearer of exchange-value... *it is itself 'exchange-value'*" (Marx, 1975, p. 198).

In short, Marx uses the term "exchange-value" in three different senses: a quantitative relation between use-values, a use-value in the process of exchange, and the exchange-value of a use-value, that is, quantities of other use-values that can exchange for the use-value in question.[12] In the last two senses, a use-value appears to both *be* and *have* "exchange-value."

But are these different concepts of exchange-value compatible with one another, and if not, how does Marx reduce one to another? Let me try to answer this question by first looking at the relation of exchange, $E$, embedded inadvertently in some of the classical, as well as Marx's own statements, and explore some feasible ways to redefine the concept of exchange-value. I will then return to Marx's different concepts of exchange-value.

Suppose three use-values $b$, $c$, and $d$, are or can be exchanged for one another in the following manner: $1b \ E \ 1c$ and $1b \ E \ 2d$. There are two distinct and mutually incompatible ways to define exchange-value. First, one can generally refer to any use-value that satisfies the relation of exchange, $E$, as an exchange-value. In this sense, use-values $b$, $c$, and $d$ are exchange-values. Second, one can define whatever comes after $E$ to be the specific exchange-value of whatever comes before $E$. In this sense, $1c$ is the exchange-value of $1b$ expressed in $c$ and $2d$ is the exchange-value of $1b$ expressed in $d$. A shorter way of writing these statements would be as follows:

1.  $1c$ is the $c$ *exchange-value* of $1b$; and
2.  $2d$ is the $d$ *exchange-value* of $1b$.

Note that in either definition, "exchange-value" expresses a relation, but it is not itself a relation. Furthermore, the two definitions of exchange-value are irreducible to one another, unless we resort to some careless generalizations to reduce the second definition to the first one. For example, if we overlook the fact that exchange-values of $1b$ are expressed in different units, the above two statements would appear as such:

1'.  $1c$ is the *exchange-value* of $1b$; and

2'.   2*d* is the *exchange-value* of 1*b*.

If we also drop the notion of 1*b* altogether, we get:

1."   1*c* is exchange-value; and
2."   2*d* is exchange-value.

That is, 1*c* and 2*d* appear to be simply exchange-values, reducing my second definition of exchange-value to the first one. More importantly, these defective statements combined make it appear that the exchange-values, 1*c* and 2*d* are somehow identical.

Now, let us return to Marx. The relation of exchange is not clearly defined by him; as a result, he refers to "exchange-value" as a relation and simultaneously as a use-value expressing a relation. Furthermore, his first definition of exchange-value already involves the kind of careless generalizations that I alluded to above; and, I believe, it is as such that he reconciles this definition with his third one. To see this, let us look back at this definition. We are told that by the "value in exchange of a thing, we mean ... the relative quantities of all other commodities that can be exchanged for the first commodity." This definition of Marx resembles my second definition of exchange-value, except that Marx has already left out the very fact that each exchange-value is expressed in a particular unit. According to this definition, by exchange-value of a use-value we can "mean" many things. For instance, using my example, by exchange-value of 1*b* we can mean both 1*c* and 2*d*.

Further generalization leads Marx to simply declare these relative quantities, that is, 1*c* and 2*d*, to be exchange-values, leaving out any notion of the first use-value, whose exchange-value is expressed by these relative quantities, that is, 1*b*. This reconciles the first and the third concepts of exchange-value and makes use-values both have and be exchange-values.

Last, since by exchange-value of a use-value we can "mean" different use-values and since these use-values are simply exchange-values, it follows that as exchange-values, these use-values are, to use some of Marx's expression, "identical," "as good as," "equal," and so forth, that is, 1*c* = 2*d*. This strengthens the idea in Marx that the relation of exchange is one of equality.

In the next section, we will see all of the above problems appearing in the derivation of value in the third edition of *Capital*. But let me add here that the same problems can also be seen in the derivation of value in *A Contribution*, as well as in the first edition of *Capital*. For example, in *A Contribution*, immediately after defining exchange-value as a relation and discussing the exchange of some use-values, Marx writes: "Considered as exchange-value, one use-value is worth just as much as another, provided the two are available in the appropriate proportion" (Marx, 1970, p. 28). Similarly, in the first edition of *Capital* he states: "As far as the exchange-value is concerned, one commodity is, after all, quite as good as every other, provided it is present in the correct proportion" (Marx, 1976, pp. 8-9).

In sum, Marx's concept of exchange-value is ill-defined. Indeed, there is more than one such concept in his writings and these concepts are not compatible with one another. Moreover, these fuzzy concepts reinforce the classical view of the exchange relation as a relation of equality.

Having examined Marx's concepts of exchange relation and exchange-value, we can now answer the question posed earlier in the section on use-value, a question which I believe to be the most important issue in Marx's derivation of value: why does Marx believe that the relation of exchange is characterized by abstraction from use-values? The answer appears to be based on the following arguments. As exchange-values, Marx argues, use-values, in certain proportion, are equal to one another. Using my previous example, this means that as exchange-values, $1c = 2d$. However, as was pointed out in the previous section, Marx knows that use-values, that is, useful objects, are not physically equal. That is, as use-values, $1c \neq 2d$. It therefore follows, Marx reasons, that the relation of exchange, "=", is characterized by abstraction from use-values!

## D.   The Logic of the Derivation in *Capital*

Let us now return to the controversial paragraphs in *Capital*, quoted and numbered earlier in this paper. In view of what has been said, these first four paragraphs deserve particular attention and analysis, since all the problems with the definitions and logic come to the fore at this point, leading Marx to the convoluted idea that the relation of exchange is in reality characterized by abstraction from use-values. In the remaining three paragraphs, Marx uses this idea to justify his abstraction from use-values and to arrive at "value." Given, however, that a proper justification for such an abstraction is lacking, these remaining paragraphs are, from a logical perspective, inconsequential, and therefore deserve less attention than the first four paragraphs.

In paragraph 1, Marx writes that "a quarter of wheat for example, is exchanged for x boot-polish, y silk or z gold." Note, once more, that the relation of exchange "is exchanged for" is embedded in this statement without Marx's awareness. From this statement, Marx concludes that "x boot-polish, y silk or z gold, etc., each represent the exchange-value of one quarter of wheat." Here, once again, the fact that x boot-polish, y silk, and so forth are different expressions of the exchange-value of a quarter of wheat is overlooked. That is, by exchange-value of a quarter of wheat we can "mean" x boot-polish, y silk, or z gold. In the next sentence, all traces of "a quarter of wheat" seem to vanish and x boot-polish, y silk, and so forth are generalized as exchange-values: "x boot-polish, y silk, z gold etc., must, as exchange-values, be mutually replaceable or of identical magnitude." Since within Marx's vocabulary the expressions "mutually replaceable" or "identical magnitude" are synonymous with "equal," this last statement is equivalent to saying that as exchange-values, x boot-polish = y silk = z gold.

Paragraph 2, which contains the celebrated equation of exchange, now appears to be nothing more than an extension of the first paragraph. The equation "1 quarter of corn = x cwt of iron" is simply a generalization of the above series of equations. From this single equation, Marx then concludes that the two things must be "equal to a third thing." What is missing here is the convoluted argument that we saw in the previous section. That is, as use-values, 1 quarter of corn and x cwt of iron cannot be equal, but as exchange-values they are equal. Therefore, there must be a "common element," a "third thing," having nothing to do with wheat and iron as physical goods, which makes these exchange-values equal to one another. How does one arrive at this "third thing"? Marx's answer obviously must be, by setting aside wheat and iron as use-values.

Before giving his answer, however, in paragraph 3 Marx tries to argue by means of his geometric analogy that the "common element," which the "exchange-values of commodities" are reduced to, cannot be another use-value, as Bailey had argued, but must be something else. Note that in this paragraph Marx switches back to the concept of commodities, or use-values, having exchange-values rather than being exchange-values. As it stands, the argument in this paragraph is too short and unclear. But if this is read in conjunction with the original and the longer version of this analogy in *Theories*, the thrust of Marx's argument appears to be the following. The measurement of the areas of all rectilinear figures entails the splitting up of these figures into triangles. The area of the triangle, however, is determined by half the product of its base, "b," and its altitude, "h." This "h $\times$ b / 2", according to *Theories*, is the common "property" or the "common element" between the areas of rectilinear figures (Marx, 1971, p. 144-145). Thus, Marx believes, expressing the areas of all rectilinear figures in the area of the triangle is of little use in geometry; it is necessary to go beyond this expression to locate the common element between the areas of such figures. In the same way, he likes to argue that the relative expression of the exchange-value of a use-value in another use-value is useless in political economy; it is necessarty to go beyond this expression to locate what exchange-values have in common. This geometric analogy, which in both works is marred with all kinds of notational and conceptual errors, not only does not "illustrate" the issue of the "third element" but creates additional problems, for the following reasons.[13] First, it is not always necessary to split up rectilinear figures into triangles in order to measure their areas; there are different ways of measuring the areas of rectilinear figures, such as integration. Second, it makes no sense to say that "h $\times$ b / 2" is the common "property," or the "common element" between all rectilinear areas; "h $\times$ b / 2" is merely a method of calculation of the area of a triangle. Third, "h $\times$ b / 2" ultimately expresses the area of a triangle in the area of a unit square, which by convention has a unit side and therefore a unit area. In other words, in axiomatic geometry all areas are, after all, expressed relatively. Yet, this is precisely what Marx is trying to avoid in his argument about exchange-value, that is, that the concept of exchange-value is something "purely relative."

Now comes paragraph 4, which contains the most crucial part of the argument, why we must set aside use-value to arrive at the common element. We are told at the very beginning of this paragraph that the "common element cannot be a geometrical, physical, chemical or other natural property of commodities." Given my analysis in the previous section, it is clear why this is so: As exchange-values, $1c = 2d$. However, as use-values, $1c \neq 2d$. Thus, as far as the exchange relation, "$=$", is concerned, we set aside use-values altogether. This means that we set aside all those natural properties which make $c$ and $d$ use-values; and, therefore, none of these properties can be the "common element." Marx, however, does not write all of this clearly. For example, he first writes: "Such properties come into consideration only to the extent that they make the commodities useful, i.e. turn them into use-values." This is then followed by the claim concerning the relation of exchange: "But clearly the exchange relation of commodities is characterized precisely by its abstraction from their use-values." Why this is so is explained only by: "Within the exchange relation, one use-value is worth just as much as another, provided only that it is present in the appropriate quantity."[14] But this is only half of the argument, that is, as exchange-values, $1c = 2d$. The other half, that is, as use-values, $1c \neq 2d$, is not mentioned at all by Marx.

Note that without prior knowledge, it is virtually impossible to understand paragraph 4. For one thing, as was mentioned earlier, if we misinterpret the term "use-value" to mean usefulness—which, given Marx's lack of clarity, is a distinct possibility—no sense can be made out of any part of this argument. In fact, if "use-value" is not read in the sense of a useful object, it is impossible to understand why none of the natural properties of commodities can be the common element. Even if we pass this hurdle, it is not at all "clear" what Marx means by the "exchange relation" and why this relation is characterized by abstraction from use-value. Indeed, the fact that no previous writer has ever questioned Marx's claim concerning the relation of exchange can partly be explained by the abstruseness of this paragraph. Had this question been raised, the remaining paragraphs, which historically have been given greater attention, would lose much of their significance. As was mentioned earlier, it is inconsequential whether Marx's argument concerning the residue of such an abstraction is sound or not, once we realize that there is no justification for the abstraction to begin with. Nevertheless, for the sake of completeness, let me say a few words about the remaining paragraphs.

Paragraph 5 reiterates the idea that use-values must be set aside to arrive at the common element. This is evident from the argument that as "exchange-values" commodities "do not contain an atom of use-value."

Paragraphs 6 and 7, at last, deal with the process of abstraction and the actual derivation of value. Let me first present what I believe to be the thrust of Marx's argument in these paragraphs, and then discuss the problems involved. It is possible to reduce these two paragraphs to the following set of statements: (1) products of labor are also use-values; (2) abstraction from use-values entails abstraction from "the useful character of the products of labor"; (3) given, however, that the useful character of different kinds of labor are "embodied" in the useful character of the products of labor, abstraction from the latter entails abstraction from the former; (4) the former abstraction, in turn, entails abstraction from the "different concrete forms of labor," leaving us with abstract "congealed" labor; and (5) thus, abstraction from use-values results in "congealed" abstract labor, that is, "value."

There are three kinds of problems with paragraphs 6 and 7. First, Marx, as usual, does not present the above argument in a clear and cohesive manner. For example, when at the beginning of paragraph 6 he states, "If then we disregard the use-value of commodities, only one property remains, that of being products of labor," he does not mean it! The next statement is actually an attempt to qualify the previous one: "But even the product of labor has already been transformed in our hands." In other words, it is not exactly the "products of labor" that are left over after the abstraction, but something else. That something else, as I indicated above, is supposed to be "embodied" abstract labor, or "value." This only becomes apparent after a careful reading of these passages. Second, the entire discussion here concerning labor and its relation to its product is premature, since such a relation is only dealt with afterward, in the second section of the first chapter, titled "The Dual Character of the Labor Embodied in Commodities," and in the first section of the seventh chapter, titled "The Labor Process" (Marx, 1977, pp. 131-138; 283-292). Third, there are some concepts in these paragraphs that are also troublesome and are in need of semantic clarification. One such concept is, of course, the notoriously ambiguous expression, "labor embodied," which also appears in these same paragraphs as "congealed" labor and "crystals" of labor. Such problems make difficult, if not impossible, any meaningful analysis of the arguments involved in these paragraphs without a prior comprehensive analysis of Marx's concepts of labor and its relation to its product.

This concludes my analysis of Marx's derivation of value. Before continuing to the final section, let me summarize my arguments in this section. Marx's derivation of value, despite his many revisions, is flawed after all. Some terms used by Marx, such as "use-value," are not clearly defined and can, therefore, adversely affect the reader's understanding of the logic of the derivation. But more importantly, some terms, such as "exchange-value" and "exchange relation," are simply ill-defined, resulting in Marx's own confusion and fallacious reasoning.

## IV.  REVISITING BOHM-BAWERK'S CRITIQUE

In light of what has been said in the previous section, it should not be difficult to see why much of what has been written by Bohm-Bawerk, and many others, on Marx's derivation of value is either inconsequential or irrelevant. To the best of my knowledge, none of these writers has ever asked what I have contended to be the most important question with regard to this derivation: what does Marx mean by the relation of exchange and why does he think that this relation is characterized by abstraction from use-value? Why this question has not been asked is also not difficult to understand. Marx's semantics has never been analyzed seriously in the previous debates on the derivation of value. Indeed, both sides of this debate often have paid no attention to the meaning of the terms used by Marx and, in some cases, have simply misinterpreted them entirely.

Consider, for example, Marx's expression "use-value." How this term is used by Marx and how this usage affects our understanding of the logic of the derivation have, so far as I know, never been pointed out. Most readers, particularly those who are familiar with the writings of the classical economists, have had a propensity to read the term in the sense of usefulness, overlooking the second and most predominant sense in which it is used by Marx, that is, useful object. This is even true of the *Dictionary of Marxist Thought*, where Marx's term "use-value" has been defined, not according to Marx, but actually according to Adam Smith, as "usefulness" (Bottomore, 1983, pp. 86, 504).[15] Some, as I have pointed out elsewhere, have gone even so far as to confuse this term with the neoclassical concept of "utility" (Fayazmanesh 1986, 1992).

This was not the case for Bohm-Bawerk, but it is clear from his critique that by Marx's "abstraction from their use-values" he understood abstraction from the usefulness of the commodities. This understanding resulted in the argument that we saw in the first section of this paper, that is, Marx confused "abstraction from the genus, and abstraction from the specific forms in which the genus manifests itself." That is, the "special forms under which the values in use of the commodities may appear, whether they *serve* for food, shelter, clothing, etc., is of course disregarded, but the value in use of the commodity as such is never disregarded." This argument is totally irrelevant, since it is not the way that commodities "serve" us or are useful to us that Marx is abstracting from, but the useful object itself.

Those writers who have criticized Bohm-Bawerk's critique have not fared much better. Hilferding, for example, never noticed any difficulty with Marx's term "use-value" or Bohm-Bawerk's understanding of it. He simply said: "A use-value is an individual relationship between a thing and a human being" (Hilferding, 1949, p. 131). Given this concept of use-value, Hilferding went on to produce a litany of irrelevant arguments against Bohm-Bawerk. Or, consider a more recent critic of Bohm-Bawerk such as Meek. In his book on the labor theory of value, instead of giving a direct reference to the term "use-value," Meek gave only a cross-reference to "utility" (Meek, 1975, p. 331). Thus, without ever mentioning the difference between Marx's term "use-value" and the concept of "utility," or realizing Bohm-Bawerk's error on this issue, he went on to argue that Marx was not concerned with "use-value as such" but only with what Bohm-Bawerk himself called "the special forms under which the values in use of commodities may appear" (pp. 160-161). In support of this argument, Meek then quoted Marx in *A Contribution*, that is, "Entirely apart from their natural forms and without regard to the specific kind of wants for which they serve as use-values, commodities in certain quantities equal each other, take each other's place in exchange, pass as equivalents, and in spite of their variegated appearance, represent the same entity" (p. 161). Here, Meek did not realize that the abstraction involved in this quotation is abstraction from the useful object and not the abstraction from the usefulness of the object which Bohm-Bawerk had in mind.

The situation becomes far worse when we consider Marx's term "exchange-value." What Marx means by this term and how this fuzzy concept affects his logic, to the best of my knowledge has never been addressed in the debates on the derivation of value or, for that matter, in any general discussion of Marx's economic categories. In dealing with this term, most writers have simply quoted Marx's varied and confused concepts.[16] Some, such as the contributor to the *Dictionary of Marxist Thought*, apparently unable to make sense out of Marx's own concept, have instead resorted to Adam Smith's definition of exchange-value as "the power to command other commodities in exchange" (Bottomore, 1983, pp. 86, 504).[17]

Given all this, it is unlikely that Bohm-Bawerk, who had a very limited knowledge of Marx's works and concepts, would have realized the problem with the term exchange-value in *Capital*. He actually used the expression "exchange-values" synonymously with the "prices of the commodities" (Bohm-Bawerk, 1949, p. 66). With such an understanding, he obviously could not have noticed the actual logical error in the derivation or the source of this error. Among the many different ways that Marx conceptualized the relation of exchange, Bohm-Bawerk noticed only one: the equation of exchange with the symbol "=" used in the sense of equality. And all Bohm-Bawerk had to say about this equation, as we saw earlier, was that it is "old fashioned," "unrealistic," and in plain words, a "wrong idea." But why a wrong idea? Because, he said, "[w]here equality and exact equilibrium obtain, no change is likely to occur to disturb the balance" (p. 68). This argument is obviously nonsense, since the mathematical concept of equality has nothing to do with the concepts of "equilibrium" and "balance."

But, if Marx's equation of exchange was a wrong idea of the exchange relation, what was the right idea? Bohm-Bawerk did not "dwell" on the issue and instead proceeded with his "critical investigation of the logical" process by means of which Marx arrived at the "common factor" (p. 69). The upshot of this "critical investigation" was, as indicated earlier, a two-part argument. First, Bohm-Bawerk proposed that Marx should have abstracted not from usefulness in general but from the specific usefulness of the product. The reasoning behind this argument was that insofar as the exchange relation of commodities is concerned, the specific usefulness of commodities "is of course disregarded." This argument of Bohm-Bawerk's, even if we put aside his confusion about Marx's term use-value, makes no sense. He had previously dismissed Marx's equation of exchange as the wrong idea, so it is not at all clear what relation of exchange he had in mind and why this relation was characterized by abstraction from the specific usefulness of the commodities. Marx's idea of abstraction from use-values had certain, however erroneous, justification. Bohm-Bawerk's argument, on the other hand, seems to be void of any justification whatsoever.

The second part of Bohm-Bawerk's argument was that if we abstract from "the use-value of commodities" we can find, besides Marx's common property of "being products of labor," many other common properties. Among these, according to Bohm-Bawerk, is the property of being "natural products." This argument shows, once again, how little Bohm-Bawerk understood what he was reading. First, as I mentioned in the previous section, a careful reading of Marx's texts indicates that the common property, after abstraction from "the use-value of commodities" is supposed to be "congealed" abstract labor and not "products of labor." Second, it is absurd to say that if we set aside "the use-value of commodities," we can still be left with such residues as "natural products." But, why did Bohm-Bawerk say such a thing? Simply because he was misinterpreting the term use-value to mean usefulness rather than a useful object.

In conclusion, much of Bohm-Bawerk's critique of Marx's derivation of value, as well as the subsequent countercritiques of Bohm-Bawerk's critique, is completely irrelevant. Neither side of this issue has paid close attention to the exact meaning of Marx's term "use-value" and, therefore, both sides often have misinterpreted the meaning of this term. None of the combatants have realized that Marx's term "exchange-value" is not properly defined and is used in different, incompatible ways. Neither side has probed deeply into Marx's concept of "the exchange relation," its source, and its flaws. As a result, no one has questioned the meaning and the correctness of the statement which is at the heart of Marx's derivation: "But clearly, the exchange relation of commodities is characterized precisely by its abstraction from their use-values."

# NOTES

1. A partial list of the works that directly or indirectly deal with the issue would include Rubin (1972), (Meek 1975), Cutler et al. (1977), Mepham (1978), Lippi (1979), Bowles and Gintis (1981), Carling (1984-1985, 1986).

2. Until otherwise stated all italics are in the original.

3. From here on, all italics are mine.

4. I have often found it helpful to use set theoretic notations to clarify these concepts and the distinction between them. For example, if we let $O = \{o\}$ represent the set of objects; $N = \{n\}$, the set of human needs at any given time; and $S$, the relation of satisfaction between the human needs and the objects, then the set of use-values $U = \{u\}$ can be defined as:

$$U = \{u\} = \{o: oSn\}$$

*The classical economists' term "use-value" corresponds roughly to the relation of satisfaction, S.* Marx's term "use-value," on the other hand, corresponds roughly to $u$, a member of the set $U$.

This mode of presentation can be helpful in clarifying a statement which we saw earlier in the *Grundrisse*: "Use-value falls within the realm of political economy as soon as it becomes modified by the modern relations of production" (also see Marx, 1970, p. 28, for similar statements). What Marx is trying to say is that the set of use-values, $U$, is not the proper subject of investigation of political economy. It becomes so, however, once we have introduced, on this set, the relation of exchange.

5. See, for example, the following statements which appear in the discussion of the process of exchange in *Capital*: "For the owner, his commodity possesses no direct use-value…. It has use-value for others" (Marx, 1977, p. 179).

6. This is not a problem of translation. The original German versions read differently (see Marx, 1983, p. 19, 1989, p. 69).

7. Here, I am using the translation of the first edition of *Capital*, since the same sentence in the latest English edition has been incorrectly translated as: "Just as, in viewing the coat and the linen as values, we abstract from *their different use-values*" (Marx, 1977, p. 135). The expression "their different use-values" should be replaced by "difference between their use-values" (see Marx, 1983, p. 25, and Marx 1989, 76.

8. Marx, of course, wants to argue that this abstraction would result in a "residue," that is, "value" (Marx, 1977, p. 128).

9. By "equivalents," Marx here means "equal values" (Marx 1971, 127).

10. For example, Ricardo wrote that water and air have little or no value in exchange because "nothing *can be obtained in exchange for* them," but gold, on the other hand, has a great deal of value in exchange because it "*will exchange for* a great quantity of other goods" (Ricardo 1976, 5).

11. An analysis of such a relation does not concern us here.

12. There is of course another concept of exchange-value in Marx, that is, the "form of manifestation" of value (Marx, 1977, p. 152). But this concept does not concern us since it obviously appears after the derivation of value.

13. For example, in *Capital*, instead of saying that the *area of the triangle* is reduced to half the product of the base and the altitude, Marx writes, "The *triangle itself* is reduced to … half the product of the base and the altitude." At first, this may appear to be either an error in translation or a simple slip. But it is neither. The same kind of error appears also in *Theories*. Here, after having assumed that a "triangle A" and a "parallelogram B" have the same area, Marx writes "$A = h \times b\ /\ 2$" instead of writing the area of $A = h \times b\ /\ 2$. This notational error is then followed by a convoluted logic: "As areas, the triangle and the parallelogram are here declared to be equal, to be equivalents, although as a triangle and a parallelogram they are different" (Marx, 1971, pp. 144-145). These are obviously the same kind of notational and conceptual errors that we saw earlier in the discussion of exchange-values.

14.   In an earlier English translation this last sentence has been translated more accurately: "Then one use-value *is just as good as* another, provided only it be present in sufficient quantity" (Marx, 1974, p. 37). For the original German, see Marx, 1989, p. 69.

15.   Even *The New Palgrave*, which has many entries dealing with Marxist economics, has overlooked this unique and important concept in Marx and has discussed only the classical concept of use-value and the neoclassical concept of utility.

16.   Paul Sweezy, for example, repeats all of Marx's mistakes by saying that "exchange-value appears to be a quantitative relation between things," and at the same time maintaining that a commodity both possesses exchange-value and is an exchange-value (Sweezy, 1970, pp. 27-28).

17.   In *The New Palgrave* the term "exchange-value," which is an important concept not only in Marxian economics but also in classical political economy, does not even have a direct entry.

# REFERENCES

Bailey, Samuel. 1967. *A Critical Dissertation on the Nature, Measure and Causes of Value*. New York: A.M. Kelley.

Black, R.D. Collison. 1987. "Utility." *The New Palgrave* 4: 776-779.

Bohm-Bawerk, Eugen von. 1949. *Karl Marx and the Close of His System*. Edited by Paul M. Sweezy. New York: A.M. Kelley.

Bottomore, Tom, ed. 1983. *A Dictionary of Marxist Thought*. Cambridge: Harvard University Press.

Bowles, S., and H. Gintis. 1981. "Structure and Practice in the Labor Theory of Value." *Review of Radical Political Economics* 12(4, Winter): 1-26.

Carling, Alan. 1984-1985. "Observation on the Labor Theory of Value." *Science & Society* 48(4, Winter): 407-418.

_____. 1986. "Forms of Value and the Logic of Capital." *Science & Society* 50(1, Spring): 52-80.

Cutler, A., Hindness, B., Hirst, P., and Hussain, A. 1977. *Marx's "Capital" and Capitalism Today*. London: Routledge & Kegan Paul.

Fayazmanesh, Sasan. 1986. "Reconsidering the Concept of Use-value." Paper presented at the Allied Social Science Association annual meetings. New Orleans.

_____. 1992. "Utility" and "Use-value." Unpublished manuscript.

Hilferding, Rudolf. 1949. *Karl Marx and the Close of his System*. Edited by Paul M. Sweezy. New York: A.M. Kelley.

Krause, Ulrich. 1982. *Money and Abstract Labor*. London: Verso.

Lippi, Marco. 1979. *Value and Naturalism in Marx*. London: New Left Books.

Marx, K. 1970. *A Contribution to the Critique of Political Economy*. New York: International Publishers.

_____. 1971. *Theories of Surplus Value*, Part 3. Moscow: Progress Publishers.

_____. 1973. *Grundrisse: Foundations of the Critique of Political Economy*. New York: Vintage Books.

_____. 1974. *Capital*. Vol. 1. New York: International Publishers.

_____. 1975. "Notes on Adolph Wagner (1879-80)." Pp. 179-219 in *Karl Marx: Texts on Method*, edited by Terrell Carver. Oxford: Basil Blackwell.

_____. 1976. *Value: Studies by Karl Marx*. Translated by Albert Dragstedt. London: New Park Publications.

_____. 1977. *Capital*, Vol. 1. New York: Vintage Books.

_____. 1980. *Öbkonomische Manuskripte und Schriften (Economic Manuscripts and Writings) 1858-1861. Karl Marx/Friedrich Engels Gesamtausgabe (MEGA)*. II/2. Berlin: Dietz Verlag.

————. 1981. *Öbkonomische Manuskripte (Economic Manuscripts) 1857-58. MEGA.* II/1.2. Berlin: Dietz Verlag.

————. 1983. *Das Kapital 1867. MEGA.* II/5. Berlin: Dietz Verlag.

————. 1989. *Das Kapital 1883. MEGA.* II/8. Berlin: Dietz Verlag.

————. 1987. *Das Kapital 1872. MEGA.* II/6. Berlin: Dietz Verlag.

————. 1989. Le capital 1872-1875. *MEGA.* II/7. Berlin: Dietz Verlag.

Meek, Ronald. 1975. *Studies in the Labor Theory of Value.* 2nd edn. New York: Monthly Review Press.

Mepham, John. 1978. "The *Grundrisse*: Method or Metaphysics? *Economy and Society* 7(4, November): 430-444.

Ricardo, David. 1976. *The Principles of Political Economy and Taxation.* New York: Dutton.

Rubin, I.I. 1972. *Essays on Marx's Theory of Value.* Detroit, MI: Black and Red.

Smith, Adam. 1965. *The Wealth of Nations.* New York: Random House.

Sweezy, Paul M. 1970. *The Theory of Capitalist Development.* New York: Modern Reader Paperbacks.

# THE INTERPRETATION OF THE "BALANCE OF TRADE": A "WORDY" DEBATE

Salim Rashid

*The features that are generally thought to be present in connection with a general name—necessary and sufficient conditions for membership in the extension, ways of recognizing whether something is in the extension, etc.—are all present in the linguistic community considered as a collective body; but that collective body divides the "labor" of knowing and employing these various parts of the "meaning" of [a word].*

— Hilary Putnam

## I

The "balance of trade" and its connection with "wealth" were two concepts closely involved in the transition of economic thought from Mercantilism to Classical Economics. In an age before economics acquired a specialized vocabulary, there are two issues to be considered in assessing the significance of the changed interpretations of well-established words and phrases. First, did a word have multiple meanings for contemporaries; second, if multiple

**Research in the History of Economic Thought and Methodology, Volume 12, pages 93-111.**
**Copyright © 1994 by JAI Press Inc.**
**All rights of reproduction in any form reserved.**
**ISBN: 1-55938-747-5**

meanings can be found, what is the relative importance of each meaning? While it is relatively simple to show that a word may have had several meanings, it is very much more delicate for us to impute the proper emphasis to each connotation. It is this difficulty of acquiring a "feel" for the proper emphasis of each connotation that makes it so important to keep context in mind, a point that can be illustrated with reference to English Mercantilism. That "Power and Prosperity" were the twin goals of (English) Mercantilism is now widely accepted, but the fact that these (political) goals have strong implications for the proper interpretation of wealth (and the balance of trade) is a point that has been often ignored. One of the goals of this paper is to document that "wealth" had multiple meanings in the seventeenth and eighteenth centuries and that one of its primary connotations was political power.

Among the major semantic changes that took place in the eighteenth century was the gradual limitation of wealth solely to its (modern) economic aspects. In failing to appreciate this change, economists since Adam Smith have misinterpreted the ideas of Mercantilism. The link between certain common words and martial activities goes back to the Greeks. Thus, "arete" was fundamental in Greek ethical systems—where it corresponded to "good" or "best"—and originally denoted the excellence of a brave warrior. This mode of thought expressed itself in many ways. For example, when the Cretan poet Hybrias writes of wealth, he clearly includes physical prowess:

> In my great spear and my sword lies my wealth (quoted in Rahe 1984, p. 271).

These martial overtones of wealth became muted during the Middle Ages, but reappeared during the more military-minded sixteenth century when a "Military Revolution" occurred that had a considerable impact upon society. As stated by Geoffrey Parker:

> the greater costs incurred, the greater damage inflicted, and the greater administrative challenge posed by the augmented armies made waging war for more of a problem than ever previously, both for the civilian population and for their rules (quoted in Black 1990, p. 2).

Students of Mercantilism have to become more sensitive to the multiple meanings of words, and particularly to the role of political connotations.[1]

Few phrases in the English language have been used and studied as much as "the balance of trade." Even before the phrase came into common usage in the mid-seventeenth century, the underlying concept had been used with some regularity and may be traced back as far as the fourteenth century. The phrase itself refers to a fairly mundane notion: if we pretend that a country is a single family, then the balance of trade merely tells us whether, at the year's end, we owe money to others or others owe money to us; if we sold more to the rest of the world than they bought of us, so that we are owed money, the balance of trade is said to be favorable, whereas if we owe money, the balance of trade is said to be unfavorable.

After 1660, "the balance of trade" came to dominate all economic discussion and Adam Smith made the phrase notorious in 1776 when he accused his predecessors of guiding economic policy almost exclusively with the aim of obtaining a favorable balance of trade. Smith explained this addiction by attributing to his predecessors the folly of Midas—the belief that gold and silver were the only true forms of wealth. In order to cure this infatuation for the precious metals, Smith pointed out that houses, food, land, and goods of all kinds were the real objects of economic policy—gold and silver only provided a means for transferring goods. Smith claimed that his predecessors had suffered from an elementary confusion between means and ends. Joseph Schumpeter is one of the few economists who has directly challenged the prevailing view. In his *History of Economic Analysis* (1954), Schumpeter refers to Adam Smith's "unintelligent criticism" in the text and goes on to make a sharper charge in the footnotes.

> Adam Smith's criticism is open to a still more serious indictment. Obviously conscious of the fact that particular change cannot be made good, he does not strictly speaking make it, but he insinuates it in such a way that his readers cannot help getting the impression, which has in fact become very general (Schumpeter 1954, p. 361, see also pp. 36, 362, 364).

For most of the nineteenth century economists believed Smith's account of his predecessors and spoke contemptuously of them. With the writings of William Cunningham, Augustus Oncken, and Gustav Schmoller in the 1880s, the Mercantilists were seen as political theorists who viewed economic policy as one of the primary sources of the power of the state. This began a controversy between economists, who tend to support Adam Smith's account, and economic historians, who consider the Smithian view to be a caricature. There is no doubt that "the balance of trade" is the most frequently used indicator of good economic policy in the seventeenth and eighteenth centuries. Jacob Viner has rightly pointed out that:[2]

> The central problem in the interpretation of mercantilist theories is the discovery of the grounds on which their belief in the desirability of an indefinite accumulation of the precious metals was based (Viner 1937, p. 15).

In view of the need for exact monetary calculation in economics, it might be expected, a priori, that economic words and phrases would have relatively precise meanings. The primary aim of this essay is to point out the considerable difficulty involved in arriving at an unequivocal interpretation of "the balance of trade." That economists such as Cunningham, Oncken, and Viner would attempt to place words in context is in itself a positive step and would surely have borne more fruit if it had coincided with the current wave of interest in hermeneutics. It is a pity that subsequent economists have not followed their example. Schumpeter's pungent footnotes attacking the standard interpretation appear to have been universally ignored and it is of some importance to elaborate upon the issues Schumpeter raised. Viner himself has also been the most careful interpreter of the phrase "the balance of trade" and so I shall begin by reviewing Viner's highly influential arguments in order to illustrate my points.[3]

# II

My aim in this section is not to provide a critique of Viner's general position on Mercantilism but only to consider one part of Viner's case. Thus, my goal is to clarify what *was* the Mercantilist's case—not necessarily to defend it. If, however, I am right in pointing out that politics and power were a constant feature of words like "wealth," then it will follow that economists, qua economists, are to some extent inappropriate judges of Mercantilist policy. Indeed, I have argued elsewhere that "Mercantilism" is more properly called "Pragmatic Political Economy" since pragmatic and political concerns appear to dominate economic thought between 1600-1776 (Rashid 1980, 1989).

The order in which Viner presents his arguments is as follows (Viner 1937, pp. 15-22). First, Viner comes to the defense of Adam Smith's characterization of Mercantilism as a confusion between the precious metals and real wealth. If the Mercantilists did not believe in the Midas fallacy, Viner tells us, then: (1) their arguments are much too laborious, and (2) we do not know how they would have talked about what we call "real wealth." After concluding his defense of the Smithian position, Viner tells us that most authors did not rely solely on such an erroneous identification; indeed, he even doubts if the pamphleteers seriously believed it themselves, and attributes the use of such concepts to the desire for popularity. Finally, Viner provides three more cogent reasons for desiring to accumulate gold and silver—(1) the needs of war, (2) to store as capital, and (3) to facilitate exchange.

Before coming to grips with the details of Viner's argument, it is worth pointing out how the issue would take on a new light if the three reasons given at the end of Viner's presentation were given at the beginning. The use of money as an instrument of war, or as a store of capital, or as a medium of exchange are all eminently reasonable and practical concerns. It is also generally accepted that the overwhelming majority of the literature of the Mercantile Ages was provoked by policy issues in which people wrote to secure some concrete practical end. Is it not reasonable that individuals concerned with such immediate policy issues would take one or more of these three grounds for granted and simply assert the consequence—namely, the desirability of obtaining gold and silver. If I may use a modern analogy, when we refer approvingly to the latest computer innovation, is it not true that we are taking for granted a whole train of ideas regarding the relationship of computers to man, the desirability of material progress, and so on? Our silence on these larger issues should not necessarily imply that we are unaware of them or permit others to infer that we possess unequivocal opinions on these issues. The difference between the two possible approaches is that Viner presents Mercantilism as essentially erroneous, containing errors that can be mitigated by auxiliary considerations, whereas it is equally possible to display Mercantilism as basically sensible, but prone to exaggeration and imprecision.

If, then, it is reasonable to assume that the Mercantilist pamphleteers took for granted one or more of these three grounds when arguing for a favorable balance of trade, then the Midas fallacy can be proved *only* if we have a specific contrast drawn between real wealth and the precious metals. This is a strong requirement but it is needed to make the Smith-Viner case. Since gold and silver formed an internationally acceptable currency, it is obvious that they are *always a form* of wealth. The Mercantilists can be shown to be in error by displaying passages where they argue that gold and silver are the *only* forms of real wealth. Viner was fully aware of this issue and provided what he believed to be representative quotes from leading mercantilist writers on this point (Viner 1937, pp. 16-18).

The entire issue can now be taken to hinge upon finding out exactly what is proven by the quotes Viner provides. Eleven quotes are provided and, of these, six use the word "riches," "rich," or "enrich;" two use the word "wealth;" and two use the word "gain;" the last one refers to gold and silver as "the only or most useful treasure of a nation," a view so qualified that it cannot count as evidence in behalf of the Viner-Smith position. How, then, are we to interpret the words "wealth," "riches," and "gain"?

Oncken and Cunningham had argued that words like "wealth," "riches," or "treasure" had a different meaning in earlier ages and that it was improper to interpret them in the modern sense. Viner disagreed and replied as follows:[4]

> If it be replied that the mercantilists meant by "wealth," "treasure," "riches," "gain," "loss," "poverty," "prosperity," "profit," etc., only money or absence of money, their arguments generally become merely laborious tautologies, and it becomes a mystery: (a) why they should have thought it necessary to present so earnestly and at such great length arguments reducing to the assertion that the only way for a country without gold or silver mines to get more bullion is to obtain it from abroad in return for goods, and (b) what terms they used when they were thinking of what we mean today when we speak of riches, wealth, gain, prosperity (Viner 1937, p. 17).

The first rebuttal of Viner lies in denying that the Mercantilists argued at great length that the only way for a country without mines to acquire riches was through the balance of trade. Here are Thomas Mun's own words on the issue:

> The ordinary means therefore to increase our wealth and treasure is by Forraign Trade, wherein wee must ever observe this rule; to sell more to strangers yearly than wee consume of theirs in value.... I will take that for granted which no man of judgment will deny, that we have no other means to get Treasure but by forraign trade, for Mines wee have none which do afford it...this mony is gotten...by making our commodities which are exported yearly to over ballance in value the forraign wares which we consume (Mun 1954, 5, pp. 14).

It will be seen that Mun finds the statement to be entirely obvious. Indeed, I do not know of *any* Mercantilist, able or otherwise, who argued that the relationship between the inflow of precious metals and the balance of trade was a point of some intellectual difficulty, requiring careful proof.

Viner's second response to Oncken and Cunningham was that if words did not mean then what they mean now, how *did* Mercantilists express the modern concepts? This is a substantive issue and will be considered later. Suppose, however, that the word "treasure" did mean only gold and silver, then the title of Mun's classic, *England's Treasure by Foreign Trade*, is simply expressing a fact of life for the English and, indeed, for any country without mines of its own. It is only when we read "treasure" in the modern sense as an exotic form of riches which makes one instantly wealthy that Mun's title becomes striking. The way in which Adam Smith refers to Mun's book (slightly misquoting the title) suggests that by 1776 we have already moved towards the modern connotation of "treasure."

> The title of Mun's book, England's Treasure in Foreign Trade, became a fundamental maxim, in the political economy, not only of England, but of all other commercial countries. (Smith 1937, p. 403)

If the above interpretation of "treasure" as precious metals is correct, then Mun was only observing the trivial fact that England would have to look abroad for its gold and silver. How can such a platitude become a "fundamental maxim?"

Of the eleven authors quoted by Viner as representative of the confusion between money and wealth, one, Thomas Mun, is later quoted by Viner as being a moderate mercantilist who did not suffer from such a confusion. Ten authors remain and it will suffice for my purposes to show that Viner's characterization of three of these cannot be taken as representative. The three are Samuel Fortrey (1663), the collection of papers known as *The British Merchant* (1748), and Joshua Gee. Together with Mun, these four form the most famous names in the list provided by Viner. What I would like to question is not the accuracy of the quotes themselves, but whether such quotes can be considered representative of the authors quoted.[5] If such authors can be shown to be familiar with our notion of "real wealth," or if they held other aims as coequal to the favorable balance of trade, or if they did clearly use words like "wealth" or "riches" to mean the acquisition of gold and silver, then Viner's interpretation of these authors is not the only one that can be sustained.

Samuel Fortrey was a gentleman of the King's bedchamber and his work, *England's Interest and Improvement*, was published in 1663, after the manuscript had been seen and approved by Charles II. I quote at length the beginning of Fortrey's pamphlet, where it will be seen that "store" corresponds to real wealth:[6]

England's Interest and Improvement consists chiefly in the increase of store and trade.

Store comprehendeth all such commodities, as either the soil, or people of this nation are capable to produce, which are either usefull at home, or valuable abroad.

Trade is the means, by which a nation may procure what they want from abroad, and vent to the best advantage, what ever may be spread of their own increase at home.

Of store there are properly two sorts, natural and artificial.

Our natural store may also be divided into three parts.

First, the annual increase of the soil, which consists chiefly in corn of all sorts, and all the best sorts of cattel.

Secondly, the product of our Mines, of lead, tin, iron, coal, allum, and the like.

Thirdly, the great plenty of fish our seas naturally afford, of which we might reap unknown advantages, were our fishing trade rightly improved.

Our Artificial store consists in the manufacture and Industry of the people, of which the chiefest in this nation are the manufactures of woollen clothes, and all other sorts of woollen stuffs, linen cloth, silk, stuff, ribbandings, stockings, laces and the like (Fortrey, 1954, pp. 7-8).

Later, while describing those commodities most profitable for export, Fortrey clearly uses "richer" in the sense of meaning "more money."

to proceed in order, and first of our natural store, and annual increase of the soil, the annual profit and increase of the soil of this kingdom, consists chiefly in corn of all sorts, flax, hemp, hops, wooll, and many more such like; and also the best sorts of cattel, as bullocks, horse and sheep; and the greater our increase is of any of these commodities, the richer may we be; for, money, and all forein commodities that come hither, are onely bought by the exchange of our own commodities; wherefore by how much our own store doth exceed those necessaries we want from abroad, by so much will the plenty of money be increased amongst us (Fortrey, 1954, 16)

Fortrey thus illustrates the multiple meanings of words used in common economic discourse.

*The British Merchant* consists of a series of papers written by several prominent English merchants around 1714 to protest the proposed Commercial treaty with France. It is generally credited with being influential in leading to the rejection of the treaty and was frequently referred to by subsequent pamphleteers as embodying considerable economic wisdom. The two quotes that follow show that increasing employment was one of the primary aims of these economists and that, in somewhat of a reversal of the usual sequence, the adverse balance of trade with France was being treated as a creator of unemployment.

> That the Trade of that Country which contributes most to the Employment and Subsistence of our People, and to the Improvement of our Lands, is the most valuable.
>
> If a Treaty of Commerce be likely to add to our capital Stock; if it shall add to the Rents of our Landed Gentlemen; if it shall increase the Employment and Subsistence of the Poor; it must needs be beneficial.
>
> On the contrary; if it don't make the Customs and Duties reciprocal in both Countries; if it diminishes our Gold and Silver; if it shall prove a means of introducing the Product of Foreign Countries to interfere with our own; if it shall lessen the demand of our own Manufactures at our own or foreign Markets, and bring our Manufacturers to the Parish and Lands for their Subsistence; every Man is able to determine that a Treaty which shall do any of these things, is destructive to the Kingdom (*British Merchant*, 1748, pp. 18, 140).

So, the balance of trade derives its importance from concerns about employment.

The third economist on the list is Joshua Gee, a merchant of some repute, who had contributed to *The British Merchant* and wrote a popular tract titled *The Trade and Navigation of Great-Britain Considered*, whose subtitle is significant in showing both the use of "riches" as "gold and silver" and the desirability of attaining full employment.

> That the surest way for a Nation to Increase in Riches, is to prevent the Importation of such Foreign Commodities as may be raised at Home That this Kingdom is capable of raising within itself, and its Colonies, Materials for employing all our Poor in those Manufactures, which we now import from such of our Neighbours who refuse the Admission of ours (Gee, 1969, title page).

In the Appendix to the fourth edition of Gee's work, there is an extensive description of the items we would include in a listing of items of "real wealth." It is noticeable that there is no attempt to describe all these items by a single word, which suggests that the concept of "real wealth," as we know it, was not really distinctly considered in the mid-eighteenth century. The few quotes to the contrary that can be found, in Davenant, Jocelyn, and Wallace for example, are probably indicative of the fact that the very meaning of "real wealth" was in the process of a metamorphosis from its older to its current meaning:

> GREAT-BRITAIN, with its Dependencies, is doubtless as well able to subsist within itself, as any Nation in *Europe*: We have an industrious enterprizing People, fit for all the Arts

of War or Peace: We have Provisions in Abundance, and those of the best Sort, and are able to raise sufficient for double the Number of Inhabitants: We have the very best Materials for Cloathing, and want nothing either for Use, or even for Luxury, but what we have at Home, or might have from our Colonies; so that we might create fuch an Intercourse of Trade among ourselves, and between us and them, as would maintain a vast Navigation, even tho' we traded to no other Parts: And as Linnen is the Manufactury wherein we have been the most deficient, *Ireland* has of late Years made a very great Improvement therein (Gee, 1969, p. 235).

The questionable validity of the quotes provided by Viner extends to other authors whom Viner labels as "extreme mercantilists." Of the four authors whom Viner refers to under this rubric, the quote provided from one of them, John London, relies on the forced interpretation of "riches" already discussed above. Another author, Lewes Roberts, can be shown to have used "riches" in several senses, while the claim that Erasmus Phillips was an extreme mercantilist is truly puzzling. Consider the two following quotes, which show how money was considered instrumental to other ends:

Even Money itself without Trade, like stagnated Water, is of little use to the Proprietor....
   Gold and Silver being only valuable as they relate to other commodities. But as the Riches of a Country does not consist in any Quantity of Gold and Silver, if it cannot keep them, or acquire more; so our utmost Attention should be to preserve those Methods [of increase] (Phillips, 1725, pp. 2, 7).

Surely, Erasmus Phillips was free of the "Midas fallacy."

Viner is quite aware that words may have multiple meanings, but he does not quite concede the difficulties in interpretation that arise therefrom:

"Riches," "wealth," "treasure" had ambiguous meanings in the seventeenth and eighteenth centuries. They meant money, jewels, and other especially precious commodities at one moment, and all goods useful to man at another moment. Very often this shift of meaning occurred within the limits of a single paragraph or even sentence, and reasoning involving, and obtaining what plausibility it has from, such shifts in the meaning given to terms constitutes a large portion of the mercantilist agreement, and especially of the balance-of-trade doctrine (Viner, 1937, p. 16).

Viner claims here that the Mercantilist case gains what sense it has by jumping between meanings. If words are truly ambiguous, then one can retort by arguing that the Mercantilist case derives what absurdity it has from shifts in the meanings of words. It all depends upon whether we are obliged to place the most or the least sensible meaning upon the words of an earlier age.

# III

A review of Viner's treatment of Mercantilism thus indicates that the deficiency in Viner's treatment is due not so much in a failure to recognize multiple meanings but rather in the relative importance assigned to the several meanings. The same point can also be made with regard to Eli Heckscher's outstanding work on Mercantilism. This is all the more curious because Heckscher begins by noting, explicitly and carefully, that power was the raison d'etre of the mercantilist state:[7]

> For him [i.e., Adam Smith] power was certainly only a means to the end...Mercantilists usually believed the reverse, and mercantilism as a system of power was thus primarily a system for forcing economic policy into the service of power as an end in itself (Heckscher, 1965, vol. II, p. 17).

Heckscher goes on to observe that the pursuit of power makes the aggressive and even malevolent policies of the mercantilists understandable:

> the goal [i.e., power] could be achieved just as well, if not better, by weakening the economic power of other countries instead of strengthening one's own. If wealth is considered as an aim, this is the height of absurdity, but from the point of view of political power it is quite logical (Heckscher, 1965, vol. II, p. 17).

Heckscher then provides cogent illustrations of this thesis from such writers as von Hornigk, Roger Coke and John Locke.

Immediately following these pages, however, Heckscher goes on to argue that

> In the last instance, the ideas were based on a *static* conception of economic life: the view that there was a fixed quantity of economic resources in the world...a particular country could change and was capable of progress, but that this could only happen through acquisitions from other countries. This was the tragedy of mercantilism. (Heckscher, 1965, vol. II, pp. 24-26).

Having just admitted that power is relative and that economic resources were the primary source of power, how could Heckscher call the mercantilist economic view "static?" So long as power is relative and economics is subordinate to politics, all such views *must* be "static." It should be made clear that, in this context, the static viewpoint is no reflection on mercantilist economics, a point Heckscher fails to raise. The misuse of "static" in this connection can only serve to provide a pejorative air to mercantilist economic thought. A similar misuse arises in Heckscher's characterization of the mercantilist attitude towards commodities as "fear of goods." In a footnote to the second edition, Heckscher fully accepts E.A.J. Johnson's explication of the "fear of goods" as "a fear of redundant stocks of finished goods." (Heckscher, 1965, vol. II, p. 59) In this last sense, however, the point is trivial—when have merchants not been afraid of unsold products lying on their hands?

This refusal to impose an order of priorities upon mercantilist thought leads Heckscher to a truly perplexing characterization of the mercantilist attitude to money and wealth. Heckscher finds the belief that only money has value to be "so obviously absurd" that we may "take it for granted" that no one actually held it. Nonetheless, there is no doubt that such expressions exist. Heckscher therefore provides several quotes for this viewpoint and comes to the conclusion that the confusion of money with wealth was typical:

> It is not my intention to prolong these quotations endlessly; they could fill many pages. It may be said that the discussions concerning national wealth which took place in England towards the end of the 17th century among less intelligent, but none the less characteristic, writers led to a pure Midas-like view of the precious metals, i.e., that all economic value consisted in precious metal (Heckscher, 1965, vol. II, p. 188).

Heckscher feels uncomfortable with this claim and again goes on to point out that the mercantilists would "not deny that people must eat, clothe themselves, and have a roof over their heads." Heckscher feels that their silence in not asserting these facts indicates an attitude but should not be pushed to grotesque lengths. However, Heckscher himself pushes the argument along this groove. He notes the mercantilist disregard for consumption goods and their habitual neglect of domestic goods as costs and concludes:

> If we attempt to pursue this argument to its logical conclusion it is obvious that the outcome could be nothing other than "treasure." ...all that remained was to direct the productive powers to the acquisition of money and precious metals.... For two centuries writers on economics were unanimous in the belief that the argument outlined here was sound. To quote them all would only be to repeat the same thesis *ad nauseam* (Heckscher, 1965, vol. II, p. 194).

Once again, the pursuit of power, which Heckscher himself had so emphasized earlier, is now neglected by Heckscher, and the mercantilists are considered as though their goal was to increase riches in the modern sense of the term. To complicate matters even more, Heckscher is emphatic in asserting that the mercantilists

> were in no way aware that they were idolised money and the precious metals (Heckscher, 1965, vol. II, p. 260).

Rather, their economic policies were guided by "unconscious elements" which served to provide the precious metals with "a halo of significance."

Despite his attempts to be fair, Heckscher cannot hide several expressions of amusement at the thoughts of mercantilists—von Hornigk is called the "Tertullian of mercantilism" and on reading Papillon "one might think that at last a perfectly sane and practical view of the actual conditions had been hit upon" (Heckscher, 1965, vol. II, pp. 22, 191). Are we then to conclude that mercantilist ideas are the "reflection" of a (nonmercantilist) subconscious and that, for over two hundred years, economic thought was guided by an unanalyzed halo?

## IV

In his pioneering work on *The Growth of English Industry and Commerce* the Rev. William Cunningham wrote of the Middle Ages that

> the very terms by which we habitually describe the industrial condition of the present day are inapplicable if we wish to analyse the circumstances of these earlier times. Labour, Capital, and Rent have all altered their connotation so much, that we run considerable risk of confusing ourselves if we are satisfied with adopting modern language to describe the period of the Domesday Survey. *This is perhaps the greatest difficulty with which we have to contend* (Cunningham, 1905, vol. I, p. 5, emphasis added).

The fact that the seventeenth and eighteenth centuries are not so dissimilar from our own age has perhaps misled scholars in their interpretation of earlier pamphlets. When Jacob Viner asks how these ages would express *our* concepts of wealth and consumption, he is, to a certain extent, also assuming that these concepts were of sufficient interest to be frequently used and unequivocally expressed. It is odd that Viner is willing to give words unequivocal modern meanings in his quotes when he himself recognizes that the seventeenth and eighteenth centuries did not share the modern notion of enjoying goods but rather focused upon the ways of growing richer:

> The emphasis on saving is shown also by the frequent exclusion of consumable goods, or goods destined for consumption instead of for accumulation, from "riches," the latter term being confined to saved or accumulated goods (Viner, 1937, p. 27).

Raymond Williams points out that the root of "consume" meant to devour or waste and that "in almost all of its early English uses, consume had an unfavorable sense," as in the disease pulmonary phthisis or "consumption" (Williams, 1980, p. 68).[8] Now, it is one sort of defect in the Mercantilist literature not to have wanted consumption; it is quite another to say that they wanted to consume (in our sense) but did not know how to achieve it. Irrationality in the choice of means can be corrected but irrationality in the choice of ends is a disease without a cure. Viner's refusal to give due weight to the noneconomic senses of the words he quoted and his readiness to discount the importance of power makes him curiously unable to find a suitable interpretative framework for the many accurate observations he provides.

Many examples can be provided to show the great fluidity in the use of words in economic discourse. Consider the words "stock" and "store." In 1659, English merchants complained that the trade with France "doth exceedingly drain us; for that thereby our National Stock is diminished and the Frenches Stock Increased a Million of Pounds" (Priestly, 1951, p. 38) Here, "stock" clearly refers to an amount of money. Four years later, while dealing with the very same topic, Samuel Fortrey used the very similar word "store" to refer to a *physical* accumulation of goods. So, these closely related words had very different meanings for economists.

The words "wealth" and "riches" are perhaps the most important one for the purposes of this essay, and it is worth demonstrating that these words retained a multiplicity of meanings right down to the time of Adam Smith. The word wealth was frequently used in conjunction with "Honor," and since Honor invariably denoted martial prowess, this provides us with a clue to interpreting "wealth." Whenever the Mercantilists spoke of pursuing wealth, they *meant* both "wealth" (in our sense) *and* power. To divest their words of this political use is to distort their intent.[9]

The close connection between wealth and power is shown in the pamphlet of Dudley North, frequently held to be one of the more brilliant precursors of Adam Smith.

> What is commonly understood by Wealth viz Plenty, Bravery, Gallantry and cannot be maintained without Foreign Trade (North, 1691, pp. 15-16).

The connotations of Bravery and Gallantry, however, have been quite missing in the literature on Mercantilism.

About half-a-century later, the French-Irish banker, Richard Cantillon, writes:

> It is this balance of trade which enriches nations in the present situation of the world, as the acquisition of bullion. of which money is made, is that which acquires to one nation, comparing with another, its superiority of power, force and influence (Cantillon, 1755, p. 33).

While such an identification of increased wealth, in the form of gold and silver acquired through the balance of trade, with national power had been made earlier by John Locke, it is more notable in Cantillon because Locke was actively a politician while Cantillon never was.

"Riches," on the other hand, meant primarily a plenty of money, as in North's statement, "Riches, or in the common phrase, plenty of money." Nonetheless, the sense of riches as a plentitude of goods was also widely prevalent. When David Hume asked whether a Rich Country could be overtaken by a poor country, he meant rich in the sense of one with more money. In a critique of Hume, the Rev. Josiah Tucker used the word rich in both senses, but primarily to imply more real wealth. Viner notes the ensuing situation as follows:

> Tucker, in the course of an attempt to refute Hume's argument, follows Hume's ambiguous terminology too closely . . and Hume, in an unsatisfactory reply, himself follows this shift in issues (Viner, 1937, p. 87).

What better proof of multiple meanings can there be than the confusion two first-rate minds can suffer? The Rev. Robert Wallace and the Rev. Nathanial Foster are widely believed to be two of the more able liberal economists in the two decades before Adam Smith—and yet, a look at their pamphlets will show that they too did not feel confident about assigning an unambiguous meaning to "riches" and "wealth." Is it not curious how almost every economist who has been held up as a "precursor" of Adam Smith still shows attention to both the economic and noneconomic connotations of "riches" and "wealth?" In this perspective, it becomes clear that one of the reasons why Adam Smith was able to obtain sharper results in the *Wealth of Nations* was not necessarily his possession of better analytics but rather his determination to use some critical words solely with their modern meaning. It is widely agreed that Smith's fundamental contribution was to the doctrine of Free International Trade. Malachy Postlethwayt was a firm believer in the merits of competition (which he called "emulation"), but his attachment to the joint concept of prosperity *and* power prevented him from viewing movements of the balance of trade with equanimity.

> The Balance of Trade, I cannot too often repeat it, is in Fact the Balance of Power (Postlethwayt, 1967, p. 322).

# V

In the Middle Ages, "the identification of gold and silver with wealth was not merely general, but universal." With such expressions did J.R. McCulloch (1845, p. 1) express the immeasurable satisfaction the classical economists felt at having overcome the fallacies of the mercantilists. Certainly, the reception accorded to the *Wealth of Nations* after 1790 makes the growth of classical economics a genuine revolution in the annals of science. A less self-confident age such as ours has to be more curious about such an unusual phenomenon, if only because of warnings such as those of T.S. Kuhn regarding the assessment of "victors" in his *Structure of Scientific Revolutions*. The problem, of course, is that the protatagonists never directly address each other, a problem Kuhn terms "incommensurability:"

We have already seen several reasons why the proponents of competing paradigms must fail to make complete contact with each other's viewpoints. Collectively these reasons have been described as the incommensurability of the pre- and post-revolutionary normal-scientific traditions, and we need only recapitulate them briefly here. In the first place, the proponents of competing paradigms will often disagree about the list of problems that any candidate for paradigm must resolve. Their standards or their definitions of science are not the same (Kuhn, 1970, p. 148).

People talk across each other, Kuhn tells us, because the same words have different meanings to the two parties:

> More is involved, however, than the incommensurability of standards. Since new paradigms are born from old ones, they ordinarily incorporate much of the vocabulary and apparatus, both conceptual and manipulative, that the traditional paradigm had previously employed. But they seldom employ these borrowed elements in quite the traditional way. Within the new paradigm, old terms, concepts, and experiments fall into new relationships one with the other. The inevitable result is what we must call, though the term is not quite right, a misunderstanding between the two competing schools (Kuhn, 1970, p. 149).

It may be worthwhile to point out that economics does not provide ambiguous words that *cannot* be translated from one framework to another. Rather, no one seems to have understood the problem and made the effort.

That words have an imprecisely defined content even in a seemingly technical subject like economics is not adequately appreciated. For all the fun they poked at the Mercantilist conception of wealth, the classical economists could not reach close agreement on this issue either and the *Oxford English Dictionary* introduced a specific entry for wealth as used by economists:[10]

> *Economics.* A collective term for those things the abundant possession of which (by a person or community) constitutes riches, or "wealth" in the popular sense. There has been much controversy among economists as to the precise extent of meaning in which the term should be used (*O.E.D.*, 1933, p. 222).

Nor is this ambiguity limited to words like "riches" and "wealth." The law courts have almost continually defined the limits of "property" while the word "manufacture" is so far from its original connotation of artificial that we almost exclusively associate it with machinery. Just because we have been using the same word for centuries, we have to be especially careful in ensuring that older documents are being read in context. We would do well to heed Ian Hacking's observation that:

> When I find that the word "determinism" begins in German around 1788, and that its usage in terms of efficient causes rather than predetermining motives begins in all European language around 1860, I am surprisingly inclined to say that a new concept comes in with the use of this word (Hacking, 1984, p. 11).

In a careful and much-quoted study of the proper methods of historical research, Quentin Skinner came to some conclusions that must depress the student of the history of economic ideas:

> The appropriate, and famous, formula—famous to philosophers, at least—is rather that we should study not the meanings of the words, but their use. For the given idea cannot ultimately be said in this sense to *have* any meaning that can take the form of a set of words which can then be excogitated and traced out over time. Rather the meaning of the idea must *be* its uses to refer in various ways.... If there is good reason to insist that we can only study an idea by seeing the nature of all the occasions and activities—the language games—within which it might appear, then there must be correspondingly good reason to insist that the project of studying histories of "ideas," *tout court*, must reset on a fundamental philosophical mistake (Skinner, 1969, p. 37).

An examination of the writings of Jacob Viner and Eli Heckscher on the balance of trade, perhaps the most influential and certainly the most careful works on this issue, reveal that Skinner's structures possess considerable justification. Nonetheless, Skinner's recommendations can be interpreted in too nihilistic a fashion. Ideas such as the balance of trade do persist in the economic literature for over two centuries; for most of this time they form a major, if not the principal, topic of discussion; as historical writing needs to have some organizing principle to bring coherence to events spanning several centuries, it is not really possible to avoid coming to grips with such concepts as the balance of trade. Nor is it impossible for a phrase to have a clearly defined social meaning for extended periods of time. No student of the period would deny two outstanding features of the literature on Mercantilism: first, that political issues generally dominated economic considerations and second, that many of the pamphlets were motivated by narrow self-interest (and recognized as such). In a seminal essay on the "Tory origins of Free-Trade policy," William Ashley provided a cogent and penetrating description of debates on economic policy in the 1670s and showed how the policy of free trade—and, by implication policies based on the balance of trade—derived primarily from political considerations and secondarily from the internal squabbles of the East India Company (Ashley, 1900, pp. 268-303). If more careful work is done along these lines, phrases like the "balance-of-trade" will perhaps cease to be a battleground.[11]

The recurrence of worry about the balance of trade for over two centuries has led economists such as Heckscher to insist that mercantilist ideas bore no relationship with reality; economic historians such as Barry Supple (1959) have retorted that the recurrence of the same economic problem is just as likely the cause for the constant use—or even rediscovery—of the concept. Every time the concept becomes significant, it is necessary to examine the accompanying political and economic circumstances in order to see whether some more reasonable explanation than the puerile identification of money with wealth is available. If words which are widely used really do possess significant multiple meanings, then the only way by which we can focus on the particular meaning intended is by a close attention to historical context; for the type of questions of interest to economists, this implies focusing upon the relationships between reality and the part of it economists use within their model.[12] In the graphic words of S.R.L. Clarke:

> Words convey more than they say, and never all that there is. We have an imaginative grasp of solid reality, but cannot think about reality except by mapping it out in our verbal language, which cannot accommodate more than a particular cut through the manifold of experienced being. (Clarke 1986, p. 49).

# ACKNOWLEDGMENTS

The author is grateful to Larry Laudan, David Levy, A.M.C. Waterman, and two referees for comments on an earlier version. One of the referees provided especially helpful references and comments.

# NOTES

1. An excellent piece that pays attention to the evolution of words is Christopher Hill (1990). For a useful bibliography, as well as a collection of classic articles, see D.C. Coleman (1969a).

2. The argument that the Mercantilists wished for an "indefinite" accumulation of gold and silver is questionable. In later work, Viner agreed that Mercantilist writings were probably best interpreted as short-run in aim, hence the question of "indefinite" accumulation will not be considered further.

As I do not read German, I am relying on Viner's presentation of Cunningham's article and of Oncken.

3. For a recent example of Viner's authoritative status, see G. Anderson and R. Tollison (1984)

The most widely used graduate text in the history of economics also follows Viner, (Blaug, 1985, pp. 11-16). (To be fair, in correspondence Professor Blaug has said that this chapter needs to be rewritten.)

4. This last qualification is probably a rhetorical gloss; if taken seriously it would negate the point of the pages spent discussing the mercantilist conception of wealth. For another such example, see note 5.

5. At one point, Viner does state that "It is impossible...to understand...common mercantilist arguments...unless they believed, momentarily at least, that all goods other than money were worthless, or were of value only as they served as means of securing money" (1937, pp. 16-17). No one would defend the "momentary" import of some sentences as a basis for interpretation, and I am sure Viner himself could not have meant such momentary illusions to form the basis of his case.

6. In "The Political Balance of Trade ...?" (forthcoming) I have argued that Fortrey is really the originator of "Mercantilism" and that the sort of economic policy depicted by Adam Smith was politically motivated, was in vogue only between 1660-1720 and its vogue died out around 1720.

7.  Heckscher's work has been criticized frequently by economic historians, most notably by D. C. Coleman (1969b, reprinted in Coleman, 1969a, 92-117). For my purposes Heckscher is not as relevant because he readily conceded the propagandistic aspects of the representation of Mercantilism in the *Wealth of Nations* and because he is not so self-consciously concerned with the proper methods of interpreting sources as Viner was.

8.  The fact that historical events had four "sorts" of causes—formal, material, efficient, and final—for writers imbued with Aristotleian ideas during these centuries is a further point to be noted. For us, cause can only mean efficient cause. (Woolf, 1990, p. 18).

9.  For wider views of the concept of Honor, see J.C.D. Clark (1985) and M. James (1986).

10.  The entry goes on to present John Stuart Mill's definition as that most commonly accepted. Among economists, only *T.R. Malthus* appears to have been acutely conscious of the need for a uniform terminology, in *On Definitions in Political Economy* (1827). Indeed, if words could have strictly defined meanings in the sense of computer science, that is, finitely encodable, then there are results which suggest that we have zero probability of getting to the "truth!" (see Gilboa, 1990).

11.  The extent to which general views dominate the interpretation of early texts is clearly visible in Klaus Knorr's carefully researched, *British Colonial Theories, 1570-1850* (1944).

12.  I am grateful to a referee for suggesting this clarifying phrase.

# REFERENCES

Anderson, G., and R. Tollison. 1984. "Sir James Steuart as the Apothesis of Mercantilism and His Relation to Adam Smith." *Southern Economic Journal* October.

Anderson, G., and R. Tollison. 1986. "Smith, Steuart and Mercantilism: Reply." *Southern Economic Journal* January.

Ashley, W. 1900. *Survey's Historic and Economic.* London: Longmans.

Black, Jeremy. 1990. *A Military Revolution?* London: Methuen.

Blaug, M. 1985. *Economic Theory in Retrospect.* Cambridge: Cambridge University Press.

*The British Merchant.* 1748. London: n.p.

Cannan, E. 1937. *An Inquiry into the Nature and Cause of the Wealth of Nations.* New York.

Cantillon, Philip. 1759. *The Analysis of Trade, Commerce, Coin, Bullion, & C.* London.

Clark, J.C.D. 1985. *English Society 1688-1832.* Cambridge: Cambridge University Press.

Clarke, S.R.L. 1986. *The Mystery of Religion.* New York: Blackwell.

Coleman, D.C. 1969a. *Revisions in Mercantilism.* London.

_____. 1969b. "Eli Heckscher and the Idea of Mercantilism." Pp. 92-117 in *Revisions in Mercantilism,* by author. London: Methuen & Co. Ltd.

Cunningham, W. 1905. *The Growth of English Industry and Commerce.* Cambridge: Cambridge University Press.

Forster, N. 1767. *An Inquiry Into the Causes of the Present High Price of Provisions.* London: n.p.

Fortrey, Samuel. 1663. *England's Interest and Improvement.* Reprinted in McCulloch 1954. Cambridge: Field.

Gee, J. 1729. *The Trade and Navigation of Great Britain Considered.* Reprinted by Augustus M. Kelley, 1969. London: n.p.

Gilboa, I. 1990. "Philosophical Applications of Kolmogorov's Complexity Measure." Northwestern University Discussion Paper No. 923, October.

Hacking, Ian. 1984. "Five Parables." Pp. 103-124 in *Philosophy in History,* edited by R. Rorty, J.B. Schneewind, and Q. Skinner. Cambridge: Cambridge University Press.

Heckscher, Eli. 1965. *Mercantilism.* London.

Hill, Christopher. 1990. "The Word Revolution." *A Nation of Change and Novelty.* London: Routledge.

James, M. 1986. "English Politics and the Concept of Honour, 1485-1642." Pp. 307-415 in *Society, Politics and Culture*. Cambridge: Cambridge University Press,

Knorr, Klaus. 1944. *British Colonial Theories, 1570-1850*. Toronto: University of Toronto Press.

Kuhn, T.S. 1970. *The Structure of Scientific Revolutions*. Chicago: University of Chicago Press.

Malthus, T.R. 1827. *On Definitions in Political Economy*. London: Murray.

McCulloch, J.R. 1954. *The Literature of Political Economy 1845*. London: Longmans.

_____. 1954. *Early English Tracts on Commerce 1856*. Cambridge. *Oxford English Dictionary*. 1933. Oxford: Oxford University Press.

Mun, T. 1968. *England's Treasure by Foreign Trade*. New York: Augustus M. Kelley.

North, D. 1691. Discourses Upon Trade. London: T. Basset.

Phillips, Erasmus. 1725. *The State of the Nation*. London.

Postlethwayt, M. 1967. *Great Britain's True System*. New York: Augustus Kelley.

Priestley, M. 1951. "Anglo-French Trade and the 'Unfavorable Blance' Controversy, 1660-1685." *Economic History Review*.

Putnam, H. 1975. *Mind, Language and Reality*. Cambridge: Cambridge University Press.

Rahe, 1984. "The Primary of Politics in Classical Greece." *American History Review*, 89(2): 265-293.

Rashid, Salim. 1980. "Economists, Economic Historians and Mercantilism." *Scandinavian Economic History Review* 28(1): 1-14.

_____. 1989. "English Financial Pamphleteers of the Mid-Eighteenth Century: The Last Phase of Pragmatic Political Economy." Pp. 3-18 in *Perspectives in the History of Economic Thought*, Vol. 1, edited by D.A. Walker. Aldershot, UK: Edward Elgar.

_____. 1993. "The Political Balance of Trade...??" *History of Economic Thought and Methodology*, 11: 73-92.

Rorty, R. 1984. "Five Parables." In *Philosophy in History*. Cambridge: Cambridge University Press.

Schumpeter, J. 1954. *History of Economic Analysis*. London: Allen and Unwin.

Skinner, Quentin. 1969. "Meaning and Understanding in the History of Ideas." *History and Theory*.

Supple, B. 1959. *Commercial Crisis and Change in England, 1600-42*. Cambridge.

Viner, J. 1937. Studies in Theory of International Trade. New York: n.p.

Williams, R. 1980. *Keywords*. Glasgow, UK: Fontana.

Woolf, D.R. 1990. *The Idea of History in Early Stuart England*. Toronto: University of Toronto.

# INGRAO AND ISRAEL'S *THE INVISIBLE HAND: ECONOMIC EQUILIBRIUM IN THE HISTORY OF SCIENCE:*

## REVIEW ESSAYS

*The Invisible Hand: Economic Equilibrium in the History of Science.*
**By Bruna Ingrao and Giorgio Israel. Translated from the Italian by Ian MacGilvray.**
**Cambridge: MIT Press, 1990. P. xiii + 491.**

### MATHEMATICS AND THE AXIOMATIZATION OF GENERAL EQUILIBRIUM THEORY
by
Roger E. Backhouse

Referring to economic theory, Gerard Debreu, in his Presidential Address to the American Economic Association, argued that:

> the effectiveness of attempts to alter the course of its evolution will gain from a detailed analysis of the processes that led to its present state (Debreu, 1991, p. 6).

In The *Invisible Hand: Economic Equilibrium in the History of Science*, Bruna Ingrao and Giorgio Israel would appear to have provided just such an analysis. The book's subject is general equilibrium theory, its main thesis being that

**Research in the History of Economic Thought and Methodology, Volume 12, pages 113-151.**
**Copyright © 1994 by JAI Press Inc.**
**All rights of reproduction in any form reserved.**
**ISBN: 1-55938-747-5**

the problem of mathematization is no secondary feature of general economic equilibrium theory but rather one of the basic reasons for its creation and development (p. x).

Its main focus, therefore, is on the development of general equilibrium theory from Walras and Pareto to the present day, covering the three issues that, the authors claim, constitute the theory's "invariant paradigmatic nucleus": namely, the problems of existence, uniqueness, and global stability of equilibrium (p. 3). The work of Walras, Pareto, Wald, von Neumann, Hicks, Samuelson, Arrow, Debreu and many others is discussed in detail. There are also, however, two very important chapters on general equilibrium theory before Walras.

In reviewing a book which covers such a wide range of material and which has potentially such wide-ranging implications, it is necessary to be selective. Rather than examine its arguments in detail, this review seeks to pick out some of the book's main themes, exploring their implications for the history of economic thought and for our understanding of contemporary economics. It is important, however, to stress that the book covers much that is of great interest but which is not discussed in this review. To give but one example, there is a fascinating discussion of Poincaré's reaction to Walras's work, which raises some very important issues.

This review is written from the point of view, which may sound old-fashioned in some quarters; that historians of economic thought should be concerned with what Schumpeter (1954) termed the filiation of economic ideas. By this, it is not intended to imply that there is only one correct way to tell the story, or that our histories are not "constructed" (of course they are). Rather, it is based on the view that the history of economic thought is like a fabric in which many different threads are woven (sometimes tangled!) together, and from which the historian can pick out different strands; or that it is like a multidimensional map in which there are many paths, in different places merging, crossing and splitting. The fact that there may be other paths, or that ideas that appear in one path may also appear in another, does not imply that it is mistaken to pick out one apparent route and to use historical evidence to ask whether the different points we see are indeed connected, or whether the appearance of a connection is illusory; or to ask whether one road is more important than another.

## A.   The Genealogy of General Equilibrium Theory

The "standard" history of economic thought, insofar as it is reasonable to speak in such terms, presents the Physiocrats as the first organized school of economic thought, with many historians echoing Schumpeter's judgement that Quesnay's *tableau économique* "was the first method ever devised in order to convey an explicit conception of the nature of economic equilibrium"

(Schumpeter, 1954, p. 242). From Quesnay, the genealogy is usually shown as passing to Adam Smith and thence to Ricardo and the English classical economists. Opposition to the Smith-Ricardo-Mill orthodoxy is recognized, but is usually presented in terms of individual dissenters.

Ingrao and Israel show that this account of the filiation of economic ideas involves a significant distortion of the historical record. Not only was the *tableau*, they argue, "the first attempt to provide both a general and a quantitatively precise representation of the flows of production and exchange in an economic system" but

> Physiocratic thought was also, in a still more direct sense, the privileged source of inspiration of almost all the attempts to mathematize social science that flourished in the last twenty years of the eighteenth century and the early years of the nineteenth (p. 45).

During the years of the French Revolution, "social mathematics" flourished, its outstanding exponent being Condorcet. Two factors contributed to its decline in the early years of the nineteenth century: the rise to prominence in scientific circles of Laplace; and the consolidation of Napoleon's dictatorship, in which there was no room for inquiries concerning the rational organization of society. It is at this stage that Say's approach (and with it Smith's influence) rose to prominence in French economics. Say departed completely from Physiocracy in calling for a naturalistic social science, excluding the use of formal abstract models whether derived from abstract analysis or statistical inquiries.

Given that "social mathematics" was a movement which, for whatever reason, died out, why is the historical record distorted by neglecting it? One obvious reason is that if we neglect social mathematics, we cannot properly understand the background against which nineteenth-century French writers on mathematical economics such as Cournot were working: they may, after the early years of the century, have been isolated, but they were not working in a vacuum. A second obvious reason is that fate of social mathematics explains how and why the early moves towards mathematical economics came to be eclipsed by "English" classical political economy, as represented in the work of Jean-Baptiste Say.

More important than either of these reasons, however, the case of social mathematics illustrates the point that the history of general equilibrium theory cannot properly be understood apart from the history of science. The inspiration for social mathematics was Newtonian:

> [Newtonian physics] was seen as proof that the universe could be conceived and represented through the concepts of mathematical knowledge ... [and] was recognized as containing not only scientific results of great value, but "*regulae philosophandi*" that must act as norms in the study of natural phenomena (pp. 37-38).

Despite this enthusiasm for Newtonian physics, however, there was an awareness of the problems involved in applying the quantitative methods of mechanics to biological and social phenomena. Condorcet, for example, intended social mathematics to encompass a wide range of formal methods. Thus, not only do we find in his work concepts such as *homo suffragans*, a mathematical abstraction analogous to the abstractions of Newtonian physics; but we also find Condorcet basing theory not on differential calculus but on a "markedly subjectivistic" idea of probability (p. 52). His subjectivism was a symptom of his desire to unite positive and normative approaches: to construct both a descriptive theory and a rational science of society.

Ingrao and Israel claim that with the suppression of social mechanics by Laplace,

> the interdisciplinary unity that had constituted the strength and originality of Condorcet's studies was lost. The scientific world gradually lost interest in the idea of applying Newtonianism outside its original sphere and paid none of the attention necessary to the specific problems thus raised in relation to the new disciplines.... The status of "science" was by now granted solely to the physicomathematical sciences' (p. 58).

This, they claim, explains why later attempts at mathematizing economics, including those of Cournot and Walras, used traditional mathematical tools and referred explicitly to mechanics. The incipient probabilistic revolution represented in Condorcet's work proved abortive.

## B.  The Marginal Revolution

In arguing that the mathematics was an integral part of Walrasian theory, and not something incidental to it, and in claiming that Walras was concerned to make economics scientific through following the example of physics, Ingrao and Israel might appear to be echoing Mirowski's claim that the key to developments in neoclassical economics is to be found in "physics envy" (Mirowski, 1984, 1990). However, though it has certain features in common, their thesis is very different from anything Mirowski has argued. The first point is that they make no mention of energetics, the branch of physics developed in the mid nineteenth century that neoclassical economics was concerned to emulate. Rather, they date much earlier the equation of science with the use of methods taken from physics and mechanics: to the Laplacean suppression, discussed above, of attempts to apply Newtonianism outside its original sphere. Though he acknowledged his debt only to Cournot, Walras was the "direct heir" of Canard and Isnard as much as Cournot (p. 91). Isnard, though not making any use of the concept of equilibrium, had formulated a system of equations, based on equality of supply and demand, to determine prices (pp. 63-66). Canard went further in providing a "clear formulation of the close dependence of all markets in a state of equilibrium" (p. 69). He even provided "a description of the process through which confrontation between buyers and sellers leads to a state of equilibrium. The description of this process is extremely interesting in that it constitutes the outline of a form, albeit rudimentary, of the *tâtonnement*" (p. 72).

Canard made *explicit* use of mechanical analogies. Walras's originality thus lay, according to Ingrao and Israel, not in formulating a set of equations of equilibrium but "in his fusion of the equations of equilibrium borrowed from statics with a theory of value based on marginal utility, or rareté" (p. 91).

Ingrao and Israel also diverge sharply from Mirowski's interpretation of developments after Walras. Like Mirowski, they draw attention to the way in which physics changed direction in the early twentieth century. However, where Mirowski claims that neoclassical economists continued to espouse a theory which was based on a physics that had become out-of-date—what Walker terms Mirowski's "first genetic thesis" (Walker, 1991, p. 617)—Ingrao and Israel argue that a crisis arose in economics too:

> The period around 1910 thus appears to have been a moment of real crisis for general economic equilibrium theory. Or perhaps it would be better to say for that version of the theory—the only one known hitherto—whose central paradigm was the model of classical mathematical physics and especially mechanics. The crisis of a great "reductionistic" project was thus coming to a head. The often-attempted unification of the methods and concepts of the two disciplines—mathematical physics and mathematical economics—finally proved impossible. The major representatives of the reductionist school in physics ... ended up proclaiming the impossibility of further attempts (p. 170).

However, where Mirowski argues (among other theses) that economists stuck to theories based on a set of physical theories that were soon discredited, Ingrao and Israel argue that general equilibrium theory went through a major paradigm-shift, analogous to the change which took place in physics:

> The central position that *mechanical analogy* had played in classical reductionism was now assigned to *mathematical analogy*. It was no longer a matter of reducing the laws of phenomena to the form of mechanical laws (the orthodox method followed by Walras in economics), but rather the formal unification of different laws by means of mathematical frameworks bringing out their basic analogy ("empty schemata of possible contents," as the exponents of axiomatic mathematics were to call it) (p. 171).

In an important sense, therefore, the decisive break came not with Walras, but after Pareto. Whereas Walras and Pareto had, like their predecessors, viewed themselves as deriving mathematical laws from nature, with the constraints that implied, for their successors,

> Not only is mathematics no longer the language of nature but all claims to derive mathematical laws from nature are dropped, along with any excessive demands for the

verifiability of such laws. Mathematics increasingly becomes a "pool" of abstract frameworks of possible realities (p. 171).

There was thus a move towards regarding economic theories as models, which might or might not be related to the real world.

## C.  From the 1930s to the 1950s

In most accounts of the evolution of general equilibrium theory since Walras (including this reviewer's, in Backhouse, 1985) the story is told in terms of the progressive refinement and generalization of existence proofs, starting with Neisser, von Stackelberg, Schlesinger, and Wald in the 1930s, and moving on to Arrow and Debreu in the 1950s. Ingrao and Israel argue, however, that the picture is more complicated than this: that associated with the movement toward mathematical modeling there developed a split between "formal" developments in general equilibrium theory (proofs of existence and so on) and what they term the "interpretive" uses of the theory, these two aspects leading "parallel lives" (pp. 175, 290). The "formal" developments, they argue, were undertaken by mathematicians, including Wald, von Neumann, and others. The main interpretive models were those of Hicks and Samuelson: although the mathematicians provided formal rigor, it was "the assimilation and the methodological filter provided first by Hicks and then by Samuelson" that gave general equilibrium theory its "unchallenged key position" (p. 178). That this was a split and not merely a division of labor is suggested by Morgenstern's very critical response to Hicks's *Value and Capital.*

Ingrao and Israel also discern an important split between different approaches to the formal analysis of general equilibrium theory, with Wald lying on one side, and von Neumann and Debreu on the other. Though Wald was concerned with axiomatization and formal proof, he used what were essentially traditional methods including differential calculus. In addition, he was prepared to work with restrictions on the properties of aggregate excess demand functions which, though they might have a clear economic interpretation, were, from the point of view of the theory's axioms, essentially arbitrary (they were not derived from restrictions on individual utility functions). Furthermore, Ingrao and Israel argue, Wald's paper "effectively blocked" further research along such lines (p. 209). Advance was possible only by resorting to new methods: by using convex analysis instead of differential calculus, characterizing equilibria using separation theorems instead of tangencies. This approach was introduced by von Neumann and was taken to its extreme by Debreu. It was associated with an even deeper split between the formal and interpretive uses of the theory.

In Debreu's interpretation, general economic equilibrium theory thus loses even its status as a "model" to become a self-sufficient formal structure. The theory's concepts are no longer viewed as the result of a process of abstracting from real phenomena; nor as the formalization of "ideas and knowledge relating to a phenomenon," to use E. Malinvaud's definition; and still less as requiring legitimation through empirical verification. The use of the formal structure as an interpretive schema for concepts referring to the world of real phenomena is both possible and suggested but does not form an integral part of the theory itself (p. 286).

It was Debreu who pushed von Neumann's axiomatic approach to its extreme, adhering completely to the canons of the "modern formalist school of mathematics" (p. 303), his choice of axioms producing a "steroetyped and simplified version [of Walrasian theory] free of all problems of an empiricointerpretive nature" (p. 304).

Though these different strands can be identified, they are not completely unconnected. Arrow, for example, collaborated with Debreu, and yet also worked with Hahn in an attempt to provide a new systematization bringing together the interpretive and formal aspects of the theory (Arrow and Hahn, 1971).

## D.   The Achievements of General Equilibrium Theory

The book ends with a discussion of the past thirty years, during which time the ever-present gap between the aims and achievements of formal general equilibrium theory seemed about to close, providing answers to the paradigmatic problems of existence, uniqueness, and stability. "These answers," Ingrao and Israel claim,

open up the way to verification of the validity of the aims the theory has pursued since its birth and comparison of its objectives and achievements (p. 289).

After reviewing the period's literature, they conclude that Debreu's results on existence constitute an advance on previous results. They have, however, been achieved at the cost of removing from the theory any interpretive significance it may once have had: unlike the models used by Walras, Hicks, and Samuelson, the Arrow-Debreu model cannot be conceived of as referring to any real economy. Furthermore, work since the 1960s has shown that in the fields of uniqueness and stability, there are no comparable existence results to be obtained: it has been proved that the axiomatic approach can, as Debreu has consistently recognized, get nowhere. Ingrao and Israel thus draw the conclusion that the research program has failed to achieve the objectives it set for itself.

We feel it is possible to conclude that the mathematical analysis of general economic equilibrium theory in the context of the classical hypotheses as codified by Debreu's axiomatization has led to one clear result. There is a contradiction between the theory's aims and the consequences derived from the system of hypotheses constituting its structure, and hence a contradiction between aims and hypotheses within the theory. The only way out of this situation is to jettison explicitly the programmatic central core that has been so carefully preserved throughout the many paradigmatic shifts (pp. 361-362).

They go on to argue that the way forward is not through "partial adjustments' or "to lower the level of analysis and clarification," but is through "a *thorough* re-examination of the theory's basic hypotheses" (p. 362).

It is helpful to compare this conclusion with the important recent statements by two leading general equilibrium theorists. The first is Debreu's 1990 presidential address to the American Economic Association (AEA) (Debreu, 1991). This is best described as an apologia for formal axiomatic theory. The phase of "intensive mathematization" of economic theory (which he dates from 1944) will, he declares, "have no successor" (Debreu, 1991, p. 1). He refers to "dazzling mathematical developments" and an "already long" list of advances. He does not, however, either give examples or state the criteria that form the basis for these judgements.

In appraising the mathematization of economic theory, Debreu refers to three, related, criteria: (1) ceteris paribus, one cannot prefer less to more rigor, lesser to greater generality, or complexity to simplicity (Debreu, 1991, p. 5); (2) it is desirable to have weaker assumptions, stronger conclusions and greater generality (Debreu, 1991, p. 4); and (3) the mathematics used should stand on up on its own. The importance he attaches to this last criterion is shown by his remark that theories should "pass the acid test of removing all the interpretations and letting the mathematical infrastructure stand on its own" (p. 3).

His only concessions are to admit that the critiques of mathematization offered by Leontief (1971) and Gordon (1976) are still relevant, and that "many members" of the AEA consider the costs of mathematization to outweigh its benefits. His only response to these criticisms, however, is to describe the professional pressures that make it difficult to change the course of the subject's evolution!

A different perspective, and a more detailed prediction than any provided by Ingrao and Israel, has been provided by Frank Hahn, who has predicted that "theorizing of the 'pure' sort will become both less enjoyable and less and less possible" (Hahn, 1991, p. 47):

It so happens that it is becoming ever more clear that almost none of them [the crucial questions facing the discipline] can be answered by the old procedures. Instead of theorems we shall need simulations, instead of simple transparent axioms there looms the likelihood of psychological, sociological and historical postulates.

He cites difficulties inherent in the concepts of rationality and profit-maximization, the history-dependence of equilibria and the need to allow for learning, and transactions costs and increasing returns, all of which cause problems for formal, axiomatic theory.

It is revealing to note that Debreu comes close to conceding that such methods may be appropriate in physics:

> physics did not completely surrender to the embrace of mathematics and to its inherent compulsion toward logical rigor. The experimental results and the factual observations that are at the basis of physics, and which provide a constant check on its theoretical constructions, occasionally led its bold reasonings to violate knowingly the canons of mathematical deduction (Debreu, 1991, p. 2).

Economic theory, however, is "denied a sufficiently secure experimental base" and as a result, "has to adhere to the rules of logical discourse and must renounce the facility of internal inconsistency" (Debreu, 1991, p. 2). In other words, Debreu seems to be saying that a pure, axiomatic approach, with all that this implies, must be adopted because, for reasons that he does not even discuss, let alone analyze in detail, economics cannot have an empirical basis.

## E.   Conclusions

It should by now be clear that *The Invisible Hand* is, in this reviewer's opinion, a very important book that is essential reading for anyone wishing to understand the nature and history of general equilibrium theory. This review has taken issue with few of the claims made in the book. In some cases, this is because this reviewer is not qualified to assess them (for example, their interpretation of the history of mathematics), but the main reason is that Ingrao and Israel are putting forward a very persuasive thesis: it makes sense of many aspects of the history of general equilibrium theory which otherwise do not fit into any interpretive scheme. There are, inevitably in a book of this scope, details with which issue could be taken (and with which other reviewers may well take issue). There are one or two passages where the exposition is not always completely transparent, though taken as a whole the argument is beautifully clear and the quality of the translation appears to be excellent. There are some places where it is possible to quarrel with the emphasis. For example, though their analysis was not "formal" in quite the sense in which Ingrao and Israel use the term, it might be argued that Lindahl (whose name is consistently spelled incorrectly) and other members of the "Stockholm school" made, relative to Hicks, a greater contribution to the conceptualization of general equilibrium than Ingrao and Israel give them credit for. These are, however, minor issues.

The book's reinterpretation of the closing decades of the eighteenth century, and its emphasis on developments in France, should be placed alongside Terence Hutchison's recent work (Hutchison, 1989). Together, they have the effect of reminding us that the filiation of ideas that is commonly stressed in histories of economic thought, though it constitutes one important strand, is not the only one. To focus on it alone gives a distorted effect of the whole fabric: one might wish to suggest that there was a "Smithian" as much as a "Ricardian" detour.

Turning to the nineteenth century, *The Invisible Hand* is valuable as providing further evidence against Mirowski's theses. The evidence that abstract general equilibrium theory has roots that go back well before the rise of energetics runs counter to Mirowski's first genetic thesis. Similarly, instead of seeing neoclassical economics as botched physics, those responsible for its development not having a proper understanding of physics—Mirowski's second genetic thesis (Walker, 1991, p. 618)—we find economic theory being developed by "good or even outstanding mathematicians" and by "scholars with a perfect mastery of mathematical formalism" (p. 177). Thus, although Mirowski is right in arguing that economists have wanted to emulate physics, and although Ingrao and Israel provide further evidence for this, their main, very convincing argument is that it is developments in mathematics, not physics, that have been the most important determinant of the way general equilibrium theory has developed.

When it comes to appraising contemporary economic theory, Ingrao and Israel carefully document the failure of general equilibrium research program to achieve its own objectives. This raises the question of what implications this has for neoclassical economics, the research program of which general equilibrium theory forms a part. In view of the great prestige attached to abstract general equilibrium theory, it would be natural to assume that the program's failure to achieve its objectives would be a matter of great significance. To make this assumption would, however, be a mistake. For all the prestige attached to working on general equilibrium theory, its relationship to workaday neoclassical theory (the theory that is used to tackle concrete problems) is very tenuous.

The simplest relationship between general equilibrium theory and workaday theory would be that between a general theory and various special cases. Once theorems had been proved for the general model, they could be used to demonstrate existence, uniqueness, and stability in simpler models. If this were the relationship between general equilibrium theory and less abstract theory, the failure of the general equilibrium program would be significant, though it would not be a disaster. Failure to prove the stability of an equilibrium, for example, is not the same as proving instability (which would be much more serious): it just means that stability has to be proved case by case.

The link between general equilibrium theory and workaday theory is, however, much weaker than this. Many (most?) of the models economists use in tackling "real-world" problems are not special cases of, say, the Arrow-Debreu model. Markets are often taken to be incomplete; agents are not fully, or even symmetrically, informed; there is uncertainty; and so on. Theorems relating to the Arrow-Debreu model have no direct bearing on such models. Thus, while general equilibrium theory may have failed to achieve its own objectives, this does not imply a failure of the broader program of which it forms a part.

This leaves the question of where we go from here. Very sensibly, Ingrao and Israel offer no instant remedies. Like Hahn, they point out the failings of pure axiomatic theory and they see a need to reexamine the foundations of the subject. The value of their approach is that, unlike many critics of general equilibrium theory, they see the value of rigorous arguments: formal, axiomatic theory has dispelled many illusions about what could be achieved in this area. Their overriding thesis, that the evolution of the subject has been determined by the demands imposed by the search for mathematical rigor, would seem clearly to vindicate Alfred Marshall's fears about the consequence of pursuing mechanical analogies, and of not keeping mathematics under control. If we accept, as Debreu appears to do, that economics cannot be an empirical subject, then there would appear to be no objection to letting the shape of economic theory be determined by the demands imposed by the available mathematical techniques. But if economics cannot be an empirically based discipline, does it matter what we do? To this reviewer, Hahn's conclusion seems more appropriate than Debreu's: it is imperative that economics does not become divorced from reality, even if this means that we are deprived of the beauty and the excitement that can be derived from a pure, axiomatic approach.

# REFERENCES

Arrow, Kenneth J., and Frank Hahn. 1971. *General Competitive Analysis.* Edinburgh, UK: Oliver and Boyd.

Backhouse, Roger. 1985. *A History of Modern Economic Analysis.* Oxford, UK: Basil Blackwell.

Debreu, Gerard. 1991 "The Mathematization of Economic Theory." *American Economic Review* 81(1): 1-7.

Gordon, Robert A. 1976. "Rigor and Relevance in a Changing Institutional Setting." *American Economic Review* 66: 1-14.

Hahn, Frank, 1991. "The Next Hundred Years." *Economic Journal* 101(1): 47-50.

Hutchison, Terence W. 1989. *Beyond Adam Smith.* Oxford, UK: Basil Blackwell.

Leontief, Wassily. 1971. "Theoretical Assumptions and Non-observed Facts." *American Economic Review* 61: 1-7.

Mirowski, Philip. 1984. "Physics and the Marginalist Revolution." *Cambridge Journal of Economics* 8: 361-379.

_____. 1990. *More Heat than Light.* Cambridge: Cambridge University Press.

Schumpeter, Joseph A. 1954. *History of Economic Analysis.* New York: Oxford University Press.

Walker, Donald A. 1991. "Economics As Social Physics." *Economic Journal* 101: 615-631.

CONTEXTUALIZING EQUILIBRIUM THEORY
by
E. Roy Weintraub

Bruna Ingrao and Giorgio Israel have written an important book. The arguments they construct, and the approaches they develop, are likely to engage historians of economics for a long time to come. My review will attempt to substantiate this appraisal.

General equilibrium theory, or equilibrium theory, is the centerpiece of what we now call neoclassical economics. Philosophers of science use this structure as a benchmark for measuring all kinds of assertions about the cognitive status of economic theories. Critics of neoclassical economics, from neo-Austrians to neo-Ricardians, from post-Keynesians to neo-Marxists, from neo-Institutionalists to radical feminists to no-growth environmentalists, all launch their attacks on "mainstream" economics with an examination, usually highly critical, of the nature and structure and limitations of general equilibrium theory.

With such eagle-eyed attention directed to the current instantiation of that theory in the assumptions, models, and mathematical formalizations taught to current students in the neoclassical mainstream, it is surprising that the history of that theory is not well developed in any systematic fashion. That is, while there is a substantial "Walras industry" and "Pareto industry," while early Classical general equilibrium theory has been presented in a developmental narrative, and while there have been portions of the later history addressed through examinations of proofs of existence of equilibrium and of dynamical theory, there has not been a sustained historical treatment of modern general equilibrium theory.

That said, I must point out that another recent book, Philip Mirowski's *More Heat Than Light* (1989), likewise develops a history of neoclassical economics and its general equilibrium core. That book has been and will be examined in other reviews, but let me here simply point out the primary historiographic difference, that while Mirowski is concerned with the interconnections between neoclassical economics and nineteenth-century physics, for Ingrao and Israel, "Our thesis is that the problem of mathematization is no secondary feature of general equilibrium theory but is rather one of the basic reasons for its creation and development" (p. x).

This leads to their two major historiographic points: first, that "the practice...of dealing separately with the history of economic ideas and with the theory's formal (i.e., mathematical) features must be abandoned" (p. x). Second, "one should take as the object of historical analysis the development of the theory...[and] the consequence of this is that one must consider a number of fields: the history of economic ideas, the history of mathematics and physics, the history of philosophy or sociological thought, and so on"

(p. xi). But before examining the fruits of this mode of writing history in economics, let me turn to the book, sketch its scope, and take up with some specificity a number of points.

Chapter 1 presents the theory itself. That is, the authors here exhibit the modern version of general equilibrium theory, its Debreu model form. The idea seems to be that since the book will concern a "theory," let the reader see its modern form, as if the history will lead "up to" that nouvelle-Debreu model. The chapter sets up an endpoint as it were, an end of history. We are set then to ask, Where did this edifice come from? and, How did it come to take this form and not another?

Chapter 2, "The Origins," looks at the Classical period, particularly emphasizing the spread of Newtonian ideas in France, a point well-established in the history of science and philosophy literatures. The authors examine the pre- and post-Physiocrats, and tell interweaved tales of mathematics, politics, and scientific literacy. Given the authors' extensive scholarly reach, I am somewhat surprised to find no reference here to Walsh and Gram's *Classical and Neoclassical Theories of General Equilibrium* (1980), the only modern lengthy treatment of the theories of which I am aware. Chapter 3, on Walras's forerunners, continues this early history and examines particularly Isnard, Canard, Depuit, and Cournot; the discussion of these writers is informed by their writings and linked by a surfaced awareness of the context, mathematical and philosophical, of their work.

The next chapter, on Walras, is an intertwined history, biography, and close reading of the relevent texts. In this chapter, we see most of the themes that were to emerge as problems for the later theoretical analyses. This chapter is paired with the next on Pareto, Walras's successor at Lausanne, which is a very well-researched history. Pareto is placed in an educational milieu of engineering in Northern Italy, and what he read and studied, and who he heard lectures from, are taken as influential in his intellectual development: the break with the Comptean perspective is recorded and explored. The authors present, in good detail, the various strengths and weaknesses in the nascent equilibrium program as it faced the criticisms of contemporaries.

To my own taste, chapter 6, "Economists and Mathematicians," is the most engaging history to be found in the book. The various doctoral theses, effective propaganda for the Lausanne school's perspective, provide a window on what historians of mathematics call "reception theory," the study of how a theory was received in the mathematical community. Opening with a discussion of Jacques Moret and the defense of his thesis before the law faculty of the University of Paris, this chapter details the confused and often bizarre interactions between Walras and the European mathematical and scientific giants. Walras's self-promotion, and his efforts to gain a hearing for his ideas, were continually dashed by opponents like Bertrand. The book reviews which so fazed Walras are all here, as are the letters in which he attempted to gain some measure of attention. The wonderfully rich story of Walras's overtures to Poincaré, and the misunderstandings which ensued, led to what the authors call a dialogue of "total incomprehension." The doctoral students and theses done in the Walrasian mode provided some solace, but it was not until the mathematicians Volterra and Picard seemed to agree with him that mathematical methods were appropriate in political economy that Walras felt some measure of vindication. The authors conclude that this reception of the theory led to a focus on particularly mathematical problems of existence and stability of equilibrium, and that this redirection was to lead away from France, with its concerns with the classical physics, toward Austria and Germany, where the axiomatic mathematization of physical problems was to be developed. The argument, that the French were hostile to mathematical modeling for a variety of reasons, is the fundamental contingency which reshaped the general equilibrium theory in its next stage of life. Of course, the European emigration to the United States was to be the second accident of history in the theory's life, but of that more anon.

The next three chapters are really a set of interlocked stories. They take up, respectively, equilibrium theory in Vienna, in England, and in the United States. This, of course, is too simple but if we use the names von Neumann, Hicks, and Samuelson the story is a bit more traditional. The authors do a nice job setting the stage for the rooting of the ideas in the Vienna of Karl Menger's *Mathematical Colloquium*. This is introduced by a prescient excerpt from Volterra, and leads to Hilbert's *Gottingen*, and the formalist program which was von Neumann's beacon at that time. The story of Morgenstern, Wald, and the first equilibrium existence proofs, is by now well known, but the authors have a fine eye for the interconnections among the principal actors. In England, the land of Marshall and Robbins, we are treated to a contextualization of Hicks's work which is clearly written and usefully linked to Austrian and Swedish authors. The chapter on "New Trends in the United States" begins with Irving Fisher, takes up Samuelson and his background, and leads through the Cowles group to the beginnings of game theory. Although the details of this history are in outline correct, the emphasis is a bit off, I think, in several regards. Samuelson's connection to the J. Willard Gibbs tradition through E.B. Wilson is noted, but not the Pareto influence through L.J. Henderson, Wilson, and the Harvard Pareto Circle which found its way to the Harvard Society of Fellows. These are well documented in the Wilson Archives at Harvard. Second, it is now becoming clear that von Neumann was thinking about game theory all through the 1930s, and Morgenstern's recollections are quite off the mark as to the theory's history. This came out with the examination of the Morgenstern Diaries at Duke University Library and the reconstruction of the von Neumann-Morgenstern collaboration in recent papers by Mirowski (1990), Leonard (1990), and Rellstab (1990) at a 1990 conference on the history of game theory.

This set of minor quibbles does, however, lead me to a bit larger point. The authors are weaker on American and English developments than they are on the French and Italian ones. That is, their reliance on secondary materials is greater the farther the contributions are from their homes. Now, this is not to say that the history is in any way unreliable, but rather that the breathtaking "thickness" of their chapter on "Economists and Mathematicians" set up expectations in this reader about what was to follow, and those expectations were not met. The 1930s material—these three chapters—is handled with care and thoughtfulness, a not so simple task as the story unfolds over two continents and in three languages. Nonetheless, these chapters are more interpretive studies of the historical record, less studious excavations or primary constructions of that record.

The last part of chapter 9, "New Trends in the United States," and the next three chapters on "Existence," "Uniqueness," and "Global Stability of Equilibrium," are rather different from the earlier chapters. In chapter 9, the authors take the story up nearly to the present, with a good discussion of Debreu and the new directions in which he took the theory. His connections to the Bourbaki group in France are discussed too schematically for the nonmathematician, but alert the careful historian to a number of issues too often missed in the elided formulation "Arrow-Debreu model." Debreu and Arrow are not as similar, nor are their concerns as easily meshed by an en dash.

It is, however, in the final three chapters on the developments of the last thirty years, the 1960s to the present, that the book takes on a different character, and is ultimately less successful. The material, while interestingly arranged, is in survey form and has hardly any historical sensibility in evidence. It is pleasant to end a history with an overview of the present state of the ideas in play, but in this case there is too much of a break with the earlier chapters. It is an issue of audience, really. Historians will not be engaged by this ending, and historically minded theory graduate students, if it is they who are addressed, will not be much interested in such a sketchy survey of all that is recent in general equilibrium theory.

How does the Ingrao and Israel book differ from what historians of economics have seen before? For my taste, this is the kind of book that general equilibrium deserves, that Walras and Pareto would have liked to see. General equilbrium theory is presented not as an economic theory but rather as a mathematization of the core insights of a generalized social science concerned with interdependence and equilibrium, coordination and stability. The historiographic point which introduced their concerns, that the history could not be separated from the mathematics, is too often lost on those misled by the Marshallian nonsense of writing in mathematics, translating to prose, and erasing the mathematics. Marshall, a Second Wrangler at Cambridge whose entire educational career was devoted to solving arcane and contrived problems in applied mathematics and mechanics as set by his mathematics coach, provided advice which must not be taken seriously. Neither should one do more, as historians, than laugh at the sonorous capstone to Samuelson's *Foundations of Economic Analysis* (1947), the quotation from Willard Gibbs that "Mathematics Is A Language." This kind of silliness allows the uneducated to think that doing mathematical economics is a matter of translating ideas from economics into mathematics, or applying specifically mathematical ideas to identifiably economic problems.

In fact, mathematics is a social activity, done in groups, in the same sense that doing economics is a social activity, located in a community. The mathematics community and the economics community share some values and language, and there are many connections between them. Writing a history of general equilibirum theory, a theory which has linked the concerns of those two particular communities by the idea of a mathematical economics, requires sensitivity to both communities. The mathematical ideas are just as alive as are the economic ideas, and using ideas from G.D. Birkhoff's dynamical systems theory is not a matter of taking a hammer and nail off the shelf to fasten two boards together. A better metaphor is the taking of some clay off the shelf to make a mold of a hammer and nail, all the while pretending that one's old newspapers are boards. We economists are always singing "If I had a hammer...." Mathematical ideas form economic ideas, and the resulting ideas are interpreted and reinterpreted in a veritable cascade of rerepresentations of contingent realities. The history which respects this intertwining has a more coherent narrative structure, is truer, more honest, and more useful than a history which insists that mathematics was "applied" to economics, and which assumes that the economic idea can be separated from its mathematical formulation.

Ingrao and Israel write history, which is true in this sense. Their accounts link stories of mathematicians confusing economists, teaching economists, and talking past economists. But better, they tell stories in which mathematics and economics are brought together in a culture which longs to marry them, to have a real scientific economics, which meant, both in the last century and in our own, a mathematical economics. Historiographically, Ingrao and Israel are wondrously attentive to the intertwined histories of mathematics and economics. They are not as sensitive as Mirowski is to the relationship of economics with physics, but their understanding that mathematics, in the last century, was usually applied mathematics—which means mechanics in fact— keeps them well focused on the interesting issues. I am less happy with their narrow interpretation of equilibrium itself.

That is, in the latter part of the last century, and through the 1930s certainly, the notion of equilibrium moved through a number of fields of thought and inquiry. Biology, physiology, and sociology all had their equilibrium systems, analogous to economists' general equilibrium systems. Some of this is spelled out in the now-classic *The Concept of Equilibrium in American Social Thought* by Cynthia Eagle Russett (1966). What this really tells us is that drawing a fence around economics will not do; putting mathematics inside the grounds as Ingrao and Israel do is better, and putting physics inside as Mirowski does is better, but best of all is to put everything inside and trace the interconnections and underlying structure of thought which manifests itself in the equilibrium theorizing of all the different disciplines and discourses.

This, of course, is a book not yet written. To be sure, Walsh and Gram wrote a part of it, Russett wrote a chunk of it, Mirowski has written a big part of it, I have written parts of it (1985, 1991), Norton Wise has written parts of it (1989a, 1989b, 1990), and now Ingrao and Israel have written a major part of this work. We who think about these issues are in their debt; I now use their book in my Economic Thought course, and it is well-received by students, who too will be in their debt.

One final observation: this book is a translation from the Italian original *La Mano Invisibile*, which appeared in 1987. I do not read Italian, but can affirm that this work in English reads well. The writing is graceful and the prose is, as Jacques Barzun would have it, simple and direct. The translator is Ian McGilvray, and he should be pleased by the result of his efforts.

# REFERENCES

Leonard, Robert. 1990. "Creating a Context For Game Theory." Mimeograph, Economics Department, Duke University.

Mirowski, Philip. 1989. *More Heat Than Light.* New York: Cambridge University Press.

―――. 1990. "What Were von Neumann and Morgenstern Really Up To?" Mimeograph, Economics Department, Duke University.

Rellstab, Urs. 1990. "On the Collaboration Between von Neumann and Morgenstern." Mimeograph, Economics Deaprtment, Duke University.

Russett, Cynthia Eagle. 1966. *The Concept of Equilibrium in American Social Thought.* New Haven: Yale University Press.

Samuelson, Paul A. 1947. *Foundations of Economic Analysis.* Cambridge: Harvard University Press.

Walsh, Vivian, and Harvey Gram. 1980. *Classical and Neoclassical Theories of General Equilibrium.* New York: Oxford University Press.

Weintraub, E. Roy. 1985. *General Equilibrium Analysis: Studies in Appraisal.* New York: Cambridge University Press.

―――. 1991. *Stabilizing Dynamics: Constructing Economic Knowledge.* New York: Cambridge University Press.

Wise, Norton, with Crosbie Smith. 1989a. "Work and Waste: Political Economy and Natural Philosophy in Nineteenth Century Britain (I)." *History of Science* XXVII: 263-301.

―――. 1989b. "Work and Waste: Political Economy and Natural Philosophy in Nineteenth Century Britain (II)." *History of Science* XXVII: 391-449.

―――. 1990. "Work and Waste: Political Economy and Natural Philosophy in Nineteenth Century Britain (III)." *History of Science* XXVIII: 221-261.

THE INVISIBLE AGENDA OF *THE INVISIBLE HAND*
by
Timothy L. Alborn

In their newly translated book on the history of mathematical economics, Bruna Ingrao and Giorgio Israel cite Leon Walras's recollection of his father's assertion, in 1858, that "two great tasks remained to be accomplished in the nineteenth century: to finish creating history and to begin creating social science" (p. 87). This assertion might serve as a paraphrase of Ingrao and Israel's programmatic aims in the book: to finish creating the history of economic thought and to begin creating economics anew. In the first of these two great tasks, they join a growing number of economists, historians of science, and general historians who have lately begun to locate the history of economics in wider scientific and social contexts. In the second, they join with other heterodox economists in an increasingly vocal expression of discontent against the methodological foundations of modern economic theory. Finally, by attempting to accomplish both goals in the same book, they add to the already-notorious effort of Philip Mirowski, in *More Heat than Light*, to perform historical revision and methodological reconstruction in the space of a single narrative (Mirowski, 1989). As in *More Heat than Light*, the result in *The Invisible Hand* is both stimulating and problematic. Although Ingrao and Israel's invective lacks Mirowski's flair, they will likely prove the more effective polemicists through their penetrating rereadings of classic economics texts and painstaking efforts to unearth forgotten figures: their light outshines Mirowski's heat. But after reading either book, the reader is left with the unsatisfying question, what next? Whereas Mirowski at least provides a promised research program and long footnote to answer that question, Ingrao and Israel coyly retreat to the neutral ground of the historian and claim that such larger issues go beyond "the expository nature of the book" (p. 359). They offer the economist few pointers for moving from a historical and logical deconstruction of general equilibrium theory to a more constructive critique.

Ingrao and Israel's reluctance to show their hand methodologically also mars their approach to historiography. They defend their choice to avoid discussing historiography with the offhand comment that "we see historical analysis as our immediate priority and share the old view that those who can, do, while those who can't, study pure methodology" (p. xi). This is indeed an old view, and it is poorly suited to the expressly *methodological* aims of the book. When old-fashioned historians (including many historians of economics) spurn the new-fangled obsession with [historians (including many historians of economics) spurn the new-fangled obsession with] historiographical candor, they most often do so because it challenges their unstated premise that a single consensus should dictate all historical work. But when the point of a book is to take issue with the consensus, as in *The Invisible Hand*, what purpose does it serve to stifle historiographical debate from the outset? In the case of Ingrao and Israel, the only purpose seems to be to make things more difficult for the reader, since they do seem to be following a consistent model for organizing their narrative: a model that can be found, in more schematic form, in the historiographical writings of Thomas Kuhn.

When Ingrao and Israel claim, in their subtitle, to place economic equilibrium in the history of science, what they are really doing is placing it in the matrix of normal and abnormal science as established in Kuhn's *The Structure of Scientific Revolutions* (Kuhn, 1970). This matrix has appealed to methodologists before, who have wielded Kuhn's classic as a sort of talisman against the excesses of the neoclassical orthodoxy (for a review of this literature, see Blaug, 1975). In the past, these applications of Kuhn have been intended as a means of nudging unreformed neoclassicals into admitting that their paradigm is in trouble; he is carted in to preside over a sort of wishful last rites ceremony which, of course, will never actually take place until orthodox economists stop and pay attention. Such uses of Kuhn are, among other things, less than faithful to the style and substance of *The Structure of Scientific Revolution*, which has received attention from historians of science less as a programmatic assault on the practice of "normal science" than as a generally sympathetic, and somewhat faulty, description of how science makes legitimate progress. Ingrao and Israel have managed to combine a more faithfull application of Kuhn with the same old wishful thinking that an exposé of inconsistencies in neoclassical economics will somehow bring the whole edifice down. Like Kuhn, the authors of *The Invisible Hand* admire normal science's capacity to turn out results, assembly-line style; like the other economists who have utilized Kuhn, they also draw attention to the inevitable tendency of the general equilibrium paradigm to crumble beneath the weight of an embarrassing array of anomalies. This makes for an ambitious, but not entirely consistent, narrative: much of *The Invisible Hand* is torn between praising the early developers of equilibrium theory for keeping their eyes open to a variety of possible outcomes and frowning on them for failing to be "normal" enough.

Ingrao and Israel position the first half of their story in the intellectual space separating economics conceived as descriptive of the real world and economics conceived as the study of idealized manifestations of life under pure competition. This "dialectic between the descriptive and the normative approaches," they claim early in the book, was "a leitmotiv throughout the historical evolution of general equilibrium theory" (p. 52). The descriptive-normative dialectic also informs the authors' idealized psychological portrait of the social scientist, who "finds it repugnant that his knowledge should be limited to the description of what exists and not cover also the clarification of the rules to be introduced or respected so as to ensure that man, society, or the economy behave in accordance with criteria of rationality (however defined)" (p. 48). They treat this repugnance as a dormant trait in economists, which sees daylight under circumstances that Kuhn would describe as "abnormal science." In practice, "abnormal science" appears in *The Invisible Hand* whenever Ingrao and Israel are able to detect the presence of a set of social or political values in the intellectual production of an economist. Hence, we find Quesney calculating ideal national production rates, Condorcet hoping to apply probability theory to jurisprudence, Walras employing mathematical economics in the service of "the reforming aims of the French petit-bourgeois" (p. 99), and Pareto "immersed...in a many-sided and ill-defined ideology" (p. 123); but at the same time, all these economists are also depicted as holding out for empirical content. As long as Ingrao and Israel can find evidence for this dialectic, which they do for most of the earlier thinkers, their strategy allows them to occupy a middle ground between critical onlookers like William Jaffé who discover "normative distortion" in Walras, and hagiographers like Schumpeter who disregard all ideology in their rush to dub Walras and Pareto as neoclassical pioneers.

In their survey of (mostly French) mathematical economics in the eighteenth and nineteenth centuries which occupies the first half of the book, Ingrao and Israel exhibit a variety of economists bouncing between the normative and descriptive poles of social thought. They assume that the revolutionary events of late-eighteenth century France helped break down the disciplinary boundaries separating Newtonian physical science from social theory. Revolutionary politics, in their Kuhnian account, paved the way for a series of fruitful but problematic attempts to combine scientific culture and social intervention, most of which were no more successful at surviving the Terror than was Condorcet himself. Ingrao and Israel similarly account for the relative absence of mathematical economic models in the generations separating Condorcet and Walras by implying that once French society settled down, physicists and economists parted ways to pursue mutually exclusive "normal" versions of their work. Without providing much detail, they suggest an almost conspiratorial rejection of the social applications of mathematics by the social thinkers at the Académie des Science Morales et Politiques, and a happy return to the nonmathematical "natural law" approach to political economy practised by the *Ideologues* and J.B. Say. These developments are crucial, since they lead up to the dilemma that for Walras, "the only way to develop the mathematization of the social sciences was not by attempting to construct a science with an autonomous status and equal dignity but rather by referring to the only 'legitimate' and 'official' model"—namely, classical physics (p. 58).

This dilemma sets up what might be called the tragedy of Walras, as outlined by Ingrao and Israel: how Walras borrowed his mathematical program from physics only to be spurned by the scientists when he appealed to them for legitimation. The authors' historiography serves them well in discussing this episode. By taking Walras's political agenda seriously, they are able to show how his fascination with the normative premises of economics prevented him from communicating with the French scientists whose support he desired. This is especially well illustrated in a detailed reading of the correspondence between Walras and Henri Poincaré in 1901, in which Walras brushed aside Poincaré's serious doubts about the empirical justification of supposing "unlimited foresight" on the part of economic agents. As Ingrao and Israel rightly observe, Walras translated Poincaré's empirical misgivings about equilibrium theory into a political puzzle: the problem, for Walras, was "no longer than of bearing in mind that men are not infinitely farsighted but *making them become so*" (p. 160, emphasis in original). In general terms, what is going on here is that Walras, whose ideological motivations cast him in the mode of "abnormal science," was courting praise from a *normal* scientist *par excellence*. Instead of receiving encouragement for his creative ambitions to mix empirical economics with political persuasion, he found himself in an "alien and suspicious world" full of scientists who refused to abandon their strict standards of empirical verification (p. 147). Ingrao and Israel conclude that the empirical difficulties and normative wishful thinking that marred Walrasian economics were more the result of intellectual isolation that methodological malaise. It appears that Walras asked the right questions, but nobody was around who cared to help him find answers. (I might add then the failure of Pareto's research program, which receives something of a parenthetical chapter in *The Invisible Hand*, is diagnosed along very similar lines: as an ambitious synthesis that falls victim to intellectual and cultural isolation.)

The second half of *The Invisible Hand* switches gears from the frustrating follies of the early neoclassicals to the exhilarating progress of the twentieth-century economists and mathematicians who translated equilibrium theory into an axiomatic form. This progress might be compared with the ascent of a hot-air balloon: the paradigm takes off once the sandbags of wished-for syntheses between normative and descriptive economics are tossed over the side. Ingrao and Israel spend the final six chapters of the book studiously charting the balloon's increasing altitude and intermittently worrying whether it will ever return to earth. They start this part of the story in the 1930s, when, they write, "[general equilibrium] theory's fortunes among the professional public of economists as a heuristic model of competition broke cleanly away from the evolution of its mathematical apparatus. The two separate lives did, of course, meet and intermingle during certain periods of fruitful exchange, but long stretches of their histories ran on separate parallel lines" (p. 175). An enormous amount of historical research on these separate lives of applied economics and formal theory is crammed into three chapters' worth of narrative covering four decades and as many different geographical contexts.

Three further chapters are devoted to a detailed exposition of equilibrium theory in its present form and a critique of its shortcomings.

Ingrao and Israel's account of the development of economic equilibrium theory since the 1930s follows a straightforward path. They first examine the game-theory approach to economics taken in Vienna by John von Neumann and Oskar Morgenstern, who ravaged the original Walrasian paradigm and spent little time worrying about real-world relevance. Then they discuss how the ground was paved for the acceptance of the theory, by examining the programmatic efforts of Hicks and Hayek in England and of Samuelson and Schumpeter in the United States. These economists are presented as integrating axiomatic methods into the mainstream of professional economics by inconsistently expressing their theories in language that made an axiomatic equilibrium theory *seem* relevant to a host of social questions. To return to my previous metaphor, people like Hicks and Samuelson benefited in a big way by keeping a few sandbags in the hot-air balloon: by continuing to provide glimpses of normative vision and possible empirical application, they established themselves as certifiable leaders of modern neoclassical economics. Only once their fellow economists had gotten used to the slightly higher altitude was it possible to jettison the rest of the sandbags, which is exactly what Gerard Debreu did in this *Theory of Value* (1959). After a summary of this work, Ingrao and Israel take their history up to the present by critically reviewing the recent attempts by Arrow and Hahn, among others, to bring the now thoroughly airborne theory of economic equilibrium back within sight of the real world of economic activity.

In their chapter on von Neumann and Morgenstern, Ingrao and Israel treat the reader to a lively discussion of the "unified science" movement which swept Vienna in the 1930s and which realized Walras's dream of cooperation between economists and physicists. Ironically, they argue, physicists only deigned to pay attention to economics once their own discourse had been purged of much concern for empirical relevance. By calling for the application of formal methods of *all* sciences, the unified science movement made it easier for physicists to discard Poincaré's empiricist misgivings in favor of a rigorous mathematical approach to economic phenomena. Although much more work needs to be done connecting what Ingrao and Israel blithely call "the crisis of physics" and the early stirrings of economic equilibrium theory, they seem to be on the right track here. What they *have* accomplished is a compelling reading of how certain eminent mathematicians like Hilbert and Weyl transmitted a penchant for formal logic to game-theory pioneers like von Neumann. What remains to be done is to discover more prescisely what "scientific culture" (an oft-used and seldom-defined entity in *The Invisible Hand*) really looked like in Vienna between the wars.

Ingrao and Israel turn from the high theory back to the more mundane task of discipline-building in their next chapter-and-a-half, in which they move swiftly through Marshall, Robbins, Hayek, and Hicks in England, and Fisher, Schumpeter, Samuelson, and Arrow in the United States. They deftly discuss how Hayek and Hicks, at the London School of Economics, tried to combine Marshall's respect for dynamic macroeconomic problems with Walras's abstract static representation of market activity. They argue that this attempt, which resulted in Hicks's pioneering work on temporary equilibrium, ultimately failed to tie up all the loose ends left behind by Walras and Pareto. Next stop is the United States, where economists like Fisher and Samuelson learned to respect mathematics from their undergraduate science teachers, then tried to apply models from classical physics to real-world economic problems. Samuelson, in particular, is taken to task for repeating Walras's mistakes by trying to wish away empirical problems while appealing to a physical model that was obsessed with empirical demonstration. Both the British and American efforts at mathematical economics are presented as falling between the cracks of formal rigor and empirical application; the only thing people like Hicks and Samuelson were really good at, it turns out, was generating support for their research programs. As Ingrao and Israel conclude about Hicks, "a methodological attitude that may even appear confused and somewhat lacking in rigor...in fact operated as a vehicle for the diffusion of general equilibrium modeling through wider circles of economists" (p. 243).

Hicks and Samuelson, and all the characters in between, perform the function of an opening act in this part of the story. Their job, in effect, was to soften up the audience of professional economists so that the headliner, Gerard Debreu, could enjoy a better reception for his more rigorous and empirically less relevant version of equilibrium theory. In a book devoted to exposing the flaws of the theory, Debreu might seem an unlikely hero. But his central place in the book makes sense, given the underlying tension that impends most of the narrative waiting to be resolved. As Ingrao and Israel move from one imperfect version of equilibrium theory to the next, the implication seems to be that if only people would get the theory right, they would see how wrong it really is. Debreu (who, incidentally, is thanked in the acknowledgements for his input on *The Invisible Hand*) receives the authors' sincere admiration for his role in speeding up the process: they report that his "rigidly analytic and general approach has, Socrates fashion, acted as a midwife for mathematical results that are disconcerting—to say the least—and that no economic interpretation has yet managed to subdue" (p. 280). To their credit, they do not simply present Debreu as a knight in shining armor. Instead, he is placed in the historical context, shared by Arrow and others, of the Cowles Commission, which marked an attempt to place the game-theory approach to economic equilibrium at the service of post-New Deal government planning. But at least with Debreu, this context is just window dressing for his real importance to the book: as a point of departure for a meticulous methodological dissection of the theory itself, focusing on its proof of the

existence, uniqueness, and global stability of economic equilibrium. (For thos
of you keeping score, the theory receives a "quite satisfactory" on the first point
mixed marks on the second, and an "unquestionably negative" on the third
see pp. 360-361).

Once Ingrao and Israel sail off into the waters methodology, the narrativ
structure that drives the rest of their book breaks down. They spend most o
the book either offering the reader scenic tours of promising roads not taker
or speeding down the highway of modern theory. In the last three chapters
this action comes to a halt and the authors appear, Nostradamus-style, witl
a lengthy pronouncement that the end (of the paradigm as well as the book
is near. The problem with this strategy is that Ingrao and Israel fail to delive
on their most basic millenarian task: to provide a hint at what the end wil
look like. They reject, wisely, the instrumentalist notion that it is possible t
go back to the roads not taken, concluding that economists must pursue "fa
different approaches" than Walras and Pareto took, "reductionism being nov
a thing of the past" (p. 362). But what these approaches might be is left cloake
in the vague call for a renewed synthesis between normative and descriptiv
concerns. This problem is compounded by the sincere respect which Ingra
and Israel consistently pay to the formal achievements of modern theory. Larg
sections of *The Invisible Hand*, taken out of context, will make a great dea
of sense to the most dyed-in-wool neoclassical, who will have no compunctio
about ignoring the final three chapters' worth of the same kind of argument
he or she has always managed to ignore before.

It is, of course, unduly severe to expect a full-blown alternative theory, o
perhaps even a blueprint for such a theory, neatly poised at the conclusio
of what is mainly presented as an historical narrative. Ingrao and Israel canno
add an epologue on the appearance of a theory that has not yet appeared
But it is not out of line to stress that they might have spent much more tim
pursuing the implications of their history which, as the saying goes, raises man
more questions than it answers. Perhaps the most compelling questio
emerging from *The Invisible Hand* involves the place of formalism in a futur
paradigm shift. In a recent review in this journal (Lavoie, 1990), it was suggeste
that the single-minded focus on positivism in present-day economics needs onl
to be tempered, not discarded, and the "formalistic prowess" needs only t
take its place beside a plurality of different methods. This would mean, amon
other things, reforming the rewards system presently practiced by th
economics profession and more generally relaxing the pressure to conform tha
is the defining trait of "normal science." Ingrao and Israel, who are anxiou
to retain the logical rigor of formalism even as they stress the need fo
economists to pay attention to the real world, barely pause to consider thi
possibility. They call for "a true paradigmatic revolution" (p. 362) but the
idealistically, and perhaps unrealistically, hope for that revolution to b
bloodless.

# REFERENCES

*laug, Mark. 1975. "Kuhn versus Lakatos or Paradigms versus Research Programmes in the History of Economics." *History of Political Economy* 7:399-433.

*uhn, Thomas. 1980. *The Structure of Scientific Revolutions*. Chicago: University of Chicago Press. (orig. 1962).

*avoie, Don. 1990. "Woo's *What's Wrong with Economics?*" Pp. 000-000 in *Research in the History of Economic Thought and Methodology*, Vol. 7, edited by Warren J. Samuels. Greenwich, CT: JAI Press.

*Mirowski, Philip. 1989. *More Heat than Light. Economics as Social Physics: Physics as Nature's Economics*. Cambridge: Cambridge University Press.

## THE PARADIGM IS THE PROBLEM: GENERAL EQUILIBRIUM THEORY AND THE INVISIBLE HAND
by
Charles J. Whalen

n 1974, E. Roy Weintraub (1974, p. 7) began his *General Equilibrium Theory* with the observation that "general equilibrium analysis is at the very centre of economic theory." Nearly two decades later, general equilibrium theory GET) is still an indispensable tool for most economists. Indeed, in the wake of recent scientific and policy developments leaving macroeconomics in disarray, GET is seen by some as their profession's only remaining "core concept."

Despite the centrality of GET, few works have focused on its history. As Weintraub (1983, p. 2) wrote in the *Journal of Economic Literature*:

> By all reasonable criteria general equilibrium analysis defines a coherent body of thought as fully articulated as Keynesian economics. Yet the historical material associated with the latter runs to the tens of thousands of pages, while that of the former hardly exists in an organized fashion. Nobel Laureates Arrow, Hicks, Klein, Koopmans, and Samuelson are all associated with this tradition, yet narrative histories of general equilibrium analysis rarely proceed beyond Walras and Pareto. The history of neo-Walrasian analysis is in the footnotes of current contributions, or in sections titled "Notes on the Literature" in modern treatises.[1]

With *The Invisible Hand: Economic Equilibrium in the History of Science*, Bruna Ingrao and Giorgio Israel—an economist and mathematician, respectively—attempt to fill this void in the literature.[2] Moreover, their effort is quite successful—*The Invisible Hand (IH)* is likely to be the definitive volume on GET for some time.

### A. Themes

Ingrao and Israel integrate a number of themes into their work. Indeed, some of these are woven into the foundation of the volume and thus help shape the entire effort. For example, they argue that "mathematization is no secondary feature of GET but rather one of the basic reasons for its creation and development" (p. x). Therefore, they insist upon a historiographic approach that permits consideration of the important links between mathematical developments and GET.[3]

Another theme is that GET has always been an interdisciplinary body of thought, one cutting across academic "fields" as defined in both the past and present. Thus, the authors seek to "take as the object of historical analysis the development of the theory ... without dissecting and isolating partial aspects and thereby losing sight of an overall interpretive key" (p. xi). Indeed, this helps explain the volume's subtitle—the "history of science" is not merely shorthand for the history of economic thought.

A third theme is that GET's development has often been influenced significantly by the scientific, philosophical, and cultural environment in which its contributors worked. This causes the authors to endeavor "to bring out and recognize the importance—the centrality even—of contacts and interaction between scientific culture and economic and social disciplines in the theory's development" (p. 35). In fact, they suggest that GET originated in the eighteenth century as

> one of the positive responses to the question, "Is it possible to apply or to adapt the methods of inquiry that have proved so effective in the physicomathematical 'exact sciences' to the study of man's moral, social and economic behavior?" (p. 33).

Still another theme is that the history of GET has not been "deterministic." The authors view this history as "long and tormented" (p. 1) and explain early in their first chapter that "it would be contrary to our intentions to present an image of the theory's historical development as monotonous progress toward its present form" (p. 3). Indeed, they state that "*one of our main aims* is to bring to light the nature of the often markedly different paradigms involved in the development of GET" (p. 3, italics added).

A related "thread running through the whole work" is what Ingrao and Israel call "the dialectic between the normative and descriptive viewpoints" toward GET (p. xii). In short, the authors explain that the *purpose* of GET has undergone nearly as many changes as the theory itself. For example, some have viewed GET as a product of empirical observation; others have interpreted it as an ideal norm; still others have seen it as the first step (or "first approximation") toward a description of reality; and yet another group has argued that GET is devoid of all empirical reference, "receives meaning only within its own logicoformal framework and should evoke no concrete images" (p. 285). Moreover, these developments have neither been cumulative nor have they produced a present-day consensus on the utility of GET.

A final theme is that "the recognition of the existence of different (or even conflicting) research programs in scientific development does not rule out the existence *also* of a process of accumulation of discoveries" (p. 3). Thus, *IH* shows that

> the highly different and even divergent programs (or paradigms) that succeed one another in the history of the theory <u>retain an almost intact core</u> that can be identified with the aim to demonstrate the *existence*, the *uniqueness*, and the *global stability* of the equilibrium (p. 3, underline added).

Moreover, it is the existence of this "invariant paradigmatic core" (p. 360) that permits the authors to conclude their volume by moving beyond historiography and into the realm of assessment. The conclusions of this assessment will be considered in a moment. First, however, it is necessary to offer a brief summary of the volume's historical account.

### B.  From Montesquieu to Saari

Ingrao and Israel begin their account in eighteenth-century France. There Newtonian physics was the scientific model for scholarly communities. Indeed, Newton's empirical viewpoint and natural-law philosophy combined to offer many intellectuals a point of reference for attempts to renew their entire society. Moreover, the intellectual climate was full of enthusiasm for efforts to use mathematical concepts in conceiving and representing knowledge throughout the sciences.

In this environment, Charles L. Montesquieu offered—in an analysis containing both descriptive and normative elements—what is perhaps the first conceptual analogy of social and mechanical equilibrium. This was soon followed by both Francois Quesnay's "Tableau economique," which used hypothetical quantitative figures to guide economic behavior according to normative laws, and the Marquis de Condorcet's "mathematique social," which sought "not so much to describe social realities as to construct the rational rules that must regulate its correct and orderly functioning" (p. 49). While the mathematics of the "Tableau" was limited to arithmetic and geometry, Condorcet employed probability calculus. Moreover, "proceeding on lines directly parallel to those followed in mechanics and physicomathematics" (p. 51), the latter introduced the concept of "homo suffragans," an abstraction leading directly to the isolated human faculty of "homo oeconomicus."

After Condorcet, the use of mathematics in studies of social phenomena fell out of favor for more than a century. Nonetheless, attempts at mathematical economics—efforts "based on the methods of infinitesimal calculus" (p. 58)—were carried on by a few individuals during the late 1700s and throughout the nineteenth century. Members of this group making significant contributions to GET include Achylle-Nicolas Isnard, Nicolas-Francois Canard, Jules Dupuit, and, of course, Leon Walras and Vilfredo Pareto.[4]

The attention to Isnard, Canard, and Dupuit demonstrates that Walras's originality has often been overestimated. According to Ingrao and Israel:

> [T]he great novelty of his work in comparison with previous attempts to formulate a rational mechanics of exchange lay above all in his fusion of the equations of equilibrium borrowed from statics with a theory of value based on marginal utility, or *rarete* (p. 91).

They also note that

> [f]rom the outset, the interest shown by Walras in the theory of exchange value and even the formation of the idea of a general market equilibrium were motivated by the search for a rigorous demonstration of the superiority of free competition as a form of the organization of production and exchange (p. 98).

Thus, like Quesnay and Condorcet, Walras's theory offered a *"normative ideal* toward which the actual functioning of markets should be directed"* (p. 98, italics added).

Pareto introduced only slight changes to the formal structure of Walras's system of equations. His most important contributions involved a new purpose for, and approach to, GET. Walras's notion of a "normative ideal," for example, was rejected and replaced with the view that "pure political economy [i.e., Pareto's GET] offers a *first approximation* to [actual] phenomena by defining the general conditions for economic equilibrium" (p. 125, italics added). Thus, both the autonomy of economics and the abstraction of "homo oeconomicus" were defended, even as the need for "successive approximations" and a broader sociological synthesis was acknowledged.[5] Pareto's shift in approach, meanwhile, led him to two of GET's most significant developments:

> the explicit and motivated replacement—albeit not totally completed—of confused theories of utility with a closely delimited theory of preferences; and the first unambiguous formulation of an equally delimited theorem of the competitive optimum—Pareto's optimum principle—which was to play its part in all subsequent developments of GET (p. 124).

The modern era of interest in mathematical economics and GET began in the 1930s. Though some—and not just those on the "right wing" of the political spectrum—sought to fully resuscitate the theory's normative side, the two most important lines of research (from a historiographic perspective) involved more descriptive work by intellectuals in the United States and United Kingdom, and Austria and Germany, respectively. Among the most important figures in these groups were Irving Fisher (founder of the Econometric Society), John Hicks and Paul Samuelson, and John von Neumann, Oskar Morgenstern, and Abraham Wald.

In response to changes within physics, this new era involved a greater emphasis upon mathematical—versus mechanical—analogies and "the emergence of mathematical modeling" (p. 179). Indeed, while the Americans and British of the 1930s were interested in retaining a link between theory and reality, an axiomatic approach (along with more sophisticated mathematical techniques) was employed on the European continent often without regard for, or claim to, verisimilitude.

By the 1940s, immigration of talented European economists made America the center of GET work. Then, in the next decade, the (individual and collaborative) writings of Kenneth J. Arrow and Gerard Debreu offered a synthesis of existing research traditions. Those works offer a frame of reference for all subsequent GET studies, including investigations by contemporary scholars such as T.J. Kehoe, Stephen Smale, Herbert Scarf, and D.G. Saari.[6]

## C.  A "Dead End"

In the "Introduction" to *General Equilibrium Theory*, Weintraub (1974, p. 14) identified three questions as central to GET: (1) does a general equilibrium *exist* for a decentralized, market system (in which agents are motivated by self-interest and guided by price signals)? (2) is this equilibrium *unique*? and (3) is it *stable*? Ingrao and Israel agree with Weintraub. Indeed, as mentioned earlier, they view an attempt to respond affirmatively to each of these questions as the "invariant paradigmatic core" of GET.

Reflecting on the history of GET, the authors are not troubled by the first question. They write:

> The results achieved by Arrow and Debreu in the 1950s (and all the subsequent results obtained in the field of research opened up by them) demonstrate the existence of general economic equilibrium under very general assumptions and without any awkward restrictions. The assumptions are, in fact, those traditionally and fundamentally inherent to Walrasian theory (p.360).

The question of uniqueness, however, "presents a very different picture" (p. 360):

> It is quite clear that uniqueness theorems can only be obtained on assumptions so restrictive as to appear unacceptable. This has serious consequences as regards the possibility of a comparative-statics analysis (in Samuelson's sense [of global dynamics]) (p. 360).

Moreover, while Ingrao and Israel acknowledge that "opinions vary" on the implications of results concerning uniqueness, they maintain that the implications concerning global stability "are unquestionably negative" (p. 361). Further, the future of research in this area is said to look "anything but promising" (361). Thus, the authors conclude that GET has proven to be precisely what Pareto found late in his career—"a dead end" (pp. 135, 358-359). Since Ingrao and Israel believe it is clear that GET cannot achieve its central aims, they call for "a *thorough* reexamination" of the entire analysis, "i.e., a true paradigmatic revolution" (p. 362).

## D.   General Remarks

The above review of themes, content, and conclusions indicates that *IH* is a dense and complex volume.[7] Indeed, this reviewer's quick overview of the book's historical account is in some respects inadequate even as a schematic device. This book was not written—and will not be read—overnight.

After digesting this work, the reader is tempted to employ all the standard adjectives and phrases associated with lavish praise—"impressive," "tour de force," "a major scholarly accomplishment," "certain to be a classic in the literature." While all would be appropriate, they also seem a bit trite. Suffice it to say that while a successful volume offers at least one of three things—new insight, an integration of existing information, or an application of current knowledge—Ingrao and Israel offer all at once. Moreover, *IH is* the "meticulously researched work" promised in the jacket abstract. Further, it contains no major shortcomings of form, organization or style.[8]

The work's subtitle, however, is somewhat misleading. With a title of this sort, the subtitle becomes crucial. *Economic Equilibrium in the History of Science*, however, misses the mark a bit.

Both the history and current spectrum of economic thought contain a wide range of views toward the notion of economic "equilibrium." For example, there are various instantaneous, temporary, and long-period equilibria, partial and general equilibria, and even "structural" (versus "market") equilibria that require balance within an entire social system. Similarly, while neo-Austrians, Marxists, neo-Ricardians, post-Keynesians, Neoclassicals, and Institutionalists might all refer to "equilibrium" at some point, most are likely to attach meanings to the term that are very different from those used in competing movements. Economic equilibrium in the history of science—or equilibrium in the history of economic thought—is a topic worthy of a serious volume; but it is *not* the subject of *IH*. Adding the word "general" to the beginning of the existing subtitle would have yielded a significantly clearer and more accurate label.

Some might find the aforementioned matter insignificant. But this entire volume builds to a call for both a complete reexamination of GET and a paradigmatic "revolution." Moreover, GET is not just any paradigm; in many respects, it is *the* paradigm—the one that defines for many the meaning of fundamental terms such as *the economy, equilibrium*, and even *economics*. Thus, the fact that the history of thought offers a number of competing interpretations of a concept as central as equilibrium is not unimportant.

The remainder of this essay is devoted to a discussion of four matters—the limitations of GET, time and money, rigor versus relevance, and the seductive notion of an "invisible hand." Each is considered in turn.

## E.  Limitations of GET

As mentioned above, Ingrao and Israel are quite critical of GET. The authors are not alone, however. In fact, *IH* indicates clearly that major contributors to GET have often been among its toughest critics. Indeed, it could be concluded from this volume's discussion of the descriptive-normative "dialectic" that GET history itself leaves only the theory's "logical framework" (p. 183) interpretation unscathed.

Scholars interested in the development of views on the limitations of GET will find valuable quotes and other important material throughout *IH*. For example, it was Walras—not John Maynard Keynes—who observed that, in reality, "the market is like a lake agitated by the wind, where the water is incessantly seeking its level without ever reaching it" (p. 109).[9] Similarly, Ingrao and Israel remind us that Alfred Marshall saw equilibrium theory as "only an introduction to economic studies." Indeed, Marshall added:

> Its limitations are so constantly overlooked, especially by those who approach it from an abstract point of view, that there is a danger in throwing it into definite form at all (p. 415, n. 5).

Of course, one economist with an entirely "abstract" viewpoint is Debreu. Indeed, Ingrao and Israel observe that an introduction (by W. Hildenbrand) to a recently published collection of Debreu papers notes, "The axiomatic method ... has never been applied in economics as *forcefully* as by Debreu in his classic monograph *Theory of Value, An Axiomatic Analysis of Economic Equilibrium*" (p. 282). Moreover, as the authors themselves write, Debreu's approach involves

> emptying the theory [i.e., GET] radically and uncompromisingly of all empirical reference. As in Bourbaki mathematics, no matter how "colorful" the language may be, it is not supposed to suggest anything more than "intellectual" images and intuitions detached from any empirical interpretation (p. 285).

Debreu himself does not overlook the limits of his work. In fact, in *Theory of Value* he writes that "allegiance to rigor dictates" that the theory "is logically entirely disconnected from its interpretations" (p. 285). Yet Marshall's point about the danger associated with formal theory remains quite valid. As Ingrao and Israel note, "Debreu's rigid axiomatic interpretation has not had—nor could it have—a wide following among economists, [who regard contemporary

GET] ... primarily as a formalization of the old problem of the invisible hand" (p. 280).

In the end, though, the assumptions necessary to demonstrate the existence of general equilibrium—not to mention its uniqueness and stability—are out of the reach of actual economies. As Milton Friedman (1982, p. 120) acknowledged in *Capitalism and Freedom*, "there is no such thing as 'pure' competition"—and in the real world there cannot be, for it is merely an "ideal type." In addition, a host of factors cause some markets to fail and others (certain forward markets) not to exist. Moreover, the purposive nature of humans—who think, develop expectations, plan, learn, and reconsider preferences in a world of uncertainty (not merely risk) and calendar time—guarantees that the best we can hope for is life upon Walras's "agitated lake."

Thus, GET offers is a first step toward understanding existing economies, but it is a strange step, indeed. In particular, it merely involves looking

to see which of the features regarded as essential for a correct representation of the real world are in contradiction with the model's basic hypotheses and thus make the compatibility [i.e., equilibrium] affirmed in the theory impossible in real terms (p. 279).

In other words, GET theorists have turned weaknesses into strengths. Smale and Debreu, for example, have each indicated that *a major, positive feature* of GET is its ability to bring its own (descriptive and normative) shortcomings into focus (pp. 287-288, 351-352).

In the context of praising GET for its shortcomings, Debreu supports his position by recalling Francis Bacon's assertion that truth emerges sooner from error than from confusion. But Debreu's aims strike this reviewer as far too modest. For example, might not truth emerge even sooner from the *avoidance* of error? Moreover, should we not try to to *eliminate* error once it is detected? As Ingrao and Israel write, the problems addressed by GET researchers are "all in all, marginal questions.... The aim of defining a different and more satisfactory context [for economic analyses] backed by the relevant mathematical results appears not only remote but not even clear" (p. 305).

Smale goes further than Debreu and suggests GET can be useful as a point of departure for new analyses:

[E]quilibrium theory plays an important role in communication within the economic profession. Since most economists are knowledgeable in equilibrium theory, they can understand new ideas more readily when presented in that context (p. 351).

The problem, however, is that this approach offers very little once a researcher has concluded that what must be jettisoned are—as Ingrao and Israel correctly observe—the fundamentals of the "context" itself.

## F. Time and Money

Critics have often attacked GET for its treatment of time. Indeed, in its most developed, axiomatic form, GET is static and atemporal in that it reduces all economic processes "to a single act of exchange occuring in one place and at one instant" (pp. 5, 9). Tatonnement, meanwhile, is said to precede all economic activity and occur in "abstract" versus "real" time (p. 27). But heterodox scholars are not the only ones to criticize this aspect of GET. Indeed, in *Theory of Value* even Smale complains that "time has an almost artifical role" (p. 352).

Unfortunately, GET researchers have refused to recognize the full significance of moving from hypothetical to historical time. Thus, scholars like Smale have responded merely by attempting "to use a mathematics of a different kind" (in particular, a return to infinitesimal calculus and differential equations) (p. 353). Like Walras, many seem to have "absolutely no inkling of the radical difference between the purely virtual tatonnement of [an] ideal simulation and a sequential process of adjustment taking place in time and allowing exchange at other than equilibrium prices" (p. 106).[10]

Money is also a concept that cannot be treated adequately in GET. This theory has always taken the pure-exchange economy as its starting point. But money can never play a role of great significance if it is merely superimposed onto an economic system. Thus, in all of mainstream economics, money functions only as an exogenously determined facilitator of exchange.

The difficulties associated with treating time and money in GET are, of course, closely related. Indeed, there are two especially important connections. First, GET's inability to recognize the full role of money is a direct result of the theory's failure to accommodate calendar time. As both institutionalists and post-Keynesians have explained on many occasions, money arises endogenously in a private-property economy in which production takes time (and both uncertainty and the desire for accumulation exist).[11] Thus, as works by both Hicks, and Arrow and Hahn, indicate, money can play no essential role in GET because the latter "is not really *in time*" (Davidson, 1977, pp. 277-285; Ingrao and Israel, 1990, pp. 240-241).

Another important connection between GET's treatment of time and money is that an attempt to incorporate more realistic notions of these concepts is likely to clash with the theory's "paradigmatic core." Hicks acknowledged this in a note of November 1932, when he wrote, "The use of money is inconsistent with economic equilibrium" (p. 235). More recently, Arrow and Hahn (1971, p. 361) have confirmed this view: "in a world with a past as well as a future in which contracts are made in terms of money, no equilibrium may exist." In short, to move significantly beyond their existing approaches to time and money, GET researchers would have to abandon GET itself.

## G.  Rigor Versus Relevance

The foregoing discussion suggests that while GET may offer "a useful 'warming up' exercise for the muscles of scientific inquiring minds," it is best viewed as an intellectual exercise—"a good game"(Davidson, 1978, p. 8; Wiles and Routh, 1984, p. 14).[12] David Dale Martin (1980, p. 363) is correct, of course, when he writes that "economic theory is more useful to those who know its weaknesses than it is to the true believers." In the case of GET, however, "usefulness" does not extend to efforts involving either a serious description of reality or accurate prediction and policy analysis.

Why, then, have economists been so reluctant to reject—and move beyond—GET? Of a large number of possible reasons, two seem among the most significant. One—which returns us to one of the central themes of *IH*—involves the role of mathematics in economics; the other—which focuses our attention on what is perhaps *the* most fundamental preconception of conventional economics—involves the seductive nature of the invisible hand. The present section focuses on the former, and the next section considers the latter.[13]

Transforming economics into a "rigorously quantitative discipline, into a mathematical science on a par with astronomy and physics," has always been "a central programmatic aim" of GET researchers (p. 1). As indicated above, GET has its origins in the French Enlightenment, a period during which mathematization in physics "aroused new hopes and indicated new directions in all branches of knowledge" (p. 38).[14] Moreover, although mathematization of the social realm fell out of favor for a period after Condorcet's death, the status of "science" was granted solely to the physicomathematical disciplines. Thus, as Ingrao and Israel note, even then many remained convinced that the only way to develop political economy was "not by attempting to construct a science with an autonomous status and equal dignity but rather by referring to the only 'legitimate' and 'official' model" (p. 58).

A belief in the need for mathematical rigor to "legitimize" economics has remained with economists throughout the history of economic thought. Indeed, today the belief might even be felt more strongly than ever. In short, mathematization remains one of the "basic reasons" for GET's existence and development (p. x).

In light of the economics profession's long tradition of seeking to introduce as much rigor as possible into its theories, it is not surprising that economists are reluctant to scrap GET. But, as Robert Heilbroner (1968, p. 10) has noted, the prestige accorded to math has given economics "rigor, but alas, also mortis." Individuals not interested in emptying their analyses of all empirical content and practical relevance have no choice—they must move beyond GET.

Heterodox scholars have often criticized the relentless pursuit of mathematization in economics.[15] But well-respected orthodox economists have also expressed their concern over this matter. In fact, in the 1970s a number of prominent American and British economists delivered presidential addresses on the subject at major professional conferences.

Robert A. Gordon (1976, p. 1), for example, complained to the American Economic Association that "the mainstream of economic theory sacrifices far too much relevance in its insistent pursuit of ever increasing rigor."[16] John T. Dunlop (1977), meanwhile, maintained that most conventional economic models and theories are intellectually exciting, challenging, and irrelevant to both policy making and vital practical concerns. G.D.N. Worswick (1972), E.H. Phelps Brown (1972), and Wassily Leontief (1971) have all made similar points. None called for an end to mathematical economics, only that, as Gordon (1976, p. 12) wrote, "our credo be: 'relevance with as much rigor as possible,' and not 'rigor regardless of relevance.'" Unfortunately, many of their colleagues were unwilling to go even this far.[17]

### H.  The "Invisible Hand"

Finally, we come to GET's philosophical cornerstone, the "invisible hand" concept. As Ingrao and Israel demonstrate, GET was erected upon—and remains wedded to—the eighteenth-century image of self-regulation. Indeed, the authors conclude that GET "is a theory of the 'invisible hand'" (a conclusion reflected in the very title of their work) (p. 361).[18]

The notion of a self-regulating social system is quite attractive. It is especially attractive to believers in a supreme being, advocates of individual freedom, and students of history's many economic-planning failures. It is also attractive to those seeking simple rules for public policy. Indeed, if an actual or obtainable economic structure were shown to possess the capacity to attain equilibrium on its own, the economist's job would be simply "to describe these laws of self-regulation, i.e., to discover their form and demonstrate their validity" (p. 331).

Moreover, the image of market self-regulation (conceived in either descriptive or normative terms) is not insignificant. In fact, as Ingrao and Israel note, many economists would agree with Arrow and Hahn's suggestion that this idea is "the most important intellectual contribution" of economic thought (p. ix). Thus, since GET is seen as "the culmination" (p. 330) of efforts to express self-regulation in analytic form, it is understandable that economists are reluctant to move away from this theory.

In short, like the relentless pursuit of a "rigorous" science, the search for a theory consistent with the preconception of self-regulation prevents economics from advancing beyond GET.[19]

### I.  Beyond GET

The study of GET offered by Ingrao and Israel leads to two fundamental conclusions. One is that GET is incapable of either describing reality or serving as an effective public-policy guide. Instead, it is perhaps best considered an exercise in logic. To offer more—by seeking to incorporate a more realistic view of market structures, time, and money, for example—is to reject GET.[20]

The other conclusion, however, is that many economists have objectives that *prevent* a rejection of GET. Mathematization and the preconception of an invisible hand, for example, are not secondary features of GET. Thus, it is likely that GET will be an indispensable part of the "tool kit" of most economists for some time to come.

Some economists will argue that the "real" reason why this form of economics has survived is that there is no alternative. As Oliver Hart (in Wiles and Routh 1984, p. 189) wrote recently, "Only when a real alternative to neoclassical theory becomes available can economists be expected to abandon it."

But mainstream economics is *not* the "only game in town." Indeed, as mentioned above, there are many competing schools of thought—and a variety of approaches to defining *equilibrium, the economy*, and *even economics*. Further, some of these approaches have a long—and, in many ways, respectable—history. Moreover, even if there were no satisfactory alternative to GET (and many may indeed find the existing alternatives unsatisfactory), the position that Hart represents seems a bit disingenuous: how can any significant alternative ever "become available" in an environment that discourages—even penalizes—those seeking to move beyond the received theory?

Perhaps Ingrao and Israel will convince a number of economists to abandon GET and work toward the development of a more "satisfactory" alternative. This reviewer, however, is not optimistic. It is more likely that *IH* will be ignored by those who would benefit most from reading it.

Nonetheless, I hope I am wrong. It has been nearly a century since Thorstein B. Veblen (1919, p. 70) wrote: "There is the economic life process still in great measure awaiting theoretical formulation." Unfortunately, while practical problems mount, not much has changed in the realm of theory.[21] Ingrao and Israel can contribute to a reversal of this tendency if their audience is listening. They have done their part. The rest is up to us.

## ACKNOWLEDGMENT

The author would like to thank Dawn Feligno and Linda Whalen for their assistance, and his colleagues Geoff Gilbert, Scott McKinney and Bill Waller for comments on an earlier version of this review.

## NOTES

1. Today, of course, one would have to add Gerard Debreu to Weintraub's list of Nobel Laureates associated with GET.

2.   Bruna Ingrao is Associate Professor of Economics at the University of Sassari and Giorgio Israel is Associate Professor of Mathematics at the University of Rome. Their volume builds on both a 1985 article by the authors and ideas exchanged at a 1986 Research Workshop organized by the European University Institute.

3.   In the opening sentences of chapter one, Ingrao and Israel write:

From the outset it has been the aim of the theory whose historical development, main achievements, and state of art are chronicled in this book to use mathematics as its basic tool in describing and analyzing economic reality. This was not a secondary feature but a central programmatic aim: to transform economics into a rigorously quantitative discipline, into a mathematical science on a par with astronomy and physics. In more modern terms—and with a certain shift in meaning—this aim would be defined as the transformation of economics into a "formalized science" (p. 1).

4.   While Montesquieu, Quesnay, and Condorcet are discussed in chapter 2, the contributions of Isnard, Canard, and Dupuit are considered in chapter 3. Walras and Pareto, meanwhile are discussed in chapters 4-6.

5.   Late in his career, Pareto concluded that "homo oeconomicus" stood as an *obstacle* to any attempt at closing the gap between theory and reality. As a result, herejected the artificial separation of human behavior implicit in economic theory—and turned instead toward sociology. Economists, however, "ignored his self-criticism and had no wish to follow his new lead" (p. 136).

6.   Chapters 7-12 of *IH* focus on twentieth-century developments in GET (with chapters 10-12 emphasizing developments since 1950).

7.   It is also a rather long book, with 362 pages of text and nearly another hundred pages of endnotes.

8.   The fact that this volume was wirtten in Italian (it was first published in Italy in 1987) presents no problem—a tribute, perhaps, to the translation work of Ian McGilvray.

9.   Walras added:

Such is the continous market, which is perpetually tending toward equilibrium without ever actually attraining it, because the market has no other way of approaching equilibrium except by groping, and, before the goal is reached, it has to renew its efforts and start over again, all the basic data of the problem, e.g., the initial qualities possessed, the utilities of goods and services, the technical coefficients, the excess of income over consumption, the working capital requirements, etc., having changed in the meantime (p. 109).

10.   As Ingrao and Israel note, some equilibrium theorists have sought to "escape from the straitjacket of tatonnement" and allow price adjustment "during which transactions between agents are permitted." One of the best-known works here is the "Hahn-Negishi theorem of global stability of non-tatonnement." However,

This provides a process of price adjustment converging at equilibria ... at the price of the very strong assumption that the markets are "orderly" at all times. [Frank H.] Hahn himself has more than once pointed out the restrictive nature of this assumption, which takes back with one hand the realism given with the other: "the assumption that markets are at all times orderly and the retention of the auctioneer casts doubt on the realism and relevance of [this] approach" (p. 343).

A 1976 work by Smale suffers from a similar shortcoming (p. 354).

11.   For an excellent discussion of the endogenous approach to money, see Wray (1990).

Evidence of this view in the work of institutionalists—and in the writings of the so-called "grandfather of monetarism," Henry C. Simons—is presented in Whalen (1991).

12.  In Kuhnian terms, we would say that GET involves "puzzle solving," not "problem solving" (Kuhn, 1970, pp. 35-42).

13.  Another reason for not rejecting GET is worthy of a brief amount of attention. It involves Friedman's (1953) well-known essay on the methodology of "positive economics." In particular, Friedman's work seems to defend theories with unrealistic assumptions. As students of methodology are well aware, however, "Friedman's essay constitutes extremely weak methodological underpinnings" (Darity, 1984, p. 7). Whalen (1988, pp. 22-61) reviews much of this literature and related issues (including the fact that there is no such thing as an entirely "objective" economic analysis).

14.  Also playing an early and significant role in the mathematization of economics was the "strongly felt" need "for a quantitative representation of economic magnitudes for the purposes of approximate measurement" (p. 36).

15.  Some institutionalists, for example, argue that "it is better to have imprecise or approximate answers to the right questions than to have precise answers to the wrong questions" (Myrdal, 1977, p. 5).

16.  Gordon (1976, p. 3) was especially critical of GET.

17.  More recent works by these authors indicate that the profession has not changed since their addresses (see, for example, Leontief, 1983; Dunlop, 1988).

18.  Moreover, *IH* insists that the division of GET issues into categories of existence, uniqueness, and stability involves merely a "formal distinction" (p. 361). The matters are, in fact, intimately linked. Together—and only together—they permit GET to give analytic representation to the idea that

a force inherent to the market ... inevitably plots the economy toward a state in which the operations of the various economic agents become compatible (p. 330).

19.  For an optimistic discussion of the consequences of abandoning the self-regulation preconception, see Whalen (1992).

20.  As Philip A. Klein (1980, p. 880) wrote a decade ago, "In economics ... the [conventional] paradigm is not the solution—it is the problem."

21.  That is, relatively little effort has gone into the development of alternatives to orthodoxy—and nearly all of this work has been ignored by the mainstream.

# REFERENCES

Arrow, Kenneth J., and Frank H. Hahn. 1971. *General Competitive Analysis.* San Francisco: Holden-Day.

Darity, William, ed. 1984. *Labor Economic: Modern Views.* Boston: Kluwer-Nijhof.

Davidson, Paul. 1977. "Post-Keynes Monetary Theory and Inflation." Pp. 275-293 in *Modern Economic Thought,* edited by Sidney Weintraub. Philadelphia: University of Pennsylvania Press.

————. 1978. *Money and the Real World.* New York: John Wiley.

Dunlop, John T. 1977. "Industrial Relations, Labor Economics, and Policy Decisions." *Challenge* 20(May/June): 6-12.

————. 1988. "Labor Markets and Wage Determination: Then and Now." Pp. 47-87 in *How Labor Markets Work,* edited by Bruce E. Kaufman. Lexington, MA: Lexington Books.

Friedman, Milton. 1953. "The Methodology of Positive Economics." Pp. 3-43 in *Essays in Positive Economics.* Chicago: University of Chicago Press.

_____. 1982. *Capitalism and Freedom.* Chicago: University of Chicago Press.

Gordon, Robert Aaron. 1976. "Rigor and Relevance in a Changing Institutional Setting." *American Economic Review* 66(March): 1-14.

Heilbroner, Robert. 1968. "Putting Marx to Work." *New York Review of Books,* December 5, p. 10.

Klein, Philip A. 1980. "Confronting Power in Economics." *Journal of Economic Issues* 12(December): 251-276.

Kuhn, Thomas S. 1970. *The Structure of Scientific Revolutions.* Chicago: University of Chicago Press.

Leontief, Wassily. 1971. "Theoretical Assumptions and Nonobserved Facts." *American Economic Review* 61(March): 1-7.

_____. 1983. "Foreword." Pp. vii-xi in *Why Economics is Not Yet a Science,* edited by Alfred S. Eichner. Armonk, NY: M.E. Sharpe.

Martin, David Dale. 1980. "The Uses and Abuses of Economic Theory in the Social Control of Business." Pp. 351-365 in *The Methodology of Economic Thought,* edited by Warren J. Samuels. New Brunswick, NJ: Transaction Books.

Myrdal, Gunnar. 1977. "The Meaning and Validity of Institutional Economics." Pp. 82-89 in *Economics in Institutional Perspective,* edited by Rolf Steppacher, Brigitte Zogg-Walz, and Harmann Hatzfeldt. Lexington, MA: D.C. Heath.

Phelps Brown, E.H. 1972. "The Underdevelopment of Economics." *Economic Journal* 82(March): 1-10.

Veblen, Thorstein B. 1919. *The Place of Science in Modern Civilisation and Other Essays.* New York: Viking Press.

Weintraub, E. Roy. 1974. *General Equilibrium Theory.* London: Macmillan.

_____. 1983. "On the Existence of a Competitive Equilibrium: 1930-1954." *Journal of Economic Literature* 21(March): 1-39.

Whalen, Charles J. 1988. "Beyond Neoclassical Thought: Economics from the Perspective of Institutionalists and Post Keynesians." Unpublished Ph.D. dissertation, Economics Department, University of Texas at Austin.

_____. 1991. "Money and Credit in Capitalist Economies: A Review." Paper presented at the Western Social Science Association Annual Meeting, April 27.

_____. 1992. "Schools of Thought and Theories of the State." In *The Stratified State,* edited by William Dugger and William Waller. Armonk, NY: M.E. Sharpe.

Wiles, Peter, and Guy Routh, eds. 1984. *Economics in Disarray.* Oxford, UK: Basil Blackwell.

Worswick, G.D.N. 1972. "Is Progress in Economic Science Possible?" *Economic Journal* 82(March): 73-86.

Wray, L. Randall. 1990. *Money and Credit in Capitalist Economies: The Endogenous Money Approach.* Brookfield, VT: Edward Elgar.

# LINDBLOM'S *INQUIRY AND CHANGE:* THE TROUBLED ATTEMPT TO UNDERSTAND AND SHAPE SOCIETY: REVIEW ESSAYS

*Inquiry and Change: The Troubled Attempt to Understand and Shape Society*
By Charles E. Lindblom.
New Have: Yale University Press, and New York: Russell Sage Foundation, 1990
Pp. xii + 314.

## CHANGE WITHOUT DIRECTION: PRAGMATIC PROBINGS WITHIN CONFLICTUAL SETTINGS
by
James M. Buchanan

*Inquiry and Change* is a challenging book, even if its central theses are somewhat obscured by stylistic ambiguity and frequency of careless assertion. Clarity and analytical rigor are not to be expected in any such broad-based attack on the conventional wisdoms in social science. As a sometimes, but continuing, critic of these wisdoms, I share with Lindblom important elements of his attack. But my differences may, in some final balancing, overweigh elements of agreement. These differences stem, in part, from the fact that, in his reckoning of accounts, agreement may be irrelevant in any case.

Research in the History of Economic Thought and Methodology, Volume 12, pages 153-168.
Copyright © 1994 by JAI Press Inc.
ISBN: 1-55938-747-5

153

Lindblom categorically rejects the whole of the modern economists' enterprise, which models the problem of economic order as a continuing search for more efficient solutions, defined as closer approximations to the satisfaction of the interests, preferences, and values held by individuals, given the available resource constraints. The key element in this enterprise is the conceptual separation between that which is to be achieved (maximized), which may be called "utility," "satisfaction," or "$X$," and the manipulation of the means that is aimed at such achievement (maximization). Lindblom rejects this analytical structure for choice, and he suggests that the ends of action do not exist at all independently of the process of selection. There exists no prior ordering of alternatives, whether these be described as commodity bundles or social states. Individuals, as they confront opportunities, create their own orderings of the emerging alternatives in the process of choosing.

The jettisoning of the orthodox model in this respect has profound implications for any effort by outside observers to be of assistance in the resolution of choice problems, at any and all levels. If individual orderings do not exist prior to choice, but are, instead, discoverable only through choice, how can choice alternatives be evaluated externally, even by some omniscient and benevolent authority? Lindblom discusses the inquiry that precedes choice in terms of the activity of *probing* which is, finally, truncated by some rather arbitrary stopping rule that may be localized to the setting.

I have no quarrel with this criticism of orthodoxy. I note only my surprise that nowhere is there reference to the work of G.L.S. Shackle.

Lindblom is not primarily interested in individual market choice. His emphasis is on the process of inquiry, of probing among the possibles, in settings that necessarily require some collective selection from among mutually exclusive alternatives, as these are again to be discovered in the probing process itself. As his subtitle indicates, his concern is with attempts "to understand and shape *society*" (italics supplied). On many critical issues, knowledge is not and cannot be sufficient to generate agreement and, indeed, the sources of disagreement are not appropriately attributable to failures in knowledge, as such. Lindblom's thesis is that, in such settings, persons are brought into agreement on beliefs by a process that involves deliberative effort by elites to impair free and open inquiry by members outside the self-anointed.

In this part of his discussion, Lindblom's argument would have been improved by some effort at clarifying the nature of the beliefs upon which agreement is expected to emerge. In this context, it is helpful to distinguish between *interest* and *theory* components of initial attitudes or preferences.[1] If persons initially disagree on some issue that requires the selection of one from among a mutually exclusive set of alternatives, such disagreement may reflect differences in interests, even if we accept (with Lindblom) that these interests may not be fully articulated until the act of selection itself. In this setting, agreement may emerge from a generalized process of "exchange," or compromise, with each party acquiescing in some ultimate departure from his/ her separately expressed volition. In this process of settlement among competing or initially conflicting interests, each of the parties may seek to persuade others, and efforts at persuasion may include impairment of the sort Lindblom seems to have in mind. An example: Dormitory roommates must agree on a single setting for the thermostat. The senior (the elite), who likes it hot, may, indeed, seek to impair the probing inquiry of the freshman (the nonelite), who likes it cold, but who is naive in the college culture. Here, talk is perhaps primarily a means of persuasion, a means to secure convergence in attitudes toward those possessed by the elite.

Consider, however, an alternative setting in which initial disagreement stems, not from some difference in interests but, instead, from a divergence in *theory*, defined as a model of how the world works. Here, discussion need not involve efforts on the part of one party to further identified interest at all but, instead, may be concentrated on the sharing of knowledge with others. Again, a dormitory example: Both students seek the comfort of a seventy-degree room. But the senior, who has experience, "teaches" the freshman that the eccentric thermostat must be set at a reading of sixty degrees to achieve the commonly desired result. In such a situation, the usage of Lindblom's elite/nonelite terminology is highly misleading and tends to prejudice analysis seriously toward an exaggeration of conflictual elements in social interaction. Lindblom's stance throughout the book reflects this prejudice and leads him to question the potential efficacy of the whole educational and scientific process in language that is frequently akin to Marxian diatribe.

If, indeed, conflicts are as pervasive as Lindblom's discussion seems to imply, it is difficult to construct a model for a viable social order at all. In this case, the next step would seem to be one that calls for radical constitutional revolution, one that reduces dramatically the number of interrelationships among persons that require collective action. If members of particular groups sense that their own volitions are systematically thwarted and that their efforts at expression are impaired by the dominating influence of some elite, exit alternatives must come into consideration and devolution, secession, depoliticization, and privatization take on relevance and importance.

Rather surprisingly, these terms rarely, if ever, appear in Lindblom's discussion. His almost exclusive emphasis is on making "voice" most effective, as opposed to making "exit" more viable, to employ both of Hirschman's descriptive terms here. Lindblom's policy agenda includes measures designed to reduce the impairment of inquiry by increasing the potential competition among ideas and by modifying the institutional structure of transmission. Perhaps more significantly, however, Lindblom urges the abandonment of the continuing search for consensus in the face of conflicts among beliefs. He seems willing to put up with much that economists would label to be inefficient and wasteful in exchange for the putative stability of muddling through. Also, he expresses little concern for the imposition of outcomes on the persons and groups who actively seek the rejected alternatives. In this, the most provocative subthesis of the book, Lindblom rejects the usage of agreement, for either criterial or epistemological purpose. The absence of concern for individual liberty, here as in earlier Lindblom works, makes my own philosophical curiosity beg for some articulation of the underlying political philosophy, for some insight into the structure of Lindblom's own utopia.

While, as previously noted, I share with Lindblom much of his basic criticism of the conventional wisdom in economics, I remain more positive in my evaluation of the contributions of social science, past, present, and future (and particularly economics), to the resolution to the continuing problems of maintaining a social order that functions tolerably well. Hardheaded scientific analysis can prove of immense use in our jointly pursued inquiry into the predicted working properties of alternative structural rules, alternative constitutions within which we interrelate one with another to play out the social game. Also, the acknowledgement of such usefulness does not, in any way, carry as a corollary the adoption of the scientistic mindset that imagines the amenability of social problems to solutions by science.

I shall illustrate the distinction here by reference to a simple, and currently familiar, example of economic policy choice. Should Japan open up its internal market to allow the importation of rice from other countries? There is no scientific answer to this question, and economists who have invoked the standard efficiency norm in the name of science surely have confused the issue. Only the members of the Japanese society, operating through their own institutions from which collectively generated decisions emerge, can resolve the issue, one way or the other, on criteria of their own. Nonetheless, in their varying deliberations on the issue, the Japanese may find it useful to consult the findings of economic *science*, both analytical and empirical. A Japanese electorate that is scientifically informed can be expected to make a "better" decision, by criteria of their own selection, than an electorate that is scientifically illiterate.

By implication, Lindblom would seem willing to accept the outcomes emergent from a pluralistic struggle among competing interests, along with the imposition of the winners' interests upon the losers, so long as the process of inquiry remains open to all participants on roughly equal terms. Somewhat surprisingly, perhaps, Lindblom's stance becomes anticonstructivist in the extreme, placing his position well beyond that of Hayek along this dimension.

Lindblom's role as radical social critic, as opposed to the critic of social science, emerges only in his discussion of impairment, which seems to dominate his ultimate concern in this book. As noted above, he classifies most public, and much private, discourse as effort by some ruling elite to control the mindset, and through this the actions, of those persons beyond the pale. I have several problems with this thesis. First, why does the individual member of a large-number elite engage in costly effort to impair the inquiry of others? The classic PD or public goods dilemma remains, and Lindblom offers no argument for a resolution peculiar to this setting. Second, by what criteria is it determined whether or not inquiry is being impaired? We may, of course, acknowledge that each and every person, from peon to professor, and whether or not a claimant to membership in an elite, probes among alternatives with a mind that is preconditioned by his/her many dimensional heritage. The mind is not, cannot be, a tabula rasa, to which all conceivable options appear as if newly imagined and for the first time observed. Persons are mentally as well as physically constrained by natural forces, including those of history and tradition. Perhaps our minds are often too narrowly confined to the consideration of alternatives that are nearby and familiar, and perhaps the whole realm of education, rhetoric, and social science tends toward a reinforcement of that which is rather than that which might be. But if we are to seek improvement through an opening of our imagination to things not dreamt of in our philosophy now, how does this focus for improvement square with the anticonstructivist stance that Lindblom adopts elsewhere? Finally, and relatedly, how do we distinguish between impairment of inquiry and the transmission of truth, the point illustrated in the dormitory example introduced earlier?

Neutrality between truth and falsehood is morally reprehensible, and it is morally irresponsible to confer legitimacy on such neutrality. Communism cannot produce goods, maintain individual liberties, and secure equality. Surely, after 1989, this statement must be acknowledged to have a higher truth content than its opposite. Is it not then irresponsible to infer that nonimpaired inquiry should remain neutrally blind in the face of historical and scientific evidence that can be helpful, although never decisive, in some final choice among alternative institutional orders? To me, Lindblom skirts very close to the edge of such irresponsibility in such statements as the following:

> the media are not impartial between, say, advocacy of communism or *dirigiste* authority and that of capitalism, or between revolution and gradualism, or even between advocacy of legal street demonstrations and advocacy of political action restricted to voting (p. 103).

What, ultimately, is Lindblom's counsel? Open up our minds, all minds, to allow for the imagination of alternatives that we have failed to consider. But, at the same time, expect little or nothing from the social scientists who claim that their analyses allow us to winnow the romantic from the real. Radicalize thought, but beware of subjecting it to discipline. Dream large dreams, but put up with what emerges from the pluralistic muddling through that describes modern Western society. Accept that which is, so long as all interests are allowed entry and inquiry is not impaired.

My own counsel is critically different, although with some relevant intersections. Radicalize thought, subject to the constraints of scientific discipline. Dream large, but *feasible*, dreams. And hold fast to the faith that we can, through the appropriate use of our critical intelligence, *reform* the structure of our institutions to produce a "better" world, defined in terms of standards that we commonly share. But, beware of coercively imposed "solutions" to alleged "problems," whether in the name of science, theology, or pragmatic practicality.

## NOTE

1. For two papers that discuss the distinctions between these components see Vanberg and Buchanan (1989, 1991).

## REFERENCES

Vanberg, Viktor, and James M. Buchanan. 1989. "Interests and Theories in Constitutional Choice." *Journal of Theoretical Politics* 1(January): 49-62.
————. 1991. "Constitutional Choice, Rational Ignorance and the Limits of Reason." Mimeograph, Center for Study of Public Choice, George Mason University.

## CHARLES LINDBLOM'S ESSAY ON INQUIRY AND CHANGE
### by
### Kenneth E. Boulding

Charles Lindblom is one of the most remarkable interdisciplinary scholars in the social sciences on the American scene. Originally trained in economics, he and co-author Robert A. Dahl ventured into political science in a celebrated book, *Politics, Economics and Welfare* (1953). It is still a classic in the field of the study of American political institutions, which, however, Lindblom somewhat repudiates in *Inquiry and Change* (p. 191). The present volume is a product of a lifetime of interdisciplinary study and thought on social systems. It is a work of remarkable scholarship (I counted 724 names of authors in the index, and even that impressive list does not include my own name). The book is also a product of a lifetime of hard thinking about the intractable patterns of the social and, especially the political, system.

The style of the book is somewhat reminiscent of that of a fugue. It is a set of variations around three major concepts as themes: volition, probing, and impairment. Part I deals with the first two themes. Chapter 2 deals with the concept of volition, which is what human beings want, or think they want. This goes far beyond the traditional economist's concept of "assumed" indifference curves and utility functions, recognizing that volitions are in some sense learned by very complex processes and that they therefore can be changed through experience, either of success or failure. This is an aspect of the human organism which economists have shockingly neglected. They apparently believe that preferences are something that we simply have to take for granted; very often they are not granted but are indeed learned and change constantly.

Lindblom does not discuss this learning process in great detail, nor does he discuss the role that genetic factors may play in it. The studies of identical twins separated from infancy have certainly indicated that genetic factors do play a role in our preferences and volitions, but exactly what role they play is mysterious.

The difference between wants and needs, important to some thinkers like John Burton, is completely neglected. If there are needs which are in some sense universal, these clearly are related to the genetic factors that we all share. Nevertheless, this should not lead us into a kind of genetic determinism. I think Lindblom is right in suggesting that volitions are in large part the product of a complex process of learning and persuasion, accommodation and consensus, and so on. If this were not so, there would certainly be no advertising or propaganda, which is certainly designed to change other people's volitions in directions favorable to the volitions of the advertisers or propagandists.

Chapter 3 takes up the second theme of the book, which Lindblom calls probing. This again refers to certain aspects of the learning process, directed particularly by the volitions of the learner. There is a certain amount of implicit learning theory involved in this concept, for instance, the distinction between single- and double-loop learning (p. 36). The latter takes place "when the formulation of a problem itself is in question and when its reformulation compels a broader and deeper reconsideration of volitions, including a cognitive reorganization." The place of probing in the overall process of learning, however, is not very clearly explored. A little more probing here might have been desirable. Just how the learning of our image of the world present in our minds is related to the learning of our volition structure is something that needs much further exploration. Lindblom does mention coherence (p. 39) as a factor in the learning process, presumably a selective factor, as we tend to be uncomfortable if our images of the world are not coherent. He points out, perhaps quite rightly, that coherence does not necessarily imply absolute consistency, as inconsistency seems to be something we are able to live with up to a point. Beyond a certain point, however, it may turn into incoherence.

Lindblom does not discuss much the various methods of learning, especially in the sciences. The role of observation, the collection of data, experiment, and the very creative role of the failure of expectations are not much developed. I have often pointed out myself that success merely confirms what we thought we knew already, and that it is the failure of expectations that is likely to lead to the reduction of error. Chapter 4, "Inquiry, Imposition and Partisanship," explores the social framework within which probing becomes creative or uncreative, and looks briefly at how the use of power, that is, threat, perverts the learning process, and how partisanship and argument may actually encourage it. If anything emerges from all this, it is the proposition that anything we all agree about is almost bound to be wrong.

Part II then develops the third theme in this fugue, which is the concept of impairment and, especially, the reduction of impairment. This refers to all those processes and institutions in society which essentially corrupt the learning process and result in a failure to eliminate error, whether this is errors of volition, that is, wanting things we should not want, or errors in probing, which is a failure to create images of the world in our mind which are reasonably free from error. A reduction of impairment is the great aim of Lindblom's thinking. The concept of impairment is related to that of human betterment. It implies that there is something in the state of the system which makes the system worse rather than better in terms of what might be called mature human judgments. In some sense, perhaps, the term is a little unfortunate in that it implies that all that is wrong with us is obstacles, hindering the movement toward a better world. But there is no use removing obstacles if there is nothing to obstruct.

The impairment concept implies, in a way, that there is a large and delightful movement of power toward human betterment which is somehow obstructed. This neglects the possibility that there may be large and powerful movements toward worsening, which have to be obstructed, as Calvinists know very well. We do not have to believe in original sin to observe that in some times and places there are large movements toward evil which need to be impaired. If we are downstream from a big flood, there is a lot to be said for having a dam with storage capacity between us and the flood. The use of threat in social systems, while sometimes beneficial, can easily become extremely pathological, as Cromwell, Napoleon, Hitler, and Stalin demonstrated. A bit of impairment here might have come in very handy.

Nevertheless, there is also much truth in the idea that movements toward a better world are impaired by obstacles. Lindblom is particularly concerned with institutions and structures in society that impair probing (chapter 5). He is particularly concerned in chapters 6 and 7 with elite structures which create situations where the right questions are not allowed to be raised, particularly where a high value is placed on conformity instead of on diversity. Chapter 8, "Convergences as Evidence of Impairment," certainly suggests that the fear of being different is one of the greatest obstacles to human learning. It is surprising that he does not go on to point out how the environmental movement, with its emphasis on the love of variety and on the value that if something is different it should be seen as interesting rather than frightening, can play a very important role in realizing the nonconvergent probing society.

On the other hand, what Lindblom does not seem to recognize is that there can be a convergence toward truth. He recognizes that there is a real world, but could develop further the concept that there is an inherent instability in error, and what we have to be afraid of is convergence on error produced through threat and various forms of social organization. It is curious that he refuses to discuss religion in this matter, regarding it as a "sleeping dog" (p. 115). It would have been useful to have seen a little more discussion of the nature of the subculture of the scientific community, particularly the ethos which has produced such an extraordinary explosion of human knowledge, as a result perhaps of a volitional or ethical system which put a high value on curiosity, on testing (a form of probing), on veracity (telling lies about your results is the one thing that will drive you out of the scientific community without any question), and also on the abstention from threat, the principle that people should be convinced by evidence and never by threat. These principles have some resemblance to the ethos of the common law, but their history is quite obscure. It would, I think, have helped the argument of the book if Lindblom had distinguished more carefully among the different subcultures which make up a society.

Part III of the book is a devastating attack on the social sciences themselves as contributors to impairment, by developing consensuses of elites, the suppression—or at least the neglect—of dissenting opinions, the substitution of agreed upon images for reality, and so on. Some of the intensity of the attack may be the result of a noticeable distaste in the social sciences for interdisciplinary activity of the kind that Lindblom has pursued over his life. His argument, that the social sciences do not adequately probe the realities of the world and tend to dismiss problems that do not conform to their subculture, at least cannot be simply dismissed.

Nevertheless, Lindblom's attack on the social sciences is weakened because he does seem to regard them as a single subculture, whereas in fact economics, sociology, political science, psychology, and anthropology have really different subcultures and, even within each discipline, there are quite sharp cultural divisions. There is a strong case for methodological critique in the social sciences. As each tends to have its own methodology and submethodologies within each of the various divisions, Lindblom's broad generalizations obscure a good deal of detail. His thesis that the social sciences are corrupted by a desire to control the social system can certainly be fortified by examples, especially perhaps from economics in the days of "fine-tuning" in the 1960s. But every desire to make the world a better place cannot simply be written off as an impairment. Chapter 10, "Professional Dependence on Lay Probing," describes the social sciences as "a candle in a lighted room" (p. 164), surely an exaggeration. Lay probing would never have given us national income statistics or detailed study of individual cultures, or even price theory and game theory. In systems as complex as social systems and the human being, lay probing, like folk medicine, can go a certain way, but when I am really sick I go to a doctor.

Chapter 12, "Professional Impairment," certainly has some points to make. Probably nothing has ever existed without some pathologies, and it is important to study them, identify them and try to cure them. It is true that in all the sciences there is something of an orthodoxy which resists change. But when the evidence for the orthodox view becomes clearly deficient and evidence for the unorthodox view mounts up, the basic scientific ethos takes over and change takes place. The plate tectonic episode in geology, which he mentions, is surely a good example, as indeed, to a degree, is the Keynesian revolution in economics. Even Lindblom's own works have shaken political scientists' orthodoxy a little!

Part IV of the book, "Toward Prescription," tries to pull things together a little to see if an interdisciplinary scholar can say anything positive. The results are suggestive, if a little obscure. One suspects that Lindblom's economic background gives him a certain prejudice in favor of "invisible hands" and self-organizing societies and a suspicion of hierarchy and government. When contemplating the follies of governments, it is hard not to have a sneaking fondness for anarchism. This sneaking fondness, however, has to be modified by a reflection that "invisible hands" sometimes slap us in the face and that there are processes of impairment in society which only seem to be arrested by the exercise of a legitimated threat power, like the police, the law, taxes, and subsidies.

In chapter 13, "Scientific Society and Self-Guiding Society," he points out quite rightly that any promise to produce a perfect cure for all human problems, whether of the body, the mind or society, is an invitation to disaster, like Marxism. In most situations, amelioration is better than solution. This does not deny the possibility, however, that more amelioration is better than less and that in complex systems, more knowledge about them is better than less. In chapter 14, "Multiplism, Pluralism, and Mutual Adjustment," he attacks centralism as likely to make more serious mistakes than a pluralistic society, which is, of course, the great message of his 1953 book. Chapter 15, "Some Questions about Professional Inquiry for a Self-Guided Society," asks quite rightly who benefits from research but, again, I think he neglects the fact that within the scientific subculture there is a strong value on individual and even idle curiosity, and that while it is true that research funds tend to go to specific problems, there is always a residue for pure curiosity and serendipity, which is often what produces the greatest result. The final chapter, "Reducing Impairment," points out quite rightly that the United States Constitution was not designed to solve social problems, but I think we could add that when it is modified by an appropriate political culture, it can show at least some successes, though sometimes at a high cost, like the Civil War.

This book is certainly a "troubled" attempt to understand and shape society. Perhaps ir raises more questions than it answers; it certainly disturbs complacency. It is, perhaps, a book that needs an answer, but it nevertheless raises questions that need answering and that have not been raised in so dramatic a form before. The very discomfort that it causes may lead to a reduction of the impairments that it so alarmingly describes.

## REFERENCE

Lindblom, Charles E., and Robert A. Dahl. 1953. *Politics, Economics and Welfare.* Harper & Brothers.

## INQUIRY AND SOCIAL CHANGE
by
Brian Fay

Economists will find much that is congenial to them in Charles Lindblom's recent book, for *Inquiry and Change* attempts to do for social problem solving what *The Wealth of Nations* did for the economy. Like Smith before him, Lindblom seeks to provide a general account of human capacity as a backdrop for understanding a particular but very important aspect of human life (economic activity in the case of Smith; social problem posing and solving in the case of Lindblom). Moreover, both books are works in what used to be called "moral science": they are admixtures of empirical evidence and informed social theorizing; of a conception of what is good for human beings; of practical wisdom as to what is possible in human affairs; and of urgent recommendations as to what should be done to better our lives. Like *The Wealth of Nations Inquiry and Change* contains a passionate vision of human possibility tempered by wide intellectual and worldly experience.

Most importantly, both share a common orientation. Both distrust Authority, whether it be government, teachers, parents, scientists, or other experts. Both devalue talk of social control and planning. Both believe that it is individuals who are the sources of innovation and improvement. Both urge that it is the removal of barriers to the power and creativity of individuals that is the most important step which we as a society can now take. Both believe in competition, in free exchange, in pluralism. Both are devoted to a broadly democratic ideal (Smith's market society; what Lindblom calls a self-guiding society), and both see their books as promoting democracy in social life.

There is a similarity in style, too. Though both employ highly technical terms and ideas, both write in a language which is largely jargon-free. Though both invoke the works of others (Lindblom's citations are an education in themselves), they do so by easily and seamlessly incorporating them into their overall perspective. Their writing is clear, accessible, and concrete—as is appropriate given their democratic ambitions. Also, both are suspicious of philosophy and avoid its higher reaches, which they see as entrapping thinkers in a play of indecisive abstractions.

Of course, Adam Smith's book is an undisputed classic. I think that Lindblom's book aspires to this same status. Indeed, it may well achieve this status—though it is too early to say: one of the criteria for being a classic is the capacity to offer repeated insight to readers in widely different situations, and whether Lindblom's book will do this remains to be seen. But, in any case, this is a significant, challenging, illuminating book of interest to anyone concerned with the future direction of social life and the role knowledge can and should play in it.

### A.

At the outset of his book, Lindblom states his aim:

> This study explores knowledge: how in the world's industrialized societies it helps social problem solving, how ignorance and faulty analysis get in the way, and whether and how people can do better (p. 2).

By "people," Lindblom means not only political and opinion leaders, or social scientists and other experts, but ordinary people as well—parents, teachers, laborers, middle managers, citizens, and so forth. The term "knowledge" is somewhat misleading, however; indeed, so is the term "inquiry" found in the title of the book. "Knowledge" suggests something completed and established, whereas Lindblom is much more concerned with the process by which ideas and judgments are formed and disseminated. "Inquiry" suggests a methodologically self-conscious, highly intellectual process typically found in science, whereas Lindblom does not want to restrict his inquiry (!) in this way. He himself uses the word "probing" and "social probes" throughout the book; this is a far more accurate word, given his purposes. "Probing" connotes being engaged in real-world problem solving; it suggests the exploratory character of such problem solving, as well as its close connection with action. (The book might have been more aptly titled *Probing and Social Change*.) Given this, a better statement of Lindblom's concern is: How do ordinary people as well as professionals probe in industrialized societies? How can they do it better? What effect does or can this probing have?

Central to Lindblom's answers to these questions is his discussion of what he calls impairment, which comprises all the ways the capacity to probe is restricted or hindered. (His discussion of it takes up one-quarter of the book.) Impairment results from advantaging certain participants; from inculcating only certain beliefs and values (as in schools); from concealing, obfuscating, and/or lying; from coercing or punishing those with different ideas; from onformist or convergent thinking; from propaganda of all sorts; and from other means too numerous to catalogue here. Lindblom's discussion of impairment is rich, subtle, and highly illuminating. He probes all its various nuances and reveals what an ubiquitous phenomenon it is even in societies like ours which are supposedly free, critical, and open.

The other side of the coin of the discussion of impairment is the notion of a self-guiding society. Lindblom does *not* mean by this a society which is centrally planned, *nor* does he mean a society of participatory democracy. A self-guiding society is one in which the vast powers of probing of all its members are stimulated and employed in all areas of life such that small elite groups cannot keep certain issues and arrangements out of the public realm. It is a society in which there is no Answer or Best Way, but only the provisional answers of lay people as they form their arrangements only to reexamine them later. It is a society that requires both what Lindblom calls multiplism (the participation of vast numbers of people socially probing) and pluralism "people in likeminded groups exercising influence on government policies and somewhat autonomous, specialized governmental officials (both elected and appointed) having multilateral influence on each other" [p. 234]). It is also a society committed to what Lindblom calls mutual adjustment, in which there are "highly multilateral exercises of power and influence, including but by no means limited to bargaining" (p. 240).

## B.

So far, much of this will be music to mainstream economists' ears. A self-guiding society is not unlike a well-functioning market society in which there is a plethora of messages and volitions (goods and services) produced and traded not as a result of a central plan but because of the free access to the system, the absence of barriers to the creative energies of its participants, and their willingness to mutually adjust their behavior on the basis of whatever outcomes result from their activities. But economists ought not to be too smug in this, for there are themes in Lindblom's book which run directly counter to certain tendencies in contemporary economic thought. These are the tendencies which value economic planning and control by central authorities enlightened by the truths economics itself supposedly provides for them. Lindblom addresses these tendencies when he discusses the nature of social scientific knowledge and its potential role in human life.

Lindblom discusses a number of problems with the idea of a socially planned society under the control of social scientific experts. Many of these are familiar: the lack of requisite knowledge and power, the authoritarian imposition of the values of one group onto others, the stultifying effects of such an arrangement, and so on. But Lindblom offers a deeper reason why experts in general, and economists in particular, cannot plan and control large-scale social interaction. This reason has to do with the nature of human preferences. It is a reason which ought to be of great interest to economists for whom preferences play a central role in their theorizing.

   To simplify the point for clarity, the standard picture of planning calls for planners to discover the wants and interests of a group of people and then to ascertain the most efficient means to satisfy those wants. There are, of course, standard objections to this picture, for it seems to treat wants and interests as merely given. But Lindblom's objection goes deeper than this. He claims that wants and interests—whether they are variable and socially formed or not—are not discoverable even in principle because they are not "objective attributes of human beings such as their metabolic rate" (p. 19): that is, they are not the sorts of things which can be discovered because they are not traits waiting to be ferreted out. According to Lindblom, wants and preferences are "volitions created, not (attributes) discovered." In other words, preferences are *choices* which people make either well or poorly informed; they are *decisions* they themselves effect, not facts about themselves they (or anyone else) can uncover; they are potentially continually revisable or alterable, not a bedrock on which to build a planned order.

   In this can be seen the essentially activist conception of human beings in terms of which Lindblom thinks. People are not pushed or caused to act by wants that arise in them, nor are these wants the result of social programming. Wants are human creations, situated as these creations may be, and each person is in some sense his or her own artist. Given this, the question to ask is not, what is a person's wants or the wants of this group? It is, rather, what was the thinking and judging which underlay these wants and how might these be improved? (Lindblom castigates economists for neglecting preference formation [p. 183].)

   It is because of this essentially active nature of human beings that the aspiration to discover general laws about human behavior is bound to be disappointed (because wants must play a central role in any such law). Without such laws, the hopes for a centrally planned society fade. Lindblom examines the kinds of explanations found in social science, and he finds that "relatively little explanation in social science closely approximates the model of scientific explanation in which an event is explained by subsuming it under a specified, carefully articulated general law" (pp. 142-143). In fact, he argues that most social scientific inquiry—reporting, evaluating, conceptual organizing, providing scenarios; posing questions—"embraces the same variety of explanations which ordinary people construct for themselves and exchange with each other" (p. 142).

   Lindblom does not deny that social science can indeed be useful, and indeed may even be necessary, for the complex tasks of contemporary society. (However, even here he is deflationary: "For all the effort and for all its presumed usefulness, I cannot identify a single social science finding or idea hat is undeniably indispensable to any social task or effort. Not even one, suggest" [p. 136].) But he points out that social scientists themselves suffer rom specific forms of impairment (pp. 195-209), and he insists that the chief ole of social science is in its enlightening of the probings of others: 'professional inquiry may achieve its influence not so much in accumulating pecialized social science knowledge that is largely removed from lay nowledge, but in constantly revising lay knowledge and redirecting lay nquiry" (p. 176).

## C.

Despite the wisdom of *Inquiry and Change*, the reader should not get the mpression that there are not any problems in it. I cannot discuss all of them ere, but I do wish to mention one which I shall call the problem of information overload (or, to speak as I have done in this review in terms of analogies drawn rom economics, the problem of inflation). I do so because I think it points o a deep difficulty in Lindblom's vision of a self-guiding society.

"Possibly the most effective single way to reduce impairment is to get into circulation a greater variety of messages" (p. 295). This is no doubt true, but Lindblom seems unaware of an unintended outcome of such proliferation, namely, that as the number of messages increases, the value of any one of them s likely to decrease. Instead of a wide variety of possibilities opened up by a plethora of new ideas and values, the result may instead be a cacophony of noise n which even good ideas are drowned in the welter of viewpoints and positions.

Moreover, though Lindblom briefly discusses so-called "democratic overload," he does not do so in this particular context. The problem here is hat freeing more and more people to probe the "social game" is likely to result n increasing demands being made on the players to respond to the expressed charges of all the others. A society of active involvement is likely to be one marked by a proliferation of demands. The worry here is that there may be a limit to the capacity of each player individually, and of society in general, o respond to such demands.

Taken together, a marked increase in messages and the multiplication of demands might well result in an overburdened public realm marred by excessive solicitations beyond its capacity to respond, and deafened by its own noise. Of course, Lindblom might reply, this might lead to a probing into the responsible limits of probing, and a consequent setting of barriers to it. But t is not clear that this would be an adequate response. As Lindblom shows again and again (see p. 235ff., for instance), probing is a social phenomenon which necessarily involves public participation and activity. An increase of probing by its very nature inevitably will lead to an expansion of the public sphere. Probers, even those bent on limiting probing, are inherently social barrier breakers and social wall violators.

I find something frightening about a self-guiding society in which all the social arrangements (even those which erect barriers to the scrutiny of probing) are open to inspection, in which a horde of probers demands justification or seeks relief. Such a society sounds too intrusive and unsettled, too loud and boisterous, too nervous and frenetic, to be a society in which it would be good to live. (Note that many criticisms of market society, especially by conservatives, make this same point.) There is a skeptical, even suspicious bent to it which downplays the importance of custom, prejudice, and settled feeling in human affairs, which underplays the intricacy of human arrangements and their consequent intractability to rational analysis, and which overlooks the importance of stability. The whirl of a self-guided society may not be as exhilarating as Lindblom suggests, but may induce giddiness instead.

# McCARTHY'S *MARX AND THE ANCIENTS: CLASSICAL ETHICS, SOCIAL JUSTICE, AND NINETEENTH-CENTURY POLITICAL ECONOMY:*

## A REVIEW ESSAY

S. Todd Lowry

*Marx and the Ancients: Classical Ethics, Social Justice, and Nineteenth-Century Political Economy.*
By George E. McCarthy.
Savage, MD: Rowman and Littlefield, 1990. Pp. 342. $37.50.

As is indicated by the title, this is a wide-ranging work whose interdisciplinary vision is laudable. It surveys the direct influence of ancient Greek thinkers such as Democritus, Epicurus, and Aristotle upon the ethical, political, and economic theories of Karl Marx, and strives to integrate that influence with an examination of the role of eighteenth- and nineteenth-century philosophers such as Kant, Hume, and Hegel on Marx's thought. If this sounds ambitious, consider the secondary nuances of the debt of the above-mentioned trio of

Research in the History of Economic Thought and Methodology, Volume 12, pages 169-174.
Copyright © 1994 by JAI Press Inc.
ISBN: 1-55938-747-5

modern philosophers to the Greeks in their own right. Also consider the eddies of method, ethics, political theory, and economic perspective to be generalized from the Greeks, Hegelian ethics, Kantian rationality, and Ricardian political economy.

Let us begin by giving the author proper credit for having undertaken this Herculean task in the interest of integrative interdisciplinary thought at a time when narrow hair-splitting monographs are, academically, the safest and most tempting publication venture. Of course, one reason for limiting one's analyses within very narrow confines of intensive investigation is that such a procedure can limit the possibility of critical reviews to a very few informed specialists. On the other hand, a broadly conceived intellectual adventure offers an invitation to legions of nit-picking specialists, each finding fault with the author's necessarily sketchy treatment of their particular field of expertise.

The proper role of the reviewer of this type of book is, in my opinion, to evaluate the skeletal structure or framework that the author has provided for a more comprehensive understanding of the subject matter, to point out possible shortcomings, and questionable lines of analysis, and even, at times, to suggest that the author has only provided a scaffolding from which to build rather than the core framing itself. The merit of this type of work remains, however, its contribution to a broader and more general level of understanding of the evolution of ethical, political and economic thought and its promotion of future synthesizing projects.

The opening sentence of the book sets its general tone:

> From his earliest days in the gymnasium to the completion of his university studies, Karl Marx was steeped in the culture and philosophy of the Ancients. (p. 1).

While it is frequently mentioned that Marx wrote his doctoral dissertation on the ancient Greek atomist and materialist philosopher, Democritus, McCarthy presents the full picture of Marx's study, which was a comparison of the views of Democritus and Epicurus. It was, however, the latter's cultural relativism that had the most profound influence on Marx's thought. As an aside, interested readers will find Leo Groarke's recent book, *Greek Skepticism*, (McGill-Queen's U. Press, 1990), to be a very readable exposition of the breadth of cultural relativist and proto-institutionalist thought on the Greco-Roman philosophical scene and its influence on modern thinkers.

In his introductory discussion of the scope of the work, McCarthy lists nine benefits from broadening the analysis of Marx's writings to include the ancients, mainly, Epicurus and Aristotle. Among these are a richer grasp of Marx's theory of democracy and individual political participation, a theory of value that is different from and deeper than the labor theory of value of Smith and Ricardo, and the integration of theories of knowledge, science, and ethics. The ninth item is "the reintegration of economics, politics, and moral philosophy into a social ethics as appeared in the Ancients" (p. 3) (sic—there a number of indications of poor proofing in the book). In pursuit of this ambitious and original agenda, the author draws on an extensive body of recent scholarship dealing with Marxist ethics and philosophy. He also demonstrates considerable erudition in recent German scholarship that he assimilated during an extended research stint in Germany while preparing this material. The weakest link in his research seems to be in the economic thought of the ancients, and in his generalizations of Aristotle's political theory.

After developing the importance of Epicurean thought in Marx's ideas in chapter I, McCarthy devotes chapter II to Aristotle. He gives an extended analysis of Aristotle's treatment of justice and ethics in three levels and extrapolates a dynamic theory of participative interaction from Aristotle's *Ethics* and *Politics*. This theory of dynamic consensus ties into Aristotle's ideas on social justice and ethics and gives us a clear picture of the source of Marx's views. The argument is made that Hegel absorbed a concept of a social ethic from antiquity, but Marx went back to the original well to include the individualist and subjectivist participative element that supports his theory of needs. McCarthy sums up Marx's sense of relativistic social justice, distribution and political interaction by quoting from Marx, *Critique of the Gotha Program*, "right can never be higher than the economic structure and its cultural development conditioned thereby" (p. 95). The point is that ethics cannot be abstracted from material and institutional realities.

The major contribution of the book is found in this and the following chapter on "needs" elaborating the Hegelian and Aristotelian senses of participative interdependence in the fabric of an economy. However, McCarthy completely ignores the extensive body of recent literature on Aristotle's economic ideas, the essay component of which is now collected in a single volume edited by Mark Blaug (1991) He relies primarily on M.I. Finley, who rejects Aristotle's relevance to economic thought, and Carl Polanyi, who generalizes robustly about Aristotle's sense of an economy. Polanyi, however, imposes a "status" theory on his treatment of distribution and exchange. Marx's own analysis of Aristotle's formulation of justice in exchange from Book V,v, of the *Nicomachean Ethics* is omitted (Marx, *Capital*, vol. 1, Chap. 1, end of sec. 3) as is Marx's analysis of exchange and use value, from Commodity-Money-Commodity, (*Capital*, chap. 3, sec. 2), which attributes the exchange formulation of goods to gold and gold to goods directly to Heraclitus, but clearly draws on the presentation in Aristotle's *Politics*, Book I. In the first instance, the discussion of *Ethics* V,v, there is an objective value connotation that needs to be confronted if the author's thesis is going to be taken seriously by economists. Marx says, "The brilliancy of Aristotle's genius is shown by this alone, that he discovered, in the expression of the value of commodities, a relation of equality" (*Capital*, vol. 1, chap. 1, sec. 3).

A second caveat in these two critical chapters is McCarthy's cavalier assurance of Aristotle's priority and originality in promulgating the theory of a dynamic participative consensual democracy. (p. 85). This line of relativistic participative thought is Protagorean—Protagoras having been alleged in antiquity to be a pupil of Democritus. He was an advisor and confident of Pericles during the heyday of the Athenian democracy, a century before Aristotle's time. This Protagorean perspective is elaborated in chapter 6 of my own *The Archaeology of Economic Ideas* (1987) and in chapter 11 of Edward Schiappa's *Protagoras and Logos* (1991). Of course, quibbling over priority is not a very fruitful academic pursuit, and McCarthy may be correct in attributing Marx's assimilation of these ideas to his familiarity with Aristotle, but in order to presume that, and even more to demonstrate it, he should be familiar with the broader picture of ancient sophistic political theory and its extensive influence on European thought.

This is a proper place to comment on McCarthy's writing style. He presents his arguments like a surging surf, wave after wave of extended sentences. The repetitive impact of his arguments obscures its lack of specificity and analytic incisiveness. We are treated to one sentence (p. 84) that is 12 lines long.

In developing his argument that Marx was primarily committed to an ethical basis for evaluating the capitalist system, McCarthy formulates his view very succinctly as follows:

> His (Marx's) critique of the economics of the nineteenth century—which is still applicable to today's economic theory—is that the complex economic and social relationships of capital and wage labor are ignored in preference to "simple determinants" and "infantile abstractions." The historical and political analysis of capitalist society is reduced to the mechanism of a simple exchange of commodities. Everything is reduced to simplistic models of exchange relation based on formal abstractions ... it is capitalism without the Industrial Revolution (p. 219).

This spirited interpretation of Marx's views follows a rather tangential discussion of monetization of the economy attributed to the *Grundrisse* and is followed by a list of six aspects of the economy that are not properly considered by such abstractions, namely, the nature of work, organizational structures, authority systems, and the state. The sixth category included "land appropriation, exploitation, wars, and imperialism for overcoming its internal contradictions" (p. 219). McCarthy then proceeds to challenge the premise that Marx had a labor theory of value of the Ricardian type and denies that there is any contradiction between volume I and volume III of *Capital*. He cites an array of secondary literature on both sides of this question and, without any specific analysis of Marx's own statements, he appeals to the authority of Aristotle to support Marx's freedom from a commitment to price theory. This appeal, however, is also based on secondary literature—M.I. Finley's classic rejection of Aristotle's relevance as a contributor to economic analysis on the grounds that he had no price theory. While Finley is quoted at length with his denial that Aristotle had any analysis of the structure of exchange and that he considered economic gain unnatural, (p. 220), we are left with a dilemma in analyzing the discussion as a reviewer.

First, in Book I of the *Politics*, which Finley is discussing, Aristotle clearly defines barter, commodities for commodities, (C:C; he defines exchange for mutual benefit using money—Commodities: Money: Commodities (C:M:C in Marx's terms). He then defines exchange with professional merchants who were interested in money that could be carried out of the economy. These merchant-foreigners (or metics) bought goods with money and resold them for money introducing the possibility of draining the community of bullion: Money-Commodities-Money (M:C:M). Aristotle found this process unrestrained by natural *needs* for consumer goods and, therefore, *unnatural*. He went a step further and rejected the moral acceptability of usury since it involved the exchange of M:M1, which he saw as exploitative since this process was conceived as consumption loans to the needy. The unnaturalness of commerce to which many classicists have referred, and which Finley follows, is in fact a very perceptive analytic distinction. It is not exchange within the community for mutual benefit that is censured as unnatural, but the exchange with metics, the traditional merchants in the Greek world, that introduces the possibility of exploitation and loss of assets by the tightly knit Greek polis. Several authors, including myself, have, in recent years developed this distinction which seems to be so elusive for classicists, but Finley, as indicated by his entry on Aristotle in the recent edition of *The New Palgrave*, did not assimilate or did not read any economics literature on Aristotle since his 1970 paper which McCarthy quotes. It is also apparent that McCarthy has not reviewed the available literature, limiting himself to Finley (1970), Polanyi (1955), and Soudek (1952) (whom he cites, but whose subtleties he does not seem to have understood).

I will not quibble with McCarthy on the issue of whether Aristotle emphasized ethics, and I also agree that he placed ethics and personal virtue at the top of his hierarchical analysis of values in Book VII of the *Politics*. But Marx apparently read Aristotle much more closely than either McCarthy or Finley, and so the use of Aristotle, erroneously interpreted, as support for vaguely argued interpretations of Marx, leaves both the Aristotelian and the Marxist scholar in a state of exasperation. We can appreciate, however, McCarthy's more convincing elaboration of the German ethical heritage that influenced Marx's thought.

I must reiterate that the author deserves credit for the breadth and historical depth of his attempt at an interdisciplinary synthesis of major European ideas on ethics, social justice, and political economy as they culminated in Marx's writings. Mastering several different disciplines to the degree that original critical synthesis can be accomplished is a challenge to the erudite heterogeneous scholar at the level of decades of input. That is not to say that premature attempts to structure and present material are not valuable contributions to scholarly development, both for the author and the reader. We look forward to future work in this same vein by the author.

S. Todd Lowry

# REFERENCES

Blaug, Mark. 1991. *Aristotle's Economics*. Brookfield, VT: Edward Elgar Publishing Company.

Finley, M. I. 1970. "Aristotle and Economic Analysis." *Past & Present*, No. 47, pp. 3-25; reprinted in *Studies in Ancient Society*. M. I. Finley, Ed. 1974. London: Routledge & Kegan Paul, (Reprinted in Blaug, 1991.)

Groarke, Leo. 1990. *Greek Skepticism*. Montreal: McGill-Queen's University Press.

Lowry, S. Todd. 1987. *The Archaeology of Economic Ideas*. Durham: Duke University Press.

Polanyi, Karl. 1957. "Aristotle Discovers the Economy," pp. 64-94. In *Trade and Market in the Early Empires: Economies in History and Theory*, ed. Karl Polanyi, Conrad M. Arensberg, and Harry W. Pearson. New York: Free Press. (Reprinted in Blaug, 1991.)

Schiappa, Edward. 1991. *Protagoras and Logos*. Columbia: South Carolina University Press.

Soudek, Josef. 1952. "Aristotle's Theory of Exchange: An Enquiry into the Origin of Economic Analysis." *Proc. of the American Philosophical Society 96*, pp. 55-59.

# THE DISAPPEARANCE OF AUSTRALIAN ECONOMICS:
## A REVIEW ESSAY

Ray Petridis

*A History of Australian Economic Thought.*
**By Peter Groenewegen and Bruce McFarlane.**
**London and New York: Routledge, 1990. Pp. xiv & 277. $54 cloth.**

In the forty years after 1920, it seemed that an Australian economics had finally emerged after a hesitant and disjointed gestation in the previous one hundred years. But by 1990, the internationalization of economics had overtaken what might have been described as this Australianness so that the student, teacher, researcher, and policymaker in economics seem indistinguishable from their counterparts in other developed economies the world over. The essential ingredients of an Australian economics and the processes in its absoption into an international economics are issues deserving of more attention than the authors of this book can afford. By the end of the book, the reader has gained some feel for the nature of this Australianness and an appreciation that this distinctive character has been gradually eroded. However, in the first chapter of their "outline history of economic thought" (p. 1), Peter Groenewegen and

Research in the History of Economic Thought and Methodology, Volume 12, pages 175-186.
Copyright © 1994 by JAI Press Inc.
All rights of reproduction in any form reserved.
ISBN: 1-55938-747-5

Bruce McFarlane address the issue of the existence of a clearly differentiated Australian economics.

## I. DELINEATING AN "AUSTRALIAN" ECONOMICS

Australia is a growing country, just over two hundred years old, still with a small population and an intellectual tradition in the universities which began only in the 1850s. Academic study of economics in the universities did not obtain a firm footing until over half a century later, and many of these academic economists were immigrants, mainly but not exclusively from English-speaking countries. It is not surprising that Groenewegen and McFarlane rule out the commonly accepted criterion of nationality and/or birthplace of author for delineating Australian economics, for this would have led to the ruling out of much of what they correctly regard as Australian economics. Instead, they chose the sensible and pragmatic criteria of residence of author and place of publication of major work. Inevitably, the application of such criteria will generate some anomalous cases, especially in the post-1960 period when Australian economists' promotion prospects were partly determined by the extent to which they had published "internationally." The criteria are sufficiently ambiguous to ensure that there will be general agreement about what constituted Australian economics. The authors rarely apply the test of their criteria after the opening statement (pp. 6-7). Instead, they examine chronologically the development of Australian economics, providing ad hoc justifications for particular inclusions as they see fit.

Unfortunately, the somewhat repetitious first chapter in which Groenewegen and McFarlane outline the economists and topics in Australian economics which they intend to examine, also leaves the reader slightly confused. On page 5, they suggest that the 1920s and 1930s saw "the demise of the brief interlude of ... a *genuine* [italics added] Australian economics" but on page 7 quote historians of economic thought as mentioning "the 1920s as the real beginning of a *genuine* [italics added] Australian economics." They conclude, not very convincingly, that they have "established the existence of an Australian economics" (p. 7) which will allow them to adopt their specific chronological approach in subsequent chapters. This is an exceedingly difficult task, for the chronology follows "various groupings of academics, amateurs, cranks and economists from government and elsewhere," and in the absence of a thematic approach or domination by one or two writers, inevitably leads to some backtracking and repetition. Clearly, there is no ideal method of dealing with material traversing so much time and ranging over such disparate themes and writers. Yet, it appears that the authors' task was made even more difficult by the stringent word limits placed on the book by the publishers.

## II. THE FIRST CENTURY OF AUSTRALIAN ECONOMICS

Four chapters dealing with the "rude beginnings, the early developments at the university, the decade of the Australian Economist 1888-98 and the nation of statisticians" dispose of the first century of Australian economics. Approximately the same period was covered a quarter of a century ago in the monumental but relatively neglected *Economic Enquiry in Australia* (1966) by Craufurd D.W. Goodwin. There are more than forty separate references and substantial discussions of the material in Goodwin's book, and Groenewegen and McFarlane are at pains to stress their debt to this earlier work, which has allowed them to devote less space to it than otherwise would have been judged necessary. Instead, they have aimed to "present new findings on the significance of some of the *dramatis personae* ... as well as changes in interpretation" (p. 8). Unfortunately, the paucity of research into this period seems to have greatly constrained their ability to fulfil this objective.

"Rude beginnings" refers to the earliest Australian economic writing which, given its dating, was non academic or popular writing, and some of it was crude indeed. The characteristic of most of this writing, as also of much later Australian economic literature, was its emphasis on the debate over policy. These early origins of Australian economics are illustrated by examining seven writers in some detail on the issues of free trade and protection, cycles of economic activity and monetary policy, land use and government regulation and the role of government in general, and a variety of sources of economic development including immigration and transport. This is a varied menu, but unfortunately much of what these early writers said was lacking in analytical rigor, drew in a crude way on the work of a few scholars from other countries, and more often than not adapted (or corrupted) their writing to suit a local political purpose.

Of the seven writers examined in "rude beginnings," only David Syme and Sir Anthony Musgrave were known outside Australia, mainly in Britain. Symes' views are particularly important because they provide a link to later developments in economic analysis and the protectionist policies adopted in Australia in the twentieth century. As a newspaper proprietor, he promoted the protectionist position in the state of Victoria, in opposition to the free trade position in New South Wales. His more analytical writings were published in a book and in British periodicals, especially in the 1870s. Interestingly, aspects of Symes' analysis were known to Alfred Marshall in the 1870s, in particular, Symes' critique of John Stuart Mill's methodology and Mill's analysis of supply and demand, and his critique of laissez faire, including the analysis which pointed to a wide range of deleterious effects associated with competition and the possibility of competition degenerating into monopoly. Furthermore, following another "Australian," W.E. Hearn, Syme was critical of the description "political economy," replacing it in the title of his book (1876) by "industrial science." In 1879 in *The Economics of Industry*, Alfred Marshall argued for the replacement of "political economy" by "economics," and in 1890 the *Principles of Economics* permanently enshrined the new usage (see Guillebaud, 1961).

The writing of Sir Anthony Musgrave was originally examined in detail in Goodwin (1966) in a thorough and scholarly analysis. Goodwin characterized Musgrave as a "pioneer of macroeconomics" for his monetary theory with its implied critique of Say's Law and its anticipations of Keynes, for his analysis of economic growth and his critique of John Stuart Mill's four propositions on capital, and for his mercantilist-slanted criticism of Mills' analysis of international trade as it was applied to colonies in the early stages of growth. William Stanley Jevons was the only prominent economist to provide much support for Musgrave's views, although he disagreed with Musgrave's analysis of trade. Thus, Musgrave received a poor reception outside Australia and some of his creative ideas failed to be taken up either in Australia or elsewhere. Groenewegen and McFarlane suggest that Musgrave's impact was limited because of his use of intemperate and hostile language to describe economic analysis and economists. Most of the remaining economists discussed in this opening chapter also expressed critical views about this imported economics. This is predictable given that Australia was in the early stages of economic development and some of the imported theories seemed better suited to countries already well progressed through the industrialization process. These early "Australian" economists, including J.D. Lang, J.E. Goodwin, "Cinderella" (not confidently identified by the authors), and A.J. Ogilvy, had little or no formal training in economics. Their writings had a certain freshness and relevance, because they adapted economic theory to support or reject particular policy positions. But the reader is left with the impression that much of this literature is ephemeral, with the possible exception of that of W.C. Wentworth, who in 1819 published the earliest known estimates of the national income of the colonies of New South Wales and Van Diemen's Land (Tasmania).

The writings of the nonacademic economists who were part of the early history of Australian economics do not provide a coherent link with subsequent developments in academic economics. Australian universities were established rather late, beginning with Sydney University in 1852, Melbourne University in 1855, and universities in the four remaining state capital cities between 1876 and 1912. A pervasive set of anti-intellectual and anti-academic attitudes seem to have been directed against economics in particular. In the new and growing colonies, there existed grave doubts and some suspicions about the theoretical musings and likely policy pronouncements of academic economists. Thus, only at Melbourne University was any economics teaching established on a regular basis from the earliest years of the establishment of the university. The best known of these academics was W.E. Hearn, whose book *Plutology* was quoted approvingly by W.S. Jevons and Alfred Marshall among others. But the teaching of economics had a halting start at Melbourne, while at Sydney University there were strong attempts to keep the economists at bay. Groenewegen and McFarlane provide brief summaries of the writings of a few economists who might be regarded as worthy of more detailed study. All of them (apart from Hearn) were based at Sydney University; Pell, Woolley, and Scott based their views on "accepted principles of economics" and only Irvine "showed heretical tendencies" (p. 60). The chapter dealing with the early academic developments at the universities is fragmentary; much of the material gives the impression of being in note form, and much relevant information is relegated to long footnotes at the end of the chapter. A better appreciation of this phase in Australian economics can be obtained if this chapter is read in conjunction with Goodwin (1966), which has a systematic treatment of "economics in the universities."

An interesting interlude in Australian economics was the establishment of an Australian Economic Association in 1887 and the publication of an unusually frequent (monthly) periodical, *The Australian Economist*, between 1888-1898. Most of the material published in *The Australian Economist* is available in a facsimile reprint (Butlin, Fitzgerald and Scott, 1986) and two chapters at the beginning deal with the origins of the Association and the contents of the periodical. Groenewegen and McFarlane provide a brief review of the contributors to and material published in *The Australian Economist*. It was a rich and varied collection, with the emphasis on practical and policy matters, even when the papers were theoretical in nature. Four contributors to *The Australian Economist* are singled out for a more detailed examination, although the authors range beyond their writings in that periodical in their review. Only Andrew Garran and Alfred De Lissa seem worthy of note, although the reader is left in some doubt about the merits of their contributions. Garran's views on the nature and methodology of economics seem akin to those of British writers such as Ashley and Cunningham. Furthermore, his discussions of a class-based system of political economy is also largely derivative. It seems to be stretching the imagination to argue that "Garran illustrates the heights of critical brilliance Australian economics of the 1890s would reach" (p. 87) in view of the footnote which states "Garran's historical knowledge (appears) somewhat limited with respect to the literature of political economy, a matter which can also be illustrated by his familiar interpretation of Physiocracy" (p. 89).

De Lissa was described as a second pioneer of macroeconomics by Goodwin (1966, p. 495) for his development of a multiplier theory. Groenewegen and McFarlane correctly interpret De Lissa's work as the rediscovery of "the Physiocratic theory of growth" (p. 75) and not as an anticipation of a Kahn-Keynes type multiplier. Again, the reader is left bemused by the subsequent summary which concludes that a "multiplier" of the Kahn-Keynes type "had important anticipations from the pen of De Lissa, more than three decades before"(pp. 75-76). Regardless of the merits of the writings of De Lissa, Garran, and others, the decade of the Australian economist undoubtedly paved the way for the even more practical work of the statisticians.

It may seem unusual to include a chapter on "a nation of statisticians" in a book on the history of economic thought (Goodwin, 1966, calls his chapter "economic statistics") and some of the statisticians discussed by the authors obviously had a rudimentary or zero knowledge of economics. It is a measure of the practical orientation of the young Australia that statistics about the economy were regarded as an essential tool of economic management from an early date. Wars and depressions also provided a strong stimulus to statistical collections in an increasingly interventionist society. Each of the seven statisticians whose work is briefly summarized in this chapter were employed by state or federal governments, and only two, T.A. Coghlan and the most famous of them, Colin Clark, could be classified as economists. However, from the time of the earliest of these statisticians, W.H. Archer, onwards, the detailed statistical collections relating to output, population, labor force, employment, and prices were used to provide an ad hoc history of economic development and to generate appropriate policy recommendations. Coghlan was an outstanding statistician and economic historian, and his work in this period is directly linked by Groenewegen and McFarlane to the subsequent national income estimates made by Clark and J.G. Crawford in the 1930s. Clark's writings spanned the contemporary period of economics, although his internationally most well known work was the *Conditions of Economic Progress* (1940), which used national income estimates to provide an "applied" theory of economic growth. At long last, through the work of the statisticians from 1850 through to the 1920s, it is possible to discern a line of development to the zenith of Australian economics reached in the period 1920 to 1960.

## III.   A "GOLDEN AGE" — A MISNOMER?

A rather short chapter, the sixth, is devoted to the 1920s and 1930s. The authors again pose the question raised in the first chapter — was this period the "golden age" of Australian economics? But at the end of the chapter, the reader is left up in the air, for the answer will only be provided in the final chapter of conclusions. There, it is revealed that the economists' contributions in the 1920s and 1930s were not superior to those of other periods and that "its golden age aspects undoubtedly derive from the perspectives provided (often in retrospect) by some of the founding fathers of Australian academic economics in the 1920s (and their close associates)" (pp. 229-230). Obviously, there is much room for disagreement about such assessments since the comparison is across time periods involving unlike economic epochs and different degrees of technical expertise and different established stocks of knowledge. A superior theory should be readily identifiable in any period — on that criterion, the 1920s and 1930s were not a golden age. Yet, there is still scope for disagreement because of the apparently superior manner in which theories were adapted and applied to generate policy proposals, which were then accepted by governments. On these grounds, the 1920s and 1930s were the "golden age" of economic policy advice.

This "golden age" of policy advice extended into the 1940s and 1950s and, to a lesser extent, beyond. Much of this is examined by Groenewegen and McFarlane in a later chapter dealing with the influence of economist advisers. As a result, the continuity from the development of policy advice in the depression and recovery, to the planning for war and postwar reconstruction is not so easily discerned.

There is a change of style in the chapter dealing with the "golden age." A much longer exposition of the economic history of the 1920s and 1930s is woven in with some of the contributions of the economists, and only four economists are singled out for more detailed treatment at the end of the chapter. Weaving economic history with economic thought and policy makes for a much more interesting exposition. Unfortunately, some of the economic history is less than satisfactory. In attempting to depict the "turbulent twenties," the authors refer to data of working days lost, without indicating the year referred to or the period covered by the statistic used. Concerns about employment levels are illustrated by quoting an employment figure of 425,000 in 1927 as "only a quarter of the 1913 result." Data from the most commonly used source show that employment in 1927 was 2,383,500, 17 percent higher than the 1913 figure of 2,043,800 (Withers, Endres, and Perry, 1985, p. 100; Shedvin, 1970). The point of the data quoted was that adverse and deteriorating economic conditions provided an environment conducive to some interventionist economic ideas.

One ongoing and persistent preoccupation in a developing country has been the role to be played by tariff protection. The Brigden Report (1929) commissioned by the Australian government presented a review of the impact of tariffs on the cost structure of the economy. Its arguments that protection allowed a small economy like Australia's to maintain a larger population at a given standard of living (an argument about tariffs and income distribution) and that the excess costs of tariffs are borne by the export industries are both well known in the literature of international economics. In Australia, much of the early debate (Viner, 1929, 1937) among economists took place in the pages of the fledgling *Economic Record* which, along with the Economic Society of Australia, has been continuously in existence since 1925. Apart from Jacob Viner, other contributors among the well-known academic economists of the time included D.B. Copland, E.O.G. Shann, and R.C. Mills who, to varying degrees, developed arguments opposed to the tariff. None of this analysis broke new theoretical ground. The noteworthy point is that at the policy level, discussions on the tariff and other issues were well informed by the availability of reliable statistics, including national accounts data.

Only one contribution at the time was outstanding. This was L.F. Giblin's development of a multiplier analysis for an open economy, explicitly taking account of the impact of the marginal propensity to import on the size of the multiplier. Giblin presented his analysis in his inaugural lecture at Melbourne University in 1930, which gave him precedence (formally) over R.F. Kahn, whose work was published in 1931. Giblin occupied the chair at Melbourne for just ten years. During this time and subsequently, his impact as an economist was made at the policy development level. This is equally true of the small band of economists discussed in detail by Groenewegen and McFarlane, specifically D.B. Copland, R.C. Mills, and L.G. Melville. Their influence on government policy was disproportionate to their numbers.

Although the earliest influences relate to the tariff debate and the Brigden Report, it soon spread to a wide range of policies. A link had been made between tariff protection and wages policy, which by the 1930s was already highly centralized through the determination of most wages by federal and state arbitration tribunals. Copland appeared before the federal arbitration tribunal to support a 10 percent wage cut in 1930, arguing from the point of view of treating wages only as a cost and dismissing the impact of a wage cut on aggregate demand. Opposed to R.F. Irvine, a former professor of economics at Sydney university, Copland's view prevailed and the 10 percent wage cut was prescribed. The authors suggest that the wage cut "affected a quarter of all wage earners" (p. 126), but it was much more pervasive, for nearly 80 percent of wage changes in the 1920s occurred via "awards" of arbitration tribunals (Hancock, 1979, p.48). The policy influence of the economists dates from this point.

Subsequently, it was the deflationary plan of the economists which was adopted by the Australian government in 1931, in preference to two other proposals. As the decade of the 1930s progressed, the economists' views appeared to undergo a sea change. By 1937, some economists were advocating reforms to the monetary system which would have including controls over the use of deposits by the banks and the establishment of a fully fledged central bank. With the advent of war, the economists played a major role in planning the economy. Copland subsequently adopted a more interventionist and Keynesian stance, guided the establishment of controls and rationing, and acted as a personal adviser to the Prime Minister. Mills played a major role in the Australian government's takeover of income taxing powers, and for a time Mills "tutored" the Australian treasurer in economics. Another economist, E.R. Walker, Professor of Economics at the young age of 32, also played a major part in the wartime planning of the Australian economy. Walker's role and contribution is underplayed by the authors, but the balance was redressed recently by a long obituary notice in the *Economic Record* (Cornish, 1991).

A separate chapter is devoted to nonacademic Australian economics, with the work of four economist/public servants/advisers, H.C. Coombs, R. Wilson, J.G. Crawford, and L.F. Giblin, being reserved for more detailed examination. Apart from Giblin, this relatively younger group of economists was sponsored by the academic economists/advisers, and perhaps the line of succession should have been emphasized more. They all had doctorates in economics; they espoused Keynesian ideas and promoted the pursuit of policies for full employment when the war ended. Surprisingly, the center of the intellectual ferment about new economic ideas revolved around them, as much as in the universities. (Coombs, 1981; Petridis, 1981). Some younger academics who later made their mark in Australian economics were also involved in the economic planning for war and postwar reconstruction. Most notable among them were T.W. Swan and R.F. Downing. It was during this "golden age" of policy advice that the favorable opinions about economists were translated into a recruitment policy for the public service. To this day, the upper echelons of the Australian Public Service are dominated by graduates with degrees in economics.

# IV. CONTEMPORARY AUSTRALIAN ECONOMICS

By 1950, the first phase of postwar reconstruction was completed, the academic economists returned to their universities, and the Australian Treasury department gradually gained primacy in the dispensing of economic policy advice. In the policy area, the Keynesian legacy lingered into the 1970s, but in the universities the change in emphasis began to emerge in the 1960s, although initially many of the academics who were recruited to teach the growing numbers of students came mainly from Britain. By 1975, Australian economics had succumbed to the attractions of the neoclassical, choice theoretic-based market clearing models of the economy. The transformation occurred in the presence of long-established institutions and practices which involved complex monetary and exchange controls, high tariff barriers, and centralized wage determination. A glib explanation for the transformation would point to the collapse of the Phillips curve and the failure of "Keynesian" policies in the 1970s. But the changes in Australian economics predated this episode. Groenewegen and McFarlane refer, almost pejoratively, to the Americanization of Australian economics as an explanation. There is no doubt that increased professionalization and internationalization played a part, but the changes were more subtle and complex, and the history of this transformation of Australian economic thought is still to be written.

To a certain extent, the history of Australian economic thought is one which began as a derivative of British economics and then changed to a derivative of American economics in the last thirty years. There have been distinctive Australian contributions in this contemporary period again related to domestic policy issues, but the distinctiveness has diminished as neoclassical economics became more dominant. Undoubtedly, the most distinctive contemporary features of Australian economics relate to Australia's unique system of centralized wage determination, which has spawned a huge, sometimes country-specific, literature. The authors probably do not place sufficient emphasis on this central focus of Australian economic attention. A great deal of the remaining Australian literature, which is concerned with public finance, monetary and fiscal issues, immigration and labour supply, foreign investment, savings rates, balance of payments equilibrium, tariffs, and competition policy, has been constructed around this central pillar. This domination of Australian economics is illustrated by various surveys of Australian economics, starting with Corden's (1968) survey, which includes a separate chapter on wages policy, as does Gruen's (1978) survey, and even the evaluation by North American economists (Caves and Krause, 1984), who provided "a view from the north." In general, the authors provide a well-balanced view of contemporary Australian economics by referring to elements of these surveys together with a discussion of the growth and content of the Australian journal literature and the growth of economics in the universities.

Some important topics, such as income and wealth distribution and Northern development, are "relegated" by the authors to a separate chapter dealing with "heretics, cranks and 'gifted amateurs,'" (p. 147). Much of this material is of very dubious analytical value irrespective of the ideological stance from which it is assessed. Some of the same topics are dealt with in the mainstream literature but are given only a passing reference by Groenewegen and McFarlane. Thus, the content, emphasis, and even need for this chapter might be questioned, despite the validity of the authors' view that some alternative, labor (union) centered policy emanated from these sources. It also seems somewhat of an injustice to include a detailed discussion of the views of R.F. Irvine in this chapter. According to the authors, Irvine's critique of Say's Law and anticipations of Keynes were extremely insightful — hardly cranky and, in the Australian context of the time, not even heretical.

The authors have selected seven economists to illustrate developments in contemporary economics. In a footnote, they note the difficulties and judgmental elements in this selection, correctly anticipating that every commentator would wish to add or subtract from the list. Would Kelvin Lancaster, who contributed so much to the theory of second best, to the choice-theoretic base of income-leisure decisions, and to the analysis of productivity-geared wages policy, qualify as an Australian? Those discussed are H.W. Arndt, T.W. Swan, M.C. Kemp, W.M. Corden, W.E.G. Salter, G.C. Harcourt and

S.J. Turnovsky. The eldest of these, Arndt, is less well known outside Australia, while the work of the youngest, Turnovsky, (apart from some work on expectations) seems to disappear into the scramble of model proliferation in contemporary economics. Swan's contributions to Swan-Solow models of economic growth, to internal-external balance, and earlier to Australian economic policy discussion single him out as the most significant of the group. But Corden's well-known contributions to the theory of international trade, Salter's work on productivity and technical change, and Harcourt's (probably the best known internationally) pathbreaking clarification of the Cambridge debates on capital theory and contributions to post-Keynesian economic theory, are also of great significance. Only Kemp and Turnovsky in this group received North American training and despite Groenewegen and McFarlane's reservations about the Americanization of Australian economics, these two seem to have had the smallest impact.

# V. CONCLUDING COMMENTS

This was an exceedingly difficult book to write because the authors were forced into the straitjacket of stringent space constraints. As a result, the knowledge and erudition of the authors is manifested in the form of detailed and fact-loaded sentences. At times, this generates an indigestible information overload. Unfortunately, the syntax fails in many places, while the editing throughout the book leaves a lot to be desired. A minor, and repeated irritation, is the inconsistent spelling of labor when it refers to the Australian Labor Party.

None of this detracts from an important and pathbreaking new book. A careful reader will discover much of interest and the appetite for more reading and research will be whetted. The final chapter provides a concise summary and a favorable evaluation of the successes of Australian economics. At this point, the authors are rather more moderate in their assessment of the American impact, and optimistically conclude that "it need not be a 'fatal embrace' if critically accepted" (p. 234). They suggest that three factors may determine the survival of a distinctive Australian economics. These are the possibility of an academic backlash to the "trivialisation of economics," the existence of conditions conducive to the further development of areas where Australian economists have a comparative advantage, and lastly, "whether economics might receive some enrichment from other disciplines" (pp. 235-237). Each of these factors carries some validity, but the authors waver between agnosticism and hope, and rightly so. A fourth factor has swamped the first three. It is the current state of policy debate and implementation of policy. In 1991, with unemployment rates close to postwar peaks and the economy staggering in an unusually prolonged trough, the discussion everywhere is of further deregulation of the economy, of more privatization of government enterprise, and of further fiscal restraint to reduce the size of government. Economics in Australia, like that of Eastern Europe, has been overtaken by pervasive internationalization (Americanization?), so it may no longer be possible to talk of an Australian economics.

# REFERENCES

Brigden, J.B. 1929. *The Australian Tariff: An Economic Inquiry.* Melbourne: Melbourne University Press.

Butlin, N.G., V.W. Fitzgerald, and R.H. Scott, eds. 1986. *The Australian Economist 1888-1898,* Vols. 1 and 2. Sydney: Australian National University Press.

Caves, R.E., and L.B. Krause, eds. 1984. *The Australian Economy: A View from the North.* Washington, DC: The Brookings Institution.

Clark, C. 1940. *Conditions of Economic Progress.* London: Macmillan.

Coombs, H.C. 1981. *Trial Balance.* Melbourne: Macmillan.

Corden, W.M. 1968. *Australian Economic Policy Discussion: A Survey.* Melbourne: Melbourne University Press.

Cornish, S. 1991. "Obituary: Edward Ronald Walker." Pp. 59-68 in *Economic Record* 67(196): March.

Goodwin, C.D.W. 1966. *Economic Enquiry in Australia,* Durham, NC: Duke University Press.

Gruen, F.H. 1978. *Surveys of Australian Economics,* Vol. 1. Sydney: Allen and Unwin.

Guillebaud, C.W., ed. 1961. *Alfred Marshall Principles of Economics,* Vol. II: *Notes.* London: Macmillan.

Hancock, K.J. 1979. "The First Half-Century of Wages Policy." Pp. 44-99 in *Australian Labour Economics: Readings,* 1984 edited by B.J. Chapman, J.E. Isaac, and J.R. Niland. Melbourne: Macmillan.

Petridis, A. 1981. "Australia: Economists in a Federal System." Pp. 405-435 in *History of Political Economy* 13(3, Fall).

Shedvin, C.B. 1970. *Australia and the Great Depression.* Sydney: Sydney University Press.

Syme, D. 1876. *Outlines of an Industrial Science.* London: Henry S. King and Co.

Viner, J. 1929. "The Australian Tariff." Pp. 306-315 in *Economic Record* 5(9, November).

_____. 1937. *Studies in the Theory of International Trade.* New York: Harper.

Withers, G., T. Endres, and L. Perry. 1985. "Australian Historical Statistics: Labour Statistics." Pp. 1-205 in *Source Papers in Economic History,* No. 7. Canberra: Australian National University.

# HEERTJE AND PERLMAN'S EVOLVING TECHNOLOGY AND MARKET STRUCTURE: STUDIES IN SCHUMPETERIAN ECONOMICS: A REVIEW ESSAY

*Thomas R. DeGregori*

*Evolving Technology and Market Structure: Studies in Schumpeterian Economics.*
**Edited by Arnold Heertje and Mark Perlman.**
**Ann Arbor: The University of Michigan Press, 1990. Pp. 351.**

Technology as a factor in economic processes is a theoretical phenomenon that both unites and divides us. For the authors in this fine volume, the lack of any explicit explanatory theory of technology in neoclassical economics is a major reason for these and other Schumpeterians seeing themselves as a dissenting perspective from the mainstream of economics. Conversely, it is the emerging Schumpeterian conceptualization of technology that is increasingly creating broad areas of commonality with other dissenting schools of

Research in the History of Economic Thought and Methodology, Volume 12, pages 187-192.
Copyright © 1994 by JAI Press Inc.
All rights of reproduction in any form reserved.
ISBN: 1-55938-747-5

economics such as the institutionalist. Thirty years or more ago, the differences between these two schools were seemingly unbridgeable; now, the convergence on a theory of technology and its role in economic processes is nothing short of extraordinary. When Franco Malerba and Luigi Orsenigo write that "recently, the Schumpeterian tradition has added a third variable: the cumulativeness of technological change" (p. 285) they have aligned themselves with a central tenet of the institutionalist tradition. In fact, they are closer to this tradition than are many contemporary institutionalists who have joined the antitechnology chorus. To some of us, an antitechnology institutionalist is an oxymoron or a contradiction in terms.

In six lucid pages of "Concluding Statement," Giovanni Dosi succinctly spells out the core propositions of the modern "Schumpeterian perspective" in economics (pp. 335-341). The first of "three features" is derived from evolutionary thought going back to Adam Smith. Simply stated, it is to "look at change." The second principle or method is that "history counts." The third is that though this "perspective" does not necessarily deny the relevance of the economic modeling based on assumptions of rationality, there is a "lower methodological emphasis on individual rationality as an 'ordering force' of economic coordination" (p. 336). For those of us who seek constructively to dissent from the mainstream in economics, these three "features" provide a common framework for many disparate tendencies, in addition to the Schumpeterians, to construct a comprehensive, operational alternative to the ruling paradigm in economics.

Acceptance of the first two perspectives ineluctably implies the third. As essays in this volume clearly indicate, an economic man who fulfills all of the assumptions of rationality is a person without culture or history. Also, deductively derived principles of rationality cannot incorporate change and other evolutionary transformations. Merely defining economics as being evolutionary opens a dramatically new perspective and sets a new agenda for inquiry. For the rationality model of economic behavior is a distillation from 18th- and 19th-century economic thought that was consciously imitating physics as defining the method of scientific investigation. Twentieth-century theorists such as Schumpeter and Veblen looked more to late 19th century biology to provide guidance for methodological insights into economic action as a form of human behavior. Further, they could argue that the founders of the discipline, such as Adam Smith, had a rich historical perspective that was ignored by many later theorists. We might add that the rational economic actor in an harmonious economic universe is more the ideology of 18th-century physics than the method of contemporary science.

Inquiry for a science that is not rational and deductive must foster research that is both theoretical and empirical. The essays in *Evolving Technology and Market Structure* are in the best tradition of quality empirical work organized toward reformulating and carrying foreword a theoretical tradition. Along with the 1988 book, *Technical Change And Economic Theory* (edited by Giovanni Dosi et al., 1988), this fine volume presents a clear, cogent, and comprehensive statement of modern Schumpeterian economics, particularly in relation to the role played by technology. Ironically, neither volume incorporates a perspective derived from a broad understanding of the history of technology. Given both the stated principles and the fact that in Schumpeter's time there was little if any worthwhile research in the history of technology, it is surprising that this type of inquiry is limited to case or country studies that cover a time span that goes no further back than the last century. This is doubly ironic considering the extensive writing of Joel Mokyr (*The Lever of Riches*, [1990a] and *Twenty-Five Centuries of Technological Change*, [1990b] for recent examples), who labels technological development as "Schumpeterian growth." In addition, Mokyr adds what should be a fourth principle of evolutionary economics, namely, that there are "free lunches as well as (more frequently) very cheap lunches" and that these lunches are the results of technological change (Mokyr, 1990b, P. 1). This latter principle, along with the first three, would not only create a framework for evolutionary economic analysis, it also would challenge the most sacred and fundamental principles of modern economics. It would not only set evolutionary economics apart from the mainstream, it would also define an essential differentiation from a number of recent critiques of economic methods by romantic back-to-nature, limits-to-growth theorists.

Christopher Freeman, in his essay, "Schumpeter's *Business Cycles* Revisited" finds that in Schumpeter, technological change drove the business cycle. It was the "clustering" of inventions and innovations that propelled the business cycle, and it was the slowing of the innovative impulse that forced an economic downturn. Profits derived from pioneering innovations fueled economic expansion and it was the "swarming" of the latecomers that squeezed the profits out of the technology in a manner reminiscent of Marx and led to stagnation which, interestingly enough, is defined as equilibrium.

As Freeman's analysis continues, it is evident that technology also drives the economy. Schumpeter, or at least Freeman's interpretation of him, begins to sound like Thorstein Veblen. Though innovation may involve discontinuities, there is continuity in the cumulating technology from which it is derived. Further, in Freeman, technology may be available for innovation but the "complex process of institutional and structural change" may present too many barriers to its utilization (p. 31). Recessions can result from a "mismatch between the techno-economic subsystem and the old socioinstitutional framework" (p. 34). Freeman's thesis that economies can "become the victims of their own earlier success" (p. 35) is remarkably similar to Veblen's "penalty for having taken the lead and shown the way." There is another surprising comparison between Schumpeter and a modern school of thought, and this one is explicitly stated. Raphael Valentino finds many similarities between Schumpeter and Latin American structuralist thought.

Since Schumpeter is so often identified with an almost aristocratic political conservatism, it will come as a shock to many to find his thinking in line with reformist if not radical doctrines (p. 111). Freeman's interesting and provocative essay incorporates some of the latest ideas in the understanding of technological change, such as the significance of "tacit knowledge" and the importance of new paradigms. What is refreshing is that these terms are used carefully and operationally and not, as so often is the case, as slogans. His task and, apparently, the intent of the other authors is not to pay mindless homage but to overcome "some real weaknesses in Schumpeter's pioneering formulation" which he correctly understands to be "the best tribute to the spirit of his work" (p. 35).

Richard Goodwin, in his essay "Walras and Schumpeter," has the unenviable task of reconciling Schumpeter's predominant intellectual bent and his attachment for the theories of Walras. It is a seeming contradiction that many modern Schumpeterians (including several in this volume) seek to resolve. Walras was the high priest of general equilibrium and the equations that expressed it. For Schumpeter, equilibrium prevails in a recession as in Keynes; otherwise, "the whole system operates in a high wind of technical change, the exponential growth of productive know-how" (p. 46). What Goodwin does is to take Schumpeter's "vision" and show that it can be represented by mathematical technique more sophisticated than those used by Schumpeter. While exploring Schumpeter's apparent felt need for the "essential logic of a unified account" of economic processes, Goodwin really does not reconcile the differences but does argue that it is "rewarding to analyze this apparent contradiction" (p. 39).

There are clear policy implications to the perspective that is being developed here both in the analysis of past policy decisions and in establishing an alternative policy agenda. William Lazonick ("Organizational Integration in Three Industrial Revolutions") sees the need for historical analysis "to confront the ahistorical methodology that neoclassical economists have been employing since the late nineteenth century" (p. 78). Lazonick goes right to the heart of the failures in our financial institutions when he boldly and correctly states that we have gone "from financial commitment to financial speculation" (p. 93). He argues that, therefore, we are not financing innovation and are suffering economic loss because of it. His simple but perceptive insights reflect the best in modern Schumpeterian thought and demonstrate some of the potential power of the analysis.

The case studies in this volume are fascinating. It is interesting that Schumpeter is barely mentioned in them and where he is mentioned, it is in the form of an opening genuflection to the master. Yet, there is a coherence and consistency to them. Implicit or even explicit in all of them are the basic principles stated by Dosi in his "Concluding Statement." Clearly, these case studies are concerned with change and in all of them, history counts. Some of them are even rather biting in their offhand criticisms of neoclassical economics. It could even argue that what is Schumpeterian about these essays is to be found in the questions that they ask and seek to answer and not in any specific theory or method of inquiry that they employ. The case studies are of high quality and are similar to articles in the many fine journals that are now published on technology or the history of technology. Some, like "Gateway Technologies and the Evolutionary Dynamics of Network Industries" by Paul A. David and Julie Ann Bunn, are absolute gems. Not only do David and Bunn offer original insight into an important problem in the history of technology, they also demonstrate the practical and operational significance of the proposition that history counts. They provide a satisfying explanation as to why Edison continued to promote DC electrical transmission after the emerging technology of AC transmission was clearly demonstrating its superiority. In the process, they show that some questions in the history of technology cannot be answered without bringing in economic analysis, or at least economic analysis of the right kind. Using the concept of gateway technologies, they show how the socioeconomic framework that these technologies engender establishes the pathway for subsequent technological development and makes a substantive contribution to the history of technology. Their unraveling of the inner dynamics of the interplay of technology and economics and other institutional forces is as good if not better than anything that I have seen in the literature of economics, including that of my own school of thought.

The importance and significance of this fine volume is almost beyond question. It provides a challenging and at times devastating critique of mainstream economics. That there is a coherent "Schumpeterian perspective" is overwhelmingly demonstrated in the consistency in the methods of inquiry used and the *overall* success in using them. Certainly, there is little if anything to criticize in them, though the case studies on Japan are more in the form of historical narratives that provide little insight beyond the presentation of data.

There is a perspective, a method, and so forth presented, but what is fundamentally lacking is a theory of technology as *a* if not *the* critical or dynamic component of a larger theory of economic change. This volume and the earlier Dosi et al. (1988) work provide many of the building blocks of a Schumpeterian or evolutionary economic theory but not the integrating elegance of an operational theory. Their perspective carries them a long way toward deciphering what happened but, with magnificent exceptions such as the David and Bunn article, we really do not understand why things happened as they did. A good theory not only helps us frame new questions, it defines causal relations that allow us to intervene in an operational causally effective manner. In a word, a good theory is essential for good policy.

As noted above, Schumpeter himself saw the need for an integrating theory. Instead of trying to reconcile Schumpeter with Walras, it would have been far more useful to explore the possibility of dispensing with Walras and filling that void with a theory consistent with the "vision" of Schumpeter and with the quality research of this book. Economists have long argued that technology was a "given" or that it was a "black box" into which we could not look. One of the editors of this volume, Arnold Heertje, has taken a similar position, namely, that technical change cannot be "explained" other than to say that there will be "more technical knowledge of a certain kind" and "new technical possibilities" in the future (Heertje, 1983, p. 38, 46). On the contrary, the articles in this book go a long way toward explaining technology, and there are numerous other evolutionary economists who have developed testable theories of technological change. The writing of economists who have attempted to open the black box are largely ignored other than references to the superb work of Nathan Rosenberg. Excluded is someone like Mokyr who is in the Schumpeterian tradition. That is the single greatest weakness of this otherwise outstanding volume. Failing to explore this rich vein of technological theory has the consequence of inhibiting the development of an economic theory that incorporates and integrates the heuristic perspective that has been so cogently presented here.

*Evolving Technology and Market Structure*, along with *Technical Change and Economic Theory*, is essential reading for anyone interested in technological change or in evolutionary economics. Having read the major works of Schumpeter many years ago, it is unlikely that I will ever return and read any of them again. And that, strangely enough, is a compliment to these volumes. Schumpeter is not locked into decades-old volumes, but was the progenitor of a rich, living tradition. Schumpeter is well served by his interpreters, whose work I hope to be interacting with for a long time to come.

# REFERENCES

Dosi, Giovanni, Christopher Freeman, Richard Nelson, Gerald Silverberg, and Luc Soete, eds. 1988. *Technical Change and Economic Theory.*London: Pinter.
Heertje, Arnold. 1983. "Can We Explain Technical Change." Pp. 37-49 in *The Trouble with Technology: Explorations in the Process of Technological Change,*edited by S. McDonald, D.M. Lamberton, and T. Mandeville. New York: St. Martin's Press.
Mokyr, Joel. 1990a. *The Lever of Riches: Technological Creativity and Economic Progress.*New York: Oxford University Press.
———. 1990b. *Twenty-Five Centuries of Technological Change: An Historical Survey.*Chur, Switzerland: Harwood Academic Publishers.

# ECONOMISTS AND RELIGION:
## A REVIEW ESSAY

Alon Kadish

---

*A History of Atheism in Britain from Hobbes to Russell.*
**By David Berman.**
**London and New York: Routledge, 1990.**

David Berman's *A History of Atheism in Britain from Hobbes to Russell* constitutes a fascinating attempt to construct the development of British atheism as a positive tradition within British theological and philosophical thought. Berman begins his account with the denials of the existence, as well as the possibility, of atheism in seventeenth- and eighteenth-century texts. He distinguishes between repression which, he argues, by dismissing atheism as an absurdity, operated as a "potent preventative medicine" (p. 42), and suppression, for example, by statutory means, which indicated the actual presence of atheism as an identifiable and feared school of thought (p. 48). The evidence for the latter claim is found, usually encoded, in the works of Rochester, Hobbes, Anthony Collins, Count Radicati, Charles Gildon, and Hume. Berman admits that "the idea of a secret history" may appear suspect, but, he adds, "for this writer the revealing of an interesting secret is one of the best reasons for writing a book" (p. 105). He explains the use of code as

**Research in the History of Economic Thought and Methodology, Volume 12, pages 193-199.**
**Copyright © 1994 by JAI Press Inc.**
**All rights of reproduction in any form reserved.**
**ISBN: 1-55938-747-5**

due to the wish "to influence the public mind without allowing it to become aware that it is being influenced", and "to communicate with others of a like mind" (p. 106). Where no statement exists as to an author's secret intention, Berman's key is: "Where the weight of argumentation (or emotion) is, there, all things being equal, we have placed conscious or unconscious purpose" (p. 106).

Berman next turns to the emergence of avowed atheism. He identifies the *Answer to Dr. Priestly's to a philosophical unbeliever* attributed to a Dr. Turner of Liverpool and published in 1782 as the first expressly atheistic publication. It was followed fourteen years later by *Watson refuted* (1796) by Samuel Francis M.D., and, in 1797, by *An investigation of the essence of the Deity*, possibly also by Francis, "the first direct and self-contained defence of atheism" (p. 123). But the first "great name" in British avowed atheism was Shelley. Berman identifies Shelley as an atheist during the period 1811-1814:

> because, firstly, he called himself an atheist,... Secondly, he also denies the existence of God in both published works and private letters. And, thirdly, far from having an idiosyncratic understanding of the words "atheist" and "God", he has an unusually firm grasp of their ordinary meaning. Fourthly, he also presents a reasoned case against the existence of God (p. 143).

Berman describes Shelley's contribution to the development of British atheism "as the irreligious culmination of British empiricism" (p. 145). Unlike practical atheism, that is, atheist behavior unsupported by a conscious rationale, speculative or theoretical atheism is seen as a development of British empiricism, part of a tradition that includes Pierre Bayle, Lord Shaftesbury, and Hume. Thus, the denial of the possibility of God is regarded as a legitimate outgrowth of British philosophy, rather than an incidental sideshow consisting of unrelated and occasional statements to be placed solely within a theological context. The timing of the emergence of avowed atheism is described as determined by "conscious opposition to the repressive denial of atheism, disbelief in the orthodox position, a reasoned belief in theoretical atheism, and a fierce belief in the value of truthfulness as derived from practical theism" (p. 178). Thus, atheism is presented as a natural outcome of eighteenth-century rationalism.

However it was only with Richard Carlile that Berman discerns "the beginning of a cohesive, more or less continuous atheistic movement" (p. 201), as well as the establishment of a "firm link ... between the denial of God and social change" (p. 205), with the result that "atheist and free-thought became closely identified with the lower classes" (pp. 205-206). Atheism became, according to Berman, an integral aspect of popular reformism. It was disseminated by the standard means of popular agitation — "the periodical, mass meetings and the courtroom" (p. 206) employed by agitators including Southwell, Holyoake, who "was largely responsible for uniting the various secular societies scattered over Britain" (p. 212), and Bradlaugh who is regarded as the "thorough atheist" (p. 218). Finally, by the end of the nineteenth century there occurred "a revival of more upper-class atheism" (p. 206) in the work of three Cambridge philosophers — G.E.Moore, J.M.E. McTaggart, and Bertrand Russell whose *Why I am not a Christian* (1927) was "probably the high-water mark of British atheism" (p. 233).

All this may appear, at best, marginally interesting to economists, and even to historians of economics. Yet, from the outset one might expect some methodological problems common to all histories of thought. Berman's "Preface" is somewhat misleading. He will, he announces, provide "a new perspective" to the subject:

> Instead of asking why nearly all people at nearly all times have believed in God [i.e. the traditional anthropological approach], I try to answer these questions: What are the psychological and social forces that have prevented the emergence of atheism in nearly all people at nearly all times? Why has atheism arisen so late, so erratically, and so feebly? What are the pressures that have made the public avowal of atheism so difficult?(p. ix).

What is wanted "is a wider examination." The result, however, remains largely an internalist history, which, while focusing on the link between atheism and philosophy, accords far too little attention to the influence of social, political, and other historical factors.

In the absence of sufficient historical evidence, a number of problems emerge. Repressive denial is understood to have effectively retarded the development of atheism, that is, a mental and intellectual reaction to the possibility of atheism controlling its coming into existence. Suppression, on the other hand, reflected the presence of atheism, that is, a reaction following the emergence of a new mental and intellectual position. The process and order of cause and effect are far from clear. There is no attempt at a detailed historical explanation of the appearance of atheism despite the alleged operation of effective repression. Berman does refer somewhat vaguely to the relevance of the Restoration of 1660 and to the attitude of the upper classes (p. 48), possibly reacting against Puritanism. But elsewhere he mentions upper-class support of religion as a means "of keeping the lower orders orderly" in order to explain eighteenth-century deism (p. 170). Assuming that upper class interests did not undergo radical change from one century to the other, it can hardly be expected, as a class, to subvert the system it had a vested interest in by cultivating atheism.

Another problem concerns the use of contemporary reactions as a means of determining a writer's intentions. Hobbes crypto-atheism is partly revealed by the accusations of his critics and the approval of fellow atheists (p. 61). Berman admits that this does not necessarily make Hobbes an atheist, but he is reasonably confident that he was one. A similar method of exposure is employed in the case of Radicati, where the evidence of Richard Blackmore and Bishop Berkeley is produced in support of Berman's textual analysis. But in discussing Shelley, Berman argues that he was misunderstood by those of his contemporaries who regarded him as a deist (pp. 141-142).

Berman may well be right on all accounts, but he does not produce the historical evidence to prove it. His account is lacking a detailed historical analysis of the various stages of the development of atheism. It is quite possible that Hobbes' contemporaries accurately understood his real meaning while Shelley's did not. But in both cases, a historical explanation is required since it is obvious that contemporaneousness does not guarantee validity. Repressive denial may had been an effective preventative and a reaction to the possibility of atheism, and suppression an ineffective reaction to the presence of atheism, but a comprehensive historical explanation of the birth of British atheism is needed in order to work out the causal order of things.

One major blunder, however, is Berman's identification of nineteenth-century atheism with working-class radicalism. Bradlaugh (1833-1891) was indeed a popular leader with a working-class following, although his constituency, Northampton, did not posses a strong labor movement (see Foster, 1979, pp. 102-104). But atheism was not adopted as a popular working-class cause. The absence of working-class worshippers in the country's churches revealed by the 1851 and later surveys was due not to atheism but to indifferentism (see, for instance, Waller, 1983, p. 224; Rose, 1986, p. 26). Berman appears to suggest (apropos the question of ascertaining implicit meaning) that the history of atheism is not merely a chronological account of the development of a philosophical doctrine but also part of the process of the general progression of society, and the working-classes in particular, toward a more equitable and rational system. By adopting atheism, the lower classes were striking a blow against traditional class hierarchy and social control. But, as Noel Annan had noted, the "free thinkers themselves were untainted by revolutionary ideas" (see Annan, 1951, p. 158). They belonged to the reformist tradition which dominated mid-century rather than late nineteenth-century working-class politics. It is significant that Bradlaugh ended his life as an anti-Socialist Liberal M.P.

It is at this point that one might bring in economics. Boyd Hilton has produced in *The Age of Atonement* (1988), an impressive and important demonstration of the relevance of theology and the history of religion to the understanding of the development of British economic thought and policy. The matter should be taken further in time but not along the lines suggested by Berman's account. The militant atheism of Charles Bradlaugh was joined with a doctrinaire adherence to classical economics. His authorities were the Mills, McCulloch, the Fawcetts, and Malthus (Bradlaugh, 1877). Bradlaugh renounced not only all religion but also all forms of collectivism in favour of extreme individualism. His view of society was atomistic whereby "the only sufficient inducement to the general urging on of progress in society is by individual effort spurred to action by the hope of private gain (Bradlaugh, 1907, p. 14). He had no vision to offer the working classes beyond the possibility of individual progression. "It is no use appealing to the future," he stated in his 1884 debate with Hyndman on socialism. "The present is here" (Bradlaugh and Hyndman, 1970, p. 23)

Doubt is the yeast of intellectual ferment, not certainty. The religious context of the late nineteenth-century blossoming of economics is to be sought not in the certainty of atheism but in doubt-ridden deism. The liberation of economics from the finality of orthodoxy may be seen as part of late Victorian and Edwardian frantic efforts to construct systems to replace the universalism and totality of religion, as well as classical liberalism, without either resorting to metaphysical dogma or to amoral materialism. Perturbed by the increasing threats of social conflict and economic regression, economists sought to uncover both the true harmony of forces and interests that lay beneath the surface of confrontation and strife, and the means of allowing the former to subdue the latter. Their universe was dynamic, not static. Their eyes were to a better future, not merely to a more efficient utilization of the present. In this, economists were not unique. According to Annan (1951, p. 243):

> the 'seventies and the 'eighties were years in which the prevailing political ethos, the system of duties and privileges on which institutions were built, and the economic structure, were all being criticised by the younger school of liberals, by the Fabians and the imperialists.

The efforts to construct alternative systems lasted well into the Edwardian period, and the reader of Jonathan Rose, *The Edwardian Temperament 1895-1919* (1986) is struck by the variety and sense of urgency in the searches for "surrogate religion."

This reviewer has studied the particular case of Arnold Toynbee, whose religious crisis in the 1870s was resolved by T.H. Green's deism whereby the metaphysics of religion was replaced by a sense of duty and the gospel of service as the true essences of faith. Accordingly, Toynbee turned from religion and a commitment to Church reform to the study of political economy and a restless search for means of social and economic amelioration, while trying to work out the general principles of harmonious progress (Kadish, 1986). Indeed, Oxford economics of the 1880s were to a large extent part of a common search for the means by which Oxford Idealism could be practically implemented. Another example may be found in Toynbee's student W.J. Ashley. Raised as a Baptist (he became a full member at the age of 15), he was married in 1888 in a Congregational church. In 1897, while at Harvard, he became an Episcopalian, and following his return to Britain became active as a lay preacher (A. Ashley, 1932). As an economist (in the old catholic sense), Ashley sought to discover through the study of history the evolutionary laws of human progress. In a sermon he gave in Birmingham in 1920, Ashley (1925) declared:

> Christianity is essentially an attitude and a temper; an attitude of confidence that somehow the Universe has a good meaning, a temper of determination to help our fellow men. Such an attitude is not inconsistent with the large lessons of human evolution, as taught us by modern science; and it is conducive to progress as our reason conceives it.

The combination of deism and the search for a systematic and dynamic explanation of the operation of the economy which, in turn, would serve as a guide to future progress was not unique to Oxford. W.S. Jevons, we are told, "believed there was a Creator, but he did not believe in the inspiration and authority of the Bible," and he "intended to show the perfect compatibility of the teaching of modern science with religion" (Black and Könekamp, 1972, p. 52). Alfred Marshall came from a family which liked to believe that it was of a well-connected clerical stock.[1] His plans to take holy orders after Cambridge and possibly join a foreign mission were dropped at the time that Henry Sidgewick was grappling with his inability to accept Christian dogma which led to his resignation in 1869 of his Trinity Fellowship. In his epilogue, Berman argues that J.S. Mill's criticism of Dean Mansel in *Examination of Sir William Hamilton's Philosophy* (1865) was the most important discernable point at which "the onus of proof passed from unbelievers to the believers" (Berman, 1990, p. 235). According to J.M. Keynes, Mansel's reply showed Marshall "how much there was to be defended" (Keynes, 1924, p. 8). Although described by Keynes as an agnostic, Marshall was also said to have "sympathised with Christian morals and Christian ideals and Christian incentives," and to have been, like Sidgwick, "as far as possible from adopting an "anti-religious" attitude" (Keynes, 1924, p. 8).[2] All of which may be seen as leading to his search for "The Many in the One, the One in the Many" (see Reisman, 1987, chap. 7.3).

More examples come to mind: J.A. Hobson's organicist view of society (Allett, 1990); and Archdeacon Cunningham's criticism of individualism, his claim for the moral superiority of the ordered national community, and the importance of religion in supporting a superior morality (Maloney, 1985, pp. 109-112). The full story of late-nineteenth-century religion and economics is yet to be written. But it is doubtful whether the advent of atheism so ably and lucidly described by David Berman will be one of its main features.

## NOTES

1. For a detailed discussion of fact and fantasy in the Marshall family history, see Coase (1990).

2. An agnostic according to Leslie Stephen held that religion demoralizes society (see Annan, 1951, p. 172).

# REFERENCES

Allett, John. 1990. "The Conservative Aspect of Hobson's New Liberalism." Pp. 74-99 in *Reappraising J.A. Hobson: Humanism and welfare.* Edited by Michael Freeden. London: Unwin Hyman.

Annan, Noel. 1951. *Leslie Stephen: His Thought and Character in Relation to his Time,* London: Macgibbon and Kee.

Ashley, Anne. 1932. *William James Ashley: A Life.* London: P.S. King and Son.

Ashley, William. 1925. *The Christian Outlook: Being the Sermons of an Economist.* London: Longmans.

Berman, David. 1990. *A History of Atheism in Britain from Hobbes to Russell.* London and New York: Routledge..

Black, R.D. Collison, and Rosamond Könekamp (eds.). 1972. *Papers and Correspondence of William Stanley Jevons.* London: Macmillan.

Bradlaugh, Charles. 1970. *Jesus, Shelley, and Malthus; or, Pious Poverty and Heterodox Happiness [1861].* In *A Selection of the Political Pamphlets of Charles Bradlaugh.* New York: Augustus M. Kelley. (Originally published 1877) Pamphlet no. 13.

Bradlaugh, Charles, and H.M. Hyndman. 19707. "*Debate Between H.M. Hynman and Charles Bradlaugh: Will Socialism Benefit the English People [1884].*" In *A Selection of the Political Pamphlets of Charles Bradlaugh.* New York: Augustus M. Kelley (Originally published 1907) Pamplhet no. 3.

Coase, R.H. 1990. "Alfred Marshall's family and ancestry." Pp. 9-27 in *Alfred Marshall in Retrospect,* edited by Rita McWilliams Tullberg. Aldershot: Edward Elgar.

Foster, John. 1979. *Class Struggle and the Industrial Revolution: Early Industrial Capitalism in Three English Towns.* London: Methuen.

Hilton, Boyd. 1988. *The Age of Atonement.* Oxford: Clarendon Press.

Kadish, Alon. 1986. *Apostle Arnold: The Life and Death of Arnold Toynbee 1852-1883.* Durham, NC: Duke University Press.

Keynes, J.M. 1924. "Alfred Marshall, 1842-1924. Pp. 1-65 in *Memorials of Alfred Marshall,* edited by A.C. Pigou. London: Macmillan (first published in *Economic Journal,* September 1924).

Maloney, John. 1985. *Marshall, Orthodoxy and the Professionalisation of Economics.* Cambridge: Cambridge University Press.

Reisman, David. 1987. *Alfred Marshall: Progress and Politics.* Basingstoke and London: Macmillan.

Rose, Jonathan. 1986. *The Edwardian Temperament 1895-1919.* Athens, Ohio: Ohio University Press.

Waller, Philip J. 1983. *Town, City, and Nation: England 1850-1914,* Oxford: Oxford University Press.

# SWEDBERG'S *JOSEPH A. SCHUMPETER:*
# *THE ECONOMICS AND SOCIOLOGY OF*
# *CAPITALISM:*
## *A REVIEW ESSAY*


*Charles E. Staley*

---

*Joseph A. Schumpeter: The Economics and Sociology of Capitalism.*
**Edited by Richard Swedberg**
**Princeton, NJ: Princeton University Press, 1991. Pp. 492. $59.50, cloth; $19.95, paper.**

Joseph A. Schumpeter's major work of mature scholarship, *Business Cycles*, was received with indifference and poor reviews (the review by Kuznets [1940] in the *American Economic Review* (1940) is perhaps the best known.) From this low point in his reputation, there has occured a veritable gale of creative reappraisal, in which interest in the entire body of his work has rebounded enormously.[1] Much as Paul Sweezy attributed the rise in the interest in Marx in the 1960s to the need of the radical left for a coherent tradition to which its members could relate, I suspect the interest in Schumpeter comes in large part from those who are looking for a coherent point of view about the

---

**Research in the History of Economic Thought and Methodology, Volume 12, pages 201-210.**
**Copyright © 1994 by JAI Press Inc.**
**All rights of reproduction in any form reserved.**
**ISBN: 1-55938-747-5**

operation of our actual economies which the increasingly highly abstract mathematical output of economic theory does not provide.[2]

Richard Swedberg has collected twelve pieces, dating from 1918 to 1950, and has provided a 74-page introduction to the man and his work. Swedberg, a sociologist at the University of Stockholm, selected two major categories from Schumpeter's enormous output: sociological articles, and writings on the state of capitalism (which, from an early date, Schumpeter believed to be declining).[3] Some of these, such as "The Crisis of the Tax State," "The Sociology of Imperialisms," and "Social Classes in an Ethnically Homogeneous Environment," have been translated and published elsewhere; others, such as "Max Weber's Work," which was originally published in German in 1920 and is published here in English for the first time, will be new to non-German readers; and "An Economic Interpretation of Our Time: The Lowell Lectures" (1941), from the Harvard Archives, will be new to everyone. (Only part of one article, "The Creative Response in Economic History" (1947), overlaps with the earlier collection of Schumpeter's essays (Clemence, 1951); Swedberg includes a more complete version).

Swedberg's biographical note briefly describes Schumpeter's boyhood, education, professorships in Austria, stint as Financial Minister of Austria, job as president of a Viennese bank, professorship at Bonn, and his long career at Harvard.[4] Turning to Schumpeter's work, Swedberg emphasizes that Schumpeter's entire work has a unity, partly because his "preanalytic vision" (Schumpeter's own phrase) was uncommonly broad, and partly because he expressed his vision within the *Sozialoekonomik* which emerged around 1900 in reaction to the *Methodenstreit*. Gustav Schmoller had argued vigorously for the primacy of the historical method to derive economic laws; Carl Menger argued for looking for "essences" in a theoretical approach. *Sozialoekonomik*, as promoted by Weber, was a broad kind of economics, which would resolve the *Methodenstreit* by including both the theoretical and historical research programs, as well as economic sociology. In Weber's view, these approaches would conduct a dialogue with each other rather than being integrated in a single analysis.[5] Schumpeter (1914), as well as several other early works, discusses *Sozialoekonomik*. Historical research was to him part of economics, as was economic theory, economic sociology, and statistics. He used this broad approach all his life, and devoted chapter 2 of *History of Economic Analysis* (1954) to a rather thorough description of these four fields, which he described as the techniques of the "scientific" economist.[6] (In a footnote on p. 21 he mentions that *Sozialoekonomie* was a parallel term to "scientific" economics.) He regarded himself as primarily an economic theorist, although his theory as expressed in *The Theory of Economic Development* (1912) was designed to be more dynamic than traditional economic theory by accounting for changes within capitalism brought about by forces internal to the economic system (the entrepreneur and his financiers, the banks). But with his enormous energy, he did not confine himself to economic theory; however, his sociological work took the form of concrete studies rather than sociological theory (these were the three mentioned earlier: on the tax state, imperialism, and social classes). In his later years he continued the *Sozialoekonomic* program; *Business Cycles* attempted to employ theory, history, and statistics, and *Capitalism, Socialism, and Democracy* focused on the "sociology of capitalism"—those forces affecting the economy which are not purely economic phenomena.

In addition to the books, several articles in the Swedberg volume show Schumpeter's continued concern for *Sozialoekonomik*—the complete version of "The Creative Response in Economic History," here called "Comments on a Plan for the Study of Entrepreneurship"; "The Future of Private Enterprise in the Face of Modern Socialistic Tendencies" (1945) which, surprisingly, advocated corporate organization in the sense of *Quadragesimo Anno* (associations of workers and enterprises to make economic decisions); and the Lowell lectures. To complete the roster of items chosen by Swedberg, there is a 1931 speech delivered in Japan, "Recent Developments of Political Economy"; a paper written for a 1940 Harvard informal seminar, "The Meaning of Rationality in the Social Sciences"; a brief outline of five lectures given in 1948 at the University of Mexico called "Wage and Tax Policy in Transitional States of Society"; and another brief outline for a series of speeches which Schumpeter had planned, but died before delivering, at the Walgreen Foundation in Chicago on "American Institutions and Economic Progress." Swedberg analyzes each of these publications briefly and concludes with this thought: "Indeed, the isolation of 'economic theory' from the other social sciences has grown considerably since Schumpeter's death in 1950. This is in many ways a negative and anomalous development, which must be overcome if economics and nearby types of analyses—such as economic history and economic sociology—are to really flourish again. In the end, this is one reason why Schumpeter's ideas on *Sozialoekonomik* are still of great interest to us today" (p. 77). The book concludes with an extremely useful bibliography of Schumpeter's writings, compiled by Massimo M. Augello, which updates Elizabeth Boody Schumpeter's 1950 bibliography.

Swedberg's interest in sociology is evident in his selection of *Sozialoekonomik* as the organizing principle for his analysis of Schumpeter's work. Other influences were also important in Schumpeter's intellectual heritage. He always acknowledged his debt to Walras, and practically everybody points out his debt to Marx. The general tenor of Austrian economics is very evident—the emphasis on disequilibrium, time, and change (Vaughn, 1990). With respect to the entrepreneur, the centerpiece of Schumpeterian economics, Streissler (1982) credits Schumpeter's teacher Friedrich von Wieser with ideas about the creative entrepreneur and the need for credit to finance innovations, and Samuels (1983) adds that von Wieser contributed ideas about the importance of a disciplined labor force and historical education in every economic system.[7]

Santarelli and Pesciarelli, 1990, find that Schumpeter's entrepreneur has elements in common with Nietzsche's overmen, and also trace influences of Bergson, Sorel and Mach.

Swedberg's introduction keeps *Socioloekonomik* in the foreground, but his subtitle, "The Economics and Sociology of Capitalism," highlights the subject matter of Schumpeter's research. Whatever piece of the apparatus of social science Schumpeter was using for a given research project, the purpose of the exercise was to study some aspect of capitalism. He surveyed "The Crisis of the Desmesne Economy at the Close of the Middle Ages" (p. 103), but that was necessary background to understand the "Crisis of the Tax State" in 1918. He wanted to understand imperialism's role in capitalism, but he found that "What imperialism looks like when it is not mere words, and what problems it offers, can best be illustrated by examples from antiquity" (p. 156). He studied Greco-Roman economics, not only because of its intrinsic interest but because knowledge of previous economics is necessary to understand the economics of today ("much more than in, say, physics is it true in economics that modern problems, methods, and results cannot be fully understood without some knowledge of how economists have come to reason as they do" (Schumpeter, 1954, p. 6).[8]

The core of Schumpeter's analysis of capitalism may be expressed in desperate brevity (a familiar Schumpeterianism) as follows:

1.  Imagine an economy in stationary equilibrium, with the same things being produced in the same way year after year, with no savings and no population growth (Schumpeter, 1908).

2.  This static circular flow is disturbed by an entrepreneur who introduces a new product or a new technique of producing an existing product. He finances his innovation with newly created bank money. The existing general equilibrium of product and factor prices is completely upset, but the economy establishes a new circular flow equilibrium in which the temporary profits of the entrepreneur and the interest he pays the bank are eliminated (Schumpeter, 1912).

3.  The time path of the economy has a cyclical motion because other entrepreneurs copy the original innovator, and there is a swarm of new investment which leads to a business cycle upswing; as the innovations are absorbed and as the original bank loans are repaid, the depression phase of the cycle follows. Historical research shows that there are actually three cycles superimposed on one another: the 50-to-60 year Kondratiefs, the 10-year Juglars, and the 40-month Kitchen cycles (Schumpeter, 1939).[9]

4.  Sometime around the beginning of the third Kondratief in 1898, classical capitalism changed under the rise of large corporations into the modern

form, where competition involves the innovations supplied by large-scale research rather than the price-cutting of pure competition (Schumpeter, 1942).

What do the articles in Swedberg's collection contribute to understanding this central core, or are they peripheral to Schumpeter's major intellectual effort? After all, when Schumpeter prepared the second German edition of *Theorie der wirtschaftlichen Entwicklung* in 1926, he shortened the book by 179 pages "mainly by omitting the seventh chapter of the first edition with its predominantly sociological themes, a move designed to emphasize to his readers that it was the *economics* of development that he felt represented his main contribution" (Oakley, 1990, p. 5).

It is no surprise that "Comments on a Plan for the Study of Entrepreneurship" is rich in expressions of Schumpeter's belief in the centrality of innovation. He is astonished at Keynes and the Keynesians who "explicitly exclude from sight what to the unbiased mind is the most striking feature of capitalist life—the incessant revolution, by a 'disruptive innovating energy', of existing industrial and commercial patterns" (p. 406). However, to the despair of model builders, the "creative response" of some entrepreneurs to the innovations introduced by others can practically never be predicted ex ante; historical research is needed to study each case ex post (p. 411). In doing the research, the historian should realize that, "The definition that equates enterprise to innovation is of course a very abstract one" (p. 413), and much of the article is concerned with specific points that historians should look for in researching the entrepreneur. This is only a sample to illustrate the importance of this article to Schumpeter's main system.

"An Economic Interpretation of our Time: The Lowell Lectures" (1945) is useful because it contains an application of Schumpeter's business cycle theory to the 1920s and 1930s. He describes the events and attempts to show that the 1929-1932 crisis was not unprecedented, comparing it to 1873-1878 (p. 350). He explains why America suffered more than Europe (speculative excesses, weak banking system, misguided Federal Reserve policy). Then he asks what was new, and answers that it was the spirit in which familiar events like unemployment and speculative excess was met—not simply indictments by professional critics of capitalism but the condemnation of the American people (p. 353). This would seem to lead to the conclusion that capitalism will end not with a bang but with a whimper except that he assures the audience that fighting for capitalism is not a hopeless task (p. 399). This article is simultaneously an example of *Socialoekonomik* and a readable review of much of Schumpeter's main system.

The big three of Schumpeter's sociological efforts—the tax state, imperialism, and social classes—fit into and fill out Schumpeter's system of capitalist development. The modern tax state grew out of the medieval prince's need for revenue to fight his wars; medieval life disintegrated and modern democracies took over his power. But this power is dependent on what it can wring from the economy—it drives its finances deep into the flesh of the private economy (p. 111). The state lives as an economic parasite, and it must not "demand from the people so much that they lose financial interest in production or at any rate cease to use their best energies for it." (p. 112). Based on this principle, Schumpeter analyzed various forms of taxation. His system prescribes that entrepreneurial profit be taxed lightly, although actual practice brutally destroys it. His charter membership in supply-side economics is obvious.

In his study of imperialism, Schumpeter contended that in a purely capitalist world there would be no need for imperialism; with free trade and competitive markets, decisions are made by the market, there is no need to own raw materials since they can be purchased at fair market prices, and energy in this society goes into industry not war. The protectionism, monopolies, and national rivalries which we see are survivals from the era of monarchies. "The only point at issue here was to demonstrate, by means of an important example, that the dead always rule the living" (p. 214). However much he disagreed with Keynes's macroeconomic analysis, they were at one on the proposition that "it is ideas, not vested interests, which are dangerous for good or evil" (Keynes, 1936, p. 384). Having said that, it comes as a shock to find, in one of the great mysteries of Schumpeterian scholarship, that in the 1930s Schumpeter changed his mind and disavowed the atavistic theory of imperialism (Schumpeter, 1939, Vol. 2, p. 696, fn 1), noting, "It is impossible here to expound the reasons why it is inadequate." He said much the same thing in the newly published Lowell lectures, without doing much to dispel the mystery: of the two theories which account for imperialism, the socialist theory linking it to big business capitalism and the theory based on atavisms, "In the light of later events we may well suspect that both were wrong." (p. 345).

The tax state is a thorn in the flesh of capitalist enterprise, and imperialism is derived from the rivalries of past days, but the social class structure is much more an integral part of the capitalist model. Each social class is a special social organism whose units are families. Families move within and across social classes; an upward movement may occur because the class member performs the tasks of his class more successfully than most, or he may *do something altogether different*" (italics in the original, p. 253). This is what entrepreneurs do; a study in the *Journal of the Royal Statistical Society* in 1912 showed that 63% to 85% of the leaders in the English cotton industry had risen from the working class (p. 251). And the descendents of the entrepreneur sink into a lower class when they merely plow back into the business a set proportion of profits, "without blazing new trails, without being devoted heart and soul, to the business alone" (p. 243). Swedberg judges that Schumpeter was more successful in linking sociology to economic theory in this essay than he was in the essay on imperialism (p. 53).

Without staying to comment on the content of the other essays in Swedberg's collection, let us summarize. Schumpeter always thought that his research was a starting point and he hoped that others would continue and complete his program ("The younger generation of economists should look upon this book merely as something to shoot at and to start from—as a motivated program for further research. Nothing, at any rate, could please me more" (Schumpeter, 1939, Vol. I, p. v). What does the Schumpeterian revival noted above show that the "younger generation" thinks was important about Schumpeter's ideas? First, many of them (including Swedberg) think that Schumpeter's mastery and use of research techniques other than economic theory is of major importance. Second, with respect to the substantive content of his theory, his theories of innovation and the entrepreneur occupy center stage (see, for example, Heertje and Perlman, 1990). Of these theories, the dynamic competition afforded by competitive innovation in oligopolies is taken by many to be the way in which competition really works in the real world (see Hanusch, 1988). Third, "The practitioners of public choice and social choice theory tend to hold onto the Schumpeterian legacy, particularly his work on capitalism, socialism, and democracy" (Heertje and Perlman, 1990, p. 2). Fourth, there is much recent interest in the long wave, which, under the name of the Kondratief, was central to Schumpeter's *Business Cycles* (see Freeman, Clark, and Soete, 1982). And what about his vision that mature capitalism must inevitably change into socialism? I wonder how he would accomodate Ronald Reagan and Margaret Thatcher into that vision? A major turnaround in the course of history or a temporary interruption? After all, "A prophet" (which, it seems, Reagan was) "does more than merely formulate a message acceptable to his early adherents; he is successful and comprehensible only when he also formulates a policy that is *valid* at the moment" italics in original, (p. 169).

# NOTES

1. For example, the International Joseph A. Schumpeter Society has 515 members in 31 countries and publishes the proceedings of its annual conferences. Interest has spread to the extent that *The American Scholar*, published by the Phi Beta Kappa Society, a journal not prone to pay much attention to economics, included an article (McCraw, 1991) in a recent issue.

2. "During our previous period" (1945—mid-1960s) "the idea of growth, however attenuated, remained a major focus of economic inquiry. During the subperiod now under consideration" (mid-1960s—mid-1980s) "economic inquiry largely abandons even this frail link to historical relevance. Economic discourse becomes characterized by a pronounced tendency to formalism, in which choice theoretics becomes the principal mode of representing the interactions of the decision-making units under scrutiny" (Heilbroner, 1990, p. 1106).

3. One of these, the record of a talk given to the U.S. Department of Agriculture Graduate School in 1936, is called "Can Capitalism Survive" and begins with the sentence "No, ladies and

gentlemen, it cannot" (p. 298). (Swedberg included this verbatim transcript to give a picture of Schumpeter's style of lecturing.) Even earlier, Schumpeter (1928; not reprinted in the Swedberg volume) concluded with the same thesis he later developed in *Capitalism, Socialism, and Democracy*: "Capitalism...creates, by rationalizing the human mind, a mentality and a style of life incompatible with its own fundamental conditions...and will be changed...into an order of things which it will be merely a matter of taste and terminology to call Socialism or not" (pp. 385-386). Indeed, his Cassandra complex was expressed still earlier in Schumpeter (1918): "Society is growing beyond private enterprise and the tax state. *That* too is certain" (p. 131).

4. Allen (1991), the definitive biography, was not available to Swedberg.

5. Shionoya (1991), describes Schumpeter's critiques of Schmoller and Weber with an emphasis on Schumpeter's research method rather than his substantive analysis.

6. Weber and Schumpeter used economic sociology as a research technique to investigate economic phenomena (for example, Weber's study of the relation of the Protestant ethic to economic growth, and Schumpeter's study of imperialism). In an interesting twist, Jensen (1987, p. 126), claims that Schumpeter introduced economic sociology as a tool to explain "the source, setting, and analytic consequences" of the motivation of the pre-analytic foundations of economic analysis. Whereas Jensen shows by quotes from Schumpeter that it is possible to describe the motivations of the doctrines of Smith, Marx, and Keynes, and set them in an economic-sociological framework, it is not for this purpose that Schumpeter introduced the tool, as Swedberg (1989, p. 508) points out. It had been part of his own research agenda from the beginning.

7. By the way, Samuels (1983), remarks that "Schumpeter was institutionalist in the scope and content of his interests, but, possibly for reasons of ideology, world view, and career, was loathe to admit it" (p. 18). The following statement of Schumpeter's may cast some light on this point:

> while in Germany that part of the work of Schmoller spoiled by errors has been put aside by most economists, there is a revival of the errors in America under the name of institutionalism. Institutionalism is nothing but the methodological errors of German historians (p. 292).

The errors were doing history without theory in the sense in which Marshall defined it, as a tool, an engine of analysis (p. 290).

8. The fact that Schumpeter's subject matter was capitalism explains why, to quote Dyer (1988):

> A serious gap remains, however, in Schumpeter's theoretical analysis of development. He never succeeds in explaining the nature of the process that alters social and economic meanings and results in a new social hierarchy...his theories of social order and social change are based on the concept of social conditions. However, he fails to specify either the exact nature of social conditions or what factors produce a change in those conditions (p. 40).

Dyer's criticism is beside the point; Schumpeter was not trying to provide a complete explanation of social life, but of what he regarded as important in understanding capitalism. For many of the important elements, he said that he could not provide the completed research but that he opened doors for others to enter. Sometimes there was nothing behind the doors, of course.

9. Oakley (1990), is an excellent analytical treatment of the core of Schumpeter's theory of capitalism. The older brief guide, by Clemence and Doody, [1950] (1966), lacks Oakley's thoughtful appraisal.

# REFERENCES

Allen, Robert Loring. 1991. *Opening Doors: The Life and Work of Joseph Schumpeter.*New Brunswick, NJ: Transaction Publishers.

Clemence, Richard V., ed. 1951. *Essays of J.A. Schumpeter.*Cambridge, MA: Addison-Wesley.

Clemence, Richard V., and Francis S. Doody. 1966. *The Schumpeterian System.* New York: Augustus M. Kelley (reprinted from the 1950 edition).

Dyer, Alan W. 1988. "Schumpeter as an Economic Radical: An Economic Sociology Assessed." *History of Political Economy* 20(Spring): 27-41.

Freeman, Christopher, John Clark, and Luc Soete. 1982. *Unemployment and Technical Innovation: A Study of Long Waves in Economic Development.*London: Pinter Publishers.

Hanusch, Horst, ed. 1988. *Evolutionary Economics: Applications of Schumpeter's Ideas.* Cambridge: Cambridge University Press.

Heertje, Arnold, and Mark Perlman, eds. 1990. *Evolving Technology and Market Structure: Studies in Schumpeterian Economics.* Ann Arbor: University of Michigan Press.

Heilbroner, Robert. 1990. "Analysis and Vision in the History of Modern Economic Thought." *Journal of Economic Literature* XXVIII (3, September): 1097-1104.

Heilbroner, Robert, 1990. Analysis and Vision in the History of Modern Economic Thought *Journal of Economic Literature* 28: (3)6 1097-1104.

Jensen, Hans E. 1987. "New Lights on J.A. Schumpeter's Theory of the History of Economics?" Pp. 125-134 in *Research in the History of Economic Thought and Methodology,* Vol. 5, edited by Warren J. Samuels. Greenwich, CT: JAI Press.

Keynes, John Maynard. 1936. *The General Theory of Employment Interest and Money.* London: MacMillan.

Kuznets, Simon. 1940. "Schumpeter's *Business Cycles.*" *American Economic Review* 30(June): 257-271.

McCraw, Thomas K. 1991. "Schumpeter Ascending." *The American Scholar* 60(Summer): 371-392.

Oakley, Allen. 1990. *Schumpeter's Theory of Capitalist Motion.*Brookfield, VT: Edward Elgar.

Samuels, Warren J. 1983. "The Influence of Friedrich von Wieser on Joseph A. Schumpeter." *History of Economics Society Bulletin* 4(Winter): 5-19.

Santarelli, Enrico, and Enzo Pesciarelli. 1990. "The Emergence of a Vision: The Development of Schumpeter's Theory of Entrepreneurship." *History of Political Economy* 22(Winter): 677-698.

Schumpeter, Joseph A. 1908. *Das Wesen und der Hauptinhalt der theoretischen Nationaloekonomie. (The Nature and Essence of Theoretical Economics.)* Munich and Leipzig: Duncker & Humblot.

_____. 1912. *Theorie der wirschaftlichen Entwicklung.*Leipzig: Duncker & Humblot. (English translation: *The Theory of Economic Development: An Inquiry into Profits, Capital, Credit, Interest, and the Business Cycle,*translated by Redvers Opie, London: Oxford University Press, 1934.)

_____. 1914. "Epochen der Dogmen- und Methodengeschicte." In *Grundriss der Sozialoekonomic, I Abteilung, Wirtschaft und Wirtschaftswissenschaft.*Tuebingen, Germany: J.C.B. Mohr (P. Siebeck). (English translation: *Economic Doctrine and Method: An Historical Sketch,*translated by R. Aris, New York: Oxford University Press, 1954.)

_____. 1918. "Die Krise des Steurstaates." *Zeitfragen aus dem Gebiete der Soziologie* 4: 3-74. (English translation: "The Crisis of the Tax State," translated by W. F. Stolper and R. A. Musgrave, *International Economic Papers,* Vol. 4, London: MacMillan, 1954, pp. 5-38. Reprinted in Swedberg, 1991.)

_____. 1919-1919. "Zur Soziologie der Imperialismen." *Archiv fuer Sozialwissenschaft und Sozialpolitick,* 46: 1-39, 275-310. (English translation: *Imperialism and Social*

*Classes,*translated by H. Norden, New York: A.M. Kelley, 1951. Reprinted in Swedberg, 1991.)

———. 1927. "Die sozialen Klassen im ethnisch homogenen Milieu." *Archiv fuer Sozialwissenschaft und Sozialpolitik* 57: 1-67. (English translation: *Imperialism and Social Classes,*translated by H. Norden, New York: A.M. Kelley.)

———. 1928. "The Instability of Capitalism." *Economic Journal* 38(3, September): 361-386.

———. 1939. *Business Cycles: A Theoretical, Historical ans Statistical Analysis of the Capitalist Process.* New York: McGraw-Hill.

———. 1954. *History of Economic Analysis.*New York: Oxford University Press.

———. 1976. *Capitalism, Socialism, and Democracy.* 5th edn., with introduction by T. Bottomore. New York: Harper & Brothers (first published 1942).

Shionoya, Yuichi. 1991. "Schumpeter on Schmoller and Weber: A Methodology of Economic Sociology." *History of Political Economy* 21(Summer): 193-221.

Streissler, Erich. 1982. "Schumpeter's Vienna and the Role of Credit in Innovation." Pp. 60-83 in *Schumpeterian Economics,* edited by Helmut Frisch. New York: Praeger.

Swedberg, Richard. 1989. "Joseph A. Schumpeter and the Tradition of Economic Sociology." *Journal of Institutional and Theoretical Economics* 145: 508-524. Vaughn, Karen. 1990. "The Mengerian Roots of the Austrian Revival." Pp. 379-407 in *Carl Menger and his Legacy in Economics,* edited by Bruce J. Caldwell. Durham, NC: Duke University Press.

# METHODOLOGICAL ISSUES IN KEYNES'S ECONOMICS:

## A REVIEW ESSAY

Richard X. Chase

*Keynes' Economics: Methodological Issues.*
Edited by **Tony Lawson and Hasham Pesaran** (for the *Cambridge Journal of Economics*).
London and New York: Routledge, 1985. Pp. 265.

## I. INTRODUCTION

"When a field of study becomes marked by dissatisfaction and disillusionment, methodological analyses and debate tend to become prominent and often provide pointers to fruitful directions for the subject to move in." So begin editors Lawson and Pesaran in their introduction to this collection of papers. (p. 1).

Considering the first part of their statement, casual observation surely indicates that the editors are right on target. The aftermath of the breakdown of the postwar "Keynesian consensus" has witnessed a definitely increased interest in matters methodological, and more broadly epistemological, in

Research in the History of Economic Thought and Methodology, Volume 12, pages 211-221.
Copyright © 1994 by JAI Press Inc.
ISBN: 1-55938-747-5

economics. Witness not only the ongoing flow of books and scholarly articles in the field, but also the recent inauguration of an "International Network for Economic Method" along with its journal, pointedly titled *Methodus*, now renamed *The Journal of Economic Methodology*. (The 1983 establishment of the series publishing this paper, *Research in the History of Economic Thought and Methodology*, only further illustrates the point.)

The volume under review adds its measure to the methodological outpouring. But by explicitly focusing (almost but not entirely) on the contributions of J.M. Keynes, its approach is, by design, personalized rather than subdisciplinary. In light of Keynes's great influence on the development of contemporary of economics, the question that arises is not why focus specifically on his methodological contributions, but rather why has it taken so long for such interest to become manifest. For, at least until recently, there has indeed been very little exploration of the methodological foundations of Keynes's economics, as Lawson and Pesaran point out (p. 1).

With the foregoing in mind, the *Cambridge Journal of Economics* observed the 1983 centenary of Keynes's birth by organizing a conference on methodological issues in Keynes's work. The Lawson and Pesaren volume *Keynes' Economics: Methodological Issues* is the result.

## II. OVERVIEW

As a collection of conference papers, the book's chapters reflect the authors' interests which are, as would be expected, rather wide ranging. As a result, there are significant gaps in the collection's coverage at the same time that there are large areas of overlap containing significant disagreements. In the interests of truth in advertising, two of the chapters are really misplaced; though of interest in their own right, they really deal with particular aspects of derivative *Keynesianism* as opposed to the methodology of J.M. Keynes per se.[1]

The nine papers in the collection that deal specifically with Keynes's methodology may be broadly grouped into three categories. First, there are two papers (by Geoff Hodgson and by Alexander and Sheila Dow) that emphasize Keynes's treatment of expectations. The authors react—the first contra, the second pro—to Keynes's approach on this matter, the germs of which may be traced to his *A Treatise on Probability* (*TP*). (1921) In the second group of five papers (by Johannes Klant, John Pheby, Tony Lawson, Hashem Pesaran and Ron Smith, and Anna Carabelli) the *TP* plays a central role. It is the foundational philosophic source for Keynes's lifelong views on particular methods of analysis, for example, induction, statistical inference, and of course, econometrics

A third group of papers deals with the strategic implications of two methodological devices employed by Keynes. The first of these (by Lawrence Boland) examines the broad idea of "liquidity"—that is, inclusive of unused physical capacity—as a device for generalizing the model of *The General Theory* vis-á-vis those of a neoclassical genre. The other paper in this category (by Victoria Chick) focuses on Keynes's use of the wage-unit as an implicit device for incorporating historical time into an otherwise static model.

## III. EXPECTATIONS AND ECONOMIC THEORY

That there is a crucial relationship between the expectations of economic actors and consequent economic activity now-a-days goes quite without saying. But incorporating a role for expectations into the theory of the modern economy was sadly lacking before Keynes. Thus, a major methodological contribution of Keynes, as Geoff Hodgson points out (chap. 2), was to explicitly rectify this deficiency.

But beyond this acknowledgement, Hodgson is critical since underlying Keynes's view of expectations is a deficient conception of "psychologistic" social behavior and a rationalist conception of action (the latter affected by contextual uncertainty). This is to say, expectations and related human action were seen by Keynes to stem from individual psychology and were thereby amenable to rational and individualistic argument and persuasion. This not only gave Keynes a mistaken view of the (altruistic) nature of government and its functionaries but also made his theory vulnerable to the subsequent counterrevolutions that would challenge it. For example, the rationality and methodological individualism implicit in Keynes is substantively consistent with the expectations approaches of both the rational expectations hypothesis and Austrian subjectivism. In these two approaches, expectations and their consequences are rationally determined and thus "explained" *within* their respective theory frameworks as endogenous variables. As a result, these approaches have been seen as analytical advances over Keynes's autonomous and (unexplained) psychology and rationalism.

In short, a key difficulty with Keynes's approach to expectations is the nature of their exogeneity—that is, their autonomous unexplained psychologistic nature. As such, his concept of expectations strongly invited rationalistic and opimization-orientated endogenization. This led to theoretical "explanations" that worked to pervert his central message concerning economic uncertainty and instability.

A way out of the problem, according to Hodgson, would be to recognize the fundamental role that institutions and culture along with their inherent imperfections—for example, contractual and normative rigidities of various types—have on both shaping expectations and enabling a market system to function effectively. By emphasizing the dependence of expectations on the existent institutional environment rather than on an autonomous psychology, expectations become endogenized and open to explanation by non-"psychologistic" rationalistic means. Along with this, societal institutions, with their necessary imperfections and rigidities, would be explicitly recognized for what they are, exogenous determinants of the system as a whole that are necessary for its effective functioning. Such an institutionalist-Keynesian approach would have profound effects for both theory and policy. For example, demand management policies would become seen as necessary but not sufficient since they would need be accompanied by wide-ranging institutional intervention and restructuring.

Yet, the central issue of expectations and consequential behavior that interested Keynes is unresolved. There is no escape from the necessity for individual action in the face of a noncalculable uncertainty. Also, as Joan Robinson once suggested, a major element in Keynes's analysis and, indeed, of his revolution itself is his "change from the principles of rational choice to the problems of decisions based on such things as guesswork, mood, belief and convention (1973, p. 3). Alexander and Sheila Dow (chap. 3) pursue these themes by focusing especially on Keynes's notion of animal spirits, a concept employed to explain the will to action despite what G.L.S. Shackle once called "the horrid void of indeterminacy and irrationality" (1973, p. 517). Within such a void, the notion of mercurial animal spirits, based on uncertain expectations, would be consistent not only with indeterminacy in the economic system (e.g., employment equilibrium could be almost anywhere) but also with the system's observed volatility. That is, the notion was consistent with even casual (contemporaneous) empirical observation.

Nonetheless, from a professional standpoint, the concept was an embarrassment, a vivid example of Keynes's tendency toward colorful prose. Also, in a scientific sense, animal spirits "explained" nothing; they were indeed a "psychologistic" fiction served up as an exogenous variable that could be consistent with any outcome.

It has already been noted how the exogeneity of behavioral parameters would serve to stimulate efforts to endogenize expectations and their consequent behavioral consequences. But Dow and Dow go further; they also point out that the eventual methodological choice of a Walrasian general equilibrium (IS-LM) framework for Keynesian analysis led by its very nature to efforts to endogenize as many behavioral parameters as possible. Backward-looking adaptive and forward-looking rational expectations approaches would be the major results. Aside from any of their analytical and/or empirical deficiencies, these approaches would constitute a logical imperative toward endogeneity of behavioral parameters, an imperative that spontaneously arises from the choice of general equilibrium as the methodological framework. But, within the context of *Keynes's* own model and methodological mode, wherein nonprobabilistic uncertainty, surprise, and entrepreneurial shift play key roles—namely, in chapter 12 of *The General Theory* (1936) and in the 1937 *Quarterly Journal of Economics* article—exogenous and unexplained animal spirits based on uncertain expectations find their "spiritual home."

# IV. FOUNDATIONS: A TREATESIE ON PROBABILITY

*A Treatise on Probability* (1921) was Keynes's earliest major work. Although published in 1921, it was essentially completed by December 1907 and submitted in support of his Cambridge fellowship, eventually awarded in March 1909.[2]

*TP* was a philosophical work, dealing as it did with matters that go to the roots of epistemology and logic. And it was here that Keynes's notions concerning the character of (uncertain) expectations and consequent behavioral tendencies found their earliest roots with his underlying concern with the nature and uses of knowledge.

Being a noneconomic work, most economists have at best a passing knowledge of the *TP*. But, as becomes clear from the various papers in this grouping, the ideas and analysis of the *TP* were to have a lifelong and profound influence on Keynes's views concerning methods of economic analysis, particularly as these related to quantitative measurement. For example, in the *TP*, Keynes, focusing on the nature of probability (frequency versus logical belief), was led to such related matters as the ages-old problem of induction and the related issue of statistical inference, to the nature of knowledge and of cause and chance, to consideration of the atomic versus the organic nature of reality, and thence to limits of mathematical reasoning.

The chapter by Anna Carabelli (chap. 9) is the most systematic one linking Keynes's economic methodology to *TP*.[3] To Carabelli, the ideas and analysis of the *TP* are clearly *the* foundations to Keynes's later and lifelong approach to economics. This is an approach, she argues, that is anti-empirical, antirationalistic,[4] and nonpositivistic. Subjective conviction rather than objective relations of cause and chance govern the sense of knowing and of belief. The latter, in turn, affect the degree of conviction attached to probability relations and, thereby, the will to action (animal spirits).

Keynes's point of view on the foregoing led him to see economics as a method of nondemonstrative argument. It was essentially a branch of logic, a way of thinking, basically in terms of models, that aided the sound thinker using the correct model to reach sound conclusions. Economics was nonpositivistic in that it did not, indeed could not, discover objective fact; it was thus a "moral" as opposed to a natural science.

Keynes's views on economics and its epistemological foundations can be seen as leading directly to his often colorful polemics, the latter often employed in combination with sharp economic reasoning. His aim was to effect belief, to persuade (in a sense, to shape probability perceptions), and thereby to stimulate desirable action. In this sense, Keynes was perhaps the most important 20th-century proponent of the methodological approach currently labeled "the rhetoric of economics." Indeed, his magnum opus, *The General Theory of Employment, Interest and Money* (*GT*) (as opposed, for example, to his

*Treatise on Money* [1930]) can be seen as much an exercise in "rhetoric" and persuasion as in theory development and model building. Witness Keynes's eloquent conviction in The *GT* concerning the primacy of ideas *both* when they are right and when they are wrong (p. 383).

The Carabelli essay suggesting such themes, both implicitly and explicitly, merits thoughtful consideration concerning the origins of Keynes's views on methods of analysis.

The remaining papers in this group go on to discuss particular methods in Keynes's economics with analytical foundations found in the *TP*. Of special interest here, of course, is Keynes's views on econometrics. These views are clear outgrowths of his *TP* views on induction generally, and statistical inference and the nature of probability more particularly.

For example, Tony Lawson (chap. 7) argues that Keynes's criticisms of econometrics go well beyond superficial argument concerning technical issues. The essence of Keynes's criticisms are far more fundamental; they stem from the epistemological roots of the inductivistic criticism developed in the *TP*. It is these deeper (epistemological) issues that must be addressed by moderns, not the mere technical questions—for example, problems of equation specification, biases and the like—that any good economtrics text analyzes.

To enable a better understanding of Keynes's position on econometrics, Lawson first summarizes his *TP* accounts of both probability and induction. He then fleshes out Keynes's position by alluding to the latter's views on prediction (in itself, it is not an adequate test of a hypothesis); by drawing a contrast with falsificationism (testing a hypothesis has more to do with degree of belief and consequent usefulness for policy than with corroboration); and finally by a perusal of the debate with Tinbergen on econometric method. Details aside, the thoughtful examination of the latter shows that Keynes was primarily interested in matters relating to induction that were fundamentally epistemological and not merely technical—namely, Keynes's interest was in "the *logic* of justification" (p. 127, emphasis added)." To Lawson, Keynes's arguments, stemming from the *TP*, are (or should be) as well taken today as they were when originally put forth.

Johannes Klant (chap. 5) builds substantially on the same philosophic base as does Lawson. However, he comes to mixed conclusions concerning Keynes's criticisms on Tinbergen and econometrics. On the one hand, Klant is highly critical of Keynes's extreme anti-empiricism, a stance that stems from his failure to resolve the Humean problem of induction in the *TP*. Because of this, Keynes was to develop a lifelong and at times unwarranted mistrust around the "slippery transition" from statistical description to inductive generalization or inference (pp. 89-91).

It was Keynes's extreme suspicions in this area—reflecting by the late 1930s, datedness along with "much ignorance and misunderstanding" (p. 91)—that led to his "rather presumptuous criticism [in the *Economic Journal* of

September 1939] of Jan Tinbergen's pioneering work in econometrics" (p. 90). Lawrence Klein called Keynes's review "one of his sorriest professional performances" (p. 90), and "Richard Stone blamed Keynes's character, bad health and rusty mathematics for it" (p. 91). Thus Keynes, according to Klant, showed himself unfamiliar with the technics of Tinbergen's simple arithmetic, preferring rather the mazes of logic (p. 91) (an emphasis entirely opposed to Lawson's!).

On the other hand, when appraised from a less technical perspective, Klant argues (now consistent with Lawson) that, "Keynes' review, all the same, contained a valuable core" (p. 91); and even more strongly, "that when Keynes rejected econometrics as a method of testing he was basically right" (p. 96). For economics is indeed, as Keynes noted, a moral science. As such, it cannot be cultivated as if its variables followed some irrelevant mechanical model; its models are judgmental and their selection is an art.

The Keynes-Tinbergen debate is refought once again by Hashem Pesaran and Ron Smith (chap. 8). This is pursued the way that generals refight old battles; not to change the outcome but to see what is left to be learned. To accomplish their exercise, the authors survey the debate from a somewhat different perspective, Tinbergen's. Their essay opens with a brief overview of his method. This is followed by a summary of Keynes's critique of Tinbergen which is organized into three separate departments. First are the technical issues (of which Klant was so critical and Lawson largely dismissive). These involve five questions concerning the specification of equations and one concerning the inductive and predictive validity of the estimates. Second are the broader epistemological issues—the methodological and logical problems dealing with induction and statistical inference, the nature of probability and the like—that devolve from the *TP* (the contributions for which both Lawson and Klant lauded Keynes). Third, and as their particular addition to the controversy, are the instrumental issues that Keynes raises, for example, what is the objective of econometrics?

The appraisal that Pesaran and Smith come to—largely consistent with both Lawson and Klant—is that despite some technical confusions, the problems Keynes raises are quite real. However, they take their criticism of Keynes a step further. They feel that methodologically and instrumentally, Keynes took much too narrow a view of Timbergen's work. That is, Keynes overlooked both the novelty and the potential for policy analysis inherent in Tinbergen's approach. Econometrics succeeded not so much because Keynes was wrong technically much less logically, but rather because it was a novel instrument whose time had come.

John Pheby (chap. 6) steps back from the details of the econometrics debate *per se* and argues that Keynes's methodology was characterized by what can be called a Babylonian eclecticism. As Pheby puts it, Keynes adopted a problem-dependent methodology that involved varying combinations of both induction and deduction supported by a critical rationalist outlook (p. 104).

Keynes's attitudes in this respect were strongly shaped by his mentors, particularly his father Neville and Alfred Marshall. For example, a major concern of Neville Keynes, writing in response to the Methodenstreit of the 1880s, was to find the appropriate balance between the inductive and deductive methods in economics along with the proper scope of the discipline. How Neville's concerns might have been reflected in Keynes's later philosophic inquiries concerning the problem(s) of induction in the *TP* is an open yet suggestive question. Furthermore, the gist of Marshall's emphasis on economics being an "engine of discovery" can be found in Keynes's attitude that economics is a branch of logic, of thinking in terms of (right) models.

Pheby also discusses aspects of Karl Popper's methodological views, particularly as they appear to be critical of Keynes. The conclusion here is that in certain key aspects, their respective methodologies are quite similar. For one thing, both are strongly opposed to instrumentalism—the idea that a scientific theory is nothing but an instrument, its truth or falsity being of no consequence—as a "soft" methodological escape from hard problems. (Perhaps this antiinstrumentalism explains why Keynes was so inclined to see Tinbergen's work with the truncated vision of which Klant and Pesaran and Smith complain!)

# V.  TWO STRATEGIC DEVICES

The final two papers reviewed here are more pinpointed in their focus than those in the first two groups. This is so in the sense that each paper seeks its insight into Keynes by spotlighting strategic implications of a particular conceptual device that he employs.

Liquidity is the device that Lawrence Boland (chap. 10) emphasizes. Boland, following Hicks, broadens the meaning of the term so as to include not only financial but also "real" liquidity, the letter referring to the existence of excess physical capacity.

The need for liquidity arises in the first instance because of the existence of uncertainty; that is, without uncertainty there would be no need for spare capacity, financial or otherwise. Furthermore, accepting the idea of incorporating this (broadened) notion of liquidity as a short-run endogenous variable into a Keynes model would serve to generalize it on neoclassical terms. That is, by using liquidity, in effect, as a proxy variable to endogenize uncertainty, *all* strategic variables would be endogenous to the model. This strategy would effectively counter the neoclassical argument that Keynes's model is a special case—that is, a case dependent upon a particular state of autonomous forces (e.g., mood and expectations) that reflect an exogenous and noncalculable uncertainty.[5]

Victoria Chick's paper (chap. 11) argues the point of a historical, real time dimension in Keynes's apparently static framework. To Chick, the device employed by Keynes that accomplishes this objective is his use of the wage unit for deflating aggregate demand and aggregate supply in money terms (D and Z) to wage units (Dw and Zw). By doing this, the latter functions are held constant in terms of money wages and thereby held independent of the historical component embodied in money wages. This allows for the development of general theoretical principles while maintaining the historical element of the wage determining process in the background. By determining and reintroducing current levels of money wages, and thereby a unidirectional real-time component, the absolute levels of prices and output can be determined (in the D and Z functions).

Chick's argument is set within the context of a pre-*General Theory* entrepreneur, or monetary production, economy. Here, firms must plan regarding costs (most importantly labor) and demand before the former is realized and the latter is known. As noted, an aggregate model in terms of the wage unit (Dw and Zw) shows the principles on which such plans are made, holding history constant (and given expectations about the future); moving to an aggregate model in money terms (D and Z) allows history to enter via the wage process (and to determine to what degree expectations have been realized or disappointed).

Chick's argument is post-Keynesian in character. For example, she seeks to develop direct theoretical links to Keynes and she is interested in the role of historic time in economic analysis. Nonetheless, she is careful to offer her argument as a strategy that is only implicit in Keynes. This is warranted since Keynes's use of the wage-unit as a deflator more than likely stems from his lifelong distrust of index numbers[6] as opposed to an objective of incorporating a real-time element in his analysis.

## VI.  APPRAISAL

As with any collection, there is some unevenness among the essays. Quality-wise, this is minimal. (As for the noted problem of the two essays that just did not belong in the book, this is really not one of authorship but rather of editorial selection.)

As for the coverage of the remaining papers, there were wide areas of overlap as were there gaps. Clearly, there were disagreements among the writers, sometimes argued to the point of contentiousness. (And what else is new in methodology?!)

If there is a single thread that runs through at least most of the papers, it is that the *TP* is the single most important source for Keynes's methodological and philosophical approach to economics. The *TP* long preceded Keynes's professional interest in economics, but as Harrod once put it, "Early influences remained of great importance through Keynes' life" (1951 p. vii). Another writer commenting on Keynes's early philosophical works, of which the *TP* is central, notes:

> Although Keynes undertook no major extension or reworking of his philosophical theories after 1921 [publication date of the *TP*], he never abandoned his interest in philosophy in general, nor escaped the particular influence of his earlier beliefs (O'Donnell, 1989, p. 19).

Thus, it would seem that deeply understanding Keynes the economist requires at least some understanding of (an earlier) Keynes the philosopher and logician. Schumpter misled economists when he remarked in his obituary of Keynes that the *TP* was essentially "an outlet for the energies of a mind that found no complete satisfaction in the discipline of economics" (1946, p. 502). It seems, to the contrary, that in the *TP* Keynes developed the fundamentals for his lifelong methodological and epistemological approach to economics. He largely held onto these fundamentals even when, as in the debate with Tinbergen, he himself felt twinges of doubt and unsureness (pp. 90-91).

Most of the essays in this volume, particularly when related to the Carabelli one, provide a convenient way for making some basic connections between the *TP* and Keynes's later work. Some might even be driven back to the (formidable) *TP* itself. If not that, then perhaps to the recent excellent studies on Keynes's philosophical and methodological roots by Anna Carabelli (1988) and R. M. O'Donnell (1989).

# NOTES

1. Chapter 4, "Expectations In Keynesian Econometric Models" by Simon Wren-Lewis, explores the consistency of the rational expectations hypothesis with large-scale Keynesian econometric models; chapter 12, "Keynesianism in Germany" highlights the contributions of Werner Sombart and Wilhelm Lautenbach in the development of Keynesian thought and policy in Germany during the 1920s and 1930s. (Because of the *Keynesian*, as opposed to Keynes, focus of these two papers, they are not further elaborated in this review.)

2. Keynes's fellowship dissertation, originally titled *The Principles of Probability*, was rejected in 1908 on the basis of reservations held by Whitehead. Keynes revised his dissertation during the summer of 1908 and the spring of 1909, and in March of the latter year he was awarded his Cambridge fellowship. The work was subsequently expanded and prepared for publication through 1912. Publication was delayed—first because of financial disagreements with the publisher and then by the World War I—until 1921, when it appeared under the title, *A Treatise On Probability* (O'Donnell, 1989, pp. 15-17).

3. This chapter is a precursor of Carabelli's later book on the subject (1988).

4. Another recent commentator argues that Keynes's philosophic orientation was indeed rationalism albeit a "thin rationalism" (O'Donnell, 1989, p. 100).

5. Boland's paper relates to Hodgson's opening one on expectations (above) in that both address the issue of endogenizing, and thus "explaining," behavioral parameters subject to

(autonomous) Keynesian uncertainty. While liquidity is the device suggested by Boland, the determining role of institutions is the approach of Hodgson. Dow and Dow (above) also address the endogenization issue. They point out, it will be recalled, that such an approach would only serve to violate the spirit of Keynes. However, if the methodological framework chosen were a "Walrasian" general equilibrium one, then endogenization of behaviorial parameter would be both appropriate and, indeed, necessary.

6. This distrust can be dated from his 1901 paper, "The Method of Index Numbers with Special Reference to the Measurement of General Exchange Value," (*CW*, XI, chap. 2).

# REFERENCES

Carabelli, Anna M. 1988. *On Keynes's Method.* New York: St. Martin's Press.

Harrod, Sir Roy. 1951. *The Life of John Maynard Keynes.* London: McMillian.

Keynes, John Maynard. 1930 *A Treatise on Money.* Vol. I *The Pure Theory of Money*; Vol. II The Applied Theory of Money. London: McMillian.

_____. *A Treatise on Probability.* 1921. London: McMillian.

_____. "The General Theory of Employment." *The Quarterly Journal of Economics*, February 1937, Vol. LI, pp. 209-223.

Keynes, John Maynard. 1936. *The General Theory of Interest, Employment and Money.* New York: Harcourt, Brace and World.

_____. 1983. *Collected Works,* Vol. XI: "Economic Articles and Corresponence: Academic." London: McMillian.

O'Donnell, R.M. 1989. *Keynes: Philosophy, Econmics and Politics.* New York: St. Martin's Press.

Robinson, Joan. 1973. *After Keynes.* Oxford, UK: Basil Blackwell.

Schumpeter, Joseph. "John Maynard Keynes: 1883-1946." *American Economic Review* 36(4).

Shackle, G.L.S. 1973. "Keynes and Today's Establishment in Economic Theory." *Journal of Economic Literature* (Fall): 11(2) 517.

# RECONCILING LEIJONHUFVUD AND THE POST-KEYNESIANS: A REVIEW ESSAY

Allin Cottrell

*On Interpreting Keynes: A Study in Reconciliation.*
By Bruce Littleboy.
London and New York: Routledge, 1990. Pp. 340.

The secondary literature on Keynes has by now multiplied to such a degree as to warrant a systematic tertiary literature: an attempt to "interpret the interpreters" and bring some order to the competing views on the nature of Keynes's contribution. Bruce Littleboy's essay in this field is not without precedent. Alan Coddington's pioneering attempt to make sense of the varieties of Keynesianism (1976, 1983) provides one reference point for Littleboy, and indeed, he carries over Coddington's taxonomy of "hydraulic," "fundamentalist," and "reconstituted reductionist" approaches. Dow and Earl (1982), Chick (1983), and Dow (1985) also deserve mention in this context, although the scope and emphasis of Littleboy's book are rather different from these works.

Research in the History of Economic Thought and Methodology, Volume 12, pages 223-232.
Copyright © 1994 by JAI Press Inc.
All rights of reproduction in any form reserved.
ISBN: 1-55938-747-5

The thesis of the work under review may be stated simply. Littleboy believes that there is scope for a fruitful reconciliation between the two main Keynesian theoretical tendencies standing in opposition to the orthodox (or once orthodox) neoclassical synthesis, namely, the approach of Clower and Leijonhufvud (Littleboy's emphasis is on the latter) and the post-Keynesian school of Davidson, Shackle, Brothwell, and others. He also believes that if these alternative Keynesianisms were to present a united front, they might be better able to exert an influence on the wider macroeconomic scene. So far as exposition of the two strands of "alternative Keynesian" thinking is concerned, Leijonhufvud gets the lion's share: a reasonably full knowledge of (as well as basic sympathy toward) the fundamentalist position is presupposed. The implied reader is a post-Keynesian who needs to be persuaded to take Leijonhufvud more seriously. As a somewhat "fundamentalist" Keynesian who has long found Leijonhufvud's work fascinating, I came to Littleboy's book favorably disposed toward his main thesis. Before discussing the way in which the thesis is worked out, however, some brief preliminaries.

A minor quibble first: the text is typeset in a sort of "Near Book Quality" mode which I hope is not the wave of the future. I daresay that cost considerations are important for a monograph of this type, but perhaps a saving could have been made on the unaccountably profligate bibliographical style, which combines a complete (and very useful) list of references at the end with full (and frequently repeated) details of all sources in the copious footnotes.

More substantively, Littleboy's prose is distinctly uneven. Minor infelicities abound, and from time to time the reader is stopped in his/her tracks by truly monstrous locutions such as: "Even if Leijonhufvud is taken to argue that in the long run, through the Keynes effect, recovery can in logic occur, though conceding in practice that other forces would swamp the benign effects of lower interest rates, he cannot allow Keynes to have a theory of interest-rate movements which can rule out even the conceptual possibility that endogenous and fully restorative mechanisms must exist" (p. 195). From an author who is at pains to point out the woeful effects of lack of effective communication between the adherents of different macroeconomic viewpoints, this kind of thing is particularly unfortunate.

Apart from stylistic issues, Littleboy's "Introduction" is poorly organized. It is too long and rambling, goes into too much detail, and introduces too many extraneous concerns, without giving an adequate overview of, or motivation for, the general structure of the argument to follow. His speculations concerning the social-psychological bases of sharp opposition between the different schools of Keynesianism seem out of place here. Coming before the substantive point—that there really is a profitable opportunity to marry the different approaches—has been established, these remarks are likely to annoy rather than edify; they would be better placed in a conclusion. Problems of organization, though not as acute, extend to the rest of the text. Following chapter 2, Leijonhufvud is left dangling while Littleboy heads off into his own explication of "Involuntary unemployment in the history of economic thought." This chapter, dealing with Keynes, Mill, Pigou, Patinkin, Barro, Lucas, et alia, is interesting in its own right, but it is not clear precisely how it is supposed to advance the main project of reconciling Leijonhufvud and the post-Keynesians. Chapter 7 heads off on a nine-page tangent concerning the aggregative procedure of the *General Theory*. Yes, the issue is raised by Leijonhufvud, but as the digression ends with the admission that "squabbles about the aggregative structure are of little importance" (p. 214), I wonder why he bothered. More generally, there is a fair amount of "cycling around" the main topics of the book. Matters are taken up, dropped for a while, and then taken up again, without much apparent rationale.[1]

Despite all this, I found the book very stimulating. Littleboy has conscientiously worked his way through a vast literature and has many perceptive points to make—far more than I can comment on in a short review essay. One does get the (most welcome) sense of a fair-minded attempt to assess the Leijonhufvudian and fundamentalist positions, and the relationships between them.

Returning to the main thesis of the book, let me summarize the nature of the reconciliation that Littleboy proposes. From Leijonhufvud, he takes the Clowerian apparatus of effective and notional demands, along with the associated analysis of the multiplier as a disequilibrium process. Leijonhufvud is presented as strong and generally convincing on the Keynesian short run. For the most part, criticisms are confined to relatively narrow matters—matters of "logic" rather than "vision" in Littleboy's terminology. For instance, Littleboy argues that Leijonhufvud's (1968) attempt to "unify" the *General Theory* via the theme of inelastic expectations is off the mark. While there are good reasons for emphasizing the importance of inelastic expectations regarding the interest rate, it is not at all clear that inelastic expectations regarding the nominal wage play an important role in Keynes's analysis of the emergence of unemployment, nor that Keynes assumes inelastic short-run sales expectations on the part of producers. Again, Leijonhufvud is faulted for not recognizing that Keynes's "finance motive" for holding money, much emphasized by the post-Keynesians, softens the dichotomy between the Liquidity Preference and Loanable Funds versions of disequilibrium interest-rate dynamics, undercutting Leijonhufvud's insistence on the superiority of the latter. More vaguely and diffusely, Littleboy finds Leijonhufvud somewhat too soft on the classics (in the long run, at any rate). Despite his own criticisms, however, Littleboy stoutly defends Leijonhufvud against most post-Keynesian attacks.

As regards the "fundamentalist" or post-Keynesian position, Littleboy willingly embraces the emphasis on uncertainty and the need to deal with an economy embedded in historical time. He is also comfortable with the idea that a monetary economy may have no significant automatic tendency to recover to full employment, even in the long run. He wishes, however, to fend off the most radical appropriations of Keynesian uncertainty (e.g., Shackle), which brings us to his bridging theme. The reconciliation he seeks is not simply a matter of collating the favored elements of the two approaches, but must involve some constructive work—the provision of a general framework within which these elements can harmoniously cohabit. Littleboy proposes to supply this framework through an extension and refinement of the idea of "conventions" as employed by Keynes in the *General Theory*. Conventions perform double duty in his argument. On the one hand, the idea of a "conventional equilibrium" licenses the proposition that monetary economies can get thoroughly stuck in underemployment states; on the other hand, conventions provide a means of taming uncertainty and preserving some degree of predictability. Having no really solid foundations in objective fact, conventions are liable to collapse from time to time, but nonetheless, as long as they do survive, they impart a coherence and continuity to macroeconomic affairs, a domain of relative systemic stability within which Leijonhufvud's style of analysis is seen as valid and useful.[2] An interesting final chapter extends the idea of "convention" from its original locus in Keynes's analysis of long-term investment and financial markets, to cover product and labor markets too, and constructs the notion of a hierarchy of conventions of differing degrees of fragility. The freedom of the system to depart from an initial stable state (whether full employment or not) is then seen to depend on the seriousness of the disturbance, gauged by the number of layers of convention it disrupts.

I find much that is interesting, and much to sympathize with, in all this. My comments, however, will have to be selective. I propose to take up one issue which occupies a good deal of Littleboy's attention (especially in the introduction and chapters 2 and 4), yet which remains somewhat obscure. If I am right in saying that the implied reader is a post-Keynesian, further clarification of this point will be useful to the purpose of the book, for the point may be a stumbling block for such readers. I refer to the Clower-Leijonhufvud analysis of "effective demand failure," endorsed by Littleboy. To put the point in context, we can distinguish two main theories in Leijonhufvud's work. Theory A (I will call it) is the basic Clowerian effective demand theory; Theory B is a theory of intertemporal disequilibrium, of saving/investment problems, and of bear speculation. Theory B is fascinating, and is brilliantly presented in Leijonhufvud's "Wicksell Connection" paper (1981, pp. 131-202.). The relationship between this theory and Keynes is now clearer than in Leijonhufvud (1968): in an important respect, it constitutes a critique of the *General Theory,* from a standpoint, as Leijonhufvud puts it, interpolated between the *Treatise on Money* and the latter.[3] The relationship between Theory A and Keynes, however, is murky in the extreme, and this theory has been the target of much fundamentalist criticism. Such reactions are discussed by Littleboy in the introduction (with respect to Dow and Earl) and chapter 4 (Davidson), but it seems to me that he does not he get to the core of the problem; indeed, he suggests that the post-Keynesians have simply misunderstood or even wilfully misinterpreted Leijonhufvud.

Let us try, then, to assess Leijonhufvud's Theory A. In a nutshell, this is the idea that an otherwise Walrasian economy which lacks the Walrasian auctioneer may get into persistent unemployment states, due to the fact that the "notional" excess demands which would guide the auctioneer's price adjustments fail to have any effect on the system in her absence. The "no auctioneer" argument implies that *if* price movements were governed by notional excess demands, the establishment of full employment would not be a problem. The key point is that, given a state of Keynesian unemployment, the auctioneer would register not only an excess supply of labor but also a corresponding *excess demand for goods* (i.e., the goods that the unemployed would buy, if they had work and therefore higher incomes). She would therefore react by both lowering the nominal wage and *raising the price of consumer goods*. This adjustment would clearly signal to producers the profitability of an expansion of output and employment. Without the auctioneer, the nominal wage may tend to sag, but the message that an expansion of employment would automatically increase the demand for output does not come across, and the unemployment will not quickly disappear.

This argument can be presented most cleanly and concisely if we assume a unit marginal propensity to consume, an assumption which Leijonhufvud makes quite explicit in one case (1981, pp. 66-67) but which seems to be lurking in the background in other presentations of the argument as well. In that case, the unsatisfied demand for consumer goods revealed by the auctioneer's enquiries is just sufficient to justify the expansion of output all the way up to full employment.

I agree with Littleboy (pp. 27-28) that it is quite wrong to suggest that Leijonhufvud assumes a unit marginal propensity to consume in general:[4] that would make nonsense of his lengthy and perceptive discussions of the saving/investment problem. The fact remains that he *does* introduce this assumption into his discussion of the effective demand problem, even if only for ease of exposition. But then, does not his argument prove too much from a Keynesian point of view? If the *mpc* equals 1, we are in a world where Keynes's Aggregate Demand Price (D) and Aggregate Supply Price (Z) schedules coincide. The "no auctioneer" theory therefore appears able to explain the persistence of unemployment in a monetary economy *even when the D and Z curves are coincident over the relevant range*.

This possibility did not occur to Keynes. He states (1936, p. 29) that if, as per the classical theory, the D and Z curves are coincident (Say's Law), "the volume of employment is in neutral equilibrium for all values of N [i.e., employment] less than its maximum [i.e., full-employment] value; so that the forces of competition between entrepreneurs may be expected to push it to this maximum value. Only at this point, on the classical theory, can there be stable equilibrium." If an expansion of employment would "justify itself" via a corresponding increase in the demand for output, Keynes sees no reason why the expansion should not occur.

Littleboy (p. 151) finds it incredible that Leijonhufvud could be accused by Davidson of assuming the truth of Say's Law in the course of an argument which is designed to bolster Keynes's rejection of that very doctrine, but there is after all something to the charge: Leijonhufvud argues that even if supply would "create its own demand" given a *general* expansion of employment, the fact that it does not create its own demand at the micro level (since newly employed workers in any particular branch of production will not purchase their own marginal products) can stymie expansion: Keynes's "forces of competition" cannot be relied upon. This is clearly *not* Keynes's argument. It might be seen as a further consequence of the distinction—held to be important by Keynes—between a "real-exchange" and a monetary economy, but Leijonhufvud does not present his argument in this light; rather, it is put forward as an exposition of what Keynes himself (must have) had in mind. While Leijonhufvud's point is not logically inconsistent with Keynes— Leijonhufvud is not bound to, and indeed does not, assume that the Aggregate Demand Price and Supply Price schedules are in general coincident—he seems to have (unwittingly?) set up a potentially *competing* explanation of unemployment, one which draws attention away from Keynes's theory and which, incidentally, appears compatible with the simple-minded "Reagan cure" for unemployment: talk every employer into hiring another worker and we will be alright (cf. Davidson, 1984).

Keynes's theory, it hardly needs said, is one in which the economy settles down at the *unique* point of effective demand, where the D and Z schedules intersect. Expansion of employment beyond this point will not be sustainable (in the absence of an increase in investment or rise in the propensity to consume) precisely because the increase in demand that would undoubtedly accompany that rise in employment will be insufficient to purchase the whole additional output at a price equal to marginal cost. Saving would exceed intended investment. Say's Law fails to operate *at the macro level,* as well as for each individual employer considered in isolation.

Having introduced the saving/investment problem, a further question arises: What happens to the "no auctioneer" argument when the unit *mpc* is dropped? If the recipients of the extra income generated by an expansion of employment will save part of this increment, then the notional counterpart to the excess supply of labor comprises: (a) excess demand for consumer goods, (b) excess demand for securities and, (c) excess demand for money. Suppose for a moment that we can ignore (c) altogether. Then the auctioneer's set of adjustment rules will include the requirement that the rate of interest should be lowered so long as the notional supply of saving exceeds intended investment. The "macro version" of Say's Law would then still operate: under the auctioneer's guidance, the economy will proceed to full employment without difficulty. In her absence, the notional excess supply of saving is ineffective, there is no downward pressure on the rate of interest, and the expansion may fail to occur. Here, we have another variant of Leijonhufvud's argument that "competitive forces" may fail to shift a monetary economy from a point of "neutral equilibrium" (Keynes) below full employment.

The difficulty with the above, of course, is the assumption that money poses no problem. If the auctioneer begins by raising the price of the consumer goods that are in excess (notional) demand and lowering the rate of interest, while lowering the nominal wage, and the result of the next round of *tatonnement* is a set of plans for increased output and employment, this will be accompanied by an excess demand for money (as the transactions demand goes up in response to the rise in nominal income and the fall in interest). Raising the price of consumer goods, it appears, was a mistake. In fact, the price level must be *lowered* to offset the effects on the transactions demand for money of an increase in real income and fall in interest. So the nominal wage must be lowered even further, to preserve the fall in the real wage that must accompany an expansion of employment under diminishing returns. But then the sharp contrast between (a) what the auctioneer would do, and (b) the simple effect of falling nominal wages in response to an effective excess supply of labor, begins to evaporate. If the auctioneer could get us to full employment, why cannot wage deflation, induced deflation of the prices of goods, and the "Keynes effect?" Or, to invert the argument, if Keynes's counterarguments (1936, chap. 19) are telling against the supposedly beneficial effects of general deflation, are they not equally telling against the ability of the auctioneer herself to generate full employment, starting from a fairly stable depressed state? In my view, the strongest of the chapter 19 arguments is the Fisherian point concerning the damaging effects of general deflation on the financial structure. To obviate these effects, the auctioneer would need the power to rescind any long-term nominal commitments entered into in the expectation that prices would not fall. Here the theme of history—always difficult if not impossible to incorporate into any kind of Walrasian view—pushes its way into the argument.

The mythical creature needed to sort out an economy suffering from large-scale Keynesian unemployment is not simply an Auctioneer, coldly registering agents' notional excess supplies and demands and moving price accordingly while taking their preferences and general "states of mind" strictly as given. What is needed is a Counselor, someone who will undertake one or more of the following tasks as appropriate: (a) to persuade entrepreneurs that they are taking an unduly pessimistic view of the profitability of long-run investments; (b) to persuade financial investors that their view of what constitutes a "normal" or "safe" rate of interest is no longer sustainable; (c) to point out to consumers that they are trying to save more than can profitably be accumulated; (d) to persuade the State that it is not imprudent to employ in public investments that portion of full-employment saving that cannot profitably be accumulated by the private sector; and/or (e) to persuade the monetary authority of the virtues of an accommodating policy. While the Auctioneer will inevitably end up trying to deflate the economy out of its depression, the Counselor tries to raise the point of effective demand towards full employment without deflation, by working on the understanding and expectations of the various economic agents. (Littleboy shows some awareness of this point, when he switches from the metaphor of the auctioneer to that of a roundtable conference [p. 152], but he does not emphasize or develop the implications of the switch.)

This, I think, is the valid core of the fundamentalist objection to Leijonhufvud's Theory A. It does not invalidate the whole of what he has to say on the multiplier and related matters, by any means, but it is a substantial point, and one which Littleboy has not brought into focus. Paradoxically, Leijonhufvud himself has drawn attention to most if not all of the elements of the above argument (see, for instance, 1968, chap. 5), but that does not in itself "get him off the hook" from a post-Keynesian point of view: if he is well aware of such points, why has he not clarified the problematic relationship between the "no auctioneer" theory and Keynes's argument? Given the opportunity to restate his views at the Keynes Centenary Conference, Leijonhufvud (1983, pp. 197-198) continued to argue that "the inability of the unemployed to back their notional consumption demands with cash is a major reason for the persistence of unemployment," and that "if price-adjustments were governed by notional excess demands, then neo-Walrasian stability theorems will tell us under which conditions" the system will converge to a coordinated, full-employment state. One novelty is the claim that the newly discovered early-draft introductions to the *General Theory*, phrased in terms of the distinction between a Cooperative and an Entrepreneur economy, justify the (previously somewhat speculative) attribution of this view to Keynes himself.[5]

Keynes's "Co-operative Economy", as it turned out, was one in which labor is bartered for goods, so that the supply of labor is always an effective demand for goods. In his 'Entrepreneur Economy' the Clowerian rule applies: labor buys money and money buys goods but labor does not buy goods. In the entrepreneur economy, therefore, effective demand failures are possible and so, consequently, is "involuntary unemployment". That, I think, should settle the matter (1983, p. 198, n. 31).

But it has not settled the matter. We can all agree that in the Cooperative Economy, unemployment can only be the result of labor's refusal to work for its marginal product. It does not follow that Keynes conceived unemployment in the Entrepreneur Economy as the result of an "effective demand failure" in the Clowerian sense, for the latter presupposes that the sum of notional demands would equal the value of output at full employment, which is precisely what Keynes thought he had refuted. Perhaps it is not an accident that Keynes, in the end, chose not to introduce the *General Theory* in this way.

The foregoing suggests that there may be more of a theoretical difference between Leijonhufvud and the post-Keynesians than Littleboy recognizes. That does not invalidate his plea for open-mindedness and comradely criticism. Further, Littleboy is not hoping for a reconciliation between the principals in the confrontation so much as urging a younger generation of Keynesians to partake of the "eclecticism that may foreshadow a formal synthesis" (p. xii), or in other words, to recognize the respective merits of two approaches that share an authentic Keynesian concern with the macroeconomic frailties of the monetary market system. Amen. Personally, I would wish to see the umbrella of healthily eclectic Keynesianism extended somewhat further, to accommodate perceptive "hydraulicists" such as James Tobin.

## NOTES

1. Symptomatic, perhaps, is the fact that one quotation from Leijonhufvud is discussed in three different places (pp. 62, 79, 156).

2. This is similar in spirit to Jochen Runde's (1991) reply to Coddington's critique of Keynesian uncertainty.

3. Michael Lawlor and I (Cottrell and Lawlor, 1991) have examined this argument in some detail.

4. This point is brought up in response to Dow and Earl (1982, pp. 181-182). The latter do talk as if Leijonhufvud consistently forgets about the fractional *mpc*.

5. I should say that this 1983 piece also offers some interesting and valuable arguments concerning varieties of business cycle theory, expectations, and monetary regimes. I have focused on the restatement of the "effective demand failure" argument because of the role it plays in Littleboy's book and because of the problems this argument has created for post-Keynesians.

## REFERENCES

Chick, Victoria. 1983. *Macroeconomics After Keynes: A Reconsideration of the General Theory.* Cambridge, MA: MIT Press.

Coddington, Alan. 1976. "Keynesian Economics: The Search for First Principles." *Journal of Economic Literature* 14(December): 1258-1273.

————. 1983. *Keynesian Economics: The Search for First Principles.* London: George Allen & Unwin.

Cottrell, Allin, and Michael S. Lawlor. 1991. " 'Natural Rate' Mutations: Keynes, Leijonhufvud and the Wicksell Connection." *History of Political Economy*, 23: 625-643.

Davidson, Paul. 1984. "Reviving Keynes's Revolution." *Journal of Post Keynesian Economics* VI(Summer): 561-575.

Dow, Sheila C. 1985. *Macroeconomic Thought: A Methodological Approach.* Oxford: Basil Blackwell.

Dow, Sheila C., and Peter E. Earl. 1982. *Money Matters: A Keynesian Approach to Monetary Economics.* Oxford: Martin Robertson.

Keynes, J.M. 1936. *The General Theory of Employment, Interest and Money.* London: Macmillan.

Leijonhufvud, Axel. 1968. *On Keynesian Economics and the Economics of Keynes.* Oxford: Oxford University Press.

————. 1981. *Information and Coordination.* New York: Oxford University Press.

————. 1983. "What Would Keynes Have Thought of Rational Expectations?" Pp. 179-205 in *Keynes and the Modern World*, edited by David Worswick and James Trevithick. Cambridge: Cambridge University Press.

Runde, Jochen. 1991. "Keynesian Uncertainty and the Instability of Beliefs." *Review of Political Economy* 3: 125-145.

# ON INTERPRETING KEYNES'S PHILOSOPHICAL THINKING: CARABELLI'S *ON KEYNES'S METHOD* AND O'DONNELL'S *KEYNES: PHILOSOPHY, ECONOMICS AND POLITICS:*

*A REVIEW ESSAY*

John B. Davis

*On Keynes's Method.*
By Anna Carabelli.
New York: St. Martin's Press, 1988.

*Keynes: Philosophy, Economics and Politics.*
By R.M. O'Donnell.
New York: St. Martin's Press, 1989.

Research in the History of Economic Thought and Methodology, Volume 12, pages 233-243.
Copyright © 1994 by JAI Press Inc.
All rights of reproduction in any form reserved.
ISBN: 1-55938-747-5

Interest in John M. Keynes's philosophical thinking is a relatively recent phenomenon that owes its origins to several factors. First, the changing fortunes of Keynesian economics in the last two decades have generated new interest in what Keynes himself had to say in *The General Theory* in contrast to what Keynesians and other macroeconomists have since said. That such a variety of interpretations of Keynes's thinking and its significance quite suddenly became possible after two postwar decades of monolithic agreement on Keynes's essential message has thus reinvigorated interest in Keynes's own writings. Second, over the last two decades, methodological and philosophical thinking in economics has come of age. Not only are methodological and philosophical discussions in economics now pursued at a reasonably sophisticated level by an increasing number of economists, but most economists have also now come to accept the proposition that methodological assumptions and presuppositions are important to substantive economic argument. Third, historical developments in the world economy have undermined both the view that economies can be centrally planned outside of the market mechanism and also the view that unregulated *laissez faire* economics is desirable or captures the actual functioning of modern economies. Keynes, as a foremost proponent of the mixed economy, has thus received new attention at the century's close.

Despite this new and deeper interest in Keynes, however, interpreting Keynes's philosophical thinking is fraught with a set of difficulties not unlike those which have accompanied interpretation of the thought of the philosopher-economists Adam Smith and Karl Marx. Indeed, as a recent discussion makes clear (Bateman, 1991), there is good reason to suppose that the classic historiographic problem that has long beset Smith and Marx scholarship—whether the early Smith and the later Smith are the same, and whether the early Marx and the later Marx are the same—also confronts the study of Keynes. In each case, real differences in reasoning, assumptions, and commitments argue for significant discontinuities in these individuals' works; yet, at the same time, each of these individuals obviously possessed abiding concerns that can be traced across the different stages of their intellectual careers. Compounding these difficulties, moreover, is the fact that although each of these thinkers was first a philosopher, they did not have much to say to say about philosophical questions after turning to economics and virtually nothing to say about the apparent complications the turn to economics suggested for their earlier philosophical positions.

Thus, did Keynes's philosophical views significantly change and develop over his career, or did they remain relatively constant and unchanging? The relevant facts in Keynes's case can be quickly summarized. Keynes wrote one, full-length philosophical work, the *Treatise on Probability* (1921), which elaborated an original philosophical foundation for the probability calculus and induction. He also wrote a number of unpublished philosophical papers (known as the Apostles papers) of uneven quality on a variety of themes, mostly prior to the

*Treatise.* The arguments of these papers are not easily connected to the arguments of the *Treatise*, and they have only relatively recently become available to a small number of scholars (Skidelsky, 1983; Davis, 1991a). After the publication of the *Treatise* (or arguably, after its writing was largely finished in 1914), Keynes made only brief and somewhat casual mention of his earlier systematic positions. Of particular importance are the much commented-upon statements he made that were clearly critical of his earlier philosophical views on two occasions: first, in 1930 in response to Frank P. Ramsey's (1978) review of the *Treatise* immediately after its publication in 1922, Keynes allowed that Ramsey was in important respects correct in his criticisms of the prinicipal philosophical claim of the book (*CW*, Vol. X, pp. 338-339); second, in his post-*General Theory* 1938 memoir of his first years at Cambridge, "My Early Beliefs," Keynes asserted that his early pre-*Treatise* views had unduly emphasized intuition at the expense of the concept of convention (*CW*, Vol. X, pp. 437, 446). Finally, it should also be noted that Keynes also made a number of remarks of a philosophical nature about the character and methodology of economics and econometrics in correspondence with Roy Harrod after the publication of *The General Theory* in 1939 (*CW*, Vol. XIV, pp. 297, 300).

From this evidence, a number of tentative conclusions emerge. First, given the clear, confident statement of his early views in the *Treatise*, Keynes's response to Ramsey registering strong misgivings about his early positions clearly suggests that there were indeed certain important respects in which Keynes's philosophical thinking changed and developed after he turned his attention to economics (Bateman, 1987). Second, this is supported by the fact that Keynes later also came to think it necessary to distance himself from important aspects of his pre-*Treatise*, Apostles papers thinking in his 1938 "My Early Beliefs" memoir. Third, that the *Treatise* and the Apostles papers are not easily reconciled, and that Keynes's early philosophical views are apparently less systematic and cohesive than they seemed prior to the recent discovery of the Apostles papers suggests that Keynes's early views overall subsumed fundamental dilemmas and divisions that may well have operated upon the development of his later thinking.

Did Keynes's philosophical thinking, then, indeed undergo significant change and development away from its earliest foundations? Though Keynes allowed that a number of criticisms of his early philosophical thinking merited attention, he nonetheless did not go on to systematically elaborate an alternative philosophical system. Accordingly, were his admitted doubts to imply a significant yet undocumented change in philosophical opinion, the evidence for such a change would essentially need to be found elsewhere, particularly, it seems fair to say, in the implicit philosophical foundations of his later economics. In this connection, the philosophical remarks Keynes made to Harrod after the publication of *The General Theory* about the character and methodology of economics and econometrics are especially significant, both because they bear directly upon the fundamental nature of economics and because they reflect a thinking that seems to introduce new ideas and emphases to what may be found in Keynes's earlier philosophical thinking (Davis, 1991b).

Yet, probably more significant in this regard is the fact that Keynes's economic thinking itself underwent significant change and development across his two major treatises in economic theory, *The Treatise on Money* and *The General Theory*, indeed, so much so that he felt it necessary to assert in the Preface to the latter that the "composition of this book has been for the author a long struggle of escape ... from habitual modes of thought and expression" due to a "difficulty [that] lies, not in the new ideas, but in escaping from the old ones" (*CW*, Vol. VII, p. viii). In contrast, neither Smith nor Marx expressed comparable doubts about their earlier works, though changes in their substantive views across their early and later works have led many scholars to argue for fundamental changes in outlook. Taking Keynes's declaration in *The General Theory* quite seriously, then, his response to Ramsey and "My Early Beliefs" memoir most likely represented in his own mind significant admissions of error, with the Ramsey response coming about the same time that Keynes began to have doubts about his *Treatise on Money*, and the comments on his Apostles papers coming soon after the completion of *The General Theory*. On this view of Keynes's later thinking, the conceptual tension between Keynes's two chief economic works signals a fundamental change in basic thinking, and concepts such as confidence, uncertainty, expectation, and convention, which bear limited relation to the conceptual apparatus of Keynes's early philosophy, represent new core notions in an alternative philosophical system corresponding to Keynes's later economics.

In light of this, Anna Carabelli's *On Keynes's Method* and Rod O'Donnell's *Keynes: Philosophy, Economics and Politics* present, in combination, a quite interesting puzzle of exegesis. Both works assume that Keynes's philosophical thinking did not change in significant respects, and argue that to make sense of Keynes's philosophical thinking, both across Keynes's career and in *The General Theory*, it is necessary to operate from the vantage point of the *Treatise on Probability*. Each in effect, then, takes on the double task of translating philosophical ideas into economic ones and of inferring Keynes's later ideas from his earlier ones. Two particular obstacles to this shared strategy of interpretation deserve brief mention. First, given that Keynes's early philosophical thinking was largely carried out before he began any serious study of economics, and given that philosophical conceptions arrived at within a discipline often bear a significantly different trajectory and format than those investigated in pure philosophy, it is incumbent upon Carabelli and O'Donnell to show just how Keynes's pre-economics philosophical thinking links up with the philosophical ideas expressed in his economics. Second, since philosophy at Cambridge during Keynes's time there underwent dramatic change from the beginning-of-the-century analytic approach of Bertrand Russell, G.E. Moore, and the young Ludwig Wittgenstein to the later dominance of the later Wittgenstein, and since Keynes, who had declared his early allegiances to Russell and Moore (*CW*, Vol. VIII, p. 20) and had been criticized for them in the later Wittgenstein's 1932-1935 Cambridge lectures (Ambrose, 1979, pp. 138-139), was certainly not unacquainted with these developments (Coates, 1990; Monk, 1990), it is also incumbent upon Carabelli and O'Donnell to show just how changes in this tradition might or might not have affected Keynes's philosophical views.

Yet, whereas Carabelli and O'Donnell share the opinion that Keynes's philosophy did not change and has its essential repository in the *Treatise*, they also differ in important respects from one another in just what they believe this philosophy to be. Carabelli argues that Keynes's thinking in the *Treatise* reflected an early, prescient attachment to themes characteristic of Wittgenstein's later philosophy, while O'Donnell argues that Keynes's *Treatise* ideas were faithful to the early Cambridge philosophy of Russell and Moore. Further, operating from these dramatically different visions of how the *Treatise* underlies *The General Theory*, Carabelli argues that Keynes's later views were ultimately to represent an ordinary language philosophy reaction to early Cambridge neopositivism, while O'Donnell argues that Keynes's later thinking was focused upon an account of rational belief and action under uncertainty. In effect, then, confronted with the dilemma that much evidence supports the idea that Keynes's philosophical thinking finds differential expression according to his changing interests in philosophy and economics, Carabelli and O'Donnell each opt to seize different horns of the dilemma they create for themselves in thinking Keynes's views went unchanged. Carabelli locates this philosophy in a framework more suited to Keynes's later years and concerns, while O'Donnell locates it in a framework more reminiscent of his earliest preoccupations. Each, it might thus be said, has correctly captured a part of the story about Keynes's philosophical development; yet each, on account of a common commitment to the notion that Keynes's views did not significantly change and that they are to be found in essence in the *Treatise*, has at the same time failed to investigate the logic of development of Keynes's thinking that culminated in *The General Theory*.

Carabelli's approach, perhaps, suffers under the greatest strain of interpretation, since, in attempting to link Keynes's ideas in the *Treatise* to those of the later Wittgenstein, she needs to be able to explain the themes of the *Treatise* in terms of a philosophical thinking that did not receive expression at Cambridge until a decade and a half after the *Treatise*'s completion (in 1914 despite its publication in 1921). Wittgenstein did not return to Cambridge until 1929, and did not begin to seriously question his early views (and those of Russell and Moore) until shortly thereafter (Monk, 1990). Thus, Carabelli's case requires that the reader believe that Keynes was extraordinarily prescient about future developments in philosophy at Cambridge (indeed, more so than Wittgenstein), despite the fact that historians of philosophy universally reject this thesis. It also requires that the *Treatise* be read in an unusually creative way, since the imprint of the early Cambridge analytic philosophy of Russell and Moore on Keynes's ideas about intuition and indefinability is quite clear (Davis, 1994). Accordingly, though the reader might well want to investigate connections between Wittgenstein's later thinking and Keynes's later thinking, it seems highly unlikely that a persuasive case can be made for linking the former and Keynes's views in the *Treatise*.

Perhaps, then, because this case is such a difficult one to make, Carabelli chooses to explain the connection between Keynes and Wittgenstein in terms of a supposed shared commitment to ordinary language forms of expression. Keynes, she argues, can be seen to have had a preference for ordinary language forms of expression in the *Treatise*, and this orientation, she claims, is characteristic of Wittgenstein's later approach. However, most historians of philosophy (e.g., Passmore, 1968, pp. 440-442) regard this as a misclassification of Wittgenstein's later thinking and associate the ordinary language movement in philosophy principally with Oxford philosophers in the 1950s (especially J.L. Austin and Gilbert Ryle). Though Wittgenstein was certainly attentive to the properties of our ordinary forms of linguistic expression, most would argue that his deeper concerns went substantially beyond those of the Oxford movement, and that to restrict his preoccupations to a preference for ordinary language seriously diminishes their importance. Whether these deeper concerns (such as what it means to follow a rule, or what is involved in describing a private mental experience) can be said to have connections to Keynes's later thinking remains an open question. There seems, however, to be little reason to think that they were foreshadowed by the arguments of the *Treatise*.

Despite these deficiencies in her argument, Carabelli is still to be commended for exploring possible linkages between Keynes's thinking and later developments in Cambridge philosophy. Indeed, though evidence of intellectual exchange between Keynes and Wittgenstein in the late 1920s and early 1930s is limited (Coats, 1990), a case can nonetheless be made for saying that Keynes's later thinking shared in a climate of ideas at Cambridge that characterized Wittgenstein's later views. Particularly important here is the central role of the concept of convention in the thinking of both men, a connection which Carabelli notes (pp. 224, 300) but does not pursue. Keynes, of course, emphasized the importance of conventions in his account of the formation of long-term investment expectations and the rate of interest (*CW*, Vol. VII, pp. 152-153, 203-204). Wittgenstein devoted much thinking to the analysis of conventional behavior and the institutions in which it operated, asserting at one point, for example, that "An intention is embedded in its situation, in human customs and institutions" (1958, para. 337). For both men, moreover, this particular emphasis upon conventions and institutions represents an important departure from their earlier thinking.

Yet, if Keynes in his later economics can be thought to share ideas with the philosophy of the later Wittgenstein, which by all accounts departs in significant respects from early beginning-of-the-century Cambridge philosophy, then it seems to follow that Keynes also must have given up some part of his early views in the transition to his later ones. As Carabelli well demonstrates in her discussion of Keynes's economics, there do indeed remain strong linkages between the *Treatise on Probability* and Keynes's later economics, especially in relation to such themes as the interdependence and complexity of relationships, belief and action, and the nature of theoretical investigation (pp. 151ff). If this picture of continuity in Keynes's thinking is to be supplemented by the suggestion that this thinking also developed in a direction taken by the later Wittgenstein's thinking, then it is fair to ask what it is that Carabelli fails to see that Keynes must have given up from his early views to have ultimately adopted a form of thinking more like the later Wittgenstein's.

Here, let it be briefly noted that in his "My Early Beliefs" appraisal of his early views, Keynes faulted his early thinking for its having made intuition of intrinsic qualities central to the business of establishing how individuals determine what they say they know (X, pp. 437ff). On this view, individuals possessing particularly strong powers of intuition simply perceive the essential qualities or relations underlying the matters under investigation, and, when two individuals' intuitions are in conflict, there is little more to be said than that one must not be properly focused on the issue at hand. This doctrine, moreover, was central to the *Treatise*, where Keynes referred to the probability relation as that "type of objective relation between sets of propositions—the type which we claim to be correctly perceiving when me make [probability judgments]—to which the reader's attention must be directed"(*CW*, Vol. VIII, p. 6). On Keynes's own later statement, however, this sort of thinking was mistaken and naive. Indeed, were one to assert straightforwardly in a study of Keynes's philosophical thinking that *The General Theory* presupposes a metaphysics of "neo-Platonism" (as Keynes termed his early thinking [*CW*, Vol. VIII, p. 438]), combined with an unacknowledged epistemology of the Cartesian subject (as he implicitly characterized it), it would be clear to most that the philosophical underpinnings of Keynes's later economics had probably not been properly addressed.

Carabelli, unfortunately, fails to see what Keynes's critique of his early rationalism amounted to, since she uses her discussion of "My Early Beliefs" as an opportunity to deny that Keynes became antirationalist or irrationalist (pp. 99-100). A more valuable task would have been to ask what Keynes's admission several years after the publication of *The General Theory* implied about the philosophical assumptions of that work. Did Keynes develop a new understanding of economic agents' cognitive behavior (as, for example, in his discussion of speculation and the "beauty contest" [CW, Vol. VII, p. 156])? Did his abandonment of essential qualities and relations as the underpinnings of judgment transform his view of the objectivity of probability judgments (as, for example, in his later discussions of uncertainty)? Questions such as these, it seems, cannot be raised in an interpretive framework that takes Keynes's Treatise on Probability to possess all of the conceptual resources needed to explain Keynes's philosophical and economic thinking. At the very least, then, some analysis of the continuities and discontinuities in Keynes's philosophical thinking seems required in order to explain both what persists and what is new in Keynes's philosophy across his career.

O'Donnell's book also suffers under the strain of its specific strategy of interpretation. Like Carabelli, O'Donnell makes Keynes's Treatise the essential repository of his philosophical thinking and argues that Keynes's views did not change in any essential respects. Unlike Carabelli, however, O'Donnell is altogether insensitive to both the development of philosophical thinking at Cambridge during Keynes's time there and its possible impact upon him. The tension this oversight imposes upon O'Donnell's book is perhaps most manifest in O'Donnell's discussions of Keynes's critical self-appraisals in the response to Ramsey and in his "My Early Beliefs," where rather than address the possibility that Keynes's remarks signaled a real change in thinking, O'Donnell first denies that Keynes was serious about these statements, and then argues that what we see in these two instances is merely a change in emphasis in Keynes's original thinking that enabled Keynes to accommodate such matters as uncertainty and confidence. Drawing upon Keynes's classification of different types of probability judgments (numerical and nonnumerical, comparable and noncomparable, known and unknown) and discussion of weight in the Treatise, O'Donnell argues that Keynes first elaborated a theory of "strong rationality, based on known probabilities and referring to weight when appropriate," and then adopted a theory of "weak rationality [for] when reason in the strong sense has reached its limits and can proceed no further" for The General Theory (p. 78).

Yet, Keynes himself never made such a distinction anywhere in his published or unpublished works, and it must thus be wondered whether this division adequately represents Keynes's own thinking or is, rather, the most ready conceptualization that O'Donnell was able to bring to bear to defend the continuity thesis. Indeed, the fact that Keynes's thinking in the Treatise operated on two distinct levels that O'Donnell does not clearly distinguish— that of the substantive apparatus of the probability calculus and that of the epistemological and ontological principles of the work—suggests that O'Donnell's description of changes in emphasis in Keynes's thinking may be confused. Specifically, since elements of Keynes's early probability calculus reappeared in his later work (e.g., the reference to weight in connection with long-term expectations [*CW*, Vol. VII, p. 148]) without apparent accompaniment by their earlier philosophical elaboration (e.g., the early theory of intuition), it is quite possible that O'Donnell's view, as an interpretation of Keynes's philosophy, mistakes continuities in Keynes's substantive probability theory preoccupations for continuities in his philosophical concerns. This view gains further support from the fact that O'Donnell's description of Keynes's philosophical thinking in the *Treatise* as "a general theory of rational belief and action under uncertainty" (p. 6) makes uncertainty—properly speaking, a substantive concern of the probability calculus in connection with unknown probabilities—a characteristic of Keynes's philosophy, though the latter should concern the form and character of knowledge irrespective of the certainty conditions under which it is exercised.

At the same time, care should also be exercised in arguing that significant continuity existed in Keynes's thinking about the substantive apparatus of the probability calculus. While some of Keynes's early positions do reappear in his later thinking, that there seem to be important changes in his later views, for example, on the Principle of Indifference (see Gillies, 1988), gives us good reason to be suspicious of the idea that Keynes generally felt the same confidence about his probability calculus at the time of the writing of *The General Theory* that he had felt about it in the *Treatise*. O'Donnell, if anything, only obscures these issues, in part because of his unhesitating commitment to the continuity thesis and in part because his characterization of the *Treatise* as "a general theory of rational belief and action under uncertainty" improperly implants in the early Keynes a concern with the type of uncertainty issues that he really only turned to much later (perhaps most clearly after *The General Theory* in his 1937 *Quarterly Journal of Economics* response to reviews of *The General Theory* [*CW*, Vol. XIV, pp. 113-114]). While uncertainty and unknown probabilities may well be correlates of a sort that permit us to make rough comparisons between Keynes's early and later thinking, to say that Keynes in the *Treatise* was concerned with just the same matters surrounding uncertainty as he investigated later on seems overbold.

For O'Donnell, then, Keynes's philosophy is essentially a theory of rationality, and we can at most detect changes in emphasis on this basic theme. Does this interpretation, one that seems to need to account for behavior in the world of *The General Theory* in terms of boundaries and limitations upon decision making (reminiscent of the disequilibrium school interpretation of Keynes), adequately capture the revolutionary impact of that work on economic thinking? Certainly one thing central to *The General Theory* is its charge that traditional or Classical theory commits a fallacy of composition, or the idea that the economy in the aggregate functions quite differently than it does at the level of its units. Indeed, Keynes's critique of the Say's Law view of savings might be said to depend crucially on the notion that the rationality of the system is of an altogether different nature from the sort of rationality traditionally associated with agents' behavior. Alternatively, it might fairly be said that there exist principles of organization operating at the level of the macroeconomy that altogether transcend rationality. Conventions, in particular, have a key role in Keynes's historical, shifting equilibrium method that has become increasingly central to scholars' characterization of Keynes's understanding of the economy (e.g., Rogers, 1989; Asimakopoulos, 1991), and whether or not conventional individual behavior may be regarded as rational seems less important than explaining just how conventions create structures of socioeconomic interaction.

It is difficult, however, to make conventions a central focus should one's fundamental vision of Keynes's philosophy be Platonist, as it is in O'Donnell. On O'Donnell's view, Keynes never really abandons the "neo-Platonism" of his early views that supposes that behind the play of everyday phenomena there exist timeless qualities and relations that are the proper objects of judgment in economics and ethics (though Keynes clearly disparages his early attachment to this thinking in "My Early Beliefs" [*CW*, Vol. X, p. 438]). Conventions, that is, are by their very nature ad hoc and indelibly historical in character, reflecting for Keynes past configurations of the economy that possess no deeper rationale than their fact of existence. Thus, when the reigning conventions regarding long-term investment expectations or the rate of interest are identified, it is hardly some underlying relation or quality that are the object of judgment, as it was for Keynes in the *Treatise*; rather, the investor or speculator is specifically concerned with transitory, historical objects of judgment. To term this a "weak rationality" on the model of a somewhat impaired "strong rationality" thus seems to wrongfully impose Plato's epistemology and ontology that Keynes employed in the *Treatise* onto a fundamentally different kind of thinking that Keynes had developed by the time of *The General Theory*.

In O'Donnell's case, then, it might well be said that it is less the particular difficulties of interpreting Keynes's later thinking in terms of his early philosophy than an essentially inadequate vision of what *The General Theory* was all about that raises questions. As has been made clear by Skidelsky, the first World War inalterably transformed Keynes's early world. Except, perhaps, for a continuing utopian spirit regarding reform politics, Keynes found little of what had made up the conceptual approaches of his early years that could be brought to bear upon the deep problems of the then-modern age. There is no doubt that he did appropriate important elements of the logical apparatus of his probability calculus of the *Treatise* to employ in his later thinking, just as important components of the *Treatise on Money* found their way into new contexts in *The General Theory*. But the philosophical basis of Keynes's later thinking has its foundation in a different set of conceptual needs that Keynes faced in the 1930s.

What is the philosophical framework in which the concepts of convention, time, and expectation are elaborated in Keynes's later thinking? An effort to explain Keynes's later philosophy as a theory of interdependent expectation is introduced by the present author in Davis (1991b), and is the subject of more lengthy treatment in a forthcoming work (Davis, forthcoming). Apart from the arguments of these works, however, one thing that seems fair to insist upon is that the interpretation of Keynes's philosophical thinking start from a philosophical examination of *The General Theory*. While for the reasons noted at the outset this may initially appear a paradoxical requirement, it must not be forgotten that the chief object of the recent literature on Keynes and philosophy has been to further understand Keynes's later economic thinking. Indeed, as the objective of this literature has it, it will only be when the philosophy of *The General Theory* has been made explicit that Keynes's standing as a figure of the same rank as Smith and Marx will have been made clear. Carabelli and O'Donnell miss this opportunity, despite the fact that their books have opened up a wealth of understanding about Keynes's early philosophy in the *Treatise*.

# REFERENCES

Ambrose, Alice. 1979. *Wittgenstein's Lectures, Cambridge, 1932-35*. Totowa, NJ: Rowman and Littlefield.

Asimakopoulos, Athanasios. 1991. *Keynes's General Theory and Accumulation*. Cambridge: Cambridge University Press.

Bateman, Bradley W. 1987. "Keynes's Changing Conception of Probability." *Economics and Philosophy* 3: 97-120.

————. 1991. "Das Maynard Keynes Problem." *Cambridge Journal of Economics* 15: 101-111.

Coats, John. 1990. *Ordinary Language Economics: Keynes and the Cambridge Philosophers*. Unpublished Ph.D. dissertation, University of Cambridge.

Davis, John B. 1990. "Keynes's Early Epistemology." Paper presented to the History of Economics Society, Lexington, Virginia.

Davis, John B. 1991a. "Keynes's Critiques of Moore: Philosophical Foundations of Keynes's Economics." *Cambridge Journal of Economics* 15: 61-77.

————. 1991b. "Keynes's View of Economics as a Moral Science." Pp. 89-103 in *Keynes and Philosophy*, edited by B.W. Bateman and J.B. Davis. Aldershot, UK: Elgar.

————. 1994. *Keynes's Philosophical Development*. Cambridge: Cambridge University Press.

Gillies, Donald A. 1988. "Probability and Induction." Pp. 179-204 in *Encyclopedia Of Philosophy*, 179-204 edited by G.H.R. Parkinson. London: Croom Helm.

Keynes, John Maynard. 1971-1989. *The Collected Writings of John Maynard Keynes*, Vols. I-XXX. London: Macmillan.

Monk, Ray. 1990. *Ludwig Wittgenstein*. New York: Free Press.

Passmore, John. 1968. *A Hundred Years of Philosophy*. Middlesex, UK: Penguin.

Ramsey, Frank. 1978. *Foundations of Mathematics*. London: Routledge & Kegan Paul.

Rogers, Colin. 1989. *Money, Interest and Capital*. Cambridge: Cambridge University Press.

Skidelsky, Robert. 1983. *John Maynard Keynes*, Vol. I: *Hopes Betrayed, 1883-1920*. London: Macmillan.

Wittgenstein, Ludwig. 1958. *Philosophical Investigations*. Oxford, UK: Basil Blackwell.

# PERKIN'S THE RISE OF PROFESSIONAL SOCIETY: ENGLAND SINCE 1880:

## A REVIEW ESSAY

A.W. Coats

*The Rise of Professional Society: England since 1880.*
**By Harold Perkin.**
**London: Routledge, 1990. Pp. xvi | 604.**

There are several reasons why Professor Perkin's new book—the sequel to his highly regarded *The Origins of Modern English Society* (1969), which covered the 1780-1880 period—can be warmly recommended to readers of this annual. It provides a valuable historical background for students of the history of economic ideas, by setting the work of Mill, Marshall, Tawney, Pigou, Keynes, Hayek, and others in the context of contemporary processes of economic and social change. Beyond this, it embodies a coherent and stimulating intellectual framework, and last but not least, it is a very good read, synthesizing a vast amount of material from the late eighteenth century right up to the contentious decade of the 1980s.

**Research in the History of Economic Thought and Methodology, Volume 12, pages 245-248.**
**Copyright © 1994 by JAI Press Inc.**
**All rights of reproduction in any form reserved.**
**ISBN: 1-55938-747-5**

Perkin's earlier book broke with more conventional accounts of the industrial revolution, which have emphasized economic, technological, or demographic factors and processes, by interpreting it as "*a social revolution*: a revolution in social organization, with social causes as well as social effects" (p. 18), including "the demise of the old pre-industrial aristocratic society and the rise of the viable class society of mid-Victorian England" (p. xi). While *The Origins* by no means ignored changes in social structure, it gave special prominence to three contending social "ideals"—those of the landed aristocracy, the entrepreneurs, and the proletariat, respectively—and some critics, especially left-wingers, reacted strongly against the shift away from the familiar categories of class and material interests toward the more intangible realm of ideals.

The choice between ideals and classes poses fewer problems in the present volume, which gives pride of place to a fourth category present, but subordinate, in the earlier period—namely, the "forgotten" but steadily expanding mid-Victorian cadres of nonbusiness professionals whose social ideal, Perkin argues, has come to dominate later industrial and postindustrial society. Though professionals undeniably have career and pecuniary aspirations as well as vested interests, their ideal cuts across class lines, for professions are vertical structures that "overlay the horizontal structures and vertical antagonisms of class" (p. xiii). Professions are often seen, and see themselves, as above the main economic battle. The professional ideal of how society should be organized, and who should organize it, is "based on trained expertise and selection by merit." It differs from the other social ideals in

> emphasizing human capital rather than passive or active property, highly skilled and differentiated labour rather than the labour theory of value, and selection by merit defined as trained and certified expertise (p. 4).

This does not mean that the professionals constitute a solid, homogeneous bloc. On the contrary, they are segmented, with significant rivalries—indeed, so much so that the rivalry between public-sector and private-sector professionals has become "the master conflict" of present-day professional society (p. 10). This is a logical outcome of industrialization, the concomitant increase of state power and responsibility, and the tendencies toward specialization, concentration, integration, and growth in organizational scale.

In England—and Perkin provides occasional glimpses of other countries (suggesting that he should undertake a systematic international comparative study at some future date)—class society reached its zenith in the 1880-1914 period. It encountered a severe crisis from 1910 to 1926, which was eventually averted through the combined efforts of professional managers, professional union leaders, and increasingly professional politicians and civil servants (p. 217). And it reached a "plateau of attainment" from 1945 to the early 1970s.

The welfare state was a practical expression of the professional ideal, its popularity being due to the growing role of professionalism in society and the influence of the professional social ideal (p. 355). More recently, there has been a backlash against professionalism and an effort to revive the entrepreneurial ideal in the Thatcherite 1880s, an era for which neither the author nor this reviewer has any nostalgia. But although class survives, the professional ideal is still dominant, though weaker than it was; a crucial question for the future is not whether professionalism will prevail, but in what form. In some respects, Perkin claims, the modern growth of vested interests represents a kind of return to a pre-industrial, pre-clan society (p. 287). But his view of Britain's current state is decidedly gloomy, since we now have

> the worst of both worlds: all the bitterness and mutual hostility of an old and obsolescent class society which refuses to die and all the greedy scramble for resources between the professional interest groups, but few of the benefits of a more fully developed professional society as in West Germany or Japan (p. 516).

As must by now be obvious, Perkin seeks to replace the Marxist version of history, emphasizing the economic factor, with one that stresses the power of ideology over political reality (p. 504) and the battle between ideologies. In this account, of course, ideas have a decided potency especially when, as frequently occurs, specific groups, interests, or even classes set out to impose their ideals on the community at large. Unfortunately for the economists, they lack professional organization and do not have a readily identifiable species of expertise with which to exert occupational, social, or political leverage.

A major issue in reviewing Perkin's general thesis is whether the concepts of profession, professionalism, and professional social ideal can bear the expanatory weight he ascribes to them. This reviewer has some reservations on this score. Nevertheless, the overall picture that emerges from *The Rise of Professional Society* is persuasive and rich in detail. Three features not hitherto mentioned are especially valuable: his analyses of elites (sic); his thoughtful distinction between earlier kinds of "absolute" property and the "contingent" property embodied in professional service; and his careful analysis of long-term changes in the distribution of income and wealth. This last element convincingly demonstrates that Perkin could, if he chose, be a good conventional economic and social historian. Fortunately he has successfully transcended that professional category.

# ACKNOWLEDGMENT

Since writing this review two years ago, Professor Perkin has informed me that he is currently engaged on precisely the kind of study I envisaged.

# REFERENCE

Perkin, Harold. 1969. *The Origins of Modern English Society*.

# NEW BOOKS RECEIVED

Adler, Mortimer J. *Desires, Right and Wrong*. New York: Macmillan, 1991. Pp. 200.

Alogoskoufis, George; Lucas Papademos; and Richard Portes, eds. *External Constraints on Macroeconomic Policy: The European Experience*. New York: Cambridge University Press, 1991. Pp. xxi, 384. $59.50.

Angresano, James. *Comparative Economics*. Englewood Cliffs, NJ: Prentice Hall, 1992. Pp. xiv, 498.

Arestis, Philip, and Malcolm Sawyer, eds. *A Biographical Dictionary of Dissenting Economists*. Brookfield, VT: Edward Elgar, 1992. Pp. xiv, 628.

Applebaum, Herbert. *The Concept of Work: Ancient, Medieval, and Modern*. Albany: State University of New York Press, 1992. Pp. xiii, 645. $24.50, paper.

Aronowitz, Stanley. *The Politics of Identity: Class, Culture, Social Movements*. New York: Routledge, 1992. Pp. x, 287. $45.00, cloth; $15.95, paper.

Asimakopulos, Athanasios. *Keynes's General Theory and Accumulation*. New York: Cambridge University Press, 1991. Pp. xviii, 207. $47.50, cloth; $16.95, paper.

Auspitz, J. Lee, Wojciech W. Gasparski, Marek K. Mlicki, and Klemens Szaniawski, eds., *Praxiologies and the Philosophy of Economics*. New Brunswick, NJ: Transaction, 1992. Pp. viii, 705. $89.95.

Balabkins, Nicholas W. *Not by Theory alone...: The Economics of Gustav von Schmoller and Its Legacy to America*. Berlin, Germany: Duncker & Humblot, 1988. Pp. 115. DM44, paper.

**Research in the History of Economic Thought and Methodology, Volume 12, pages 249-260.**
**Copyright © 1994 by JAI Press Inc.**
**All rights of reproduction in any form reserved.**
**ISBN: 1-55938-747-5**

Barnett, William A., James Powell, and George E. Tauchen, eds. *Nonparametric and Semiparametric Methods in Econometrics and Statistics*. New York: Cambridge University Press, 1991. Pp. xi, 493. $65.00, cloth; $22.95, paper.

Barthes, Roland. *Incidents*. Berkeley: University of California Press, 1992. Pp. 73. $12.00.

Beiner, Ronald. *What's the Matter with Liberalism?* Berkeley: University of California Press, 1992. Pp. viii, 197. $25.00.

Bensman, Joseph, and Robert Lilienfeld. *Craft and Consciousness: Occupational Technique and the Development of World Images*. 2nd edn. New York: Aldine de Gruyter, 1991. Pp. xxiv, 395. $49.95, cloth; $27.95, paper.

Bernstein, Richard J. *The New Constellation: The Ethical-Political Horizons of Modernity/Postmodernity*. Cambridge: MIT Press, 1992. Pp. 358. $35.00, paper.

Bicchieri, Cristina, and Maria Luisa Dalla Chiara, eds. *Knowledge, Belief and Strategic Interaction*. New York: Cambridge University Press, 1992. Pp. xiv, 413. $64.95.

Black, Edwin. *Rhetorical Questions: Studies of Public Discourse*. Chicago: University of Chicago Press, 1992. Pp. xi, 209. $24.95.

Blaug, Mark. *The Methodology of Economics*. 2nd edn. New York: Cambridge University Press, 1992. Pp. xxviii, 286. $54.95, cloth; $17.95, paper.

Bohman, James. *New Philosophy of Social Science: Problems of Indeterminacy*. Cambridge: MIT Press, 1991. Pp. x, 273. $32.50.

Boland, Lawrence A. *The Methodology of Economic Building*. New York: Routledge, 1991. Pp. 194. $10.99, paper.

Boller, Paul F., Jr. *Memoirs of an Obscure Professor*. Fort Worth, TX: Texas Christian University Press, 1992. Pp. xii, 257. $24.95.

Boudon, Raymond. *The Analysis of Ideology*. Chicago: University of Chicago Press, 1989. Pp. vii, 241. $39.95.

Bourdieu, Pierre, and Loic J.D. Wacquant. *An Invitation to Reflexive Sociology*. Chicago: University of Chicago Press, 1992. Pp. xiv, 332. $38.95, cloth; $13.95, paper.

Braaten, Jane. *Habermas's Critical Theory of Society*. Albany: State University of New York Press, 1991. Pp. x, 191. $44.50, cloth; $14.95, paper.

Breton, Denise, and Christopher Largent. *The Soul of Economies*. Wilmington, DE: Idea House, 1991. Pp. vi, 366. $24.95, cloth; $14.95, paper.

Brewer, Anthony. *Richard Cantillon: Pioneer of Economic Theory*. New York: Routledge, 1992. Pp. x, 210. $72.50.

Brint, Michael, and William Weaver, eds. *Pragmatism in Law and Society*. Boulder, CO: Westview Press, 1991. Pp. xii, 400. $49.94, cloth; $16.95, paper.

Britton, A.J.C. *Macroeconomic Policy in Britain, 1974-1987*. New York: Cambridge University Press, 1991. Pp. xiii, 365. $59.50.

Bromley, Daniel W., and Kathleen Segerson, eds. *The Social Response to Environmental Risk: Policy Formulation in an Age of Uncertainty*. Boston: Kluwer Academic Publishers, 1992. Pp. 216.

Brown, JoAnne, and David K. van Keuren, eds. *The Estate of Social Knowledge*. Baltimore, MD: Johns Hopkins University Press, 1991. Pp. xxvi, 266. $39.95.

Brown, Richard D. *Knowledge is Power: The Diffusion of Information in Early America, 1700-1865*. New York: Oxford University Press, 1989. Pp. xii, 372. $16.95, paper.

Buhite, Russell D., and David W. Levy, eds. *FDR's Fireside Chats*. Norman: University of Oklahoma Press, 1992. Pp. xx, 326. $24.95.

Burawoy, Michael. *The Radiant Past: Ideology and Reality in Hungary's Road to Capitalism*. Chicago: University of Chicago Press, 1992. Pp. xvi, 215. $24.95.

Calhoun, Craig, ed. *Habermas and the Public Sphere*. Cambridge: MIT Press, 1992. Pp. x, 498. $45.00.

Caves, Richard E. *American Industry: Structure, Conduct, Performance*. 7th edn. Englewood Cliffs, NJ: Prentice Hall, 1992. Pp. ix, 132. Paper.

Cipola, Carlo M. *Between Two Cultures: An Introduction to Economic History*. New York: Norton, 1991. Pp. x, 198. Paper.

Clifton, Gloria. *Professionalism, Patronage and Public Service in Victorian London*. Atlantic Highlands, NJ: Athlone Press, 1992. Pp. x, 239. $80.00.

Coats, A.W. *On the History of Economic Thought: British and American Economic Essays*. New York: Routledge, 1992. Pp. xi, 495.

Combe, Jerry, and Edgar Norton, eds. *Economic Justice in Perspective: A Book of Readings*. Englewood Cliffs, NJ: Prentice Hall, 1991. Pp. xi, 260. Paper.

Cornell, Drucilla, Michel Rosenfeld, and David Gray Carlson, eds. *Deconstruction and the Possibility of Justice*. New York: Routledge, 1992. Pp. x, 409. $52.50, cloth; $16.95, paper.

Craib, Ian. *Anthony Giddens*. New York: Routledge, 1992. Pp. ix, 209. $49.95, cloth; $15.95, paper.

Craven, John. *Social Choice*. New York: Cambridge University Press, 1992. Pp. x, 152. $49.95, cloth; $15.95, paper.

Creedy, John. *Demand and Exchange in Economic Analysis: A History from Cournot to Marshall*. Brookfield, VT: Edward Elgar, 1992. Pp. xi, 212. $59.95.

da Fonseca, Eduardo Giannetti. *Beliefs in Action: Economic Philosophy and Social Change*. New York: Cambridge University Press, 1991. Pp. xiv, 256. $39.95.

Darder, Antonia. *Culture and Power in the Classroom: A Critical Foundation for Bicultural Education.* New York: Bergin & Garvey, 1991. Pp. xix, 170. $37.95, cloth; $13.95, paper.

Dardi, M., et al, eds. *Alfred Marshall's Principles of Economics, 1890-1990.* 2 vols. Quaderni di storia dell'economia politica, Vol. 9, nos. 2-3 (1991), pp. 1-421, and Vol. 10, no. 1 (1992), pp. 425-626. Milan, Italy.

de Marchi, Neil, and Mark Blaug, eds. *Appraising Economic Theories: Studies in the Methodology of Research Programs.* Brookfield, VT: Edward Elgar, 1991. Pp. ix, 566. $109.95.

Derber, Charles; William A. Schwartz; and Yale Magrass. *Power in the Highest Degree: Professionals and the Rise of a New Mandarin Order.* New York: Oxford University Press, 1990. Pp. x, 275. $30.00.

Desmond, Adrian, and James Moore. *Darwin: The Life of a Tormented Evolutionist.* New York: Warner Books, 1991. Pp. xxi, 808. $35.00.

Diakonoff, I. M. *Early Antiquity.* Chicago: University of Chicago Press, 1991. Pp. xxiii, 461. $49.95.

Dierkes, Meinolf, and Bernd Biervert, eds. *European Social Science in Transition: Assessment and Outlook.* Boulder, CO: Westview Press, 1992. Pp. 640.

Diesing, Paul. *How Does Social Science Work?: Reflections on Practice.* Pittsburgh: University of Pittsburgh Press, 1991. Pp. xii, 414. $29.95.

Dornbusch, Rudiger, and Sebastian Edwards, eds. *The Macroeconomics of Politics in Latin America.* Chicago: University of Chicago Press, 1991. Pp. ix, 402. $65.00, cloth; $21.95, paper.

Dostaler, Gilles, Diane Ethier, and Laurent Lepage, eds. *Gunnar Myrdal and His Works.* Montreal, Canada: Harvest House, 1992. Pp. ix, 259. $35.00.

Dugger, William M. *Underground Economics: A Decade of Institutionalist Dissent.* Armonk, NY: M.E. Sharpe, 1992. Pp. xxx, 368.

Ehrenberg, John. *The Dictatorship of the Proletariat: Marxism's Theory of Socialist Democracy.* New York: Routledge, 1992. Pp. viii, 203. $49.00, cloth; $14.95, paper.

Einhorn, Robin L. *Property Rules: Political Economy in Chicago, 1833-1872.* Chicago: University of Chicago Press, 1991. Pp. xvii, 295. $34.95.

Eisenberg, John A. *The Limits of Reason: Indeterminacy in Law, Education, and Morality.* New Brunswick, NJ: Transaction, 1992. Pp. vii, 184. $32.95.

Ekins, Paul, and Manfred Max-Neef, eds. *Real-Life Economics: Understanding Wealth Creation.* New York: Routledge, 1992. Pp. xxi, 460. $85.00, cloth; $23.00, paper.

Eribon, Didier. *Michel Foucault.* Cambridge: Harvard University Press, 1991. Pp. xvi, 374. $27.95.

Fabra, Paul. *Capital for Profit: The Triumph of Ricardian Political Economy over Marx and the Neoclassical.* Savage, MD: Rowman & Littlefield, 1991. Pp. xxviii, 345. $47.50.

Feenberg, Andrew. *Critical Theory of Technology.* New York: Oxford University Press, 1991. Pp. xi, 235. $35.00.

Fforde, John. *The Bank of England and Public Policy, 1941-1958.* New York: Cambridge University Press, 1992. Pp. xix, 861. $125.00.

Fitzpatrick, Peter. *The Mythology of Modern Law.* New York: Routledge, 1992. Pp. xv, 235. $72.50, cloth; $16.95, paper.

Foreman-Peck, James, ed. *New Perspectives on the Late Victorian Economy.* New York: Cambridge University Press, 1991. Pp. xv, 353. $54.50.

Fry, Michael, ed. *Adam Smith's Legacy: His Place in the Development of Modern Economics.* New York: Routledge, 1992. Pp. xv, 203. $35.00.

Furubotn, Eirik G., and Rudolf Richter, eds. The New Institutional Economics. College Station: Texas A&M University Press, 1991. Pp. viii, 376. $35.00, paper.

Gardiner, Michael. *The Dialogics of Critique: M.M. Bakhtin and the Theory of Ideology.* New York: Routledge, 1992. Pp. 258. $57.50, cloth; $16.95, paper.

Gareau, Frederick H. *The Political Economy of the Social Sciences.* New York: Garland, 1991. Pp. xxi, 351. $47.00.

Garretsen, Harry. *Keynes, Coordination and Beyond: The Development of Macroeconomic and Monetary Theory Since 1945.* Brookfield, VT: Edward Elgar, 1992. Pp. ix, 228. $59.95.

Gellner, Ernest. *Reason and Culture.* Cambridge, MA: Blackwell, 1992. Pp. xiv, 193. $44.95, cloth; $17.95, paper.

Gerrard, Bill, and John Hillard, eds. *The Philosophy and Economics of J.M. Keynes.* Brookfield, VT: Edward Elgar, 1992. Pp. xiii, 253. $59.95.

Giersch, Herbert; Karl-Heinz Paque; and Holger Schmieding. *The Fading Miracle: Four Decades of Market Economy in Germany.* New York: Cambridge University Press, 1992. Pp. xiv, 302. $39.95.

Gladwin, Christina H., ed. *Structural Adjustment and African Women Farmers.* Gainesville, FL: Center for African Studies and University of Florida Press, University of Florida, 1991. Pp. viii, 413. $34.95.

Goldfarb, Jeffrey C. *The Cynical Society: The Culture of Politics and the Politics of Culture in American Life.* Chicago: University of Chicago Press, 1991. Pp. xi, 200. $22.50.

Goldin, Claudia, and Hugh Rockoff, eds. *Strategic Factors in Nineteenth Century American Economic History.* Chicago: University of Chicago Press, 1992. Pp. ix, 491. $60.00.

Goldman, Alvin I. *Liaisons: Philosophy Meets the Cognitive and Social Sciences.* Cambridge: MIT Press, 1992. Pp. viii, 336. $39.95.

Goldman, Harvey. *Max Weber and Thomas Mann: Calling and the Shaping of the Self.* Berkeley: University of California Press, 1991. Pp. xi, 284. $12.95, paper.

Gottlieb, Roger S. *Marxism 1844-1990: Origins, Betrayal, Rebirth.* New York: Routledge, 1992. Pp. xvii, 248. $49.95, cloth; $19.95, paper.

Granovetter, Mark, and Richard Swedberg, eds. *The Sociology of Economic Life*. Boulder, CO: Westview Press, 1992. Pp. vi, 399. $65.00, cloth; $19.85, paper.

Griffin, Roger. *The Nature of Fascism*. New York: St. Martin's, 1991. Pp. x, 245. $45.00.

Groenewegen, Peter, ed. *The Origins of Laissez Faire in Retrospect and Prospect*. Sydney, Australia: Centre for the Study of the History of Economic Thought, 1990. Pp. viii, 72. Paper.

Grossman, Gene M., and Elhanan Helpman. *Innovation and Growth in the Global Economy*. Cambridge: MIT Press, 1991. Pp. xiv, 359. $29.95.

Gunning, J. Patrick. *The New Subjectivist Revolution: An Elucidation and Extension of Ludwig von Mises's Contributions to Economic Theory*. Savage, MD: Rowman & Littlefield, 1991. Pp. xiii, 265. $43.50.

Guthke, Karl S. *B. Traven: The Life Behind the Legends*. New York: Lawrence Hill Books, 1991. Pp. xiii, 478. $24.95, cloth; $14.95, paper.

Haber, Samuel. *The Quest for Authority and Honor in the American Professions, 1750-1900*. Chicago: University of Chicago Press, 1991. Pp. xiv, 478. $39.95.

Habermas, Jurgen. *The New Conservatism: Cultural Criticism and the Historians' Debate*. Edited and trans. by Shierry Weber Nicholsen. Cambridge: MIT Press, 1989. Pp. xxxv, 270. $14.95, paper.

Halliday, Terence C., and Morris Janowitz, eds. *Sociology and Its Publics: The Forms and Fates of Disciplinary Organization*. Chicago: University of Chicago Press, 1992. Pp. xvii, 429. $29.95, cloth; $14.95, paper.

Hamouda, O.F., and B.B. Price. *Verification in Economics and History: A Sequel to "Scientifization."* New York: Routledge, 1991. Pp. x, 182. $39.95.

Harrison, Lawrence E. *Who Prospers? How Cultural Values Shape Economic and Political Success*. New York: Basic Books, 1992. Pp. vii, 280. $22.00.

Harrison, Peter. *"Religion" and the Religions in the English Enlightenment*. New York: Cambridge University Press, 1990. Pp. ix, 277.

Hawthorn, Geoffrey. *Plausible Worlds: Possibility and Understanding in History and the Social Sciences*. New York: Cambridge University Press, 1991. Pp. xiii, 192.

Hayek, F.A. *The Trend of Economic Thinking: Essays on Political Economists and Economic History*. Edited by W.W. Bartley III and Stephen Kresge. Chicago: University of Chicago Press, 1991. Pp. xi, 388. $40.00.

Hechter, Michael, Karl-Dieter Opp, and Reinhard Wippler. *Social Institutions: Their Emergence, Maintenance, and Effects*. New York: Aldine de Gruyter, 1990. Pp. vii, 342. $49.95.

Herman, Edward S. *Beyond Hypocrisy*. Boston: South End Press, 1992. Pp. 239. $13.00, paper.

Hennessy, Elizabeth. *A Domestic History of the Bank of England, 1930-1960*. New York: Cambridge University Press, 1992. Pp. xv, 449. $125.00.

Hiley, David R., James F. Bohman, and Richard Shusterman, eds. *The Interpretive Turn*. Ithaca, NY: Cornell University Press, 1991. Pp. x, 322. $39.95, cloth; $12.95, paper.

Hodgson, Geoffrey M. *After Marx and Sraffa: Essays in Political Economy*. New York: St. Martin's Press, 1991. Pp. xiv, 279. $69.95.

Hodgson, Geoffrey M., and Ernesto Screpanti, eds. *Rethinking Economics: Markets, Technology and Economic Evolution*. Brookfield, VT: Edward Elgar, 1991. Pp. vi, 206. $55.95.

Honneth, Axel. *The Critique of Power: Reflective Stages in a Critical Social Theory*. Cambridge: MIT Press, 1991. Pp. xxxii, 340. $35.00.

Housman, Daniel M. *The Inexact and Separate Science of Economics*. New York: Cambridge University Press, 1992. Pp. xi, 372. $59.95.

Howard, M.C., and J.E. King. *A History of Marxian Economics*, Vol. II: *1929-1990*. Princeton, NJ: Princeton University Press, 1992. Pp. xv, 420. $60.00, cloth; $19.95, paper.

Hsieh, Ching-Yao, and Meng-Hua Ye. *Economics, Philosophy, and Physics*. Armonk, NY: M.E. Sharpe, 1991. Pp. xxxvii, 169. $39.95, cloth; $16.95, paper.

Hsu, Robert C. *Economic Theories in China, 1979-1988*. New York: Cambridge University Press, 1991. Pp. xii, 198. $42.95.

Hunt, E.K. *History of Economic Thought: A Critical Perspective*. 2nd edn. New York: HarperCollins, 1992. Pp. xiv, 658.

Huntington, Samuel P. *The Third Wave: Democratization in the Late Twentieth Century*. Norman: University of Oklahoma Press, 1991. Pp. xvii, 366. $24.95.

Hutchison, Terence. *Changing Aims in Economics*. Cambridge, MA: Blackwell, 1992. Pp. xi, 186. $22.50.

Inchausti, Robert. *The Ignorance Production of Ordinary People*. Albany: State University of New York Press, 1991. Pp. xi, 175. $12.95, paper.

Kadarkay, Arpad. *Georg Lukacs: Life, Thought, and Politics*. Cambridge, MA: Basil Blackwell, 1991. Pp. xv, 538. $29.95.

Kahan, Alan S. *Aristocratic Liberalism: The Social and Political Thought of Jacob Burckhardt*, John Start Mill, and Alexis de Tocqueville. New York: Oxford, 1992. Pp. viii, 228. $39.95.

Kadish, Alon. *Historians, Economists and Economic History*. New York: Routledge, 1991. Pp. xii, 305. $14.99, paper.

Katsenelinboigen, Aron. *Indeterministic Economics*. New York: Praeger, 1992. Pp. xiii, 315. $65.00.

Kirkham, Richard L. *Theories of Truth: A Critical Introduction*. Cambridge: MIT Press, 1992. Pp. xi, 401. $35.00.

Klinck, Dennis R. *The Word of the Law*. Ottawa, Canada: Carleton University Press, 1992. Pp. xii, 458. Paper.

Knight, Jack. *Institutions and Social Conflict.* New York: Cambridge University Press, 1992. Pp. xiii, 234.

Krugman, Paul. *Geography and Trade.* Cambridge: MIT Press, 1991. Pp. xi, 142. $17.95.

La Botz, Dan. *Mask of Democracy: Labor Suppression in Mexico Today.* Boston: South End Press, 1992. $14.00, paper.

Laidler, David. *The Golden Age of the Quantity Theory.* Princeton, NJ: Princeton University Press, 1991. Pp. xv, 220. $35.00.

Lamont, Michele. *Money, Morals, and Manners: The Culture of the French and the American Upper-Middle Class.* Chicago: University of Chicago Press, 1992. Pp. xxix, 320. $35.00.

Lavoie, Don. *Economics and Hermeneutics.* New York: Routledge, 1991. Pp. xii, 323.

Lazonick, William. *Business Organization and the Myth of the Market Economy.* New York: Cambridge University Press, 1991. Pp. xiv, 372. $39.95.

Lee, Frederic S., and Warren J. Samuels, eds. *The Heterodox Economics of Gardiner C. Means: A Collection.* Armonk, NY: M.E. Sharpe, 1992. Pp. xxxiii, 362.

Levy, David M. *The Economic Ideas of Ordinary People.* New York: Routledge, 1992. Pp. xxv, 341. $49.95.

Loasby, Brian J. *Equilibrium and Evolution: An Exploration of Connecting Principles in Economics.* New York: Manchester University Press/St. Martin's Press, 1991. Pp. ix, 119. $35.00.

Lukacs, Georg. *The Process of Democratization.* Albany: State University of New York Press, 1991. Pp. x, 179. $44.50, cloth; $14.95, paper.

Mair, Douglas, and Anne G. Miller, eds. *A Modern Guide to Economic Thought.* Brookfield, VT: Edward Elgar, 1991. Pp. xi, 281. $67.95.

Marshall, Alfred. *Alfred Marshall on the Method and History of Economics* (Circa 1870). Edited by Peter Groenewegen. Sydney, Australia: Centre for the Study of the History of Economic Thought, 1990. Pp. xxiii, 21. Paper.

Marz, Eduard. *Joseph Schumpeter: Scholar, Teacher and Politician.* New Haven, CT: Yale University Press, 1991. Pp. xx, 204. $30.00.

McClelland, Charles E. *The German Experience of Professionalization.* New York: Cambridge University Press, 1991. Pp.x, 253.

McCloskey, Donald N. *If You're So Smart: The Narrative of Economic Expertise.* Chicago: University of Chicago Press, 1990. Pp. ix, 180. $17.95.

McCormick, Brian. *Hayek and the Keynesian Avalanche.* New York: St. Martin's Press, 1992. Pp. xiii, 289. $59.95.

McFarland, Floyd B. *Economic Philosophy and American Problems.* Savage, MD: Rowman & Littlefield, 1991. Pp. xii, 235. $44.50.

McMullin, Ernan, ed. *The Social Dimensions of Science*. Notre Dame, IN: University of Notre Dame Press, 1992. Pp. xvii, 299. $37.95, cloth; $19.95, paper.

Meeks, J. Gay Tulip. *Thoughtful Economic Man: Essays on Rationality, Moral Rules and Benevolence*. New York: Cambridge, 1991. Pp. ix, 160. $29.95.

Milgate, Murray, and Shannon C. Stimson. *Ricardian Politics*. Princeton, NJ: Princeton University Press, 1991. Pp. xiii, 169. $32.95.

Miller, D.A. *Bringing Out Roland Barthes*. Berkeley, CA: University of California Press, 1992. Pp. 55. $12.00.

Moggridge, D.E. *Maynard Keynes: An Economist's Biography*. New York: Routledge, 1992. Pp. xxxi, 941. $37.50.

Moure, Kenneth. *Managing the Franc Poincare*. New York: Cambridge University Press, 1991. Pp. xiv, 306. $59.50.

Neill, Robin. *A History of Canadian Economic Thought*. New York: Routledge, 1991. Pp. x, 297.

Nelson, Robert H. *Reaching for Heaven on Earth: The Theological Meaning of Economics*. Savage, MD: Rowman & Littlefield, 1991. Pp. xxvii, 378. $24.95.

Neuman, W. Russell, Marion R. Just, and Ann N. Crigler. *Common Knowledge: News and the Construction of Political Meaning*. Chicago: University of Chicago Press, 1992. Pp. xvii, 172. $10.95, paper.

Norris, George W. *Fighting Liberal: The Autobiography of George W. Norris*. Lincoln: University of Nebraska Press, 1992. Pp. xxvii, 419. $14.95, paper.

O'Donnell, R.M. *Keynes and Philosopher-Economist*. New York: St. Martin's, 1991. Pp. x, 255. $45.00.

Ohrenstein, Roman A., and Barry Gordon. *Economic Analysis in Talmudic Literature: Rabbinic Thought in the Light of Modern Economics*. New York: E.J. Brill, 1992. Pp. xviii, 152. $43.00.

Oman, Charles P., and Ganeshan Wignaraja. *The Postwar Evolution of Development Thinking*. New York: St. Martin's Press, 1991. Pp. xv, 272. $49.95.

Pack, Spencer J. *Capitalism as a Moral System: Adam Smith's Critique of the Free Market Economy*. Brookfield, VT: Edward Elgar, 1991. Pp. viii, 199.

Pareto, Vilfredo. *The Rise and Fall of Elites*. New Brunswick, NJ: Transaction Books, 1991. Pp. 120. Ppaer. $14.95.

Pavel, Thomas. *The Feud of Language: A History of Structuralist Thought*. Cambridge, MA: Basil Blackwell, 1992. Pp. viii, 178. $18.95, paper.

Peacock, Alan. *Public Choice Analysis in Historical Perspective*. New York: Cambridge University Press, 1992. Pp. 231. $49.95.

Peacocke, Christopher. *A Study of Concepts*. Cambridge: MIT Press, 1992. Pp. xv, 266. $29.95.

Pearce, David W., ed. *The MIT Dictionary of Modern Economics*. 4th edn. Cambridge: MIT Press, 1992. Pp. xi, 474. $15.75, paper.

Pippin, Robert B. *Modernism as a Philosophical Problem: On the Dissatisfaction of European High Culture*. Cambridge, MA: Basil Blackwell, 1991. Pp. viii, 218. $42.95, cloth; $21.95, paper.

Popper, Karl. *In Search of a Better World*. New York: Routledge, 1992. Pp. x, 245. $27.50.

Porta, Pier Luigi, ed. *David Ricardo: Notes on Malthus's "Measure of Value."* New York: Cambridge University Press, 1992. Pp. xxi, 62. $34.95.

Poster, Mark. *The Mode of Information: Poststructuralism and Social Context*. Chicago: University of Chicago Press, 1990. Pp. vii, 179. $39.95, cloth; $16.95, paper.

Potier, Jean-Pierre. *Piero Sraffa-Unorthodox Economist [1898-1983]*: A Biographical Essay. New York: Routledge, 1991. Pp. x, 109. $30.00.

Raven, Diederick, Lieteke van Vucht Tijssen, and Jan de Wolf, eds. *Cognitive Relativism and Social Science*. New Brunswick, NJ: Transaction, 1992. Pp. xxviii, 297. $29.95.

Resch, Robert Paul. *Althusser and the Renewal of Marxist Social Theory*. Berkeley: University of California Press, 1992. Pp. xi, 436. $40.00.

Rigby, S.H. *Marxism and History: A Critical Introduction*. New York: St. Martin's Press (Manchester University Press), 1987. Pp. vi, 314. $22.95, paper.

Roberts, Bruce, and Susan Feiner, eds. *Radical Economics*. Boston, MA: Kluwer Academic Publishers, 1991. Pp. vi, 252. $57.50.

Rose, Margaret A. *The Post-Modern and the Post-Industrial: A Critical Analysis*. New York: Cambridge University Press, 1991. Pp. xiv, 317. Paper.

Rosenau, Pauline Marie. *Post-Modernism and the Social Sciences*. Princeton, NJ: Princeton University Press, 1992. Pp. xiv, 229. $35.00, cloth; $12.95, paper.

Rosenberg, Alexander. *Economics–Mathematical Politics or Science of Diminishing Returns?* Chicago: University of Chicago Press, 1992. Pp. xvii, 266. $32.50.

Rothenberg, Winifred Barr. *From Market-Places to a Market Economy: The Transformation of Rural Massachusetts, 1750-1850*. Chicago: University of Chicago Press, 1992. Pp. xiv, 275. $37.50.

Rymes, Thomas K., ed. *Welfare, Property Rights and Economic Policy*. Ottawa, Canada: Carleton University Press, 1991. Pp. ix, 181. Paper.

Sachs, Wolfgang, ed. *The Development Dictionary: A Guide to Knowledge as Power*. Atlantic Highlands, NJ: Zed Books, 1992. Pp. 306. $59.95, cloth; $25.00, paper.

Sacks, David Harris. *The Widening Gate: Bristol and the Atlantic Community, 1450-1700*. Berkeley, CA: University of California Press, 1991. Pp. xxvii, 464. $45.00.

Sanderson, Stephen K. *Social Evolutionism: A Critical History.* Cambridge, MA: Basil Blackwell, 1990. Pp. xviii, 251.

Scaff, Lawrence A. *Fleeing the Iron Cage: Culture, Politics, and Modernity in the Thought of Max Weber.* Berkeley: University of California Press, 1991. Pp. xiv, 265. $12.95, paper.

Schultz, David A. *Property, Power, and American Democracy.* New Brunswick, NJ: Transaction, 1992. Pp. xi, 223. $39.95.

Scott, Christina. *A Historian and His World: A Life of Christopher Dawson.* New Brunswick, NJ: Transaction, 1992. Pp. 266. $34.95.

Shackle, G.L.S. *Epistemics and Economics: A Critique of Economic Doctrines.* New Brunswick, NJ: Transaction Publishers, 1991. Pp. xxi, 482.

Shapiro, Ian. *Political Criticism.* Berkeley: University of California Press, 1992. Pp. xii, 338. $15.00, paper.

Shaw, G. K., ed. *Economics, Culture and Education: Essays in Honour of Mark Blaug.* Brookfield, VT: Edward Elgar, 1991. Pp. xiv, 214. $64.95.

Shils, Edward, ed. *Remembering the University of Chicago: Teachers, Scientists, and Scholars.* Chicago: University of Chicago Press, 1991. Pp. xxi, 593. $24.95.

Simmel, Georg. *The Philosophy of Money.* 2nd enlarged edn, edited by David Frisby. New York: Routledge, 1990. Pp. xlii, 537. $14.99, paper.

Smart, Paul. *Mill and Marx: Individual Liberty and the Roads to Freedom.* New York: St. Martin's Press, 1991. Pp. vi, 202. $49.95.

Smith, Vernon L. *Papers in Experimental Economics.* New York: Cambridge University Press, 1991. Pp. xvi, 812. $64.95.

Starr, June. *Law as Metaphor: From Islamic Courts to the Palace of Justice.* Albany: State University of New York Press, 1992. Pp. xli, 243. $16.95, paper.

Steidlmeier, Paul. *People and Profits: The Ethics of Capitalism.* Englewood Cliffs, NJ: Prentice-Hall, 1992. Pp. xv, 368. Paper.

Swedberg, Richard. *Schumpeter: A Biography.* Princeton, NJ: Princeton University Press, 1991. Pp. vii, 293. $24.95.

Swingewood, Alan. *A Short History of Sociological Thought.* New York: St. Martin's, 1984. Pp. x, 355. $29.95, cloth; $12.95, paper.

Szenberg, Michael, ed. *Eminent Economists: Their Life Philosophies.* New York: Cambridge University Press, 1992. Pp. xvi, 304. $34.95.

Taylor, M.W. *Men Versus the State: Herbert Spencer and Late Victorian Individualism.* New York: Oxford University Press, 1992. Pp. xi, 292. $65.00.

Teich, Mikulas, and Roy Porter, eds. *Fin de Siecle and Its Legacy.* New York: Cambridge University Press, 1990. Pp. xii, 345. $54.50, cloth; $17.95, paper.

Thomas, Brook. *The New Historicism and Other Old-Fashioned Topics.* Princeton, NJ: Princeton University Press, 1991. Pp. xvii, 254. $22.95.

Thompson, E.P. *Customs in Common*. New York: The New Press, 1991. Pp. xii, 547. $29.95.

Townshend, Jules. *J.A. Hobson*. New York: Manchester University Press (St. Martin's Press), 1991. Pp. viii, 192. $39.95.

Turgot, A.R.J. *Turgot: Extracts from his Economic Correspondence with Du Pont de Nemours, David Hume, Josiah Tucker, Condorcet, Morellet and Others, 1765-1778*. Edited by Peter Groenewegen. Sydney, Australia: Centre for the Study of the History of Economic Thought, 1992. Pp. xvii, 58. Paper.

van Caenegem, R.C. *An Historical Introduction to Private Law*. New York: Cambridge University Press, 1992. Pp. viii, 215. Paper.

Vercelli, Alessandro. *Methodological Foundations of Macroeconomics: Keynes and Lucas*. New York: Cambridge University Press, 1991. Pp. xv, 269. $54.95.

Vickers, Jeanne, ed. *Rethinking the Future: The Correspondence between Geoffrey Vickers and Adolf Lowe*. Rutgers, NJ: Transaction, 1991. Pp. xvi, 239. $34.95.

Viroli, Maurizio. *From Politics to Reason of State: The Acquisition and Transformation of the Language of Politics 1250-1600*. New York: Cambridge University Press, 1992. Pp. ix, 329.

Vovelle, Michel. *Ideologies and Mentalities*. Chicago: University of Chicago Press, 1990. Pp. 263. $29.95.

Wartenberg, Thomas E., ed. *Rethinking Power*. Albany: State University of New York Press, 1992. Pp. xxiii, 353. $16.95, paper.

Waterman, A.M.C. *Revolution, Economics and Religion: Christian Political Economy, 1798-1833*. New York: Cambridge University Press, 1991. Pp. xvi, 310.

Weintraub, E. Roy. *Stabilizing Dynamics: Constructing Economic Knowledge*. Durham, NC: Duke University Press, 1991. Pp. x, 177. $39.50.

Werhane, Patricia H. *Adam Smith and His Legacy for Modern Capitalism*. New York: Oxford University Press, 1991. Pp. 219. $29.95.

Wilber, Charles K., and Kenneth P. Jameson. *Beyond Reaganomics*. Notre Dame, IN: University of Notre Dame Press, 1990. Pp. xi, 309. Paper, $12.95.

Winiecki, Elisabeth, and Jan Winiecki. *The Structural Legacy of the Soviet-Type Economy*. London, UK: Centre for Research in Communist Economies, 1992. Pp. 133. £6.50, paper.